INGRID BERGMAN

An Intimate Portrait

INGRID BERGMAN

An Intimate Portrait

by

JOSEPH HENRY STEELE

DAVID McKAY COMPANY, INC.
New York

Library of Congress Catalogue Card Number: 59-9389

MANUFACTURED IN THE UNITED STATES OF AMERICA

VAN REES PRESS • NEW YORK

To

HANNA LUKE BOULAD

–this ancient debt

Contents

To Begin With . . .

IN the winter of 1947, after she had won the highest honor the American theater can bestow—the Antoinette Perry "Tony" Award for the finest performance on Broadway—for her portrayal of Maxwell Anderson's *Joan of Lorraine*, a gentle soft-spoken priest, whose hair matched the blizzard that muffled Manhattan, came up from Philadelphia to see me by appointment. It was Ingrid Bergman whom he had wanted to see—as did thousands of others—but, as I was her public-relations representative and general factotum, all communications and requests were first referred to me.

He showed me a few architect's drawings of a modest little church then in process of construction in his city. It was to be known as the Church of Joan of Arc, and the design envisioned a marble bust of the sainted Maid in the center niche above the entrance.

Would Miss Bergman be kind enough to pose for it?

Frankly startled at the proposal, I regretfully explained that it did not seem quite proper. "After all, Father, Miss Bergman is only an actress."

Chagrined by the failure of his mission, he took reluctant leave, and, trusting I had acted wisely, I went up to the twenty-sixth-floor suite of the Hampshire House, which then served as Ingrid's run-of-the-play home.

"Oh, my goodness!" she said, her cheeks like Svenskt porcelain. "Isn't that wonderful?" Then the hint of a shadow crossed her face. "But you did right, Joe. Wouldn't it be a terrible thing if I ever got into a scandal? I can just see them tearing down poor Joan and smashing her to pieces."

INGRID BERGMAN

An Intimate Portrait

1.

Minnesota

I FIRST met Ingrid Bergman as a result of the United States Navy's myopia.

In 1918 I had held a sergeant's "spear" in the super-production of "World War I." When the show was revived on an even more grandiose scale, I tried to get in on the act. Most of 1942 I spent in endless, exasperating, and often humiliating mental and physical examinations as a candidate for a public-relations commission in the Navy.

My chief sponsor was one of the authentic screen stars of his day, Richard Barthelmess, then a lieutenant stationed at Norfolk, Virginia, whose publicity director I had been for five years. Sponsorships and inquisitions notwithstanding, I was ultimately rejected upon the brass adjudication that my show-business background was inconsistent with mystic service standards.

Canceling the order for my uniforms and gathering the remnants of my self-respect, I plunged into a lesser war: I became publicity director for David O. Selznick, self-acknowledged hydra-headed genius of that Nirvana of geniuses, Hollywood.

Undaunted by the mortality of a long line of harried predecessors, I took on the job. I had a family to support. Still, despite Selznick's reputation for eating publicity men for breakfast—without cream or sugar—the precarious post was highly sought after for the prestige it leant those who labored in the shadow of the man who had made *Gone With the Wind*.

Selznick's pride and joy were the stars he had under personal contract: Jennifer Jones (whom he later married), Joseph Cotten, Gene Kelly, Shirley Temple, Joan Fontaine, Dorothy McGuire, and Ingrid Bergman. The group was referred to as Selznick's "Stable of Stars," and of them all, Ingrid Bergman was the prize entry.

Ingrid had already been seen in *Intermezzo*, *Adam Had Four Sons*, *Rage in Heaven*, *Dr. Jekyll and Mr. Hyde*, and *Casablanca*. Just prior to my going to work for Mr. Selznick, she had finished her role as Maria in Ernest Hemingway's *For Whom the Bell Tolls* and had returned to her family and temporary home in Rochester, New York. Thus I had yet to meet her.

The anomalous residence in the East was occasioned by her husband's studies at the University of Rochester, where, making the transition from dentistry, he was qualifying for an American M.D. in neurosurgery.

My Selznick predecessor, Whitney Bolton (who took the veil and returned to the New York *Morning Telegraph* as drama critic), had previously arranged for Ingrid to stop off in Minnesota, on her way back to Hollywood. There she was to make a propaganda film for the Office of War Information entitled *Swedes in America*. Simultaneously, *Look* magazine was to cover her adventures for an extensive feature layout.

Arriving in Minneapolis a day ahead of Ingrid, on February 2, 1943, I stepped out of an overheated train into an icebox of subzero weather. My Southern California wardrobe felt like a sieve, but what hurt most were my unaccustomed ears. A sympathetic native advised earmuffs, so I hied myself to a store. Looking over an assortment, I selected dark blue ones, as befitting my conservative tastes. An invincible saleswoman, however, out-talked me into a dazzling red-plush pair, arguing that my *tout ensemble* was enhanced thereby. Thus it happened that when Ingrid Bergman detrained at the Great Northern Station she was greeted by a tall, dark, thin man, whose head suggested a traffic signal. And ever after, whether it was New York, Ottawa, Sicily, Stromboli, or Rome, regardless of the temperature, these identical aural comforts, donned at the instant of arrival, became a token of our happy first meeting. Her gurgly, throaty laughter was reward enough for my silly appearance.

The OWI and *Look* staffs, plus the local press and all the fans the station could hold, awaited her arrival as the train from Rochester rumbled to a stop. Several passengers alighted, and behind them loomed Ingrid.

She was attired in black low-heeled shoes, a full-length mink coat, and her head incongruously encased in what looked like a child's red-white-and-blue knitted bonnet secured by a tie under the chin. This was her practical solution for concealing the boyish haircut she had to adopt in *For Whom the Bell Tolls*.

My first impression was of her size, assuredly the biggest actress I had ever seen. As I was to learn, her aversion to high heels was not an affectation, but due rather to sensitivity about her height—almost five feet, nine inches, of sturdy, peasant structure. Few persons realized how large she was because most of her leading men—such as Gary Cooper and Gregory Peck—towered well over six feet. Small men, like Charles Boyer, had to stand on boxes when appearing with her in intimate scenes.

Close behind Ingrid, in the Pullman's vestibule, stood her handsome Negro maid, Mabel, bearing in her arms four-year-old, yellow-haired Pia, a miniature reproduction of her famous mother.

I quickly stepped forward. "I'm Joe Steele, Miss Bergman." Utterly devoid of guile, her countenance shone with warmth, friendship, and a disarming girlish eagerness seldom seen in an actress. She had a way of looking directly into one's eyes. The word "straight" kept recurring to me. Even the mink coat—symbol of Hollywood caste—seemed subdued by the simplicity of its tenant. She was anybody's cousin come to spend a weekend.

"Halloo," she said, pronouncing it that way.

"The press would like to photograph you here. And then they'd like to get some pictures in the USO room upstairs. Do you mind?"

"Not at all. I shall be happy."

The Nicollet Hotel in Minneapolis assigned her to what they dubbed "The Nordic Suite." I remarked how appropriate this was, but she assured me that the name was the only thing Nordic about it. Immensely enjoying the misnomer, she led me around the rooms, pointing out Chinese lampstands, Louis XIV chairs, and Grand Rapids bedsteads.

"But it is so big and comfortable," she said.

Ingrid was punctually ready at seven the next morning for the two-hour drive over snow-drifted highways to Chisago City, population 746. There, for several days, she would live as a guest on C. E. Swenson's model Glenwater Farm, where the initial scenes of the film were to be shot. It was still dark when we started out.

As we were about to go, Ingrid hesitated a moment, glanced around the spacious apartment, then abruptly went to the bedroom. She snapped off the lights one by one and repeated the same performance in the sitting room.

"Oh, don't bother, Ingrid," I said. "The room maid will take care of all that. And besides, nobody ever turns out hotel lights."

"Yes, I know," she said. "But still I do not feel right about it."

At the farm she was immediately adopted by octogenarian Charles Swenson and his strapping, good-looking, middle-aged bachelor sons, Henry and Gilbert. After five minutes of solid talk—in inseparable combined English and Swedish—the screen star and the farmers were old friends.

Irving Lerner, the film's director, called her to work, and Ingrid went through her paces until sundown. By that time Henry was "Hank" and "Miss Bergman" had given way to informal Ingrid. Easily, unconsciously, she had become "family."

Assigned an upstairs bedroom, Ingrid was up at five in the morning. She bathed, dressed, breakfasted, and reported to the poultry barn at the appointed hour of six for scenes of candling eggs with Hank Swenson.

By nightfall the chief topic was our leading lady's undiminishing energy and exuberance. "No pose, no temperament," said Lerner. "Just look at that face. Makes you want to eat rose petals." *Look* photographer Frank Bauman summed up all our feelings with a corny old vaudeville gag, "And to think I'm getting paid for this."

One evening the elder Swenson invited Bauman, Lerner, *Look* writer Isabella Taves, and me to dinner. The food was traditional "farm style," fit for giants, and the Swensons ate like giants. The table talk was simple and friendly, strictly homey stuff. Ingrid took Hank and Gilbert to task. "Why aren't you two men married? My goodness, what fine husbands you would make! It's a shame! You would make some nice girls very happy."

And Hank, ever the spokesman, blushed like a schoolboy. "Oh, we will. When the right girls come along."

Two incidents occurred during our Minnesota sojourn that, I think, are testaments of character. The first took place at a home for the aged. A matron ushered us into the presence of several inmates. None of their furrowed faces had ever gazed upon a Bergman movie; none was aware of her identity.

The matron was about to introduce Ingrid when she, catching her breath at sight of the venerable gallery, impulsively fell to her knees and, grasping the gnarled hand of the nearest woman, spoke to her in Swedish. Her self-effacement in the presence of these folk at the midnight of their lives cast a hush over the room. For a few minutes our professional reason for being there was forgotten. We just stood and looked.

Later, on our way down the sleet-slippery walk, I took her arm, groping for something to say.

"I love old people," she said. "I cannot help it. I love them more than any other. When I was a child they were kind to me. My dearest memories are of old people."

Our next stop was a small frame house in neighboring Scandia, where Ingrid was filmed with an eighty-nine-year-old woman as she worked at an antiquated spinning wheel. Sitting on a footstool beside the tiny bent figure, Ingrid watched the "sere and yellow leaf" of her hands as they deftly spun the thread.

"Please show me how you do it," said Ingrid, and the immigrant child of 1868 proceeded to show her. She smiled a wrinkled smile at the luminous young face beside her; this was a person to whom the old lady responded. "What is your name?" she asked.

As natural as one child to another, the "hottest" star in the movie world replied, "Ingrid."

As yet ignorant of her personal habits, I one day offered her a cigarette. "Oh, no, thank you," she said. (Her replies usually began with an "oh," sounding more like "aw" in her accent.)

"I'm sorry," I said, apologetically.

"Please don't worry," she said. "I don't mind others smoking, but I do not like it for myself. I have learned to chew gum, because while my friends smoke I want to do something too."

From that day forward, wherever chewing gum was on sale, each of us bought our wartime quota of one pack and gave it to her. Bergman never chewed so happily.

One evening, while driving back to Minneapolis from a location, we debated where to dine. "How about a Swedish restaurant?" I ventured.

"I have eaten Swedish food all my life," she replied, "and I like it very much. But I want to know about other foods too. I want to try all other kinds of food. I want to know all about them and about the people who eat them." We decided on a German rathskeller.

Upon arriving at the hotel I enquired as to how soon I should call for her.

"In fifteen minutes," she said. Then, noting my dubious expression, she repeated, "Fifteen minutes–plenty of time."

"Okay. Have it your way."

I went to my room, muttering to myself: Hmmm . . . she's been working all day . . . she's all bundled up in sweaters and ski shoes and things . . . sitting in the car for the last two hours . . . no, I must have misunderstood . . . she meant *fifty* minutes, not fifteen.

In exactly fifteen minutes I knocked on the door. She was ready and waiting, looking bright as cut glass. Her short, unruly hair was brushed and framed a face well pinked by a hot tub. She had on a plain gray-wool gabardine suit, a tailored white blouse, and gun-metal gray slippers.

"It's not true!" I declared, as I held the mink coat for her. "You're entirely fictitious."

"But why . . . ?"

"Because no woman can do the trick in less than two hours. And for a movie star . . ."

"I do not understand," she said, genuinely perplexed. "Why should I take so long?"

Her secret, of course, lay in her fabled complexion. She was twenty-seven at the time. Even today she retains the vivid full glow of rugged health. Her eyebrows remain uneven and unplucked, and only in recent years has she added a light touch of rouge to her lips. Her sage-honey hair requires but three or four strokes of a brush and, behold, it is dressed. Hollywood make-up wizards tried to get at her eyebrows and the laughter creases around her mouth, but she said no, very grimly, and they threw up their hands in resignation. David Selznick once told me that soon after he met Ingrid Bergman, he put his finger to her lips to find out how much rouge she used. He found none.

As the Minnesota assignment was ending, the imminence of good-bys casting a pall over everyone, the talk was of Ingrid. "She has never complained once," said Director Lerner. "Never saw anything like it. She never seems to peter out toward the end of the day, like every other actress I've ever worked with."

"She's so goddam healthy," said Bauman, summing her up about as definitively as I've ever heard.

We finished the assignment in a slumberous village named, of all things, Lindstrom. Ingrid was then and still is an incurable camera bug, snapping pictures everywhere she goes. When she spotted the toy gingerbread depot, she let out a whoop. Out came the ubiquitous sixteen-millimeter movie camera and the "Lindstrom" sign was recorded from every conceivable angle.

"Petter will not believe it unless I show him," she said, giving his name its Swedish pronunciation, as the Lindstroms did until Americanization began to set in.

The last scene shot, we bade farewell to the hospitable Swensons, the snowbanks, and the incomparable sweet butter upon which we had gorged ourselves. (Ah, wartime rationing!)

Our railroad accommodations to Los Angeles were the best obtainable—three roomettes; one for Ingrid and Pia, one for Mabel, and one for me. (For anyone who hasn't been in one, a roomette is about the size of two telephone booths.)

We retired early and, despite a night that seemed as though I were on a streetcar that stopped at every corner, I fell into a heavy sleep and woke up at ten. I dressed and immediately went to see how Ingrid had fared. Finding her door closed and not wishing to disturb her, I looked in on Mabel. There was Pia, cheery and cherubic.

"How did Miss Bergman make out?"

"Oh, Mr. Steele," Mabel wailed, "she couldn't sleep with Pia without crowding her—you know, she's a *big* woman!—so she got up and walked up and down the train all the night long. Never even bothered to wake me. Soon as Pia got up, Miss Bergman brought her to me, then *she* went to bed. That was about seven o'clock."

Toward the middle of the afternoon Ingrid was up and around. I demanded an explanation; why didn't she wake me up? She could have taken my roomette, it was better that I walk the train than she. How could she have taken such a chance? But she shrugged the whole thing off.

"Please don't worry, Joe," she said. "I am all right. The motion of the train kept throwing me against Pia, and I could not sleep. So I got up, put on my robe, and went up and down the train. Everything was black, so I could see nothing outside. Then I went to the dining car (nine cars away!). I thought maybe I could sleep in a chair, but there was a nice old man there, and we talked for a long time. He was very interesting."

"Nevertheless," I said, in paternal wrath, "tonight you will take my roomette and *I* shall do the patrolling."

I told the conductor of our predicament and he gave me a vacated upper berth for the rest of the journey, while my three charges luxuriated in separate cubicles.

On the second day, toward the aperitif hour, a tragedy befell us. We made the distressing discovery that there was no bar, that not even wine was served in the dining car. It was a troop train. Worse, in my haste in getting away from Minneapolis I had forgotten to stow away a bottle for emergencies, as I was wont to do on my travels.

Resigned to this, I collected my assorted ladies and began the long trek to the diner, weaving in and out of doors, stumbling over luggage. Arriving at the dining car we came upon the usual, understandably restive, queue of hungry soldiers and civilians.

It was too much to ask of Pia to wait in line for another possible hour. And besides, all around us it was being rumored that the food supply was limited and would doubtless be gone by the time our turn arrived. The situation seemed palpably hopeless.

We backtracked our empty stomachs, snuggled in a roomette, and held a council on what to do. As we brooded over our dilemma, Ingrid burst out with an inspiration, "Oh, my goodness! Why didn't I think of it before? The Swensons gave me two pounds of cheese to take home. I have it in my bag!"

Now we were getting somewhere, but what to do about bread? Naked cheese, two thousand miles to California, was not a totally appealing prospect, particularly for a four-year-old.

"I have an idea, Ingrid. Listen carefully," I said. "This milk train stops at every hamlet for at least ten minutes. You and I will stand by the door. As soon as the train stops we'll jump off, and you run to the station. There has to be a lunch-counter in or near it. Buy a flock of sandwiches, milk or cokes, or any fruit or candy you can find. The sandwiches probably won't be great, but we'll throw out the fillings and eat the bread with the cheese. While you're doing that I'll make for the nearest store, grab a bottle, and rush back to the station. You wait there for me."

"Oh, that's wonderful!" she said. "Let's go!"

Before long our train pulled up, the door unlatched, and we leaped off. Ingrid made a beeline for the deserted depot while I paused a second to scrutinize the lay of the land. No electric sign even vaguely hinted at what I sought. Then I spotted a drug-store, one challenging block away. I ran for it.

I ran fast, but did some faster thinking: That's quite a distance . . . maybe they don't sell liquor . . . can I make it in time? Ingrid standing there waiting for me . . . Mabel and Pia going off without us . . . oh, the devil with it!

I nearly fell on my face as I wheeled around and tore back to Ingrid. There she stood, flushed with excitement, clutching two bulging grocery bags.

"All abaaawed!" foghorned through the still night. "Good Lord," I panicked. "Can you run?"

"Try me," she said. I grabbed one of the bags and we sprinted for our car. The train was in motion as we hopped aboard.

"Where'd you go, Mummy?" said Pia, utterly oblivious that her million-dollar Mummy was almost left behind.

2.

Stockholm

INGRID BERGMAN—an only child—was born on August 29, 1915, on the top sixth floor of an old-fashioned apartment house in Stockholm, Sweden. Her father, Justus Bergman, operated a camera shop on the ground floor of the same building. (On a sentimental exploration in the summer of 1958 Ingrid discovered that the shop now housed the Swiss Airlines ticket office.)

On the first anniversary of her birthday she snuggled in her mother's lap and was photographed by her father with a 35 mm. motion-picture camera which he had rented for the occasion. When Ingrid was two, her mother died, at the age of thirty-seven, from an acute inflammation of the liver. If the film was shown later, Ingrid has no recollection of it. As the years passed and she became one of Sweden's best known screen stars, she often thought of having it run for her, but she shrank from doing so because she wanted to be alone when first she viewed this record of her early childhood.

More than a score of years later, when she had come to Hollywood to stay, her husband, Petter Lindstrom, had the film reduced to 16 millimeters and sent it to her. She sat alone in a Selznick projection room and watched the picture unfold.

"It was a strange, uncanny feeling," she told me, "to see my mother as a living personality—someone I never remembered. I cannot describe the experience."

In her maturity, any vague recollections she may have had of the mother were fused with the memory of her spinster aunt, Ellen, an elder sister of Justus Bergman, who had moved into the home to assure her care.

"When I was born," said Ingrid, "I was named after the Swedish princess who then was two years old. Most girl babies in those days were named after Princess Ingrid, who is now the Queen of Denmark.

"Mother was German—born in Hamburg—and she was eighteen years younger than my father. Her family name was Adler. He said she had four names and it was such a nuisance when it came to filling out passports and official papers. So he insisted that I be given only one name.

"My father was only a little younger than Aunt Ellen and, though they were kind to me, it was difficult growing up with only two old people in the house. The days and years were filled with a terrible feeling of aloneness. I became extremely shy and withdrew into a dream world of my own imagination, with creatures of fantasy who were less oppressive than the people around me. To amuse myself I began inventing characters—villains and heroes, witches and fairies, and even animals. I made up stories as I went along and all these characters became familiar and friendly.

"At school my abnormal height and clumsy shyness prevented me from making friends. I barely passed from grade to grade, due partly to boredom with the regular subjects, but mostly because of my inability to stand up before the class and answer the teacher's questions. Self-consciousness would choke the words in my throat.

"I remember so well how, when school finished, I used to stand outside and watch the mothers come for their children. It seemed to me that they were very beautiful mothers, all perfumed and smartly dressed in their fancy hats. I would just stand there and watch them go off together. Then I would go home by myself.

"I went to the theater for the first time when I was eleven. My father took me and I remember it so clearly. I had on a grown-up dress lent to me by Aunt Ellen—you can see how big I was. It was red and I guess that's why it has always been my favorite color. I like red in almost everything.

"The play was by Hjalmar Bergman, who was no relative of ours. It was called *Patrasket*. I remember how amazed I was to see adults playing parts the same as I did at home. I think maybe this was when I decided to be an actress."

About a year later Justus Bergman died of a stomach cancer.

"Sometime after he passed away I accidentally opened a box and found many of his and Mother's letters. Reading them, I learned a great deal about how they felt and their attitude toward each other. They were apparently as divided in personality as two people can be.

"Father was an artist. I have several of his paintings—a beautiful one of my mother—and I am sure that if he had concentrated on his natural talents he might have become a great painter. He also sang, and when I was about ten years old he organized a mixed choir and took them on a tour of the United States. They were known simply as 'The Swedes.'

"I remember when he came home after the tour, he brought me an orange from California. It was wizened and old, with a skin like leather, but it was my first touch with America and I thought it wonderful.

"Reading the letters they had written to each other, I learned that my mother was typically German, extremely practical, systematic and orderly. But Father had all the Bohemian traits of an artist. It was he who had finally made all the compromises his marriage demanded. Painting was an uncertain livelihood, so he ended by giving up his deepest ambitions and opening a camera shop because it offered more security.

"My father became a business man against his real nature."

Seven months after her father's demise, Aunt Ellen passed away.

"She died in my arms when we were all alone," said Ingrid. "I telephoned and telephoned directly after, but it was a long time before anybody came to help me."

Twelve-year-old Ingrid was then taken to live with an elderly uncle, named Otto, and his five children—four of them older than she. It was her first experience living with children. Her body outran her years, and of this segment of her life Ingrid described herself as "all arms and legs, knocking things over because I was so awkward."

"The first years with these young cousins were an agony for me. They continually teased me about my appearance. They would say, 'What kind of an actress can you be when you are so clumsy?' I retreated more and more into myself. I determined more than ever to become an actress, because in that world of make-believe was the sanctuary I needed. I could submerge all my inhibitions and play-act at being the things I was not."

Defensively, the hypersensitive young girl sought the seclusion of her own room. There she would read aloud from published plays to the accompaniment of the family phonograph, tuning it high enough to drown out her histrionics.

"But whenever I escaped into this fantasy world of mine, I got nothing but ridicule and loud laughter from my cousins. I must say their behavior was understandable, because I was far from pretty with my long, thin body, and so inarticulate that I seldom opened my mouth to speak. Uncle Otto, instead of also laughing at me, used to get angry, because he was fanatically religious and believed the theater was the work of the devil.

"My father had left a little money, so I was sent to a private school, the Lyceum School for Girls. By this time I had become so terrified of anyone my own age that I was in constant misery. I made up my mind to overcome it. One day my chance came. Our gymnasium class was called off without anyone letting us know. So there we were in the big hall, but with no teacher and nothing to do. I got an idea which scared me, but I told myself I mustn't be afraid of my own schoolmates.

"I went up on the stage and said, 'I will entertain you.' They all laughed at me, but I said, 'I will put on a play and act all the parts myself.' Then they quieted down and I started. It was a French farce, very funny. It was called *The Green Elevator*. I played all six parts and my schoolmates laughed and clapped. But when I had played only two acts a teacher came in and threw us out.

"Then we all went to a public park and I played the third act with my audience sitting around me on the lawn. This was surely one of the most wonderful moments of my life. I got over my fear of being laughed at and my terror of kids. I was so happy I thought I would die.

"I guess I have wanted to be an actress almost as long as I can remember."

In her early teens Ingrid discovered Joan of Arc in the course of her schoolwork. Joan's dignity and courage and faith made an indelible impression upon her formative years. Joan became her favorite character and she liked portraying this role the most.

"Joan was warm and human; she wanted to get married and have children. Although I was brought up as a Lutheran, I adopted Joan as my own saint. I especially loved her sense of humor. I admired her for never being trapped by the questions of her inquisitors. For instance, when she was asked, 'In what language did you and Saint Michael speak?' she replied, 'In better French than yours.'

"As wonderful as she was, Joan showed her own humaneness when, in a moment of weakness, she denied her 'voice.' Somehow, this part of her story always had a special significance for me.

"My next favorite was the love story of Tristan and Isolde. It had a strong appeal for my romantic young girl dreams, because Isolde was a symbol of earthly love. This was a very precious dream for the unattractive girl that I was."

Once a year the state-owned Royal Dramatic Theater School held scholarship examinations to which young aspirants came from every corner of Sweden. In a series of rigid tests candidates were required to demonstrate their talents in comedy or drama or voice. Their material was of their own choosing.

By the time Ingrid graduated from high school, her future course lay clear and positive—acting was to be her career and her life. She determined to enter the Royal School competition.

Now seventeen, she broached the subject to her uncle, whereupon he exploded in outrage. Not only was the theater born of evil, but this gawky girl's notion of becoming an actress was in itself absurd.

"One of my good faults was a tremendous stubbornness," said Ingrid. "I kept after my uncle day after day. I never let up. Then, seeing that he was just as stubborn as I was, I threatened to kill myself if he prevented me from achieving my ambition. He finally relented, but nevertheless he was sure that I would fail in the very exacting tests.

"There were more than a hundred applicants that year, and because only a few of them would be picked, I worked that much harder preparing myself. I chose three subjects—the crazy boy from Rostand's *L'Aiglon*, the goddess in Strindberg's phantasy of a dream, and a big fat country girl part from something I've forgotten. I think that nothing will ever mean so much to me as the night of the tryouts."

Auditions were held in a regular playhouse with a panel of judges, comprised of staff instructors, grouped to one side on the stage. The auditorium was packed with standees. Backstage, the jittery hopefuls shuffled in silence, awaiting their big moment.

"I stood under a bright spotlight and all the rest of the theater was in blackness. When I read the speech of the crazy boy I became so moved I forgot all about the judges and the audience. So far as I was concerned I was standing there all by myself, acting only for me.

"There were about twenty judges and usually after each reading they indicated their reaction by applauding. But when I finished there was not a sound. Some whispered to each other, and one of them waved his hand as if to say 'You may leave the stage.' They gave me no chance to read the other two parts I had practiced. I went out and slowly walked home, not knowing what their judgment was.

"A couple of days later I was notified that I had been selected. One of the judges explained to me that the members of that jury had been so affected that they sat there in the darkness and they couldn't clap, and they couldn't move. They just sat there till the lights were turned on, and then the mood burst and they cheered. But I had already left the theater.

"Two other contestants that night became important Swedish stars—Irma Christensen and Gunnar Bjornstrand.

"Up until I went to the dramatic school I had never had a boy friend. They simply were not attracted to me and, I guess, I didn't try too hard to attract them. I was too self-conscious. But at dramatic school I found myself sought after; suddenly I *was* somebody. The school considered me to be one of its best pupils, and the realization of this made me delirious with joy. My happiness was reflected in everything I did, in my work and in my day-to-day life.

"About two months after I entered the school I was introduced to my future husband. It was on a blind date arranged by the boy friend of a girl I knew. I had just become eighteen and he was nine years older than I, but he was very popular and had many friends who were writers, painters and musicians. Funny thing, at that time I regarded him as quite an old man! But, because I was still a bit awkward and lacking in social ease, I felt very flattered that my company was not boring to him."

Petter Aron Lindstrom, the younger of two sons, was born on his father's farm in the sawmill town of Stöde (population 757), Medelpad, a rugged boulder-strewn region of northeastern Sweden. He was six feet, two inches of tough sinew.

"Every once in a while Petter took me to lunch or dinner and, for the first time in my life, I saw beautiful restaurants and expensive shows. He was a very successful dentist and part of the time he taught at a dental college. He owned a car and lived in a nice apartment. All this made a strong impression on me.

"Petter was very busy during this period and I was more interested in my classmates with whom I had more in common. For this reason, it was a long time before we became what you call 'a steady twosome.' "

Progressively, the dentist Lindstrom displayed a growing interest in her work and in her personal problems. His maturity and granite solidity appealed strongly to the young girl who had been fatherless for so long. More and more she found herself looking to his counsel and judgment.

The dramatic classes were an easy task for Ingrid, a mere expression of her second nature. She had been preparing for them all her life. It was not surprising, therefore, that shortly she was cast in leading roles in school presentations. Local motion-picture companies, ever on the lookout for promising talent, began to take notice. In the spring, towards the end of the first school year, she was flooded by movie offers.

"Although I liked the young men of the theater, I felt that I could rely more on Petter's intelligence and common sense. So, when I faced the making of an important decision about my career, it was to Petter I turned. With his advice and encouragement I decided to leave school in the fall and go into the movies."

She signed a contract with Svensk Filmindustrie, one of the largest companies in Stockholm. Her initial role was that of a maid in a cheap hotel in the slums. For this picture she was paid the equivalent of two hundred dollars, which she promptly spent on a leopard fur coat and a second-hand phonograph.

Later she played opposite Gösta Ekman, the Swedish John Barrymore, who had been her childhood idol. Ekman treated her with special consideration, bolstered her confidence, and predicted a glowing future. Her immediate popularity among associates and colleagues effected a marked change in her former shyness and reticence. She found their company stimulating and frequently dined out or attended a play with them.

"I enjoyed the atmosphere of the studio, the different kinds of personalities and the liveliness that was everywhere. The work itself came very easily to me. I memorized dialogue almost without trying. My uncle was very surprised at my success, because I think he still had his doubts. I went ahead full of confidence, because in the background was always Petter. Even when I didn't see him for some time I knew he was always there to help and advise me.

"A few months after I went into the movies Petter decided he wanted to be a doctor of medicine. He began to study at night and that, with all his other work, left him little spare time. But, in spite of that, we would manage to have dinner on a Saturday night or go picnicking in the country on Sundays.

"You know how Swedes like to walk; when we went picnicking, we'd leave his car and walk for miles into the woods, each of us carrying a knapsack. Mine was filled with the food I had prepared, but I noticed that Petter never opened his. One day I got curious and asked him what he had in it. He opened his knapsack and showed me—there were five bricks!" She laughed merrily as she added, "Petter said it was good for the muscles."

Of her courtship with the young dentist, Ingrid said, "It was not love at first sight, but it grew into something which, to both of us, became very important and impossible to live without. I cannot remember a formal proposal, nor can Petter, but with great happiness we decided to become engaged. On July 7, 1936, we went to the home of my mother's relatives in Hamburg and announced our engagement. We then went to the same church where my parents were married, and exchanged rings.

"Several weeks afterward, when I reached twenty-one years of age, I was finally free to move from my uncle's house and into an apartment of my own. It had one room and a kitchenette. This first taste of freedom was tremendously meaningful for me. It was good to be able to come and go as I pleased.

"During this period my uncle was quite ill, and I remember how attentive Petter was to him. His kindness and consideration touched me deeply. I soon discovered that this was not unusual in him. He was very generous and always ready to help. Old and young came to him for advice or just to cry out their troubles on his shoulder. Everybody said how happy they were for me to have found such a fine man. And so was I."

Picture by picture, Ingrid Bergman rose steadily towards stardom, while Petter Lindstrom reduced his dental practice to four days a week and intensified his medical pursuits. During long intervals between pictures Ingrid visited with her mother's family in Germany and there, with her natural facility for languages, she learned to speak and read German.

On July 10, 1937, they journeyed to the Lindstrom home in Stöde and were married in a shining little white Lutheran church. Tall and slim, Ingrid wore a flowing white silk gown which reached from her neck to her heels. A Juliet cap crowned her flaxen hair and from it fell a shoulder-length veil of silken mesh. On her arm she carried a spray of white and pink flowers—orchids, stephanotises and lilies-of-the-valley. The groom was attired in a black cutaway, striped pants and a top hat.

"Before the wedding my thoughts were mixed up with a lot of questions," said Ingrid. "My work meant everything to me. I loved it very much and I wondered what marriage might do to it. There were no simple answers, but I was sure of one thing–I didn't want to lose Petter.

"While we were in Stöde his parents showed me the utmost kindness and made me feel comfortable and at home. The father was a big strong man, but Petter's older brother was even bigger. He was like a giant. They were constantly busy doing something, never resting or taking it easy. I noticed that the father always ran from the barn to the house, although it was only a hundred yards away."

On their honeymoon they drove by car through Norway and then to London and Brighton in England. Upon their return to Stockholm, Lindstrom's apartment became their home. He now assumed the management of all her business affairs with her gratitude and blessing, since her sole concern was the artistic aspects of her career into which he did not inject himself.

Months later, when Ingrid became pregnant, she was asked how, as a rising young actress, she felt about it. "I have no feelings whatsoever about it," she replied. "Why shouldn't an actress have babies? It's perfectly natural."

Presently she began to receive tempting offers from Hollywood and German film companies. But Hollywood had an awesome sound, and the prospect of mastering a new language filled her with apprehension. She decided to first test herself on alien ground in Germany. "Besides, I felt more comfortable and secure not being too far away from Petter."

In the spring she went to Berlin and made a picture for the UFA studio, entitled *The Four Apprentices*. One day, unexpectedly, Ingrid saw her husband sitting in the lobby of her hotel–the Adlon. He told her that he had taken a room in a small, obscure hotel across the street; that he came unannounced and wished his presence to remain secret because it wasn't good for an actress to have her husband hanging around. "Thereafter," the main topic. Petter gave me the name of a doctor, said 'Good evening and welcome,' and they left. I stood there, frustrated and boiling mad.

"Next day he called and asked me to come to their apartment. When I arrived, their lawyer was present and Ingrid sat quietly knitting. Petter laughed and joked about our first meeting. He said they had had no previous engagement at all; they had come to size me up. They had expected some kind of a monster—a big, fat, hard-boiled businesswoman. They said they'd think about Selznick's offer and let me know."

The thought of far-away Hollywood, legendary Mecca of Moviedom, dismayed the young Swedish actress. And yet the prospect undeniably thrilled her. Secretly, Ingrid had hoped for this, the ultimate accolade in her profession.

"I wanted very much to go to Hollywood," Ingrid told me, "but I worried about my Pia, who was too tiny to take on such a long journey. I ached at the thought of leaving her, even though it would be only for a short time. Petter was working hard at his medical studies, and I felt that nothing should interfere with them. It would have been wrong for him to interrupt them for a few months.

"And when Kay talked about a seven-year contract I was terrified. One picture wasn't too bad, but seven years—I just couldn't imagine it! Stockholm was the only home I had ever known. I felt safe and secure there. And I wondered whether I'd like Hollywood or not, but, worse than anything, I guess I was scared to death that Hollywood might not like me."

When they were alone the Lindstroms discussed the pros and cons. "You must not worry about the baby," he said. "Between the housekeeper and the nurse she'll be well cared for. Besides, you won't be leaving for some time; she'll be that much older. This is a great opportunity and I know how much it means to you. It won't take too long, anyhow; you'll be back home before you know it. Afterward we'll see how you like it over there, and how the picture comes out."

Thus, with her husband's wholehearted endorsement, Ingrid yielded to the Selznick lure and signed for one picture, with the

Ingrid said, "when I came to the hotel after the day's w
Petter was waiting in the lobby."

Soon after her return to Stockholm she costarred with G
Ekman in *Intermezzo,* the story of an idyllic love affair betw
a married concert violinist and his fair accompanist. Four mon
after the completion of this picture, which was to effect a ma
turning point in her life, Ingrid gave birth to a daughter. She w
born on September 20, 1938, and was christened Friedel Pia, tl
former name for Ingrid's mother, and the latter an arrangemer
of the initials of the parents' given names, Petter Aron and Ingric

Ingrid adored her first-born and for several months was conten
to be mother and housewife. At the turn of the year *Intermezzo*
was released and became an instant hit. A print of the film found
its way to New York.

David O. Selznick's New York representative, Katherine (Kay) Brown—a trenchant, archetypical young career woman—saw the picture and recommended that it be remade in an English version. Selznick, that astute sniffer of talent, not only bought the story but determined to snag a far more valuable quarry and Miss Brown was delegated to deliver Miss Bergman.

In London, Miss Brown enlisted the collaboration of John Hay (Jock) Whitney of the wealthy New York family, who was then a vice-president of the Selznick company. She put a call through to the Lindstroms in Stockholm from a telephone booth, with Whitney standing by—his cupped hands brimming with coins. When contact was finally established, Dr. Lindstrom agreed to reserve a room for her at the Grand Hotel.

"When I checked into the Grand," said Miss Brown, "I called the doctor and told him I'd be glad to come and see them at their convenience. But he said no, they'd come to see me. Late that afternoon they arrived. I'll never forget Ingrid. She was holding a tiny bouquet of blue flowers to welcome me.

"We talked a while about everything except what I had come for. It was all pretty stiff. Then I asked them to have dinner with me, but Petter said that he was sorry but they had a previous engagement. I had a terrible earache and my head was all wrapped up. I guess I was a sight. Suddenly my earache became proviso that she would do more if all parties were pleased with the first. With the aid of an English tutor she immediately went to work learning the language.

On May 6, 1939, when Pia was seven months old, Ingrid arrived unheralded in the port of New York on the "Queen Mary." Kay Brown met her at the dock and put her up at the Chatham Hotel. After five bedazzled days in the big city, during which Ingrid discovered the wonders of hamburgers and hot fudge sundaes, Miss Brown took her by train to Hollywood.

She was established in a small but comfortable apartment in Beverly Hills, and that night Selznick entertained with a lavish party as a means of introducing her to the film colony. Among the guests were the Selznick stars and Gary Cooper, Greer Garson, Katharine Hepburn, Tyrone Power, directors George Cukor, Victor Fleming, King Vidor, Ernst Lubitsch, and many others.

"Ingrid sat in a corner by herself most of the evening," said Kay Brown, "dazed by the company she was keeping. I remember Lubitsch looking at her and saying, 'She's just a big peasant.' "

Selznick himself was enchanted by Ingrid Bergman's fresh, crisp beauty and unaffected personality. His wife, Irene, daughter of Louis B. Mayer, the film capital's foremost tycoon, gave her a warm welcome. An enduring attachment was born between the Nordic blonde and the striking, black-eyed, black-haired matron and Ingrid became a frequent guest at the Summit Drive mansion in Beverly Hills.

"David and Irene were so kind and wonderful to me. On my first trip to America I was very fortunate to find friends like them. But even so, I found it very hard to extend myself to the people I met. In Sweden our language is formal and filled with reserve. We always speak in the third person: 'Will Mr. the Doctor have some more coffee?'

"Being in a strange land made my old self-consciousness even worse. It was an ordeal for me to enter a restaurant and walk to my table. American informality is wonderful, but it is puzzling, too. The way people call each other by their first names, even nicknames, and act like old friends with everybody. I was so anxious to be liked."

Whether American or foreign, an actor's initiation into Hollywood invariably involves an alteration in name. For some odd reason the change is usually to that of an ordinary, colorless Anglo-Saxon cognomen. The Jeans, Janes and Joans are numerous. Ingrid was no exception.

"When I was attending dramatic school I got the notion that Ingrid was not a good artist's name. I longed for a French-sounding name because I was so impressed by those I saw in French movies, specially those who were known by single names, such as Raimu and Fernandel. They seemed lusty, forceful, and with music in them.

"There was a French actress known only as Anabella, and I thought I would like something similar. So I secretly chose Isabella because it sounded so much like Anabella. When I first came to Hollywood David Selznick wanted to change my name because he said it sounded too German. I said, 'Why? It's my name, isn't it?' But what was in the back of my mind was that my contract was only for one picture—*Intermezzo*—and then I was to return to Sweden. I refused to change my name for this one picture, thinking that if the picture failed I would be going back home having accomplished nothing but a change of name. I didn't want to be a phony with a new name in Sweden."

One half mile down the street from the Selznick studio, in Culver City, was the Metro-Goldwyn-Mayer lot, Louis B. Mayer's bastion. At MGM there was an English coach named Mrs. Ruth Roberts, whose charges were the studio's European players—among them Hedy Lamarr. Of Swedish descent, tall as Ingrid, raising three strapping young sons by a husband long since estranged, Mrs. Roberts had come to Hollywood from her native Detroit where she had taught English to the foreign-born.

"I had seen the Swedish *Intermezzo* and was fascinated by Ingrid's loveliness and fine performance," said Mrs. Roberts. "I was sure that some studio would bring her over. When I read in the papers that David Selznick had signed her, I immediately went to Billy Grady (MGM casting director) and asked him if he would recommend me as a coach to Mr. Selznick. He did, and that's how I came to be hired."

Early in June, 1939, *Intermezzo* was put into production under the direction of Gregory Ratoff, with Leslie Howard, the English actor, as leading man. Ratoff's thick, almost unintelligible Russian accent was a challenging hurdle for any beginner in English.

"Greg sure was funny," said Ingrid. "Many times he shouted in the middle of a scene, 'Vy don' you spik English! Say it like I do!' "

"When I first met Ingrid," said Ruth Roberts, "I didn't tell her I could speak Swedish. At one point during the shooting Ingrid was unable to understand what Ratoff was saying and, since Ingrid's English was limited, I reverted to Swedish in order to explain what he wanted. 'My goodness!'–she looked at me in surprise–'why didn't you tell me you could speak Swedish?' I said, 'Because if I had, you would have insisted on speaking it and that would have made it even more difficult for you to learn English.' "

Ingrid's own sturdy qualities readily responded to the earthy, thoughtful character of this woman. A staunch and lasting friendship sprang into being. When they were away from the studio the English lessons were assiduously continued and, step by step, Ingrid conquered the intricacies of the language.

As the filming of *Intermezzo* progressed, David Selznick became increasingly convinced of Ingrid's potential as a great star. He spoke of a brilliant future and urged that she come back to Hollywood to stay. She said she would first have to see how the picture was accepted, but if she did come back, her dream was to do the life of Joan of Arc. The producer agreed that it was a powerful subject, and promised to put it on his schedule.

Towards the end of August, with the completion of *Intermezzo*, Ingrid returned to her family, torn with qualms regarding her work in an alien land. "I prayed that I had done well, and that David would want me back. I loved working in Hollywood and I loved the people I worked with. I wanted so much to come back, but I had to think of my baby and Petter's studies. It all seemed so complicated."

The family reunion was joyous; Pia had flourished and Petter was nearer his goal. It seemed there would be no end to her tales of America and Hollywood. Then, suddenly, Hitler marched and war engulfed central Europe. Lindstrom's first thought was of danger to his family; Sweden seemed certain to be involved.

The English version of *Intermezzo* was released and press and public acclaimed a new star. Selznick telephoned from Hollywood and gave her the good news; saying that he was exercising the option on her services and summoning her to come back.

"I cried all that day in Stockholm," Ingrid said. "When we were making the picture I had seen some of the rushes. David and Gregory Ratoff and other people said I was good, but I didn't trust them. It was wicked to feel that way, but when I learned that audiences were pleased, then, and then only, was I convinced and satisfied."

Lindstrom now urged his wife to grasp the opportunity—to take Pia and flee the impending threat of war. In addition, he well understood her own eagerness to return to Hollywood. "Take Pia and go," he said, "and don't worry about anything. As for me, it won't be too long before I can join you."

"Leaving Petter behind was a very difficult decision for me to make," Ingrid told me. "We feared that any moment Sweden would become involved in the war. In the end, Petter made the final decision, as always. He drove us across Europe to Genoa, Italy, where we arrived barely in time to catch the last steamship, the 'Rex,' which carried civilian passengers. We sailed on New Year's Day, 1940. Later, the 'Rex' was sunk in the war.

"Around the third day out, I received a radiogram from David Selznick saying that my next film would be *Joan of Arc.* My dearest dream had come true. I became so excited and affected by the news that I went into the ship's chapel, got on my knees, and gave thanks."

Disembarking in New York after twelve rough days at sea, during which "everybody was seasick but me," she was met by Kay Brown and the usual contingent of photographers. But instead of the traditional display of "cheesecake," the reporters found a big Swedish girl in flat heels, bearing on her back fifteen-month-old Pia, encased in a fur leg-warmer turned inside out.

"New York looked so good to me that I trembled with anticipation, but I didn't know I was in for a shock. The publicity man said that a press conference had been arranged, and that if I was asked any questions about making *Joan of Arc,* I was to be 'very vague.'

"This upset me very much and I wanted to know why. He could only answer that 'the plans have been changed.' My dream collapsed and I remained in misery until I saw David. Some time after, David explained that, due to the war, it was not propitious to film the life of Joan, because in the story it was the British who burned her."

Kay Brown imparted the further disheartening news that Selznick had no immediate picture plans for her; she might just as well enjoy New York while marking time. All her expenses would be paid; she was on salary as of now. Miss Brown took Ingrid and Pia to stay in her home at 1035 Park Avenue, and a few days later engaged a maid for her named Mabel.

Describing her reaction during this period, Ingrid said to me, "In Shakespeare, Ibsen, Strindberg, men have all the good parts—the best parts. But in history there were great women I wanted to portray, such as Queen Christina and Charlotte Corday and, most of all, Joan of Arc. I was sure I looked like Joan, who was a big peasant type. From the very first time I discovered her, when I was a little girl, I wanted to play her trial. So I felt a terrible disappointment when David changed his mind, but even more when Kay told me that he had nothing else for me. I waited and waited."

Touring the sights, seeing every movie and every play—bad or good—falling in love with the throbbing city, Ingrid bided her time. "One day she disappeared and I became worried," Kay Brown said. "She had said nothing about her plans or what she might do. As we were getting ready for dinner, and I was going crazy, she popped in. She had got it into her pretty head to visit the World's Fair at Flushing Meadows on Long Island. I never did get it straight how she got there and got back."

Inactivity is the bane of Ingrid's life. She implored Selznick to let her do a Broadway play. He acceded and Kay Brown put out the feelers.

Play producer Vinton Freedley submitted a manuscript of Ferenc Molnar's *Liliom*, which Ingrid read and returned with apologies: the role of Julie's friend was not quite her type—it called for someone short and round.

Freedley looked at her in astonishment. "But that's the minor role," he said. "I wanted you for the star part—for Julie!"

So she reread the script and accepted the role of the hot-blooded Viennese servant girl who falls in love with a carnival barker. The play was limited to a run of three months at the Forty-fourth Street Theater. Burgess Meredith, her leading man, was compelled to wear lifts in his shoes to approximate her height.

"When I first met Burgess," Ingrid said, "I immediately relaxed. He had such a free and easy manner. In Sweden you have to be careful about saying the correct thing and doing the correct thing. Everyone hides inside himself, afraid to be himself. But Burgess made me feel comfortable right away. He would call me 'You big Swede,' and I laughed and loved it."

It was remarkable that Scandinavian phlegm and frigidity could be transmuted into Molnar's tempestuous Julie. But "the big Swede" accomplished it nightly as she gripped her emotional reflexes and kindled the role to life.

At the end of May, 1940, *Liliom* closed and Ingrid went to Hollywood. There she leased a modest two-bedroom furnished apartment on Shirley Place in Beverly Hills. She took her maid, Mabel, with her, and with Pia settled down to an unmovie-starrish life. She renewed her association and English lessons with Ruth Roberts, rented a blue Ford coupe, packed her own groceries, and explored the region.

In midsummer Lindstrom, homesick for his family, boarded a Swedish freighter and came to New York where Ingrid joined him. They occupied a small suite on the thirty-fourth floor of the Hotel Pierre.

"Petter didn't like New York," Ingrid said. "He was very

uncomfortable living in a room so high up. After two weeks he went back to Sweden."

In September, Selznick loaned her to Columbia Pictures for *Adam Had Four Sons*, which was based on a popular novel. With Warner Baxter as costar and Gregory Ratoff once again as director, she essayed the role of a governess who had to contend with the resistance of the boys to their father's love for her.

In November, with but a few days' respite, she went to MGM, again on loan, to do *Rage in Heaven* with actors Robert Montgomery and George Sanders. The role of a secretary courted by two rivals offered meager scope for her talents, but she, nonetheless, was happy to be back before the cameras. Other stars could complain of being rushed from one picture into another, but not Ingrid. She thrived on work.

By the end of December, *Rage in Heaven* was completed and, after a ten-day "rest," MGM brought her back for *Dr. Jekyll and Mr. Hyde*, a remake of the classic with Spencer Tracy. In agreeing to do *Jekyll*, however, Ingrid rejected the leading female part—ultimately played by Lana Turner—in favor of the lesser but more vivid role of "the bad girl."

It was typical of this dedicated actress to seek off-beat roles, characterizations invested with some oddity or idiosyncrasy that set them apart. "I like crazy parts," she said. "Something I can get my teeth into. Deliver me from these straight, goody-goody leading ladies."

Jekyll was directed by Victor Fleming of *Gone With the Wind* fame. A Viking of a man, Fleming was more than twice Ingrid's age, but he was ageless. Six feet three, part Cherokee, silver-maned, he was vibrant and vital, and sexier than any male star he ever guided.

At various times on our travels Ingrid spoke of Fleming, and I gleaned from her words and her manner that she experienced an emotion for him which I doubt she ever felt for any other man. A curiously chaste relationship, it was circumscribed, it seemed to me, by their own individual marital loyalties. There were many occasions when I was a charmed observer of their tender mutual adoration. He never addressed her by name; it was always "Angel."

Fleming was once asked in an interview to discourse on Ingrid Bergman. Unhesitatingly, he said, "She's an angel."

"Can you amplify that, Mr. Fleming?"

"That's all," he said. "She's an angel."

3.

Hollywood

AS THE Bergman career burgeoned in the film capital, another career was in the making in Stockholm. It is a commonplace in Hollywood for a screen star's husband to take the easy route, play at selling real estate or managing a professional football team, the while he basks in his wife's prominence and perquisites. But this sort of subordination was not in Petter Lindstrom's nature. At a belated stage of life—now thirty-seven—he tenaciously approached a doctorate in medicine.

But Stockholm was two hearts distant from Hollywood, and day by day he became increasingly lonesome. Homesick for his wife and daughter, he explored the possibilities of completing his studies in America. Ingrid broached the matter to David Selznick, and through the intercession of his medical acquaintances Lindstrom was admitted to the University of Rochester, New York, in September, 1940.

The Swedish medical student started from scratch in a language that often seemed beyond his reach. "It was so hard for Petter," Ingrid said, "especially with medical terms. He already had studied some English, but he knew only the basic words, so the Swedish-English dictionary and his instructors had a pretty rough time of it. Goodness, how hard he worked! To help both of us we tried always to speak English with each other, but once in a while we'd get stuck and fall back on Swedish."

In Rochester, Lindstrom rented a small nondescript house and, between pictures, Ingrid took Pia and the maid and went through the motions of being an ordinary housewife. Or, more correctly, of trying to be; for the transition from the world of glamor was not as smooth as it appeared on the surface. Buying groceries, cooking, keeping house, and the busy work that housewives get involved in might be a welcome change for a week or two, but as a steady diet, say for several months, it was a bit too much for one whose heart was before the cameras.

"Rochester was a quiet, plain city," Ingrid said, "and it was wrong for me to have expected more. But for me it was unbearably dull, with nothing to do. The only people I met were Petter's doctor friends, and when they came to the house all the conversation was medicine. This was surely natural and the way it should be, but for me, it was not easy.

"*Dr. Jekyll* finished at the end of February, 1941, and I went to Rochester with no definite work to look forward to. After a while I got so bored I couldn't stand it. I called Kay Brown and went to New York for a few days."

In the big city she caught the new plays, saw the latest movies, strolled along her beloved Fifth Avenue. She browsed through the Museum of Modern Art, gorged on chocolate ice cream and hot fudge sundaes at Schrafft's, and savored the specialty of Hamburger Heaven. But after several such excursions the yearning to work obsessed her.

"It's awful to sit around for months trying to find something to do. I couldn't understand the reason for these long layoffs. David Selznick was too fussy; nothing was good enough. Either the story wasn't right for me or the part wasn't big enough. I didn't care how short the part was as long as it was a good acting part."

She hounded Selznick for an assignment and, to appease her, in August he staged a production of Eugene O'Neill's *Anna Christie* at the 800-seat civic playhouse, the Lobero Theater in Santa Barbara, California. John Houseman directed the play, which is concerned with a prostitute who returns to the home of her estranged father. Ingrid was lauded for her performance and subsequently repeated it at San Francisco's Geary Theater and in summer stock at Maplewood, New Jersey.

"After *Anna* I took Pia to Rochester," said Ingrid, "and moped around for several weeks, waiting for a call to go to work. Then I took Pia back to Hollywood, thinking that if I was there something would be more likely to pop up. People used to say, 'You're getting paid for it, so why are you worrying?' They had no idea what I was talking about. I never played for money, or for audiences either. I played to satisfy myself. When I wasn't working I was miserable."

Purposeful activity was the core of her existence. Assiduously, she crammed at her English, then added singing lessons though she nurtured no illusions about her wispy mezzo-soprano. She delved omnivorously into biographies and novels and published plays. She read the lives of Sarah Bernhardt and Eleanora Duse. The craving to learn and grow kept prodding her.

"Just loafing around kills me," she once told me. "I hate everything that moves slowly. I hate slowness in thinking, and slow crowds in the streets drive me crazy. Goodness, I even wash my own hair because I can't bear to sit still under a drier."

The "idle" months transformed her into a fanatic movie fan. Accompanied by Ruth Roberts—now an inseparable companion—she would attend a double-feature matinee, have dinner, see another double-feature, rush somewhere else for the late show, and get to her apartment long after midnight. Five movies in one day!

A fraction of this frenetic zeal could be ascribed to the need for diversion, but mainly it was a desire to take stock of her colleagues, their techniques and accomplishments. And on these forays time-out-for-dinner usually meant the Beachcomber, off Hollywood Boulevard, which enchanted Ingrid with its South Seas decor and artificial rain. She sampled its rum masterpieces and relished rumaki, an appetizer of spiced chicken liver and water chestnuts wrapped in crisp bacon.

She frequented the open-air Farmer's Market, dallied at the stalls of lush comestibles, and loaded up on fruits and cheeses. Seldom was she recognized, for she never affected the mannerisms she might have. Her costume was usually unbecoming dark slacks, a peasant blouse, or the dreadful dirndl of the day. She rarely was recognized as a star.

She was happy about this because it left her free to take long walks or go window-shopping, or stand in a theater queue. Whatever her attitude, if Ingrid's outward appearance induced a measure of anonymity, it was due more to lack of taste than design; the early Bergman simply had no feeling for style or self-adornment.

"I abhorred playing society women who were terribly clever and who were all dolled up like window models. Clothes didn't interest me. Off the screen I put on anything that was easy to wear, mostly because of laziness. I couldn't be bothered going from store to store to match a hat and gloves."

She considered jewelry ostentatious, and neither owned nor wore any save a plain gold wedding band. She bought a pea-green Ford coupe and kept handy on the seat a battered Panama hat to keep her hair from blowing. Her correspondents received chatty letters typed on a portable with four fingers.

Her lusty frame posed a perpetual dietetic problem, solved only by sheer will plus a suicidal regimen three or four weeks in advance of a picture. Her normal weight fluctuated between 130 and 136 pounds, six or more of which she would lose by the time she stood before a camera. To quell the pangs of hunger between meals she nibbled on Swedish biscuits and cheese, and consumed countless cups of scalding black coffee. Her dresses were size 14 and shoes 7-B.

She was between pictures when Ernest Hemingway's *For Whom the Bell Tolls* rose to top the best-seller lists and was purchased by Paramount Pictures. Ingrid read it and forthwith harangued Selznick to get her the role of Maria. But Selznick needed no urging; he had already set out to do so. "A tremendous part for you," he told her. "I won't rest until you get it. And I promise you this–if you play it you'll win the Academy Award."

Paramount, however, was lukewarm; they scrutinized her films, and shook their Olympian heads. The hefty Swede was not their conception of the Spanish miss who went abundling in the battlefields of the Spanish civil war. Month after month a procession of candidates tested for the coveted role—Olivia de Havilland, Susan Hayward, Joan Fontaine, a ballet dancer named Vera Zorina, and a host of others.

David Selznick connived with his brother Myron, head of a powerful talent agency, to persuade Hemingway to endorse Ingrid. The author half-heartedly did so, but Paramount remained unconvinced.

Ingrid was at the winter resort of Sun Valley, Idaho, skiing with her husband, when a message was relayed to her; Hemingway was in San Francisco enroute to China and could a meeting be arranged? Ingrid took a plane and Hemingway took one look. "I guess I needn't have worried," he said. An instant rapport was struck between them. Elaborating on his heroine's personality, he described how Maria's hair should be shorn like a boy's. Before they parted he presented her with a copy of the book. On the return flight Ingrid read what he had inscribed, "For Ingrid Bergman, who is the Maria of this story."

Soon after the Lindstroms returned home and Paramount proclaimed that Vera Zorina had been awarded the acting plum. Ingrid's dejection hit bottom.

"I got hold of Ruth and cried on her shoulder," she recalled. "She commiserated with me and said, 'This isn't the end, Ingrid. Who can tell why things happen as they do? In the end we often find out that our deepest disappointments were the best things for us.'

"After I left Ruth I was still feeling low, so I stopped at a drugstore and had a hot fudge sundae. Then I walked a few blocks and had another one. I got in the car and drove to Santa Monica. I walked along the Palisades park and stared at the ocean. Then I had another sundae and went home, feeling a little bit groggy."

Fortunately for her state of mind, Ingrid was shortly signed for Warner Brothers' *Casablanca* with "tough" actor Humphrey Bogart. She played a refugee who, thinking her husband dead, works her way to the Moroccan city and there meets the American, Bogart. The synthetic role offered her scant scope, but she managed to raise it to her level and eventually the picture was widely acclaimed.

Concurrently, *Bell Tolls* started shooting with great fanfare, but before long word seeped throughout the industry that all was not as rosy as the publicity. A fatal error had been made in casting; the role of Maria was not coming off as desired. After two weeks of costly filming the picture was halted.

Missing no bets, David Selznick hammered at the Paramount gates and, in late August, 1942, when *Casablanca* was completed, Ingrid donned a pair of pants, a dirty shirt, cropped her own hair with a pair of house scissors, and stepped into the role of the contested Maria.

"My only change of costume," said Ingrid, "was when sometimes I rolled up my sleeves or rolled them down. I loved it."

Few actresses prepare for a role as intensively as Ingrid Bergman. If the screenplay is based on a book she'll pore through that book several times and frequently follow it up with a bibliography of pertinent tomes. I borrowed her copy of *For Whom the Bell Tolls* and found it studded with penciled underlines, noting descriptions, moods, character analyses, and even dialogue. For example, "Her hair was the golden brown of a grain field that has been burned dark in the sun but it was cut short all over her head so that it was but little longer than the fur on a beaver pelt"; ". . . her legs slanted long and clean from the open cuffs of the trousers as she sat with her hands across her knees and he could see the shape of her small, uptilted breasts under the gray shirt"; "He looked at her face . . . suddenly hungry and young and wanting"; " 'I cannot kiss,' she said. 'I do not know how.' " Screen writers have lost many a disputed point with Ingrid Bergman, thanks to her careful preparation for a role.

For three months in the California High Sierras, where the picture was filmed under the direction of Sam Wood, Ingrid shared lean, long-legged Gary Cooper's cinematic sleeping bag. Rumors trickled down to the Hollywood lowlands and the movie gossip-mongers drooled happily, "There's more than meets the eye between that Western star and the European import." But the rumors turned out to be a press agent's invention and eventually were lost in the shuffle of succeeding rumors about other stars in other pictures.

When the *Bell* ceased tolling at the end of October, 1942, Ingrid made her last journey to Rochester. Three months later I met her in Minneapolis on the OWI assignment.

On March 2nd she was reunited with Gary Cooper and director Wood in the screen version of Edna Ferber's popular *Saratoga Trunk*. She covered her scraggly Hemingway haircut with a brunette wig and again demonstrated her versatility as Ferber's unbridled, unvirtuous Creole.

At Warner Brothers, where the picture was made, Sam Wood said to me, "Bergman's loveliness is more than external. It comes from in here (he patted his abdomen). When she plays a love scene she blushes—real blushes. And when her cheeks get pink you can see it on the screen because there's no make-up to hide it. It's a beautiful sight to see."

If there was a real-life prototype of a part she was about to portray, Ingrid hunted them out, examined and absorbed their uniqueness. Her next picture, *Gaslight*, produced by MGM studios, presented such an opportunity, the role of a wife driven to the verge of insanity by a husband (Charles Boyer) who wishes to get rid of her.

"George Cukor was the director," said Ingrid, "and he arranged through a doctor friend for me to visit a private neuropsychiatric hospital. There I followed the head doctor around as he went from patient to patient. There was one young woman who especially interested me. A lot of her strangeness went into my part."

She scouts her leading men the way a football coach scouts an opposing team, by seeing them in action. In the Selznick projection room she ran all of Charles Boyer's pictures before commencing *Gaslight*. Gary Cooper, Robert Montgomery, Humphrey Bogart, Spencer Tracy and others were subjected to the same microscopic examination.

Nonetheless, despite this artistic consecration, when the day's last scene is shot the play-acting goes into storage, and Bergman reverts to Ingrid.

For charge accounts she signed herself as Mrs. Petter Lindstrom. For fans her name was scrawled in a style reserved for that purpose, on the notion that her true signature, the "I" and the "B" stroked in a broad flourish, was a strictly private matter.

At one-thirty one morning, by mere chance, I caught her walking in a drizzling rain on a deserted street in Beverly Hills. She wore a light trench coat and the usual flat-heeled slippers. She was hatless. I drew my car up and called in alarm, "Ingrid! What the devil are you doing at this crazy hour?"

"I'm taking a walk," she said calmly. "What's wrong with that?"

"Well, that might be all right for anybody else, but for you to . . ."

"I think that's silly. What could happen to me?"

She refused to be driven to her car parked three blocks away, so I joined her. In the American tradition I shifted to the curbside two or three times as we crossed streets or altered directions.

"Why do you keep doing that?" she said.

"It's polite, that's why."

"Ugh, what a foolish custom," she said. "No sense to it. And men taking their hats off in a crowded elevator, pushing their elbows, making it worse. They don't know whether to hold it up or hold it down, or in front or behind . . ."

Returning home from a Community Chest function one evening we dropped by for a daiquiri at Perino's cocktail lounge. The affair had gone off well, and her spirits were high.

A smartly attired woman nearby kept eyeing Ingrid. As we sipped our cocktails, she and her escort got up to leave. Pausing a moment at our table, manifestly feeling no pain, she said, "Want to tell you something, dearie. I've been watching you. You laugh too much. If you didn't laugh so much you'd look exactly like Ingrid Bergman."

"Thank you very much," said Ingrid, whereupon she laughed louder than before. The benevolent lady grunted her disapproval and stalked out.

On several occasions, because of her incredibly fresh appearance, the legality of her age, currently twenty-seven, was questioned by a bartender or waiter, at which time I would whisper her identity.

"Why do you have to tell him that?" Ingrid would say with displeasure.

"How else can I convince them? You don't carry your passport, do you?"

On my birthday her maid delivered a laundry basket to my home containing sundry articles bedded in a sea of crumpled tissue paper. A card was attached to the handle in her own handwriting, "Happy birthday to Joe—from Ingrid."

To each article was attached one of these separate cards:

On a package of chewing gum, "May you stop smoking."

On a bar of candy, "May you stay sweet."

On a bottle of vitamins, "May you stay young."

On a fifth of champagne: "May you stay happy."

On an apple, "To keep the doctor away. Stay healthy!"

On a bottle of aquavit, "When you run out of Scotch!"

I phoned to thank her. "Oh, I'm glad you like them," she chuckled. "But please return the basket—that is not part of the present!"

Back in Rochester, meanwhile, Petter Lindstrom completed the required courses, then, in September, 1943, transferred to Stanford University at Palo Alto, California, for postgraduate training. The college is just outside San Francisco, roughly 480 miles from Hollywood.

Periodically, Ingrid flew north to spend a weekend with him, but because he roomed in a campus dormitory, they took a small apartment in any San Francisco hotel that was available. Like tourists they dined at the famous restaurants, haunted Fisherman's Wharf, climbed the narrow streets of Chinatown, and motored through the moist green countryside.

Wearied by the task of mastering medical terminology in a foreign language, Lindstrom fell back on his native tongue during these weekends. As a consequence, when Ingrid returned to work on Monday morning her accent was obviously more pronounced, which entranced the listener but drove the sound recorders frantic.

One weekend, having worked late on Saturday night, she skipped the conjugal tryst and stayed home. On Monday morning, back on the *Gaslight* set, the sound engineer suddenly tossed off his earphones and yelled with joy: "I hear that you're not speaking to your husband, Miss Bergman. That's great! Stay mad until the picture's over, will you?"

One day, seated in her portable dressing room on the set, I probed around for material for a magazine story I wanted to write. Among my questions was what quality she admired most in her husband.

"Oh, no," she said. "I don't want to talk about that."

"I don't mean anything of a personal nature," I said. "Something abstract—like tolerance, for instance—tolerance for other people's ideas, viewpoints, failings . . ."

She mulled it over for a second, then said, "Yes. You can say that."

Early next morning my secretary buzzed that Miss Bergman was calling. Before I could complete a hello, she said, "Halloo, Joe? This is Ingrid . . ." Invariably, her phone calls, even to intimate friends, were prefaced by this self-identification, as if one might fail to recognize her vibrant voice. This singular quirk persists to this day.

She wanted to see me and within a few minutes I was on the set.

"I've been thinking about that 'tolerance,'" she said. "I don't like it. It is not true. Petter is not tolerant about anything." I promised to have it stricken.

Some time later, still digging for usable publicity items, we discussed whether if she had to choose between her work or her home she would give up her career.

Her jaws snapped grimly and she slowly shook her head. "Never," she said. And that was the end of that question.

Moved by the desire to excel in anything she undertook, she added ballroom dancing to her schedule, with emphasis on the tango, rhumba and, of all things, the jitterbug. The Hollywood Canteen, a converted barn which became the dream-goal of furloughed service men, saw her often, doling out sandwiches or dancing with the gobs and GI's. She took part in Canteen shows along with many other top stars. Once she did an act with comedian Jack Benny during the course of which they were to engage in a tussle. Those present will long remember how Ingrid, underestimating her own strength, hurled Benny across the footlights into the laps of startled enlisted men squatting on the floor.

She maintained a small library of huge personal scrapbooks, and was hard put to it to keep them up-to-date. Seeing her pasting away one day, I turned the pages of one and noted that unfavorable reviews of her pictures were calculatedly placed alongside the laudatory. When I asked her about it, she said, "It is good for me to remember the bad ones as well as the good ones."

Throughout this early period of introducing Ingrid Bergman, I was charged with countless other duties at Selznick, publicizing not only an ambitious production entitled *Since You Went Away*, but also his stable of top ranking stars, innumerable starlets, several directors, and Selznick himself.

One of the few genuine giants of the film world, Selznick's quasi-pathological addiction to written memoranda is well known. The top of my desk blistered with prime examples.

On rare occasions he would invite my appraisal of a missive aimed at someone else. One such instance was a peppery memo to producer Walter Wanger, pertaining to the presentation of the forthcoming Motion Picture Academy Awards; Wanger was an officer and Selznick chairman of the Documentary Film Division of that organization.

After digesting the document I entered his king-size office. "David," I said, "I can't understand how you can do a thing like this. Wanger is a very good friend of yours–after his house caught fire you sent him five hundred books to replenish his library. How can you now say such things to him? This will alienate him forever. What can you gain by it?"

Accepting my criticism with characteristic grace, he agreed to reduce the two-page philippic to one or two moderately couched paragraphs. The secretary was summoned and the rewrite begun.

The words flowed easily, the temper restrained; then abruptly, as if the desk imprisoned him, he raised his portly form and strode around the vast chamber. Never groping for the right word, never fumbling for the apt phrase, he paced up and down, dodged between furniture, encircled the room, plopped into a chair, instantly got up, grabbed a murderous shillelagh, whacked at the couch, and glanced fleetingly to note my reaction. He never missed a beat; a torrent of magnificent vituperation gushed like a fire hose. Moderation was smothered in a paroxysm of adjectives. He was sage and philosopher, poet and cannibal. The hapless memo was right back where it started.

But of all the Selznick targets the most convenient and vulnerable was the publicity department. Scarcely a day passed without one of his acrid effusions. As the year waned their numbers increased, acerbated by phone calls at three or four in the morning, or being needlessly paged on a golf course of a Saturday afternoon. My stomach began to act up.

For me there was one sure release from the inquisition—Ingrid Bergman. A never-failing source of repose, a few minutes with her was anesthetic and elixir. One mid-afternoon I called upon her about some publicity matters. On the agenda for discussion was a personal appearance at a charity show sponsored by a local newspaper.

"No, I don't care to do that," she said.

"But look, Ingrid, other stars are appearing—it's for charity, not for the paper. You don't have to make a speech or anything—just take a bow . . ."

She suddenly froze. "I said I didn't want to do it," she said, "and I won't! If I do it for one paper, I'll have to do it for all the others. Don't try to argue me into it!"

I gazed at her a long moment, then quietly said, "Very well. Hereafter if there's anything you want, see my assistant—or anybody else in the department." I picked up my papers and left.

I gave the incident no more thought, but six weeks later, unable physically and temperamentally to stomach the rigors of my office, I resigned.

Paradoxically, I not only admired and respected David O. Selznick, but was fond of him as a person. My impulsive resignation left me with mixed feelings, but my doctor cheered, for long had he prescribed that I "either get out of the business or go away for a long rest. There's no medical cure for what ails you."

As my wife and I drove south along the coast toward Ensenada, Mexico, Ingrid Bergman was flying in the opposite direction aboard an Army cargo plane to spend Christmas and New Year's entertaining troops in icy Alaskan outposts.

There had not been one word from any of the Selznick stars—including Ingrid Bergman.

4.

In Many Directions

SHORTLY after I had belatedly inserted a 1944 calendar in the desk holder, the telephone rang. My automatic greeting was arrested by a familiar accent I had not heard in thirteen weeks.

"Halloo, Joe? This is Ingrid." The same emphasis on the first syllable.

"Hello, Ingrid. How are you?"

"Fine, fine!" she said cheerily. "Are you busy now? I mean are you doing anything?"

"Oh, I'm handling Ronald Colman again, and doing some magazine pieces. Why?"

"Uhh, I have been asked by the Treasury Department to go on a Bond Tour. I said I would like you to go with me. Can you go?"

"What about Mitch Rawson (my successor at Selznick)?"

"I said I wanted you," she said.

"What does David say?"

"Oh . . . he didn't care much for the idea, but he finally gave in. You know how stubborn I am."

Unaware that I was embarking upon the most gratifying segment of an erratic career, I agreed.

"And come early," she said, "so you can see the new house we bought. The address is 1220 North Benedict Canyon Drive—a little ways back of the Beverly Hills Hotel."

On the appointed day I arrived with a chauffeur-driven limousine provided by the Motion Picture War Activities Committee, under whose auspices these junkets were conducted.

The Lindstrom home, the first they ever owned, was an oversize mountain lodge, situated in the foothills a mile from the shopping district. Constructed of chiseled stone and hand-hewn redwood, it nestled in heavy foliage at the end of an ascending driveway.

I climbed the stone steps, crossed a tiled veranda, and rang the bell. The door was flung open.

"Dr. Lindstrom?"

"Yah . . ."

"I'm Joe Steele."

"Oh, come in—come in!" He grasped my hand like a vise and drew me inside. A team of horses could not have pulled me back. Pinkish white skin, an up-tilted nose, dark hair curling back over a high smooth forehead—the immediate impression was of an overgrown country boy.

"That you, Joe?" Ingrid's voice came from the rear. "Be with you in a minute. Let Peter show you the house. . . ." She called him Peter; the Americanization of the Lindstroms had begun.

Grinning jovially, he led me around. "Ingrid calls it the 'Barn,' " he said, then chuckled irrepressibly. The vaulted living hall, with a great stone fireplace, was as big as two barns. Sprouting from it, like sawed-off branches, were: a coppered bar-and-grill, a master bedroom, a den-office, a kitchen, and a servant's room converted into a child's room for four-year-old Pia. Meals were served at the kitchen end of the huge hall. The furnishings, adapted from the Swedish, came with the house. The Lindstrom staff comprised a housekeeper and cook; Miss Mary Jackson, Pia's governess; and Miss Doris Collup, their secretary.

"Please, I wish you would watch Ingrid's eating," Dr. Lindstrom said confidentially. "Don't encourage her. She's getting too fat."

Ingrid emerged from the bedroom, glowing with anticipation. "Now we can go," she said. She wore a plain gray suit and no hat. I relieved her of a small suitcase and a heavy Persian lamb topcoat.

"Is this all you're taking?" I said, seeing no make-up kit, hat box or anything else.

"I have all I need in here," she said.

She kissed her husband and daughter good-bye. She was like a race horse at the starting gate, eager to be off. As the car backed out of the driveway and out of sight, she slid down against the seat with a gesture of abandon. "Isn't it wonderful!" she said. "How I like to keep going! I hate to sit still . . ."

In her drawing room aboard the Santa Fe "Chief" I said, "I'll give you twenty minutes to make yourself comfortable. I'll get myself settled and then come back and we'll have a drink."

As the drab rail-side yielded to golden citrus groves, highballs in hand, we sipped a "Skoal!" to each other.

"Now tell me," I said, "why you wanted me to come with you."

"I knew you were going to ask me that," she said sheepishly. "I decided that you were honest—I could trust you."

"Who went with you to Alaska?"

"Nobody. Only entertainers were allowed by the War Department. My, it was fun. That's when my jitterbug came in handy. The men, goodness, most of them were just boys, they loved it. There was one soldier, he looked like a baby, he just sat there and stared. Pretty soon I couldn't stand it any more so I turned and stared back at him. He got very flustered and said, 'Excuse me, ma'am. I haven't seen a woman in three years.' I could have cried."

Throughout the war years, between picture assignments, Ingrid journeyed near and far to speak or entertain or merely lend her magnetic presence on behalf of some war effort; traveling by car or Pullman or day coach, by passenger plane or military aircraft. Her housing accommodations ranged from rooms that shared a community bath to de luxe hotel suites; in temperatures from arctic to tropic. I had learned from others that, on the flight to Alaska in the Army cargo plane, she eased herself against bags of freight and quietly went to sleep.

"Tell me about Peter," I said. "Is he through at Stanford?"

"Yes, he's all finished with school. I'm so glad for him. He worked like a horse—and now it's all over. He's at the County

General Hospital, doing what he always wanted to do. I think it's wonderful!"

"It certainly is."

"I'm very proud of him. The work he's doing now is so much more important than my work."

Ingrid's wartime pilgrimages occurred intermittently throughout the hostilities and took her in many directions. Here are a few highlights, not necessarily chronological:

Indianapolis

By prearrangement, we were police-escorted from Chicago's Dearborn Station to the airport to enplane for Indianapolis. The sky was in ferment; mountains of boiling black clouds turned the late afternoon into night. Barbs of lightning split the clouds and boomed in a thundering fugue. Dust and rubbish and old newspapers swirled in blinding nebulae. No birds were in the air.

All commercial ships were grounded, waiting for weather clearance. We sat in an executive's office and waited. An hour passed; Ingrid grew restive. "My goodness, Joe. What are we going to do?" she asked.

Thinking of a possible solution, I called the nearest Air Force Base and stated our predicament: Ingrid Bergman was here at the behest of the War Department to headline a War Bond rally in the Indianapolis Coliseum; six thousand people would be waiting to see her.

They would take it up with the Commanding Officer and report back. In a few minutes they called: "The only ships that can make it in this weather are P-48s—fighter planes—be kind of crowded, but it'll get you through."

"Good enough. How soon can it be here?"

"In about twenty minutes."

Ingrid relaxed. I got her a pack of chewing gum. Thirty, forty minutes passed. I was wanted on the telephone.

"Bad news for you. The C.O. has decided it's too risky even for a P-48."

"Oh, this is just awful," said Ingrid, visibly distressed. "All those people waiting there."

There remained one last resource, private planes. After several inquiries I was directed to a leather-jacketed individual busily tinkering with the sole engine of a vintage four-seater. I posed our problem, but when I mentioned Ingrid's name, he said, "Who?"

When I elucidated, he mumbled vaguely, stepped outside the hangar, and scanned the skies. He reminded me of Wallace Beery, with a potbelly, bulbous nose, and shaggy hair. His belted trousers drooped precariously below his bulge. He was not Hollywood's notion of a pilot.

"Yeah, we can make it," he said. "That'll be forty bucks."

In fifteen minutes we were airborne, cooped inside a noisy, stifling, gasoline-drenched crate. It quivered and rattled and bounced like a roller-whip in an amusement park. Both David Selznick and Peter Lindstrom would have had my head examined, or chopped off.

From the beginning there had been no comment from Ingrid. I glanced to see how she was taking it, but she was absorbed in the spectacular heavenly display. I touched her arm and nodded at the squat, unheroic figure at the controls.

She broke into a smile, leaned her head close, and whispered: "Clark Gable." Quietly, she laughed at her jest.

Pittsburgh

A henna-haired amazon weaved down the aisle of the dining car. Spotting Ingrid, she turned around, gave her a jarring slap across the shoulder, and whooped, "Hiya! Y'know, when you just walked through the club car, a man said, 'Now there goes a gorgeous woman!' I said, 'Why, don't you know who that is? That's Ingrid Bergman, the picture star, that's who that is!' You know what the dope said? 'Never heard of her. I haven't seen a movie in ten years. But that's my idea of a gorgeous woman!' "

Henna-hair gave Ingrid another whack and disappeared. The normal sounds of diners were stilled; eating tools remained poised over plates; all faces converged on Ingrid.

She gulped down the mouthful she'd been holding, turned a

salmon-pink, and stammered, "I think my coffee's cold—maybe I'll have dessert—no, I'd better not . . ."

On these wartime junkets Hollywood players were invariably furnished with literary material volunteered by screen writers. The Indianapolis speech was stuffy and verbose, utterly unsuited to Ingrid's personality. She, however, approached every personal appearance as a challenge not to be sloughed off. In her compartment, stretched out on the berth fully clothed, she wondered if there wasn't something else she could do in Pittsburgh.

"The rally is going to be held in the ball park, eight o'clock tonight," I said. "That means ten or fifteen thousand people. The speaker's stand will probably be where the pitcher's box is, and the whole place will be floodlighted. Paul Whiteman and his band, and a couple of young actors—Lieutenant William Holden and Private John Payne—are on the program.

"Are you familiar with 'The Battle Hymn of the Republic'? (She shook her head.) For my money it's the most thrilling of patriotic songs—every American knows the chorus . . ."

To the clickety-click of the speeding train I ventured a qualmish rendition—"Glory, glory, Hallelujah!"

"The Allies have just invaded Normandy. It's the beginning of the end for Hitler. The first verse goes this way—'Mine eyes have seen the glory of the coming of the Lord.' I'm not sure of the rest.

"Let's throw out your speech and write a short one, one that sounds more like you. When you come to the end of it you start reciting the first verse as if it was a part of the speech. Then about the third line we'll get Paul Whiteman to sneak in with music. When you come to the chorus you sing right out and the band comes in full.

"He must have a vocalist who can come to the mike and help you. Then all of us pitch in, and at that point the vocalist signals to the audience to join in. It can be very effective."

"But you don't know the words," Ingrid said. "How can I learn them in time?"

"I'll get someone to dig up a copy while you're visiting the hospital."

"You think Whiteman can do it on such short notice?"

" 'Course he can. He's an old trouper. The worst he can do is ad lib it, and that'll be merely perfect."

The tours were meticulously organized to get the utmost benefit from the performer's service and at the same time consider his or her well-being. Ingrid, however, had the stamina of a bulldozer and frequently upset the best-laid plans.

From the Pittsburgh rail station we were driven sixty miles to the De Shon Army Hospital, where one hour was allotted for bedside visits with the wounded. This would allow time for the drive back, time to freshen up, have dinner, and be at the ball park at 7:30.

The medical officer who had us in tow knew of the rigid schedule and, in his zeal to spread her time as much as possible throughout the huge institution, he hustled Ingrid from ward to ward, where shattered men stared in disbelief at the Nordic apparition. She was being pushed and I could feel her tensing.

The hour was quickly over. He had his instructions, said the young officer. The Bergman temper burst into full bloom. She waved an open palm under his nose.

"Why? Why?" she cried. "This is not right! I cannot go now—we must spend more time. I will not be rushed away from them!"

It was sooty-dark when we reached our hotel; a quick shower, nervous attendants, sandwiches sent up, panicky officials, but we made the ball park precisely at the appointed hour.

While Ingrid paced around, oblivious to the usual backstage hubbub, memorizing her new speech and "The Battle Hymn," I talked with Whiteman.

"Sounds all right," he said, "but I don't have an arrangement for the boys." The great music man brooded a moment, then said, "It's okay. We'll improvise."

An hour later, without a rehearsal, without an orchestration, without a flaw, these showfolk, who had only just met, collaborated in a spine-tingling patriotic performance. The Stowe classic resounded across the night-shaded stadium as twelve thousand voices muted the tiny tones of the big girl from Sweden.

"Miss Bergman," said Paul Whiteman, when the show came to

an end. "That was as fine a piece of trouping as I ever saw. I thank you."

The "Chamber of Commerce" speech back at Indianapolis catalyzed Ingrid's determination to make of each personal appearance a finished professional performance. When not engrossed in a movie script, she gradually assembled a formidable repertoire of verse, stories, and quotations. Long and short, dramatic and humorous, she drew upon them to fit the particular occasion.

She adopted Paul Gallico's prose-poem, "The Snow Goose," Ben Hecht's "The Miracle on the Pullman," Carl Sandburg's "Threes," and several whimsies from Samuel Hoffenstein's "Poems in Praise of Practically Nothing." Her favorite was an apocryphal quotation attributed to a soldier on the field of battle, "Dear Lord: I shall be very busy this day. I may forget Thee, but do not Thou forget me."

Canada

He studied Ingrid with deep absorption, like an author in search of a word. He was Gregory Clark, Canada's foremost war correspondent. The setting was backstage of the Auditorium at Toronto; the occasion, a rehearsal of a radio broadcast for the Canadian Victory Loan. Ingrid stood before the microphone narrating "The Snow Goose" as Percy Faith and his orchestra supplied the background music.

Clark, standing beside me, pensively said, "Now I know what it is she has. A girl in Paris said it for me.

"It was right after the American occupation; the city was beginning to come alive. Once again, girls rode their bicycles on the streets, and I was fascinated by their loveliness and chic appearance. I wondered how they accomplished this, considering their hardships and limited means. That evening I remarked about it to a young Parisienne.

" 'Class,' she said, 'is not what you wear, but how you *feel.*' "

The Canadian unit consisted of Ingrid, stage star Ralph Bellamy, singer Evelyn Knight, and the comedy team of Barry Wood and

Patsy Kelly. It was the raucous Miss Kelly, before an audience that jammed a frigid public square in Ottawa, who stopped the show with,

"What's Ingrid Bergman got that I can't have fixed?"

A genial transplanted American named Guy Herbert functioned as *chargé d'affaires* of our northern sojourn. Timorously, he imparted the news that, despite his protestations, Miss Bergman was to be the honored guest at an unscheduled dinner sponsored by one of the most prominent hostesses in the Canadian capital.

"But why must I?" said Ingrid. "All of us are here only to help sell Bonds, not to decorate somebody's party."

"I know," said Herbert, "I have strict orders to that effect from Hollywood. But, here, whatever our hostess says goes. She's already invited two hundred of the biggest names in society, the government, and the embassies. Even the Prime Minister might be there. If you refuse now it'll cause a lot of bad feeling and bad publicity."

"Ugh. It is not right," said Ingrid. "But I don't want to make trouble for anyone."

Ingrid was seated at her hostess's table. Ottawa's elite, bedecked in formal vesture, toyed with their cocktails and buzzed with chit-chat.

It was my policy at similar affairs to sit away from Ingrid so as to minimize my professional presence as much as possible. This arrangement was tacitly understood between us, but she knew that I would be constantly glancing in her direction for any sign of distress.

Presently, there was the familiar signal, a fleeting frown imperceptible to anyone but me. I casually stepped to her side and bent my ear.

"Have you met the Swedish Consul?" she whispered.

"I don't think so."

"Neither have I. Find out if he is here."

To avoid making a scene I beckoned Guy Herbert into the vestibule and asked him to please fetch our hostess. "Anything wrong?" he said. "I don't know," I said. "We'll soon find out."

Repressing her annoyance, she left her table.

"I'm sorry to trouble you," I said. "Miss Bergman wants to know if the Swedish Consul is here."

"No, he isn't," she said, rather stiffly. "He wasn't invited."

Ingrid, having excused herself from the table, joined us.

"No, he's not here, Ingrid," I said. "He was not invited."

"And why not?" she flared. "I am a Swede. If this party is in my honor, why wasn't the Swedish Consul invited? Every other country is represented, but not my country. Get him here right away or I shall leave!"

In twenty minutes the hostess was presenting to Ingrid her hastily procured countryman—a Nordic backwoods Lincoln; six feet, three or four inches of gangly bone, a tuxedo hanging on him like a clothes rack. Awkwardly, he looked down at a timid little woman at his side and introduced her as his wife.

Ingrid rose from her chair and greeted them warmly, then, pushing her chair to make room, indicated she wished them beside her. Chairs were brought and an animated conversation ensued while the rest of the table seemed strangely quiet. A false sense of peace reigned for a few minutes; then, that familiar signal again.

"I am very tired, Joe," Ingrid said, quite audibly. "I think we go. Yes?" As I pulled her chair out she beamed at the hostess, "I'm sorry but we have so much to do tomorrow. Thank you for a very nice party."

The Swedish diplomat and his wife promptly rose, bowed politely, expressed their thanks, and followed us out. We got into their nondescript car and were driven to the Consulate, a small weather-beaten frame house far on the edge of town.

It was nearing midnight when we left them to head for our hotel, the Chateau Laurier, after a *souper intime* of aquavit, scrambled eggs, and indecipherable Swedish.

The Earl of Athlone, Governor-General of Canada, and his charming diminutive wife, Princess Alice (sister of George V), held a reception for the troupe at Rideau Hall, the official residence.

When Guy Herbert and the Earl's emissary came to escort us,

they were aghast that Ingrid was bareheaded; it was unthinkable for a woman to appear hatless before royalty in daylight.

Unruffled, Ingrid dug into her suitcase and drew out the only hat she owned—a rumpled mannish black felt, brought along in case of bad weather. She unrumpled it, pulled it on, gave it a rakish tilt, and said: "How's that?"

The startled gentlemen surveyed the ensemble—flat-heeled slippers, a semiformal silk frock, and the incongruous bonnet. They nodded dubiously, but Ingrid Bergman was not fazed one whit. She strode toward the elevator, the personification of grace and dignity.

After we bade our hosts good night, I asked why she didn't buy herself a stylish hat.

"I just don't feel comfortable in one," she said. "I have a pinhead—it's too small for my body."

"But you wear them in pictures and they look fine."

"Oh, that's different. Then it's part of my costume."

The daily schedules—frequently expanded by local committees—would have evoked the worst tantrums from any actress. There were official luncheons, teas, cocktail parties, and suppers, with an occasional breakfast thrown in; expeditions to hospitals and military centers; press conferences and radio interviews; photographs with the mayor or the governor or the current hero. But there was never a peep from Ingrid Bergman; naught but an astonishing, unflagging zest for the job to be done.

In Toronto, on the last day, she attended a luncheon of women's clubs, did a radio interview, shopped to buy something for Pia, was made an honorary sergeant of the oldest regiment in Canada, the Queen's Own Rifles, spent three hours chatting with hundreds of recently returned wounded soldiers at the Christie Street Hospital, and sent her husband a wire ending with "AND JOE WON'T LET ME EAT."

With barely enough time remaining to make our plane, she granted an interview to Morley Callaghan, known as "Canada's Hemingway." Subsequently, Callaghan wrote in the *New World* magazine:

"...and while she talked...I was trying to find out what it was in her face that suggested such mobility of expression, such availability and warmth. First I thought it was her eyes because they brighten easily, and laughter comes into them, and she uses them mischievously. They are the attractive eyes of a gay and eager woman, and not at all like the eyes of a first-year university girl to whom Miss Bergman is often likened. Then suddenly it was plain that it was her mouth; everything that she was, and wanted to be, and promised to be, was there in her mouth: the smile, the eagerness, the breathless expectancy, then the sudden laughter; it was all there in her full generous mouth."

Traveling soon became a habit with her. No sooner had the director commanded "Cut!" on the final scene of a film than Ingrid was itching to be off on some war effort or on a play-going trip to New York.

Time spent at her lovely home, in her swimming pool (which came later), or at Palm Springs, or Sun Valley, or at any of the spots where other film stars customarily relaxed increasingly palled on her. "Taking it easy" for Ingrid was not easy.

Oddly enough, Dr. Lindstrom, as head of the family, evinced a bland acquiescence in his wife's compulsive flights. Perhaps it was a rare comprehension born of the mysterious things that go on in private lives: an understanding of her deeply ingrained restlessness. Wherever the truth lay, the facts were that Lindstrom yielded time and again, even encouraged such hazardous wartime jaunts as Alaska and Germany; and their recurrent good-byes were devoid of dissonance or shadow.

Leaving the housekeeper, cook, and Pia's governess to look after things, Ingrid would embrace her child and her husband—if he had not already gone to the hospital—and enter the hired limousine aglow with thoughts of adventures to come and, as always, when the car rounded the corner, she leaned back, sank into repose, and said, "Here we go again!"

On one occasion I heard her ask her husband, who handled all the finances, how many War Bonds they had bought. "Why do you want to know?" he said.

"I haven't the stomach to ask people to buy more bonds," she replied, "if we haven't bought all we can ourselves."

"Ahh, don't you worry," he said. "We have all we can afford."

Minnesota Revisited

In view of her successful previous visit, the state of Minnesota appealed to Ingrid to spearhead the state Bond Drive. Ingrid promptly responded and we were on our way. In the plane she reached into her small purse (they were all small, since she carried virtually nothing) and showed me a fine new wristwatch.

"Well, well!" I declared. "So you finally blew yourself to something."

"Oh, no. It's not for me," she said. "I bought it yesterday to take with me. If we get some place where people aren't buying enough bonds, I'll pretend it's my own watch and auction it off to the highest bidder."

"Smart girl," I said. "How much was it?"

"That's not important."

"How much?"

"One hundred and forty-five dollars," she said, "but don't you go writing about it."

Ben Hecht's "Miracle on the Pullman" told of a carload of apathetic passengers who are so roused by the spirit of a dead soldier being borne home on the same train that they stage an impromptu bond rally and end by singing "My Country 'Tis of Thee." The spirit's name was Joe and his thoughts were revealed in a running conversation with the train whistle.

Ingrid had a special fondness for this fable because it was not only pertinent to her mission, but offered twelve speaking parts, and the voice of the train whistle particularly appealed to her sense of fantasy.

The voice of the whistle would go: "Woooo-Jooooe-you okay? Enjoyin' the scenery, Jooooe?" And Ingrid would give it all she had; in public squares, factories, clubrooms, halls, theaters, and aircraft plants; wherever a War Bond might be sold.

The noontime scramble inside a big city bank would seem as unlikely a site for a bond rally as a New York subway at 5:30. Yet

Ingrid was steered into Minneapolis' Midland Bank, presented to the officials, and invited to take over. Without batting an eye she pushed aside the vice-president's name plate, mounted the desk, and raised to her full height and gauged the situation.

Someone announced her presence to the heedless audience, and Ingrid launched into the Hecht story. Depositors streamed through the revolving doors, footsteps clattered over the marble floor, and marbled walls re-echoed her monologue.

I signalled for a change of material, but she only glowered at me and continued, never raising her voice above the din. Gradually, one by one, the tellers' cages muffled into stillness, depositors turned to listen, and newcomers through the revolving doors intuitively joined the tableau.

Riding to another rally in St. Paul, Ingrid said, "Why did you try to stop me?"

"I thought it was a mistake to do 'Miracle' under those conditions."

"I don't care," she said, testily. "I wanted to find out something and I did. If you address a group of people as if you were talking to each one personally, they can't help but listen."

Free of obligations on Thanksgiving Day, 1944, we went to Chisago City and renewed old friendships with the farming Swensons.

"My goodness, you're not married yet," she said to Hank and Gilbert. Then in feigned disgust: "Ugh, you are two selfish old men."

Late afternoon we motored to Stillwater for a turkey dinner at the Lowell Inn. Forewarned that the noted tavern was arid, we fortified ourselves at the hotel with a vacuum bottle of martinis, the only species of "dry" we would put up with.

The journey was executed in ten-mile spurts, pausing for oases of toasts which began with ourselves, embraced each member of our families, encompassed friends, and, as we parked at the end of the line, Winston Churchill and Franklin Delano Roosevelt.

So many events were crowded into these tours that chronological time blurred out of focus. It seemed we had been away so long, though actually it was but a few days. Nostalgically, Ingrid was eager to get back to the hotel to hear a two-hour radio broadcast from Hollywood on behalf of the government's Bond Drive.

As we listened raptly to the finest talents in our home town the flaxen-haired emigrée—having changed into a blue-gray flannel robe and boudoir slippers—sprawled on a chaise longue, a vision of sweet tranquillity. Her eyes were on the radio, mentally picturing the *mise en scène*. My eyes were on her, and my musings of a Bergman in transition.

Family and fame were hers, and the immeasurable riches of the future shone in her eyes like the dreams of day. Her Americanization was fact, explicit in a vanishing accent and the ready idiom. She could say "lousy" as freely as any leatherneck. She reacted happily to the native wisecrack, and adapted to the informality of social intercourse. She liked the unstuffiness of people in high places and the absence of subservience in those of humble station. It was implicit in her pride in Hollywood as home, pride in her profession and her colleagues; and her quick resentment of an outsider's thoughtless detraction. "You have no right to say that," she would retort. "Hollywood is a town just like yours, and Hollywood people are human beings just like you."

The broadcast was a touch of home, touching her deeply. Ronald Colman, Bob Hope, Bette Davis, Jimmy Durante, Frances Langford, Bergen and McCarthy—the airwaves rang with laughter and love of country. Washington interrupted to announce the bombing of Tokyo by land-based B-29s. Then it was twelve of midnight; Hollywood signed off, but only the laughter ended.

"Oh, Joe, aren't they all wonderful!" said Ingrid of persons she hardly knew.

Superior, Wisconsin

When the twelve-o'clock siren blared in the Butler Ship Yards on the western tip of Lake Superior several hundred employees gathered before an unshielded platform to hear an actress from Hollywood. The mercury was six below zero and a saw-edged wind slashed across the waterside.

Enclosed in a topcoat of Persian lamb, her head completely uncovered (my knees knocking), Ingrid tentatively teed off with a light humorous poem by Samuel Hoffenstein.

As she spoke, the burly assemblage stirred self-consciously; here and there someone laughed. They seemed resentful of being herded, at giving up half their lunch period, at being "counted" for what bonds they pledged for.

Ingrid's was not the kind of "sales pitch" they had expected; now she reached into her mental storehouse and gave them a Sandburg poem to match their hairy chests. It started out with ringing words and ended up on this ribald note:

> "And I met a marine of the U.S.A., a leatherneck with a girl on his knee for a memory in ports circling the earth and he said: Tell me how to say three things and I always get by—gimme a plate of ham and eggs—how much?—and—do you love me, kid?" *

A roar of laughter thawed the frozen yards. Skillfully timing herself, Ingrid unclasped the wristwatch and held it high for all to see. The far ranks shuffled in for a closer look.

"I'm going to auction off this watch to the highest bidder," she said, carefully avoiding an outright deception that it was *her* watch.

"One hundred," said a young giant.

"Five hundred!" said a man wearing two mackinaws. The bidding mounted by the 50's and 100's until a grizzled Paul Bunyan of the shipyards bellowed an unchallenged "three thousand two hundred and fifty dollars!"

"Come and get it!" cried Ingrid, feeling pretty good about the whole business.

New York

"I saw a picture without Ingrid Bergman in it" was the current wisecrack of Broadway in the winter of 1945. What gave rise to this backhanded compliment were three films—*The Bells of St.*

* From *Smoke and Steel* by Carl Sandburg. Copyright, 1920, by Harcourt, Brace and Company, Inc.; renewed by Carl Sandburg. Reprinted by permission of the publisher.

Mary's, *Spellbound*, and *Saratoga Trunk*—all running in competition with each other, all playing to packed houses.

Flattering as this was, Ingrid found herself bogged down in another occupational vacuum; her next picture, *Notorious*, was six months off. She appeared on radio for the Heart Association, entertained and visited with the bedridden at the Naval Hospital in Long Beach, California, and Birmingham Military Hospital in San Fernando Valley. She took singing and French lessons. She drove Pia to the Hawthorne Public School in Beverly Hills, then called for her when school was over. She fussed around the house, getting in the servants' way, trying to keep her mind occupied. But the days stretched into weeks of desuetude. It was agony to stay put.

She hadn't been to New York in more than two years. Manhattan was anodyne: theaters, restaurants, Central Park, Fifth Avenue, art galleries; where people walked and walking was fun; where there were friends like Kay Brown and Irene Selznick, and things to talk about besides pictures—the new plays, the Picasso exhibition at the Museum of Modern Art, or a daring new drama produced at an obscure Greenwich Village playhouse; where she could sit in the little theater of the Museum of Modern Art and see such classic old movies as *The Informer*, *Tol'able David*, and all of the Greta Garbo unforgettables. And so, soon there were good-byes again on Benedict Canyon Drive, and, "Here we go again," as the car swung towards the airport.

At Ingrid's request, Kay Brown made reservations for a matinee and evening theater performance every day of Ingrid's hasty holiday, including a Sunday night benefit. During a second-act intermission one evening, Ingrid became bored with the playwright's platitudes and suddenly announced, "Let's go see a movie."

"It's after ten, Ingrid."

"We have time. I'd like to see Bogey."

The reference was to Humphrey Bogart, in a picturization of Ernest Hemingway's *To Have and Have Not*. The girl in the box office said only balcony seats were available.

"That's okay," said the actress whose neoned name adorned the ramparts of Times Square.

The "available seats" were in the uppermost crags of the popcorn-laden alps. Engulfed by love-birds, crackling paper bags, and unclassifiable odors, Ingrid gazed contentedly at the distant screen.

It was well after one o'clock when the picture ended and the magic of make-believe was brusquely dispelled by the house lights. The audience came alive in a single mass movement, poured through the cluttered aisles into a torrent of sweaty, chattering, jostling humanity, and convoyed us into the street.

"Oh, isn't Hollywood wonderful?" sighed Ingrid. "I enjoyed that so much!"

The picture was lousy.

The next day we had matinee tickets to see Mae West in *Catherine Was Great*, a bawdy caricature of the Russian empress.

"Why in Heaven's name do you want to see that show?" I said. "The critics murdered it."

"I don't care," she said. "She's a tremendous personality. I want to see if there's anything I can learn from her. It may come in handy sometime."

When ultimately the curtain fell on the two-hour *double-entendre*, I hoped she was satisfied.

"Well," she said, "at least I learned this is not for me."

Paris

In the summer of 1945 Ingrid set out to entertain American occupation forces in Germany and France in company with Jack Benny, harmonica virtuoso Larry Adler, and singer Martha Tilton. Her only regret was that she would not have an opportunity to visit her native Stockholm. As in the case of the Alaskan junket, only those who could entertain were permitted to go.

"If you could only dance or sing or do tricks," she said.

"But I can tell jokes."

"Maybe that's why the War Department won't take you," she said.

Following an ordeal of passports (as a resident alien) and inoculations (typhoid, etc.), she arrived in New York and was promptly bedded with a bad cold. I sent off a telegram to which she replied by letter, dated June 20th, and slightly flavored with Ben Hecht's train whistle:

> Hello, Joooooe. . . . Thanks for the wire. It was very nice and very funny. I am sick, or rather have been very sick, but today I am happy because the doctor said I can leave Monday.
>
> You know, after having gone through so much so that I would be allowed to leave this country, and then go and catch cold—that almost killed me. After three days on the air-conditioned train I stepped right into misery. I can take cold, but this heat, never!
>
> I have suffered as never before and, of course, pretty quick I couldn't talk, an ear infected, sinus infected and so on. Thank God it is better but I do feel worried about going on a strenuous trip right after a cold. But what can I do? Jack left four days ago and I want to join him as soon as possible. I'll be careful this time and let Jack do all the cheering; I'll just sit and smile. Everybody has been terribly nice and anxious to help since I didn't have you here with me. Well, goodbye, Joooooe . . .
>
> Ingrid

With the aid of a flying box-car, she finally caught up with the Benny troupe and played her part in a score of German encampments. From there they went to Paris and checked in at the Ritz Hotel for several days while they made the rounds of nearby military installations.

An incident occurred in the French capital which not only illustrates her changing attitudes, but was destined to leave its mark on her whole outlook. Bob Capa, most famous of war photographers, was the "mark," and I shall recount it as he did to me.

"Irwin Shaw (novelist and playwright) and I were in the Ritz bar looking for some female companionship. All our phone numbers had previous dates.

" 'How about Ingrid Bergman?' I said. 'You know, the movie actress. I saw her go up in the elevator.'

"Irwin said, 'You're crazy. But even so, how'll we ask her?'

" 'Easy,' I said. 'Send her a note. The worst she can do is tear it up.'

"So I got some of that classy Ritz stationery and scribbled on it: 'Dear Miss Bergman—We would send you flowers and invite you to dinner, but we don't have enough money to do both. If you can have dinner with us, come to the bar and wear a flower in your hair so we can recognize you.' Then we signed our names.

"We had our little joke and sat there watching the door. Then all of a sudden there she was—*the* Bergman—wearing a flower in her hair!

"Irwin said, 'My God, it worked!' We jumped to our feet and brought her to the table. You know how dark the Ritz bar is—well, boy, she lit it up like the lobby of the Music Hall."

"How was she dressed?" I asked.

"Who cares? Anyhow, it wasn't anything I can remember."

"What was the flower she wore?"

"Something red—maybe a rose. I asked her where she got it. She said her room was full of flowers."

"Did she know who you guys were?"

"That's the funny part of it. I thought she'd at least know who Irwin was, but she didn't. She said the note amused her and she wanted to see what we looked like. Well, we didn't look like much in our war correspondent's getup; we weren't officers or even GI's.

"She was like a school kid. 'You said you were going to take me to dinner,' she said. 'I hope you have enough money, because I'm very hungry.'

"We took a cab to Fouquet's and after dinner we did the town from Maxim's to Montmartre. We even let her pay some of the bills. When I saw her the next day, I said, 'We had a lot of crust sending you that note; what did you think when you got it?'

"She said, 'Oh, I wanted to see Paris. If you had turned out dull, I would have left you.' "

Bob Capa, an American citizen of Hungarian birth, was a short, stocky, somber concentration of nerves. His black-brown eyes glistened fiercely from beneath an unbroken line of thick black eyebrows and, combined with the black turtle-neck sweaters he affected in civilian life in lieu of shirts, invested him with a sinister mien.

Capa's forbidding façade, however, belied the candor and sensibility and catholic humanism that propelled him through life. Acutely sensitive to the injustices he stumbled upon in the course of his many wanderings, he was at once rebellious, irreverent, humble, and acutely civilized. There was about him a perpetual tension, a trigger-ready quality that might explode at any moment. He was imbued with a reckless courage and a furious lust for life—the most unfettered man I ever knew.

Disinclined to play anything safe, scorning money as a staff of security, it was inevitable that poker would be his grand passion.

An afternoon session of this peerless sport, two days after he met Ingrid, found him with a pair of thorny problems—he was broke, and he was taking her to dinner. Nothing daunted, he took Ingrid's arm and started out. As they crossed the Place Vendôme he spied an equally celebrated colleague, Margaret Bourke-White. "Margaret," he said, "let me have ten thousand francs—quick!"

Miss Bourke-White casually peeled out the equivalent of thirty-five American dollars and handed it to him, as Ingrid stared in amazement. It took her a long time to get used to the idea of a man borrowing money from a woman, but for the present she adjusted her sights and insisted on sharing all expenses, which Capa accepted with customary indifference.

"Why not?" he said, when he related one of these episodes to me. "She's rich. All movie actresses are rich."

When I asked Ingrid to verify this story, she laughed with warm recollection. "Yes, it's all true," she said. "I've never known anybody like Capa (she always referred to him as Capa, never Bob). He's wonderful and crazy, and has a beautiful mind."

Then, thoughtfully, she said, "I like him, Joe. I like him very much. He says what he thinks, and lives the way he wants to live. There's nothing false about him. His honesty is almost shocking."

5.

Beverly Hills

THE mantelpiece over the fireplace of Ingrid's house on Benedict Canyon Drive bore the legend, HILLHAVEN LODGE. A varied array of trophies, awards for popularity or special performances, lined the timber shelf. Facing the gaping stone oven was a semicircular built-in seat embracing a round table. A long library table backed against the seat, isolating the area from the huge rectangular hall of the "Barn."

The house was in truth a haven for the Lindstroms, and its heart, the focal point of all gatherings, was this area in front of the oven. Captain's chairs were drawn up as needed and guests would sit close to each other, promoting the atmosphere of intimacy and informality that Ingrid loved. When there were guests, one or any number, she would go into the kitchen, fix a wooden tray of crackers, biscuits, and many cheeses, and bring it to the round table. Mixing drinks, even a simple highball, was a knack she never quite mastered; if her husband was absent, a male guest assumed the chore. Expecting servants to serve was something she had yet to learn. "It is not easy for me to give orders," she once told me.

Ingrid was orderly by habit and uncluttered of mind, systematic, thorough and tireless. Everything was in its place, and she always remembered where that place was. Her home was spotless and hummed with activity and cheer. There was talk of the possibility of building a swimming pool, and maybe having a Finnish steam bath.

It was the Lindstroms' first home and the pride and joy of ownership permeated their lives. This house was designed for the sound of friends, for music and gaiety and free-wheeling conversation; a haven from strictures and stuffiness. This was the promise that it held for Ingrid, and the promise was exciting and exulting and good.

That's the way it was in the beginning, in 1944.

Ingrid refused to endorse commercial products or lend her name to advertising tie-ins. She would not stand for being exploited and, similarly, decried the exploitation of others.

Hedda Hopper, a syndicated movie columnist, printed that Ingrid Bergman's gown for the 1944 Academy Awards dinner was being specially designed by the noted couturier Travis Banton, and that it was *paid for* by David Selznick. Furious that the Selznick publicity office had taken the liberty of issuing this item, she forthwith telephoned Banton, canceled the costume, and declared she would wear the oldest dress she had, the same one she had worn to the previous year's function. And she did.

At the Awards in March she was touted as the probable winner for her performance in *For Whom the Bell Tolls*. Selznick's prophecy, however, ironically shifted from Ingrid to another of his stars, Jennifer Jones, for her portrayal of the beatified young girl in *The Song of Bernadette*.

Jolted by the disappointment, Ingrid nevertheless took it in good grace. "When I saw the picture last year," she said, "I cried all the way through it, because Jennifer was so moving, and because I realized I had lost the Award."

In July, 1944, she went into *Spellbound*, second and last of the Bergman films personally produced by Selznick. A newcomer, Gregory Peck by name, was leading man; the director, Alfred Hitchcock, master of the "whodunit."

September came, the picture was completed, and Ingrid faced another protracted period of idleness. Dr. Lindstrom's hospital hours in surgery were long and uncertain, sometimes far into the night. Ingrid redoubled the English, French, and singing lessons, shopped for groceries (seldom for clothes), visited with Ruth Roberts, or attended a movie matinee. She played games with five-year-old Pia, read her the classic children's tales, and dramatized them with both playing parts, be they fairies or witches, ogres or animals.

The contrast between her prehouse independence and the constraints of her domestic routine surreptitiously intruded itself, though she sensed it but vaguely. She sought release in going away on some government service, often asking the Hollywood Committee—long before a film was finished—to arrange an itinerary for a military hospital tour or a War Bond selling campaign. But these excursions were of short duration, and the letdown which followed her return only emphasized her incipient restlessness.

The journeyings among strange peoples in strange places left their imprint in other ways; in self-assurance, assertiveness, and an unmuzzled articulation of ideas. Inhibitions induced by a lifetime of restraints slowly yielded to new horizons.

Shortly following the filming of *Spellbound*, director Leo McCarey approached Selznick about borrowing Ingrid to costar with crooner Bing Crosby in *The Bells of St. Mary's*. McCarey was a cinematic stylist whose chief stock in trade was a highly lucrative sentimentality that barely missed the maudlin. Though he dwelt in a Never-Never Land in which kiddies choraled "Wishing Will Make It So" and "Aren't You Glad You're You," his directorial touch was delicate and actors were better actors for having worked under his tutelage. Since Ingrid placed more value on the quality of the director than any other element in the making of a picture, she was eager to work with him.

"But David says no," she said. "He has three good reasons and it's hard to argue with him. First, the idea is a sequel to *Going My Way* (a tremendous box office hit) and David says sequels are never successful. Second, he says I'll probably go all through the picture just listening to Bing sing. But worst of all, McCarey has no shooting script and David says he can't judge a part without seeing a script."

"He's right on all three counts," I said, " but he doesn't know

Leo McCarey. Several years ago I was an associate of Douglas MacLean, one of the top comedians of his day, at Paramount when we produced a comedy that Leo directed. I got to know him pretty well. About five years ago I was Leo's assistant on *Love Affair*—a very fine picture with Charles Boyer and Irene Dunne. And he made that without a script.

"If Leo's got an idea for a sequel, it has to be good, and I doubt it'll be anything like *Going My Way*. As for listening to Bing while he croons, I can't believe that Leo would want you unless he has a strong part in mind."

"What can I do?" said Ingrid. "I can't fight David."

"Why don't you ask Leo to the house and let him tell you what he has in mind? Even if nothing comes of it, you'll enjoy meeting him."

"David will be furious when he hears about it."

"So what? Are you a woman or a mouse?"

"Very well. Will you arrange it? Any time he wants to come."

At two o'clock of the next day they met and talked for nearly three hours. At five o'clock I arrived to find Ingrid in high elation.

"Oh, you just missed him," she said. "He's full of wonderful ideas—I wish you could have been here. I like him very much. It's a beautiful part—a nun, but she's very human, not at all the way we think of nuns. The story he told is so beautiful . . ."

"Yes, I'm sure of that," I said, "but what he told you won't be the story he'll put on the screen. When Leo gets through with it it'll be better than the story you heard; that's why it's hard for him to have a shooting script to start with. Believe me, working with him will be one of the happiest experiences you've ever had."

Ingrid brought every ounce of her Nordic obstinacy to bear before Selznick finally capitulated.

Her earnings under the Selznick contract averaged two thousand dollars a week for forty weeks—roughly eighty thousand dollars a year. For her services on loanout to Warner Brothers for *Casablanca* Selznick received one hundred and twenty-five thousand dollars, and one hundred and fifty thousand dollars from

Paramount for *For Whom the Bell Tolls.* Her presence in a picture was worth millions at the box office as he well knew.

But for the lending of her unique talents and personality to RKO Studios, who were to finance the film, he negotiated a deal which will stand forever in the annals of Hollywood as a classic in tradesmanship.

After weeks of haggling and howls of pain RKO threw in the towel. Frank S. Nugent, writing in the *New York Times* on December 16, 1945, pointed out that in return for twelve weeks of the big blonde's services Selznick received: (a) a commitment for the use of a studio director; (b) all remake rights to Louisa Alcott's *Little Women;* (c) all remake rights to the John Barrymore film, *A Bill of Divorcement,* which catapulted Katharine Hepburn into stardom; plus (d) one hundred and seventy-five thousand dollars in cash. The total market value was estimated at four hundred and ten thousand dollars!

Once the transaction was consummated Ingrid tremulously awaited the initial conference with McCarey. The call came sooner than she expected; a luncheon date was made for one o'clock at Lucey's Restaurant, across the street from RKO.

At twelve o'clock—pacing the length of the living room—Ingrid decided to get going, drive leisurely, take a lot of time; that would bring her to the appointed place at the appointed hour. Grasping the wheel of her car she dragged down Benedict Canyon on a journey that would normally take but fifteen minutes. After a mile of this slow motion, the Bergman nerves rebelled; she stepped on the accelerator.

At twenty minutes before one she parked her car and glanced at her unbejeweled wristwatch. Twenty interminable minutes! What to do? She thought, I'll take a walk around the block. It wouldn't be good to be the first to arrive and sit there alone.

She started down the sidewalk, but on turning the corner she sighted McCarey pacing back and forth.

"Leo!" she cried. "What are *you* doing?"

"Aw," he stammered, his Irish face embarrassed. "I just couldn't wait. I've been wearing out this sidewalk since twelve o'clock!"

In February, 1945, the picture went before the cameras and

Ingrid ecstatically gave life to Sister Mary Benedict, the unsanctimonious nun who possessed a rollicking sense of humor, and who sang and played baseball with the children of the orphanage.

Midway in the production she was nominated for an Academy Award for her work in *Gaslight*, but her previous disappointment left her tensely apprehensive. Jennifer Jones, who was to make the presentation to the current winner, tried to bolster her. "You've just got to win, Ingrid, or I won't know what to say. My speech is all about you. If someone else gets it, I'll just stand there tongue-tied."

Ingrid sat in the theater between Dr. Lindstrom and David Selznick. Her hands betrayed the turbulence underlying her cool exterior. Lindstrom rescued one hand and pressed it reassuringly; Selznick grasped the other.

On the stage golden statuettes were being meted out for supremacy in the glittering realm of motion pictures. Now came the category for the finest performance by an actress in a leading role; a name was announced. Ingrid didn't hear it, but Selznick let out a whoop, "It's you, Ingrid! It's you!"

She turned to her husband for verification. He leaned over and kissed her, then rose to let her pass. "Go get it," he whispered.

That same evening Bing Crosby received the best actor award, and Leo McCarey the best director award, both for *Going My Way*. On the *St. Mary's* set the following morning Ingrid was given a memorable reception; the technical staff had stretched out a long, old red carpet, garnished it with withered prop flowers, and installed a "throne" of three collapsible canvas chairs. Seated between the newly crowned kings, Ingrid wept with joy as they sipped a champagne toast to each other.

Recalling the event, she said, "I thought I could never be so happy again."

Ingrid began to make use of the friendly sanctuary that fronted the big fireplace, inviting friends and co-workers to come at the aperitif hour. She invited those whom she liked regardless of station. The size of their incomes meant nothing: David and Irene

Selznick; the Alfred Hitchcocks; French director Jean Renoir and his wife; Ruth Roberts; Howard Grodé, her singing teacher; and Kay Brown, when she was on from New York. No games were played–just conversation, dynamic conversation on many subjects.

Four-letter words or suggestive stories were never heard; not because of any voiced objection, but because that kind of talk simply turned sour in her presence.

Unsure of her own attitudes, she compensated for it by a profound interest in other people's ideas, asking questions, listening, absorbing and digesting. Unneeded were the flaming logs in the fireplace, for the heat of human camaraderie was warmth enough. To Ingrid Bergman, hungry, growing, feeling the wings of achievement, these sessions were catharsis.

On nights when Dr. Lindstrom was detained in surgery, owing to the wartime shortage of medical men, Ingrid would go unescorted to parties to which both had been invited. She welcomed such occasions and reveled in the immunity from being closely watched or tacitly prohibited. She could drink and eat as much as she liked, which was never excessive, and she could speak her mind freely without fear of subsequent censure.

Once, at a David Selznick party, she and actor Joseph Cotten dressed as butler and maid, and served canapés and cocktails to the guests. Their masquerade would have gone undetected had it not been for their insistence that guests hold two drinks in their hands instead of one.

"Just think," said Ingrid, the next day, "how little attention people pay to the ones who serve them."

Dr. Lindstrom made valiant efforts to enter her world. When it happened that he came home while Ingrid sat with a friend or two, he would greet them effusively, draw up a chair, pour himself a drink, and strive earnestly to share the prevailing spirit. Ingrid would become suddenly subdued, the atmosphere leaden. The disharmony was too pronounced, his interests too divergent from theirs. The doctor tried hard, exceedingly hard, but the end result was hollow. An inhibitive austerity pervaded the air.

As the months slipped into years, the haven before the great fireplace grew quieter and quieter. With one excuse or another, colleagues stopped coming, and presently Ingrid started meeting them at restaurants or, if working in a picture, she'd set up snacks and refreshments in her dressing room, and soon after six o'clock quitting time the room would hum with lively palaver. Then she'd linger until the last possible minute before tearing herself away and going home. Otherwise the domestic routine remained unchanged, except that now Pia attended Hawthorne Public School in Beverly Hills, where Ingrid, when she was working, would drop her off on the way to the studio, and when not working, call for her after school.

Integration, resolution and direction were still in the primary explorative stage. Now thirty years old and a veteran of the competitive show world, Ingrid was still naïve and childlike in many ways, and yet, paradoxically, she gravitated towards the strong, the worldly, and the disenchanted, shunning the milk-and-water types like the plague. She was drawn by opposites like Victor Fleming, Alfred Hitchcock, David Selznick, Irene Selznick, Bob Capa, Kay Brown, Ernest Hemingway; and her husband, too, who was the epitome of strength, any way you looked at it, and whose disenchantment lay in an egregious distrust of everybody and everything. The single exception was gentle, Quakerish Ruth Roberts, who was for Ingrid a mother substitute in the pupal Hollywood years.

Ingrid was particularly fond of Kay Brown, quintessence of Madison Avenue sophistication, who, on business trips to Hollywood, frequented the halls of Hillhaven Lodge. One evening Miss Brown and Dr. Lindstrom became embroiled in some kind of squabble and she stormed out of the house, swearing she would never re-enter it. I was not a witness to the row and Ingrid was unwilling to give me the details.

Dr. Lindstrom's conduct of her business affairs was colored by his awareness that he was "in the driver's seat" in undisputed control of the "hottest" star in all filmdom. Harsh and obdurate in his dealings, studio executives came to dislike him venomously, while at the same time they respected his horsetrading acumen.

On one occasion, when I came to discuss certain publicity matters, Lindstrom was in the den-office immersed in household paperwork. As usual, Ingrid and I sat at the little round table with the built-in seat. Hearing my voice, Lindstrom dropped whatever he was doing and joined us. The temper of the confab was most amiable, with Ingrid acceding to my proposals. At one point Lindstrom, in an even tone, said, "No, I don't think that is good for you to do."

"Oh, I don't see any harm in it, Peter," said Ingrid, pleasantly. Instantly, he stiffened and leveled a rigid finger close to her face.

"I said it is not good. And you will not do it!" he said.

Ingrid turned pale, gave no other sign, got up and walked quietly to her bedroom, entered and quietly closed the door.

Not long after this incident I sat with Ingrid in her compartment aboard the Santa Fe "Chief" en route to New York. She was in the rare mood of talking about herself.

"We Swedes are not supposed to show our emotions in front of strangers. That's the way we're brought up. On the set, when I'm working, they think I'm so placid, and the fan magazines keep saying I'm so normal and simple. But you know me better.

"I wish I could rage and throw things, but if I did I'd feel foolish and wonder how I looked. So when I get angry I think to myself, will I lose my dignity? And I hold it inside and wait until I'm alone in my bedroom, then I throw myself on the bed and scream and cry."

Another time Ingrid told me how Pia once caught her in this state, and asked her mother if she was mad at her.

" 'Pia, I'm not angry with you,' I said. 'No matter what I do, it has nothing to do with you.' I had a bad time at the studio one day and I came home and shut myself in the bedroom and cried and cried. Pretty soon Pia came in and stood there looking at me. She looked so sad. Then she said, 'That's all right, Mother. I forgive you.' "

When summer came and *St. Mary's* was finished and ready to be shown, Ingrid decided it was time Pia, now nearly seven, be given a glimpse of her mother on the screen. Heretofore she had thought that her roles were not quite proper for a growing child to see.

Pia sat next to her mother in the studio projection room as the picture unreeled. She stared at the screen with hypnotic absorption, motionless, making no sound. Twice Ingrid broke the spell by asking how she liked a certain scene, only to have Pia turn on her impatiently and say, "Sh-sh!"

The picture became an outstanding success, attracting a new kind of audience not interested in sex-ridden themes or stories of violence. The luminous character and cloistral habiliments of Sister Mary Benedict invested its interpreter with an unsought halo. The role became a symbol and the symbol became incarnate in the person of Ingrid Bergman.

Forgotten were the "bad girls" she had previously portrayed, which had never fooled anyone anyway. Through all the painted women of her former films had shone the artless, virginal look, which her adherents now insisted was the true Bergman.

It was not unusual on our travels for doting mothers to bring their young daughters over and ask if they might meet Ingrid. "She wants to be like Miss Bergman," they would say, "and it makes me very glad. I couldn't want for a finer example."

It was a perilous pedestal, and Ingrid Bergman didn't like it.

Meanwhile Dr. Lindstrom advanced to senior resident in neurosurgery at Los Angeles County General Hospital and, because Ingrid displayed an avid interest in his work, he sometimes brought home X-rays and photographs of operations and explained their significance. On one occasion several of these macabre brainscapes got mixed up with a batch of studio stills and startled a squeamish guest.

"You see!" laughed Ingrid. "My husband makes pictures too!"

In an unguarded moment I blandly asked if it were possible sometime to watch him perform a brain operation.

"Yes, sure," he said. "I'll let you know. You can come with Ingrid; she wants to see one, too."

I gave it no more thought until a few days later when, trapped by my own innocent remark, I found myself at the hospital seated beside Ingrid in the front row of the surgery amphitheater. The patient was a nine-year-old Negro boy with a malignant brain tumor. My watch read 7:37 A.M.; I wished it were P.M. There were no other spectators to lend me the comfort of their presence.

"We are early," said Ingrid, astonishingly casual.

Directly below were faceless figures in white, moving silently, methodically, like a well-rehearsed ghost story. They encircled a tiny dark form, lying prone and immobile, its head and limbs like an unfinished charcoal drawing.

An anesthetist administered to the unseen, down-turned face; a doctor prepared an arm for plasma, another did the same for a limp black leg. Another doctor shaved the dark hair down to the neck, while nurses readied instruments and other mysterious paraphernalia.

Dr. Lindstrom had not yet put in an appearance. As was fitting, the real star of the show would make his entrance when the scene was properly set.

When my son was a cherubic three years of age he snagged a vicious splinter while playing on a toy slide. Unable to dislodge it, I hurried him to a nearby clinic. The doctor laid him on his stomach, bared his behind, and, using a surgical knife, made a slight incision at the injury. I, a war veteran, promptly passed out.

Now, perched in the front row of the amphitheater, a surge of nausea swept through me at the recollection. I reswallowed my breakfast and glanced at Ingrid, praying that she was weakening and wanted to go home. But all I got back was a stoic, "Interesting, isn't it?"

I wondered where the lavatory was, and how fast I could reach it; maybe if I gave in to the sickness now I could hold out for the main event. No, Ingrid was sure to suspect; my face was a dead give-away; I didn't dare "chicken out." I can take it, if she can, this unperturbed female, looking as cool as orange sherbet.

I mentally counted up to one hundred, went through the alphabet, recited parts of "Gunga Din," sang "Jingle Bells"—nothing worked. Imagination would not be routed. I got sicker by the second. Mobilizing every ounce of will-power, I hazarded a downward glance; and then, at that instant, stumbled upon a glorious discovery!

A protective iron railing stretched before me. By leaning at a certain angle this barrier came between my line of vision and the child's head. All that was needed was to maintain this posture and Dr. Lindstrom could work away as he pleased, I would see none of the bloody mess.

My head cleared; I turned to Ingrid and smiled. "Wouldn't have missed this for anything," I said, with a note of triumph.

"There comes Peter," she said, as I quickly resumed the strategic position.

For three hours Dr. Lindstrom sliced and sawed at the little cranium. I gazed on in sublime tranquillity, seeing only the peripheral activity beyond the self-imposed blindspot. Ingrid, equally tranquil, but for different reasons, leaned forward on the railing for a closer look.

Suddenly a vagrant thought crashed the gates of my smugness; suppose, when this is all over, Peter asks for my impressions? What can I say? If I try to bluff it out, he will sure as hell discern it. I'll never hear the end of it.

Slowly, delicately, I inched away from the blindspot until finally the whole spectacle was in view. No sooner had I recovered from the sweet reality of being unaffected, than a nurse approached and said, "Mr. Steele, Dr. Lindstrom would like you to come down."

"May I go, too?" said Ingrid.

"I'm afraid not, Mrs. Lindstrom. It's quite crowded as it is."

Following the nurse into an anteroom, I was fitted with a white gown and mask, then led into the surgical chamber.

"Here, come close," Lindstrom beckoned.

Edging in between him and the anesthetist, I peered down into the living insides of a human head. Oddly, I felt no emotion.

An assistant kept draining the blood which overflowed the coils of brain tissue. Dr. Lindstrom probed with a rubbered finger, then indicated a walnut-sized nodule at the base of the open skull.

"This is the tumor," he said. "A pretty bad one—should have been operated on long ago."

I nodded mutely. It was like watching a mechanic tinker with the engine of your car. All identification, all empathy, had dissolved. Expressing my thanks, I rejoined Ingrid, and presently we were homeward bound.

"What a priceless experience," I said. "Tremendous to see the way Peter works, the infinite patience and skill, so sure of himself."

"Isn't that so?" she said. "It was fascinating—much more interesting than the other time."

"You have been there before?"

"Oh, yes, a few weeks ago. He operated on a man's spine . . ."

For a long time I puzzled about this incident, striving to reconcile Ingrid's simplicity, naïveté, and consummate femininity with the ability to look for hours, apparently unaffected, upon a living child's head being torn apart. She had asked Ruth Roberts to come with us; but Ruth, with infinite wisdom, had said, "If I do, Peter will have two patients to take care of."

The answer, I think, lay in Ingrid Bergman's complete, unequivocal control of her emotions, stemming from a lifetime of withholding and covering up, of hiding her true feelings, of escaping into the privacy of her bedroom to scream and cry; a psychic subterfuge born of necessity, bitterly acquired, and now become a salient component of her character.

A week or so after my harrowing hospital experience, the Los Angeles *Times* published the following news story, here condensed:

"A desperate young mother, on her knees at the General Hospital bedside of her stricken seven-year-old daughter, yesterday laid her slim hopes for the beautiful child's recovery from a grave brain injury at the feet of Him who once proclaimed that children were 'of the Kingdom of God.'

"The child for whom medical science has done its very best, and for whose recovery a whole neighborhood has been working and praying since she was mowed down by an automobile Christmas Eve, is Margaret Eades, of 11107 S. Grand Ave.

"The left door-handle of the car . . . pierced Margaret's brain in the accident . . . as the child went on a last minute errand. Surgeons told the mother, widowed only two weeks ago, that it would require the services of an expensive brain specialist to remove the metal from Margaret's brain.

"Margaret's mother . . . not only didn't have the money, but the rent on her modest cottage was already overdue. And there were two other children to care for, with another anticipated within a few months.

"A noted brain specialist was located . . . and immediately agreed to operate if his own examination indicated the advisability of surgery.

"It did, and because Margaret's condition was too critical to permit her removal to Children's Hospital he operated at General.

"His fee? Nothing. Only anonymity."

I gave the *Times* story but casual notice, suspecting nothing. It was not until the second of January that I learned that the "anonymous" surgeon was Lindstrom, and I learned it only because Howard C. Heyn of the Associated Press had finally run the story down.

Heyn phoned and asked what I knew about it. I drew a blank. He wanted to know if an interview could be arranged, but I enlightened him regarding Lindstrom's athletic proclivities and the fieldstone steps he would likely encounter. Heyn wanted to know if Ingrid would talk about her husband.

"She knows better," I said. "He'd break her neck if she did."

I proposed that since he was a reporter and as such had access to General Hospital why didn't he invade those precincts and corner the lion himself. He thought he would.

That evening I questioned the doctor, "Why don't you tell me about these things?"

"Ah, no," he said, noncommittally. "A reporter came to the hospital today and got me on the telephone while I was in one of the wards. He asked if I was the little girl's doctor. I said no and gave him the name of the doctor in charge of her ward. That was the truth; technically I was not her doctor."

And that's as far as the reporter got.

At strategic points in Hollywood and its environs there are peddlers of pamphlets in which are listed the home addresses of film stars, and directions as to how to find them. In due course, the Lindstrom residence got on the list and for a price the worshipful and the vulgar could take a peek. Hillhaven Lodge became a tourist "must," and in self-defense Lindstrom closed off the estate with a high steel fence. The high steel fence created an impenetrable island, their own domain, breathing unity and permanence.

The family roots dug deeper into the adopted soil. In August, 1945, the Lindstroms stood hand in hand in the Federal Building and filed an application for American citizenship.

Contracts were signed for Ingrid to costar with Cary Grant in *Notorious*, with Alfred Hitchcock directing for RKO Studios. Instantly, the news was spread around that it was her final picture under the Selznick aegis. Producers and agents transferred their overtures for her future services to her husband, but the surgeon's long irregular hours at the hospital made him difficult to reach. On the other hand, I was accessible at all times. It was natural, therefore, that efforts were made to reach Ingrid through me, or to take advantage of my closeness to her, for by now my attachment was more sentimental than financial. This circumstance was destined to exert a marked effect upon her life and mine.

As a free-lance artist Ingrid had the advantage of choosing her own subject, making as many films as she wished and pocketing all of the huge price she now commanded.

In evaluating an offer she carefully considered its three principal ingredients: story, director, and cast. Anxious that her initial independent venture be an important one, she rejected proposition after proposition until she reached a point of deep discouragement.

The most promising offer came from Enterprise Pictures, a newly organized company headed by David Loew, son of the founder of the Loew theater chain, and Charles Einfeld, formerly chief of Warner Brothers publicity and advertising. Ambitious to launch their company with a blockbuster, they had purchased the rights to Erich Maria Remarque's *Arch of Triumph*, which was a best-seller owing chiefly to its author's name. What made it look promising were two of the three basic elements—the male star, Charles Boyer, and the director, Lewis Milestone. The third quantity for success, a screenplay, was not yet written. David Lewis, who was to produce *Arch*, tried to interest Ingrid but left her unimpressed.

"Let's think about it a minute," I said to her. "You've worked with Boyer and you like him. He has a big following. You two make a good team. Milestone directed *All Quiet on the Western Front*, one of the great pictures of all times. I'm sure you'll like him as a person. You'll enjoy working with him. It all depends on the treatment of the book. Milly (Milestone) has a fine story mind; with him in there the script's got to be good. With these combinations I don't see how it can miss."

"Oh, Joe," she said, helplessly. "I don't know what to do."

"It'll take at least six months to set up the production, and that long to write the script. So by the time you do *Notorious* and maybe take a trip somewhere, it'll be ready for you. You've got to make some kind of decision or you won't have anything on your schedule next year. How about letting me talk with Charlie Einfeld and see what I can find out?"

"All right, if you want to. But don't promise anything."

"Certainly not."

When I met with Einfeld, whom I hadn't seen in years, he painted a glowing prospect: an all-star supporting cast, lavish sets, an unequalled publicity campaign–nothing would be stinted. "If Bergman will do it," he said, taut with anticipation, "we'll make *Arch* one of the biggest pictures ever made."

"Let me suggest this," I said. "Ingrid doesn't know Milly. Why don't you have him call her, go to the house, and tell her how he visualizes handling the story. Ingrid puts more store in the director than she does in anything else. Also, I'm confident she'll like him personally, which is very important."

The upshot of our meeting was that Milestone and Ingrid did get together, and Ingrid agreed to do the picture. Einfeld was in seventh heaven. Overnight, the embryo Enterprise became a giant. He asked me to see him.

"Joe," he said, "I can't begin to tell you how much we appreciate your help in this. Are you too busy with Ingrid and Ronnie Colman to take on anything else?"

"No, not too busy, Charlie."

"How about coming with us for the picture? David Lewis said he'd like to have you as his assistant, and at the same time you can coordinate Ingrid's problems with the publicity department."

"I'll be happy to."

Our session was as brief, straightforward and uncomplicated as that.

Within a few days Lindstrom concluded the business details and everybody was happy. Ingrid was to receive $175,000 in cash, plus 25 per cent of the net profits.

For several weeks before the start of *Notorious* in late September, Ingrid was required to make numerous trips to the studio for story conferences, rehearsals, costume fittings and so forth. I came upon her one morning, more than two blocks down the street, squeezing into a tight parking space between two cars.

"Why do you go to all this trouble?" I said. "Why don't you drive into the studio and park near your dressing room?"

"But how can I?" she said. "The lot is so crowded."

When the matter was brought to the studio's attention they were delighted to accommodate her. Miss Bergman could have anything she pleased. Asking for special privileges never occurred to her.

On the second day of shooting she asked that arrangements be made to have coffee and cakes on the set every mid-afternoon, available to every member of the crew and cast, as had been her custom on every picture. She, of course, would pay the bill.

Consultations ensued in the executive offices with the result that the studio "regretted the existence of an iron-clad rule against this custom because it was thought to interfere with the work." Ingrid accepted the ruling in good grace and went about her work. An hour later the property man appeared with a cup of hot coffee and a sugared bun.

"What is this?" she asked.

"They said it was all right for you to have it, Miss Bergman," he said.

"Then take it away," she said, testily. "If the others can't have it, then I don't want it."

Word of this sped throughout the studio and presently the "front office" found itself on the horns of a dilemma. It promptly extricated itself. The ban was lifted for the duration of the production.

An irresponsible columnist intimated that Cary Grant, her costar, "couldn't see straight because he was madly in love," leaving no doubt as to who the object of his affection was. Grant raged at the insinuation and dispatched a castigating note by messenger. Normally the soul of decorum, he warned in unadorned language that when next he saw the gossip columnist, even though in a public place, he would "kick her square in the ass."

Indignation sizzled throughout the entire *Notorious* company. In her dressing room Ingrid found a missive from the make-up man, "Never mind those leading men. Who ain't in love with you? Include me in! (signed) Layne Britton." A petition was drawn up by the sound recorder, John Cass, addressed to the hapless columnist, declaring that "we, the undersigned, are all in love with Miss Bergman," followed by the signatures of every technician and mechanic on the set.

In the spring of the year (1945) a union of studio workers went on strike, but failed to win any support from the more powerful key union of the Screen Actors Guild. Picketing had little or no effect on shooting schedules. As the filming of *Notorious* progressed the seven-month-old strike reached an alarming stage of bitterness and violence. Mass picketing went into effect and touchy groups assembled outside the studio gates. Ingrid decided she had seen enough; she would not again cross a picket line.

On Tuesday, October 23, at 1:50 P.M., her maid phoned to say that William Dozier, production manager of RKO, had been trying to reach Miss Bergman. Would I look into it?

I called Dozier, who proposed that Ingrid ride into the studio grounds in an armored bank car; three of their top stars had all agreed to do so if Ingrid Bergman would. He further said their dressing rooms would be equipped with all the comforts of home; they could sleep there nights; they would be supplied with food, drinks, anything their hearts desired. Moreover, he would arrange that they be brought in under the cover of night; no strikers would see them. They could do it tonight.

Dozier asked that Ingrid do this "only until the end of the

week," declaring the strike would not last, but that if the crisis had not ceased by that time he would not ask any more of her.

I listened patiently until the cajolery terminated. "Bill, you don't seem to get the picture," I said. "Ingrid's not physically afraid; if she wanted to get into the studio she'd walk through the picket line, not sneak in in an armored car. She's got her own reasons for taking the stand she has, and nobody's going to change it."

The following day Dozier again called and asked if Ingrid would attend a conference outside the studio with Grant, Hitchcock, and one or two executives. She said she would and at three in the afternoon we arrived at Lucey's Restaurant and were shown to a small upstairs room. Around a table sat Grant, Hitchcock, Dozier, and two lawyers whose names escape me.

One of the lawyers opened the conference, speaking at length and expounding in legalistic polysyllables that the strike was a jurisdictional dispute between opposing unions, that the studio companies were not themselves involved, and that Miss Bergman by her "persistent attitude" was unjustly multiplying production costs, ad infinitum.

"I don't understand, Miss Bergman," he said, "why you take this stand now, when last spring you didn't object to crossing picket lines to work on *Bells of St. Mary's*. The situation hasn't changed. It's still the same strike."

"I didn't know then what the strike was all about," Ingrid said, soberly. "I was confused like many others. I am still confused and still don't understand what they're fighting for.

"I only know this: Now things are different—people are getting hurt. They are going to jail and going to hospitals—families are suffering. And something should be done to stop it!"

RKO, which then was one of the big major companies, shut down completely, affecting the entire industry. Whether or not Ingrid Bergman's intransigence had any bearing on it, I cannot say. But, coincidence or not, the strike abruptly ended a few days later.

In the meantime, Hillhaven Lodge was undergoing a transformation; a swimming pool was in process of replacing the sloping front lawn. Lindstrom had shopped around for the best bargain he could obtain, but as the rectangular hole sank deeper a maze of underground conduits was encountered, necessitating radical revisions in the original estimate. The result was that the cost of the pool tripled by the time it was finished; a bitter medicine for the medicine man.

There was one sultry day when I came to the house and discovered Lindstrom in shorts, loading dirt and debris into a wheelbarrow and pushing it to a temporary dump at the far end of the grounds; the hired laborers paid no attention.

"What's the idea?" I said. "Saving a little money?"

"Aah, no," he laughed. "It's very good exercise."

An instructor of ballroom dancing was brought in, and there were occasions when I arrived to find the big braided rugs in the living room rolled up, a swing record blasting away—and the surgeon and the Academy Award winner in the throes of a jitterbug that would have done credit to any hepcats.

Their passion for dancing led to night clubs. Once I went with them. He carried a briefcase, took it to the table and set it on the floor.

"Good heavens, what's that for?" I said.

"You wait and see," he said, cryptically.

As the evening progressed they never sat out one dance. After several rather strenuous rounds on the floor, he returned to the table with Ingrid, his shirt drenched, black tie askew, and collar creased like a concertina. Mopping his dripping brow, he picked up the briefcase and vanished into the men's room. In two minutes he reappeared, completely refurbished.

"Now you see," gurgled Ingrid. "Every time we go out dancing he always takes three extra shirts."

One morning I was met at the house by a small, shapeless, raspy mongrel, as unattractive a canine as ever yiped at a dog-lover. Entering the front door, which Ingrid habitually left open when I was expected, the beast followed close on my heels.

"Ingrid!" I shouted above the din.

"Here, Joe! I'm in the kitchen."

At the kitchen door I stood transfixed, staring incredulously at the idol of millions, the biggest single box-office bait in the country, perhaps in the whole world. There was Ingrid Bergman, poised on top of a high stool scrubbing the ceiling!

"That doesn't seem very bright. Trying to break a leg?"

"It's nothing. Somebody has to do it."

"What's the matter with the servants?"

"My goodness, they already have too much to do. I'm almost through . . ."

"And where did you get this awful animal?" I said, keeping a wary eye on the squirming mutt.

"Oh, we thought it'd be nice to have a dog around, so Peter went to the City Pound. He got it for five dollars."

Around the middle of November, soon after *Notorious* was finished, Ingrid decided on a four-week vacation in New York. Calling for her, I entered the steel gate, ascended the fieldstone steps, and on the veranda nearly tripped over a cluster of iron bars and iron disks of varying sizes—weight-lifting apparatus. As I stared a moment, Lindstrom appeared, wearing shorts.

"What the devil is this?" I said.

"Aah!" he chuckled. "See if you can lift."

Having no illusions about my physical prowess, I made a faint-hearted show of trying. He gave a jolly laugh, added two or three more of the larger disks, then with a slight effort raised the contraption above his head. All of a sudden an arm buckled and a couple of disks slipped off the end of the bar. I leaped back as they clattered onto the floor and splintered a dozen tiles.

"Very good exercise," he laughed as we entered the house. "Sit down; I want to talk to you.

"You know I like you. I trust you; that's why I don't worry when you go with Ingrid on these trips. You always take very good care of her, but I want you to watch her eating and drinking. She puts on weight fast, and sometimes she has too many cocktails. She shouldn't stay up too late."

He spoke earnestly, with a certain gravity, and impressed me as being quite unhappy about having to say these things.

"And one thing more, Joe," he said. "Try to be careful about who she sees or who she goes out with. And she shouldn't see too much of–[naming a prominent woman agent who was a close friend of Ingrid's]. She's not a very good influence for Ingrid. Okay?"

I nodded mechanically, but with considerable inner reservations.

"Do the best you can," he concluded, relieved that he had unburdened himself. "I wouldn't say anything to Ingrid about this little talk."

I sensed no connection between the admonition and the fact that the three men he had singled out were all bachelors. I had not the slightest inkling that the marital silver-lining had a cloud.

As we pulled out of Union Station, in Ingrid's drawing room aboard the "Chief," I drew out a cigarette and lit it.

"Let me have one," she said casually.

"Are you kidding?"

"Not at all. I have to smoke in *Arch*, so I might as well start to learn how."

Holding the weed gingerly, she puffed out spurts of smoke like an Indian signal. But, as in all things, she was an apt pupil and presently gave no evidence of the novitiate.

"Mmmm, I think I'm going to enjoy it," she said cheerily. Then, musingly, "Wait until Peter finds out."

Previous jaunts to Manhattan had posed a problem with regard to general press conferences that included the Scandinavian correspondents. Understandably possessive about their celebrated compatriot, the latter, numbering more than a score, invariably monopolized Ingrid's attention to the disgruntlement of the Americans. To obviate a repetition of this impasse I had wired RKO's home offices to plan separate sessions for each group.

"Ingrid," I said, "they always ask me if I speak Swedish. I want you to teach me how to say a couple of things so I can answer them."

Under Ingrid's tutelage, by the time we checked into the Drake Hotel, the phrases were well on tongue. In mid-afternoon her countrymen jammed into the conference room, drew up chairs, and waited for someone to break the northern ice. A familiar face took a look at me and said, "You learn to speak Swedish yet?"

"*Yah*," I said. "*Förbannade Svenskar* (damned Swede)—*dra åt helvete* (go to hell)."

The stiff, formal atmosphere was shattered by startled laughter. My tutor beamed with pride.

After the first few days I made the disconcerting discovery that something new had been added to our joint sojourns, or should I say subtracted? An incipient rebellion was manifesting itself. For her own protection it had been the custom to refer all her incoming telephone calls to me before passing them on to her. Now she instructed the hotel switchboard to ring her directly. Moreover, she began to make engagements without including me, or even informing me.

I was doubly troubled because: (a) I felt keenly the responsibility of looking after her welfare, which was hardly possible if I was ignorant of her whereabouts or her escorts; (b) her husband's admonition at the outset, which ultimately would confront me when New York was left far behind.

Warily, tentatively, I felt my way in the dark. As though I were merely indulging in casual conversation, I delicately probed, "Have fun last night?"

"Yes."

"Good. Whitney Bolton took me to dinner at Bleeck's, all the newspaper people hang out there, I'll take you sometime. What did you wear?"

"The Bonwit suit."

Undertones of irritation cautioned that I rest my case.

Several days passed and I went to RKO's publicity office on business. One of the men insinuatingly remarked, "Hey, what gives with your lovely lady?"

"What do you mean?"

"A friend of mine said he saw her and Bob Capa Thursday about four o'clock in the morning—very chummy in a dark corner of some Village hot spot."

"So what? They're old friends."

When next Ingrid announced she had a dinner engagement, I tiptoed gingerly, "Don't eat too much."

"Oh, no," she said in high humor. "You don't have to worry."

Then, unwittingly, it came out, "Got a date with Bob?"

Instantly, she bridled, flung her head back, and said, "Why? Why do you want to know?"

"Nothing, Ingrid, nothing. I'll feel easier if I know where you are, that's all. If anything should happen to you . . ."

"Nothing's going to happen to me. I'm sick and tired of being watched."

Under my door the following noon, May 26, 1946, there was a note in Ingrid's handwriting:

I. I am going shopping.
II. Seeing paintings with Cary.
III. Maybe a drink with Cary.
IV. Going to the bathroom.
V. Changing clothes (black bolero).
VI. Dinner (not with Cary).
VII. Home?

That was all. Significantly, it was unsigned. Precisely three years later I had reason to recall the note and the date it was written.

This was Ingrid Bergman's declaration of independence.

This, our first and only real collision, produced a salutary result; I ceased playing the reluctant guardian, and Ingrid blossomed in the sun of her partial liberation.

When she said she had gone shopping it was to buy gifts and pretties for Pia and gifts for special friends; not for herself. (She brought me an expensive Countess Mara necktie featuring a hand holding a pencil—"because you always carry a pencil.")

Her wardrobe was deplorably meager, but to all my importunities she answered, "We can't afford it." After a couple of weeks of luncheons, cocktails, dinners and late suppers, theaters and fashionable nightspots, the paucity of her apparel impressed itself. Still she hesitated.

Exasperated with her timidity, I pointed out that one of her fellow Selznick stars had recently come to New York and bought five thousand dollars' worth of clothes in a matter of two weeks.

"And what's more," I said, "she had no objection to it being publicized. Clothes are an essential part of a star's props. It's nothing for someone in your position. Besides, it's all deductible, anyway."

"Oh, all right. If I get my head cut off it'll be your fault."

A whole afternoon was dedicated to this minor Rubicon; Bonwit Teller, Bergdorf Goodman, gazing at gowns on statuesque models, riffling through racks, trying on jackets, suits and dresses. When I caught Ingrid once, examining price tags, I sidled up and muttered, "Will you please stop that! You embarrass me. Don't worry about the cost."

That was all the moral support she needed. A new kind of release enveloped her. Eight purchases were consummated, some of them in colors and styles she vowed were "not right for me—I'm too big." Dresses in beige, green, chartreuse; a tweed jacket of black, white and red; a red dress with a navy blue bolero jacket; a black cocktail dress with cowl neckline. When they were delivered to our hotel, the Drake, the sums on the sales slips totalled $837.17.

"That's not too much, is it?" she said, seeking reassurance. I shook my head hopelessly.

The David Selznicks divorced, he married Jennifer Jones, and Irene Selznick, a woman of extraordinary perspicacity, moved to New York with the intention of producing plays.

One day when Ingrid was attending a matinee with Irene, Bob Capa called and proposed we meet at the "21" bar.

"I guess you think I'm a dirty dog," he said, as we sat at a wall table.

"Why?"

"You know I've been seeing a lot of Ingrid," obviously wanting to unburden himself.

"Yes, I know. My spies keep me informed. I just hope it doesn't break out in one of the columns."

"Why?" he asked, with a note of belligerence.

"Her husband would raise hell."

"Yeah, I know."

"Well, it's natural, isn't it?"

"Up to a point—maybe. You know something, Joe? I know

Ingrid better than you do. She's all tied up in a million knots. Ever since she's been a kid, she's been told where she could go, who she could see, what she should say. Ever since her father died everybody's been fathering her.

"For a grown woman, she's so naïve it hurts—a great big woman steered around like a child. If she's got an idea of her own she stifles it, because her watchdogs say she mustn't. And that goes for you, too."

"Has she been complaining about me?"

"No, she hasn't. But I've got eyes—you watch every move she makes. She's afraid to let go. She says she's not afraid, but she is—scared to death. Scared to bust out of that goddamn built-in conformity.

"The world's her oyster, but you think she realizes it? You know better. Safeness and security—that's what motivates her. She hasn't the vaguest notion of what the world's about. It's a stinking shame.

"Ingrid's one helluva lot of woman—a damn sight more woman than actress. And people like you should stop treating her like an adolescent schoolgirl—or like a saint."

Just about that time, Kay Brown, along with everybody else, urged that we see an Italian picture called *Open City*, which had been running many months in a small theater on 49th Street in New York. We stood in a long line, Ingrid unrecognized, got our tickets and sat enthralled in the stuffy auditorium. The raw, realistic and searing account of life in German-occupied Rome in World War II moved us profoundly. We felt that mutual rapport that is born of identical sensations.

I never swore in her presence, she wouldn't have stood for it. But as we came out into the lobby, I exclaimed, "Christ, what an experience!"

"Oh, my!" she said, her face animated with excitement. "Wasn't it wonderful! It makes our pictures look silly."

We hadn't quite caught the director's name. We scanned the posters in the bustling lobby. It was directed by someone named Roberto Rossellini.

Most persistent wooer of Ingrid's professional services was

Howard Hughes, an improbable-looking but nonetheless authentic tycoon whose vast holdings encompassed the Hughes Tool Co., Hughes Aircraft, TWA Airlines, plus whopping chunks of stock in a multitude of diverse corporations.

Having inherited the fabulous Tool Company—fabricator of an indispensable oil-well drilling device—Hughes came to Hollywood in 1926, when he was about twenty years old. He formed a film company and subsequently bedazzled the industry with an extravaganza called *Hell's Angels*, which made Jean Harlow famous. In later years he made another bid for film fame with a consistently banned Western titled *The Outlaw*, which introduced, in the person of an actress named Jane Russell, a revolutionary new element of "talent," a prodigious mammary appendage.

A tall Texan—six feet, two—Hughes somehow reminded me of a dangling, loosely draped puppet. Due to a partial deafness, his quizzical countenance was invariably cocked to one side to favor the better ear. He spoke softly, often inaudibly. At times he was shy and reticent and fumbling as a country bumpkin.

Colorless as seemed the exterior, however, the inner Hughes was a complexity of the aggressive, the adventurous, the relentless, and the calculating. His aerial exploits were testimonials to unbounded courage. Designing and piloting his own planes, he circumnavigated the globe for a world record, and was not deterred from further adventures until he was plucked, unconscious and half-alive, out of a flaming crash into a Beverly Hills mansion.

Because he was a bachelor and possessed untold wealth, Hughes was the ruthless target of every bosomy, unattached female in Hollywood. But though he craved this ornamental companionship and seldom was seen in public without it, few women apparently succeeded in denting his defenses.

On the other hand, Ingrid Bergman's seeming inaccessibility presented a tantalizing challenge to the ego and might that so enamored everyone else. On occasion the two had met, but whatever impression he had left on Ingrid was negative. His deputies had courted her about doing a film, only to depart empty-handed. Howard Hughes was not accustomed to such indifference.

His chief buffer and henchman was an ubiquitous gentleman named Johnny Meyer, a person of generous girth and inexhaustible wit. His glibness was as smooth as the top of his head. Officially, he was labelled Hughes' "public relations director."

They were in New York throughout our entire stay and hardly a day passed without a call from Meyer suggesting cocktails or dinner or a nightclub, anything that would lure Ingrid. But the headstrong Swede kept shrugging them off, until one day I said, "For Heaven's sake, Ingrid, what's the harm in it? I know Peter doesn't like Howard [Hughes]—why, I haven't figured out. But I find him quite pleasant and no strain to be with. Besides, he's a very important man in our business, and some day you may want to make a picture for him. Actually, his persistence is a compliment to you. You can't hold that against him."

"Oh, he likes to go out with cuties. . . ."

"Have you been to the Copacabana? Joe E. Lewis is there, a very funny man. Howard wants to take you there tomorrow night, just you, Howard, Lana Turner, Johnny Meyer and me."

"Ugh," she said huffily. "He just doesn't interest me. But if you want me to I'll do it. But no big party, Joe—I don't want a lot of people sitting around staring at me."

The dinner came off very well, thanks in the main to Meyer's pungent persiflage. Hughes' attentions were chiefly directed at Miss Turner, giving no indication of any special interest in Ingrid. He appeared to be content merely to have her at his table.

Nearing the end of our trip Howard Hughes proposed that he fly us back to California in his private plane—a twin-motored Lockheed Lodestar. Cary Grant and Alfred Hitchcock, he said, would be aboard. Unable to conjure up a logical reason for turning down the invitation, I prevailed upon Ingrid.

"What time would you like to take off?" asked Hughes.

Concerned solely with Ingrid's welfare, I said, "I don't know, Howard. The only thing I'd like is to cross the California mountains in daylight."

"Then we'll figure on about 7:30 tomorrow night," he said. "I'll have a car pick you up around seven."

At La Guardia Airport he showed us into an office, then, leaving the others, took me out to see his luxurious air-yacht, the Lodestar. Told it would be ready shortly, I returned to the office. Almost half an hour later Hughes appeared at the door and beckoned me to come out.

"There's a bug in one of the motors, Joe," he said, "and I don't feel right about taking off with it. But I don't like to keep Ingrid waiting. There's another ship all ready to go. It isn't fixed up as well as this one, but it'll make the trip okay."

"Let's take it, Howard. Ingrid's tired and I want to get her home."

Ingrid immediately went to sleep on the single bunk; Grant opened a magazine; Hitchcock squeezed into a seat like a pouting Buddha and sank into slumber. The copilot saw to everyone's comfort, then retired to a rear cabin. I settled in the cockpit next to Hughes as he took over the controls and expertly guided the big craft westward.

We landed at Kansas City, Missouri, taxied up to the TWA hangar, and I followed Hughes outside. I was about to see the head of an empire in action. Four men in TWA work uniforms lined up about thirty feet away, their attention focussed on Hughes, awaiting orders. Others went about refueling and checking the plane. Nearby was a four-engine Constellation, dwarfing our smaller ship. Presently, as Hughes and I chatted, two of its motors started revving up. Hughes made a sign and one of the four men stepped forward.

"What are they doing?" Hughes demanded.

"They're just testing, sir," said the fellow.

"Well, tell them to stop it! Miss Bergman's asleep!"

The Constellation was instantly silenced.

An hour or so later, Hughes, who was piloting the whole night long, set down the ship like a feather at Albuquerque, New Mexico. The trio of celebrated passengers were sound asleep. For sixty or seventy minutes a squad of mechanics gave the ship a thorough going-over. The Sandia Mountains loomed through the dawnlight as another plane landed and taxied close by.

"Howard," I said, "that looks familiar—looks like the Lodestar."

"It is," he said, as if it were an everyday occurrence. "I told them that if they got the bug out to follow us in case we had trouble."

A cargo-less vehicle, perhaps costing a quarter of a million dollars, had followed us across the country with the casualness of one automobile following another.

A few minutes out of Albuquerque, Hughes opened a large map and studied it a moment, then, noting my curiosity, he pointed out our position. The Grand Canyon caught my eye and I asked how far it was.

"About a hundred and fifteen miles north," he said, raising his voice above the roar of motors. "Have you ever seen it?"

"No."

"Has Ingrid?"

"No."

"Would you like to?"

"Yes."

Before long we were suspended over the heart of the awesome gorge, flying virtually at rim level. It was at once terrifying and thrilling and beyond comprehension. I went to Ingrid and shook her.

"What is it?" she said sleepily.

"Get up! Get up and see the Grand Canyon!"

"Oh, I'm so tired."

"I don't care—you've got to see it!"

Ingrid took the copilot's seat and stared at the jagged peaks and tortuous chasms below. There was Hughes, imperturbable; Ingrid, softly radiant and savoring each morsel of thrill. Now wide awake, she remained fixed in her seat until our capable pilot set us down on his private runway in Culver City, California.

Dr. Peter Lindstrom never forgave me.

An undercurrent of dissonance jarred the homecoming and, I suspect, Ingrid's. Since David Selznick no longer steered the Bergman bark the press got into the habit of referring to me as her "manager," which understandably elicited Dr. Lindstrom's displeasure. It was naturally and generally assumed that a resident surgeon of a big city hospital was an unlikely person to undertake the management of an actress, even though she be his wife.

In order to obviate this general misunderstanding, I asked the doctor to permit me to make known his true managerial status, but he demurred, correctly, on ethical grounds. This false position in which I found myself was further aggravated by the New York trip. Pointed allusions to Ingrid's behavior, Howard Hughes, and the flight west with him, combined to breach our hitherto amicable relations.

The emotional climate surrounding us was never the same again.

Endless were the requests for Ingrid's personal participation in various public causes. It was our policy, concurred in by Lindstrom, to spread her services as impartially as possible among all religions and charities and civic activities.

Culling a batch of requests one day I came across an invitation to attend, on Sunday, December 16, 1945, a "Welcome Home, Joe" dinner, "to pay tribute to America's fighting men and women." Ingrid was to present an award to Lt. Edwina Todd, an heroic American nurse already cited by the government for her work in the Philippines. The roster of honorary guests included writer Dorothy Parker, California State Attorney General Robert W. Kenny, GI cartoonist Bill Mauldin, war hero Col. Evans Carlson, boxer Barney Ross, screen-writer Dore Schary, musician Artie Shaw, singer Frank Sinatra, and others.

The affair was under the auspices of an organization called American Youth for Democracy, whose underlying character was unknown to me. Our acceptance was motivated solely by the avowed purpose of the function.

The speeches and presentations over with, Ingrid left the dais and, beckoning me, said, "Joe, there is a soldier over there in the back; I want to say hello to him. He was in Alaska. He went with me to the PX and helped me buy cleansing tissues and chewing gum."

Among the six hundred guests she had singled out a GI whom she had briefly met two years before. Following their reunion, on our way home, she spoke of the nurse she had honored.

"Wasn't she sweet," she said. "She's so little and quiet. It's hard to imagine all the things she did. You never know what's inside of people."

Precisely one month after the Welcome Home dinner, January 16, 1946, Ingrid received the following telegram:

IT IS REPORTED THAT ON DECEMBER 16 YOU PARTICIPATED IN A PROGRAM HELD UNDER AUSPICES OF AMERICAN YOUTH FOR DEMOCRACY AT AMBASSADOR HOTEL, LOS ANGELES, TOGETHER WITH FRANK SINATRA AND OTHERS. ABOUT SAME TIME J. EDGAR HOOVER, SPEAKING BEFORE CATHOLIC YOUTH ORGANIZATION OF NEW YORK CITY, ASSERTED THIS ORGANIZATION WAS SUCCESSOR TO YOUNG COMMUNIST LEAGUE AND WAS POSITIVELY ORGANIZING CAMPAIGN UNDERMINE OUR AMERICAN GOVERNMENT. DID YOU APPEAR AT THIS BANQUET WITH AN INTELLIGENT UNDERSTANDING OF ITS SPONSORSHIP OR WERE YOU INNOCENT VICTIM OF A SLICK PROGRAM COMMITTEE? COPY OF THE TELEGRAM HAS BEEN FORWARDED TO CONGRESSIONAL COMMITTEE FOR INVESTIGATION OF UN-AMERICAN ACTIVITIES AND J. EDGAR HOOVER. ANSWER TO 420 FARWELL BLDG., DETROIT, MICHIGAN.

G. L. K. SMITH

Ingrid ignored the malicious missive. On January 30th, 1946, Gerald L. K. Smith, Detroit rabble-rouser and self-styled America Firster, appeared before the House Un-American Activities Committee and demanded an investigation of columnist Walter Winchell, comedian Eddie Cantor, Frank Sinatra, actor Orson Welles, Ingrid Bergman, and many others of like eminence and incorruptibility.

Nothing, of course, came of his foul mouthings, but there were some in Hollywood who questioned the propriety of her appearance at the dinner.

"Aah, you are all being very silly," was Ingrid's response. "I did it to honor a great woman."

I accompanied Ronald Colman on a ten-day tour of military hospitals for the War Department, which took us from Santa Fe, New Mexico, to Shrevesport, Louisiana. On my return I had lunch with Ingrid at the Beachcomber's.

"I have exciting news for you," she said. "You know how much I've wanted to play Joan of Arc all my life. At last I'm going to do it."

"A picture?"

"No. Let me tell you all about it. Last spring, Maxwell Anderson came to see me and said he had a play for me. 'What is your play about?' I asked.

"He said, 'Joan of Arc.'

" 'I'll do it,' I said."

"Without reading it?"

"Yes, without reading it. That's how badly I wanted to do Joan. When the chance came, I was determined to grab it."

"How come you never told me about this?"

"I didn't want to talk about it to anybody until I was sure it was set. Then started those damned business talks—talk, talk, talk, between lawyers, agents, Anderson and Peter. Terms, percentages, angles, clauses—ugh, I was getting sick. Maybe these business talks are necessary, but I've always wished you could say to a person 'I want to do this picture or that play,' and that would be enough of a contract.

"The dickering and bickering has been going on for months. I began to think I'd never get to do it. Whenever I asked questions I was told not to bother my pretty little head—these were matters beyond my understanding. Then last Tuesday, while you were away with Ronnie, Max Anderson came to the house. It was a very nice day so I suggested we drive to Santa Monica. We sat on the beach and commiserated about all the trouble in the world and the trouble our managers were making. Poor Max; he was so low and discouraged. And I was, too. Suddenly, I said, 'Have you a contract with you?'

"For a second he didn't know what to make of it, but he said yes, he always carried a copy with him.

"I said, 'Give me your pen.' And I signed the contract.

"Two or three days later, Peter said, 'I think we're working out a good deal on the play.'

"I said, 'You'd better, because I have already signed the contract.'

"When Peter finally recovered from the blow, he went over the contract again, word by word. When he got through he looked very relieved. He said, 'It's all right. You can always get out of it.'

"I said, 'But I don't want to get out of it!' So now I'm all set to start rehearsals when *Arch* is finished. Isn't it wonderful?"

Details of the contract were amicably worked out with the Playwrights' Company, who would produce the play, a group comprised of dramatists Anderson, Elmer Rice, Robert E. Sherwood, composer Kurt Weill, and financier John F. Wharton.

Several weeks passed and I dropped by the house to leave some press clippings. Ingrid and Ruth Roberts—pencils in hand—were deeply engrossed in work on a manuscript. The table was littered with scribbled sheets of paper.

"What are you girls up to?" I said.

"We're making notes about the play," said Ingrid mildly. "Max has plenty of time to fix it before we start rehearsals."

"Are you crazy?" I said. "Maxwell Anderson is one of our great playwrights. A play isn't a movie script; the editing and the changing are done during rehearsal, and only if the author okays them. Nobody can change a word but the man who wrote it. It's not like the movies, where the producer, the director and the stars do anything they like with the writer's work. You can't tell how the scenes are going to play until you start rehearsing."

The ladies looked at each other vacantly, then Ingrid said, "Well, I guess we'd better stop it. I'm glad, I was getting awfully tired of it."

With the approach of the Academy Awards event in March, 1946, there was a feeling extant throughout the movie colony that Ingrid was a cinch to win for her role in *The Bells of St. Mary's*. With this she did not concur.

"There have been too many good performances last year," she said.

Dr. Lindstrom, keenly sensitive to professional ethics, diligently avoided his wife's spotlight and gave me strict instructions to keep his name out of her publicity. However, when word got out that he would escort his wife, along with Leo McCarey, to the Awards at the Chinese Theater, photographers openly schemed to snap the elusive surgeon. I warned him to be on the lookout and when later I asked how he made out, he grinned complacently.

"Oh, I let Ingrid and Leo get out of the car first," he said. "Right away all the photographers crowded in front of them. Then I sneaked out and stood to one side watching the whole show. Nobody paid any attention to me until I started to laugh—everything struck me very funny. I laughed so much that one of them noticed me and started taking my picture. But I don't think he got a very good picture—I was laughing so hard."

Joan Crawford won a well-deserved sentimental victory for her performance in *Mildred Pierce*. When her name was announced, Ingrid, standing in the wings of the theater, cried, "I'm glad! I'm so glad!" Her only regret was that the custom of former years, the previous year's winner presenting the Oscar to the new one, had been changed. She would very much have liked personally to express her pleasure that Miss Crawford had been chosen.

Miss Crawford, absent from her great moment, in a sickbed, was equally gracious. After expressing her own surprise and happiness, she added, "I voted for Ingrid Bergman, myself."

The next day I ran into Cary Grant and a couple of executives in a spirited discussion of The Big Night.

"Cary has a good idea," said one of the men. "He thinks the Academy should have a special award and give it to Ingrid Bergman every year—whether she makes a picture or not."

Toward the end of June, 1946, Charles Einfeld and David Loew jubilantly launched their initial production, *Arch of Triumph*, with Ingrid as Joan Madou, the forlorn would-be-suicide who has a doomed romance with a hunted political refugee. Nothing was stinted to make her comfortable and happy. Subordinate roles were cast with the finest actors obtainable, regardless of cost. The virginal Enterprise Studio luxuriated in a state of giddy euphoria.

At another studio Loretta Young was starring in *The Farmer's Daughter*, essaying the role of a Swedish maid-servant in Minnesota who successfully runs for Congress. Destined to win an "Oscar" for Miss Young, the role had originally been proffered to Ingrid but, theorizing that the required dialect was too obvious a piece of casting—and thus no challenge—she rejected it.

Between Ingrid and Miss Young a schedule was worked out to share in Ruth Roberts' tutorage.

"In the morning," said Miss Roberts, "I erased Ingrid's accent, and after lunch I took it over and gave it to Loretta."

Bob Capa, now free-lancing, came to town and became a daily visitor on the set, often spending the whole day snapping pictures of Ingrid while she worked. He was not on assignment from any publication, but nevertheless shot hundreds of pictures of the woman he adored. She asked him to the house and he came once or twice, but the apathetic atmosphere soon discouraged that.

Almost every evening, when work was finished, producer Lewis's office became the hub of scintillating, Bohemian gatherings. There were things to eat and libations aplenty, good talk and liberated laughter. Capa was welcomed into the club.

On Ingrid's thirty-first birthday, August 29th, the company staged a party. Champagne corks cluttered the sink, and thoughtful, affectionate gifts were showered upon her.

Ruth Roberts chose our joint present, a record album of *Joan at the Stake,* an oratorio by Arthur Honegger and Paul Claudel. For the gift card I composed a limerick.

"There was a nice daughter named Ingrid
Who in Russian and Italian sing did
Her tune was so hot
For her birthday she got
This for crooning as swooningly as Bing did.
(signed) Papa and Mama."

This shameless effusion instigated a rash of limericks, including one from Ingrid:

"The nicest man we ever could know
Is a thin guy we all know as Joe
His legs and his neck—oh
Were designed by El Greco
But he is worth any gal's dough."

Ingrid's employment of native idiom was significant. Her Americanization was progressing apace.

As *Arch of Triumph* neared completion, Ingrid could talk of nothing but the Anderson play, now titled *Joan of Lorraine*, scheduled to go into rehearsals on October 5, 1946, a couple of weeks hence.

"Ingrid, I can't figure you out," said director Milestone. "Here you are on top of the world, the biggest star in Hollywood, and yet you're letting yourself in for a beating. Endless rehearsals, cold drafty theaters, a lousy little dressing room, and monotony—the same show eight times a week, week after week; laying yourself wide open to the critics. It isn't the money, because you can make ten times that much making pictures. Why do you do it?"

"It's good discipline," she answered soberly.

The cash consideration in her *Arch* contract was paid in weekly installments of $17,500. One week, instead of the check being mailed to Dr. Lindstrom, it was delivered to Ingrid by mistake. She stared at it in astonishment.

"My goodness!" she exclaimed. "That's a terrible lot of money. Do I get that every week?"

"Well, for ten weeks anyway," I said.

"Why, that's more than I got for a whole picture in Sweden—even the last ones."

"How much did you get?"

"Seven thousand dollars." She shook her head slowly, still wrestling with the revelation.

William Fields, publicity director of the Playwrights' Company, queried us about a character study of Ingrid to be used on the cover of the theater playbill. Ingrid possessed an old black ski sweater on the back of which was stitched an inch-wide yoke of white. She brought it to the studio, rearranged her hair, donned the sweater backwards and, striking a Joan of Arc pose, had herself photographed. The instant transformation was startling. Mr. Fields was highly pleased with the result.

Two or three times a week during the luncheon period we literally dashed across the street from Enterprise to the Western Costume Company for fittings of the mail and armor she would wear in the play. She couldn't get there fast enough. With countless variations I heard her say, "Think of it—eight months in New York! Isn't it exciting?"

As the weeks went by, the costume grew piece by piece; and when it was finally assembled, she put it on and for a long, pregnant moment appraised her reflection in the mirrored wall. A lifelong dream approached fulfillment.

On the way back to the studio she said, almost reverently, "Oh, Joe, I am so lucky."

One late evening in early October, 1946, when her work in *Arch* had finished, Ingrid and her husband sat before the fireplace of Hillhaven Lodge. All the day long and all through the evening dinner which she had hardly touched, a bedlam of thoughts had rioted through her consciousness. Little had been spoken between them, and that little of no consequence. She stared at the wavering flames until the riot subsided.

Then she heard herself say, "Petter, give me a divorce."

When twelve years later, at her country house in France, she told me about this incident, Ingrid said, "He looked at me stunned. He just looked at me. He couldn't say anything. And I was surprised at myself. I don't know why I said it. No, there wasn't another man, or anything like that. It was just that we had grown apart; we had very little in common any more."

Beyond this she refused to say more. What Dr. Lindstrom ultimately said, only he and Ingrid Bergman know. All that is known is that the threatening storm passed. At least for the time being.

6.

Joan of Lorraine

MAXWELL ANDERSON, one of America's foremost dramatists, a heavy-set, mild-mannered, professorial-looking gentleman, wearing a clipped moustache and rimless eyeglasses, told of how he came to write *Joan of Lorraine*.

"I have always wanted to write a play about a play in rehearsal," he said, "because I have wanted an audience in the theater to share the excitement of seeing a play come to life on a bare stage. Over and over again I have seen this miracle happen in an empty theater, with no costumes, no sets, and nobody looking on except the actors not in the scene, the stage manager, and myself.

"It's a kind of miracle, a new living world set out on a bare floor with a devilish worklight shining in everybody's eyes and constant interruptions and most of the actors reading their lines from blue-backed parts. And this first magic, this first flash of fire, is never quite repeated. The sets and costumes actually seem to get in the way. I wanted, when I wrote *Joan of Lorraine*, to catch this fire for an audience, to give them a glimpse of that first miracle. The only way to do it was to show a play in rehearsal and hope that the magic that I had so often seen would be repeated for many people—for the hoped-for full house.

"And in choosing the subject for the play in rehearsal I took one that came close to the question that has been my own torment—along with most of the human race—during the last decade. The problem of what to believe, and how a man defends his belief in a world of power politics and disillusionment, is hard to write about directly, but it's not a new problem. It was Socrates' torment, and Lincoln's, and Joan of Arc's, and many others. I chose Joan because she lived far from our time, and the scenes from her life would offer a complete contrast with the rehearsal—would give the actors a real chance to make a new world and set it down on a bare stage.

"When the play was written, and my wife had typed it, the question of who could play Joan came up. My wife said instantly that by far the best actress for Joan was Ingrid Bergman.

" 'But,' I said, 'she's at the very top of the Hollywood list. Who would give up such a sure thing to gamble on Broadway?'

" 'Nevertheless,' said my wife, 'you should try for the best there is. See her. Ask her. Give her a chance to decide.'

" 'It's one chance in a million,' I answered. 'Not more than two or three film stars have ever come back to Broadway and made a success. It's too much to ask of anybody.'

"But my wife insisted. I went to California, met Miss Bergman, and here she is."

On October 5, 1946, *Joan of Lorraine* went into rehearsal at the Alvin Theater, just off Broadway. The role of the director of the play-within-the-play was essayed by Sam Wanamaker, and the Dauphin by Romney Brent. The over-all production was directed by a personable young woman from Texas, Margo Jones, and designed by Lee Simonson, a veteran of many Broadway hits.

Ruth Roberts was brought along, to remain until the New York opening, all her expenses paid but no salary. "Peter didn't think I needed her, but I wanted to give her a trip," said Ingrid. "It will be a nice vacation for her."

I sat with Max Anderson and his wife, Mabel (Mab), down front in an otherwise empty orchestra and watched the rehearsals get under way. When the first of the three-week rehearsals ended I became imbued with misgivings about Miss Jones' static, stylized direction, and the costumes designed for Ingrid by Simonson.

The last—no doubt authentic, as claimed by Simonson—did not

take into consideration Ingrid's big-boned body, entirely unsuited for the ruffled, ballet-like conception insisted upon by the designer.

I spoke to Anderson and his wife, whose opinions seemed to carry weight with him. I suggested that he call these matters to the attention of Miss Jones and Mr. Simonson.

"Please, Joe," Anderson said, "I wish you would do it yourself. Don't feel any hesitancy about it. Your concern is Ingrid's success. It is our concern, too. We want her to be happy and comfortable. I can only put my ideas on paper. I'm not capable of arguing with the people who stage it. You have a perfect right to speak up if you feel something can be improved. I'm sure no one's going to be offended. I do wish you'd take over."

Mab Anderson added her own encouragement and I cautiously proceeded making suggestions. Aware that from the Broadway standpoint we were vulnerable as Hollywood upstarts, I employed all the tact I could muster. But as I met with more and more resistance I became increasingly insistent. All of which delighted Ingrid and helped to soothe her own concern.

The abbreviated, ruffled skirt, over her leotards, looked like a caricature. I told Ingrid I had an idea. I took her to Stroock's Theatrical Costumers and suggested she try on something of the Robin Hood period. The second costume she tried on did the trick. Of a subdued fawn color, it draped gracefully and underemphasized her large frame. Ingrid immediately took on a more relaxed turn of mind.

When Simonson saw the costume at the next rehearsal, he turned on me with resentment, "So you're a costume designer, too!" With which he walked out of the auditorium and seldom was seen again.

It was a cinch that if the play failed or if Ingrid appeared in an unfavorable light, she would bear the brunt of critical appraisal, no one else. A movie star invading the sacrosanct precincts of Broadway was always fair game. Since neither the author of the play nor anyone else seemed willing to fight the good fight, it seemed incumbent upon me to stick my neck out and assume a responsibility that was beyond the usual duties of a public-relations man.

While the rehearsals progressed, Dr. Lindstrom took a flying trip to Sweden to clean up some private property matters. He wrote me a short but jolly note, saying that Sweden was a "fine land and in good condition," but that the same could not be said for its "lost son," Peter, who was slowly deteriorating from seeing and skoaling with new "old friends" everyday. He said that he had taken refuge in the woods of his home town in order to reorient himself so that he wouldn't end up taking a plane "to Russia instead of the U.S.A." He said that the reports about *Joan of Lorraine* sounded "grand and I am getting all excited," and he asked that I reserve seats for the Washington and New York openings, both for himself and for friends.

Events of special significance to Ingrid were in the offing, particularly a big party immediately following the Broadway premiere. Ingrid possessed nothing in the way of a striking gown, new or old, to wear to this, her great moment. Kay Brown recommended that she have Madame Valentina, the celebrated couturière, design something. "She's expensive," said Miss Brown, "but it's time you owned a dress that isn't store-boughten."

Ingrid spent an hour with Valentina, looking at fabrics, studying sketches, exchanging ideas. Two days later she returned to be shown a drawing of the gown-to-be. She posed before a mirror as yards of material were draped around her body to approximate the finished article.

"My, it is going to be lovely," said Ingrid. "I would never have dreamed I could wear anything like this."

"I am pleased that you like it," said Valentina. "It will be ready for you when you return from Washington."

The gown was unconventional and dramatic—made of black moiré, with a green apron effect held in by a red sash, and a bit of red silk ribbon at the nape of the neck. The sleeves were bell-shaped and the neckline draped into a plunging "V" in back. The skirt was floor length in front and trailed slightly in the back. The whole was dramatically set off by red satin slippers.

Bob Capa, the constant, returned from a European assignment

and for several evenings Ingrid stepped out on her own. On the morning of October 20th I found in my hotel mailbox a post card illustrated with a reproduction of a mural by Adolph Dehn which graced a nightspot known as Cafe Society, at No. 2 Sheridan Square in the Village.

The drawing depicted the dazzling figure of a tall, befurred, bejeweled blonde entirely surrounded by a group of silk-hatted, swallow-tailed playboys. Under it, Ingrid had written, "Having a wonderful time. All taken care of! Joan of Lorraine."

The following day I met Dr. Lindstrom at La Guardia Airport, on his return from Sweden. He had brought back with him an old but fine set of surgical instruments which Customs took four hours to clear. He also had acquired a new hat, a stiff, broad-brimmed, light gray felt; an incongruous touch of Texas in an otherwise conservative get-up. I resisted the impulse to comment on it. Upon arriving downtown he immediately went to the Alvin Theater.

Ingrid spied him from the stage and, giving a cry, ran down into the orchestra to greet him. Spotting the new headgear, she laughed gleefully, "It looks like a cowboy hat—wait till Joe gets hold of you!" The next day he bought a new one before flying to California.

Since Ingrid's dream of Joan of Arc was now a reality on the legitimate stage, there only remained to put the Maid on film. Dr. Lindstrom broached the proposition to William Wyler, one of Hollywood's top directors, who, with director George Stevens and producer-executive Sam Briskin, comprised the independent company of Liberty Pictures. With great enthusiasm, director Wyler entered into a tentative agreement; he and Ingrid were in complete accord that the story adhere to history and steer clear of dramatized versions. Lindstrom and Briskin began working out the contract details.

In New York the Playwrights' Company broke a precedent with regard to Ingrid's comfort at the theater. Broadway theaters are notorious for dreary cell-like cubicles called dressing rooms. At the Alvin Theater a wall was knocked out between two rooms. They then were decorated and furnished like a miniature apartment. Ingrid loved it and on matinee days she kept on her make-up, and stayed there, writing letters, holding interviews, receiving guests, or napping on the couch before the evening performance.

Within a few days of our arrival in New York a group of young fans clustered around the Hampshire House, where we stayed, and followed her to the theater. They patiently waited there until Ingrid had finished, then followed her back to the hotel. Ingrid adopted them and enjoyed their well-behaved manner. They dubbed themselves the Alvin Gang and remained loyal throughout the years, staunchly standing by her in the midst of her greatest trials.

Throughout her life Ingrid had read everything about Joan of Arc she could lay hands on. Even now, during rehearsals, Ruth Roberts dug up new material and Ingrid avidly devoured it. Despite her eagerness to essay the Maxwell Anderson version, she bemoaned the fact that every word about the Maid was not historical fact.

"Finally I've decided," she said one day, "to forget the real Joan and play Max's Joan. This is a good play, so from now on I'll concentrate on this Joan."

Joan of Lorraine was overly long, verbose, and heavy with ponderous speeches, but Ingrid memorized them with amazing ease. Her photographic memory made assiduous study unnecessary. Her familiarity with *all* the roles was evidenced when she herself would prompt a faltering minor actor.

Joan of Arc medallions poured in from all over the country. Ingrid had her personal maid, Lillian Smith, a motherly Negress in her fifties (whom the Playwrights had recommended), sew one on each of her costumes for luck.

She saw an advertisement of the show in a daily paper to the effect that "seats would be on sale for twelve weeks in advance of the New York opening."

"Suppose we close after one week," she said to business manager Victor Samrock, "what'll you do with the tickets?"

"That's the least of our worry, Miss Bergman," he smiled.

In the play Ingrid had a soliloquy that ran five minutes. She complained to Anderson that Margo Jones continually postponed its rehearsal because Ingrid might not be up on her lines.

"That's all right, Ingrid," he said. "Don't read any lines. Just you come out and smile, and that'll be a scene."

In keeping with stage tradition it was everyone's opinion that she should make an entrance in the manner of all stars.

"But why?" she argued. "This is supposed to be a rehearsal; everybody is on stage when the curtain goes up. It's logical for me to be there, too."

"It's a concession to theater," said Margo Jones.

"I think making an entrance is out of character," Ingrid said. "It is not truthful to the part."

Nevertheless, despite the sound basis for her argument, she was overruled for the sake of show-business tradition.

Although Ingrid had completed her work in *Arch of Triumph*, the company continued to shoot other scenes in the picture after her departure. From New York every Sunday night she dispatched a night wire to director Milestone so that he would receive it first thing Monday morning on the set. The first of the series read simply, "DEAR MILLY. TI AMO (Italian for "I love you," her final death-scene dialogue at the climax of the picture)." She signed it, "JOAN DE ARC DE TRIUMPH."

Remembering a rather heated argument they had over the interpretation of a scene, she sent him a pair of plain gold cuff links for his birthday, September 30th, on which was engraved another quotation from *Arch* dialogue, "Are you going to beat me, too?"

Back came a telegram in verse:

Oh, sing me a saga of Joan,
Whose actions we cannot condone.
From Boudoir to Altar
Her steps never falter.
She quips 'Get me God on the phone.'
Who is this pure maid of Lorraine?
Whose voices she cannot explain?
From a life so licentious
She is turned so repentious,
It's driven her simply insane.

Oh give me the Joan called Madou,
Her memory we fondly review.
Calvados, not force,
Changes history's course—
Those judges would never burn you.

It was signed by Milestone, David Lewis, Charles Boyer, cinematographer Russell Metty, and assistant Norman Lloyd.

A speech in *Joan of Lorraine* ended with "...a miracle will happen." At a rehearsal after reading the line she suddenly looked down at Anderson in the orchestra and said, "That's a very brave line, Max. I hope the audience doesn't expect too much."

During a break Sam Wanamaker observed, "She's like a piece of silk hung on a string. When she sits or falls it's as if the silk was released."

Following a rehearsal of the dedication scene—the soliloquy—Margo Jones persisted that it be repeated.

"Everybody said it was perfect," Ingrid flared. "Why keep on rehearsing it? Let's put it in alcohol."

Around this time, motion-picture trade papers published the following announcement issued from Hollywood:

"Articles of incorporation have been filed through which Ingrid Bergman and Walter Wanger will be associated in picture making. The corporation has been named the EN Corporation, 'en' meaning 'one' in Swedish.

"Although the corporation does not have the exclusive rights to Miss Bergman's services it will make or assist in making arrangements for three pictures in which she will appear.

"Officers and directors of the corporation are: Walter Wanger, president; Ingrid Bergman, vice-president; Dr. Peter A. Lindstrom, secretary and treasurer; Mendel Silverberg, director."

Questioned about the "EN" Ingrid said, "Nobody could think of a good name, so I thought of 'en' because I am the company's only property."

On our schedule for the play was an out-of-town tryout of three weeks at the Lisner Auditorium in Washington, D.C. Several days before the opening date, Tuesday, October 29th, 1946, I received a letter from the National Association for the Advancement of Colored People asking if I was aware that Negroes would not be permitted to see *Joan of Lorraine* at the Auditorium. I showed it to Maxwell Anderson and Victor Samrock.

"The Playwrights' Company," said Anderson, "has received similar letters and protests from several organizations. So far as Negroes are concerned, discrimination is traditional in Washington. It is to be deplored, but this is a condition which has existed since the founding of the Republic. I'm afraid there's nothing we can do about it."

"Ingrid will hit the ceiling when she hears about this."

"Would Ingrid be willing to take on the added burden of a special Sunday show restricted to Negroes?" Anderson asked. "That would be a partial solution, but better than nothing."

"I'm sure she'll be happy to," I said.

"We haven't much choice right now," said Samrock. "It's too late to cancel contracts and make arrangements to hold the tryouts in some other city."

Ingrid was furious when I told her of the situation, but immediately agreed to give a special Sunday performance. However, when the proposal was transmitted to the NAACP they rejected it on the ground that "it would only serve to emphasize segregation."

"They are right," said Ingrid. "I never thought of that. Then I will tell the press what I think about the whole mess."

It was felt by Anderson, Samrock, and publicist William Fields that unsolicited statements at this time would only aggravate the situation with possibly serious consequences.

It was finally determined that Ingrid should publicly express herself after our arrival in the capital. Fields had already set up a press conference with the four local drama critics; he now invited the wire services and the city sides, intimating that Ingrid Bergman would have a newsworthy statement to make.

At 11:30 A.M., Sunday, October 27th, we took the train to Washington and checked into the Carlton Hotel. Twenty-four members of the press, including photographers, came to her apartment. For nearly an hour they plied her with questions about her work, the play, movies, future plans and so forth. We waited in vain for the all-important prime question, but there seemed to be a tacit agreement to bypass it.

"Miss Bergman, the underground has it that *Joan of Lorraine* is not one of Anderson's better plays," said a scholarly-looking gentleman, with a twinkle. "What is your opinion of it?"

"If I didn't like it, I wouldn't be doing it," she replied, good naturedly. "You critics may not like it, but I don't care whether you like it or not. I think it is a good play."

As hearty laughter followed this uncommon forthrightness, a senior journalist rose to his feet and, speaking for all, said, "We thank you, Miss Bergman. This has been a real pleasure. I'm sure we all wish you great success."

Ingrid bowed her appreciation, then as they edged towards the door, she said, "Please—there is one thing more. I have been waiting for you to ask me one question which you haven't asked. But if you're not going to ask it, I am going to answer it anyway.

"When I agreed to do the play in Washington I did not know there was such a thing as racial discrimination here. I never dreamed that it could be true in the nation's capital. When I found out, it was too late, contracts had been signed. If I had known about it in the beginning I would have refused to play in your city."

The statement was published throughout the country, and sympathetically acclaimed by her professional colleagues. A flood of wires and letters commended her stand. The union of theatrical players, Actors Equity—which heretofore had raised no voice in that direction—now debated the question. Whether or not this discussion and pursuant action were initiated by Ingrid's declaration of principle, I cannot say with certainty. But wherever actors gathered it was generally conceded that she had sown the seed.

As one fact follows another, the presumption would seem to be borne out. Within a few short months the powerful Equity ruled Washington "out of bounds to its members" until racial discrimination was abolished in its legitimate playhouses. And not too many months after a drought of the spoken drama the capital rescinded its archaic law.

A few minutes after the press departed, Frederick Polangin, Washington representative for Enterprise Pictures, came to my room and submitted a batch of requests for interviews and sundry functions.

"Miss Bergman's schedule is very tight," I explained, "and she's quite tired. I think we'd better not count on any of these with the exception of the Swedish Legation's invitation. She may want to accept that."

Ingrid, who telephoned her Beverly Hills home almost every day, discussed the Legation matter with her husband, who promptly vetoed it because "she already has enough to do."

As dinnertime approached Polangin came up with another invitation. Because of *Arch of Triumph* and *Joan of Lorraine*, French Ambassador and Madame Bonnet would like to hold a reception at the Embassy in Ingrid's honor. They would defer to her convenience—any day, at any hour—say, five to seven, so as not to tire her too much.

Ingrid—a Francophile at heart—was delighted, and a date was set for three days hence. After dinner that evening the company rehearsed until way past midnight. The stresses of the past several months, going into the play almost immediately after *Arch*, plus her own emotional problems, were now beginning to show on her normally placid countenance.

The staging of the play was woefully ragged, auguring a dismal outlook for the impending premiere. An undercurrent of anxiety permeated the cast. "If you'll forgive me, old boy," said actor Romney Brent to me, "this show wouldn't even open if it were not for Ingrid."

"Oh, Joe, the stage business—our positions and crosses—are just awful," said Ingrid, distressed. "I wish something could be done."

"I'll try," I said.

Dr. Lindstrom flew in the following day and sat with the Andersons and me as we watched a technical run-through to check lighting, props and so forth. At a couple of points I quietly stepped over to Margo Jones and made a suggestion or two, which she accepted graciously. When I returned to my seat the second time, Lindstrom remarked, wryly, "Hoah, I see you have become important." I made no reply.

The run-through ended around five o'clock and the company was dismissed until the 8:30 dress rehearsal. Riding to the Carlton Hotel with Polangin, Lindstrom, in an expansive mood, said, "Say, Mr. Polangin, you know a nice place for dancing tonight after the work?"

Tactlessly, I blurted, "Good God, Peter, what're you thinking about? Ingrid should go to bed. She's got a big opening tomorrow."

He gave a jolly laugh, "Yah—yah." Then ensued a moment of frozen silence. Ingrid stared straight ahead, making no sound.

"The Shoreham has a beautiful room and good music," said Polangin, "but you can't get anything to drink after twelve. That's a law here—none of the public places."

"Oh, no," said Lindstrom.

"There's Henderson's Castle, a private club. If you want, I can get you guest cards."

Lindstrom thought that sounded interesting. "I'll take care of it," said Polangin. "They'll be expecting you."

Shortly after our return to the hotel, Lindstrom came to my room, his manner foreboding.

"Ingrid has told me about the French Embassy," he said. "After I said no to the Swedish Legation, how can you say yes to the French? If we accept any invitations at all we should accept her own country's first."

"I did not turn down the Legation, you did. I didn't beat her over the head about the Embassy. I merely presented it as a good piece of public relations and she was very enthusiastic."

"This Polangin," he said, "is working for Enterprise; it's just a publicity stunt for *Arch of Triumph*."

"I can't imagine the French Ambassador falling for a publicity stunt. But suppose it is—what's wrong with that? You own twenty-five per cent of the picture. The French Embassy affairs are the most popular in Washington—some of the most important people in government and diplomatic circles attend them. The truth is that the Swedish Legation planned only a small affair—they said so—with only a few people present."

"You will have to cancel the Embassy," he said frigidly.

I got Polangin on the phone, who remonstrated that canceling such an acceptance once it was done was unthinkable; that it would result in unpleasant repercussions. "Nevertheless, see what you can do," I said. He said he would call me back.

Lindstrom paced the room as we waited. In five minutes the phone rang.

"Jesus, Joe," wailed Polangin, "we're in trouble. Madame Bonnet was extremely upset. Because the time was so short they rushed out the invitations right away—last night—two hundred people have been invited. It puts her in a very embarrassing spot."

When Lindstrom heard about this, he said, "It doesn't matter. You are going to have to cancel it."

"I am going to cancel nothing," I said. "I wouldn't know what logical excuse to give. You're Ingrid's husband—you get on the phone and you cancel it!"

Without further ado he picked up the phone, called the Embassy and, after a bit of involved protocol, made contact with the Ambassador's wife.

"This is Dr. Lindstrom," he said, "—about Mrs. Lindstrom—Ingrid Bergman—you were so kind to invite her—there has been a bad mistake—I did not know about it—I wasn't told—I am very sorry, she has no time—she is here to work—she cannot accept your kind invitation—here for only a few days—you understand—the Swedish Legation wanted her, too—I am very sorry—"

He must have talked for ten minutes before hanging up.

"It's all right now," he said. "You don't have to worry." Then he left the room. How Ingrid felt about this entire episode, I never learned. She never alluded to it.

Close to the curfew hour, following the dress rehearsal, we entered Henderson's Castle, Ingrid, Lindstrom, Ruth Roberts and I. A weathered, dreary old mansion, in the outskirts of Washington, it looked like something out of *Wuthering Heights*.

Despite the French Embassy incident our foursome was gay and charged with the excitement of impending events. Lindstrom immediately ordered champagne and we skoaled to the opening of *Joan of Lorraine*, followed in rapid order by skoals to Ingrid and anything else we could think of. After each skoal, however, Lindstrom's glass required a complete refill.

A second bottle was quickly followed by a third. A three-piece orchestra brightened the gloomy room and the Lindstroms danced. The only other patrons, perhaps a dozen, occupied tables on the far side. In an hour or so, under the stimulus of gulped champagne, dormant moods rose to the surface. In truth, I was still rankling under the French Embassy incident and derived little humor from the present forced gayety.

"Good Lord, Peter," I said, "that's not water you're drinking."

And that started it; he began needling me.

"Aah, Joe has changed," he said. "He's not like he used to be. Now he's getting very important, but God knows he isn't getting rich."

"What the devil is eating you?" I snapped in anger. "Somebody had to step in or this show would be one big mess. It's still sloppy —wait until the critics get at it."

"Please don't quarrel," said Ingrid, but made no move to defend me.

"Yah, Joe's getting very important," the doctor pursued. "He wants to walk proudly into the French Embassy with Ingrid on his arm."

"Look here, Peter, everything was peaceful until you entered the picture. You have no understanding of what our problems have been, and you have no appreciation of our work. Ruth here is supposed to be on a vacation, but she's been working every day, and nights too, helping Ingrid with her dialogue and doing lots of other things.

"Whatever I have done, I have done solely for Ingrid. I thought the French Embassy thing was okay. I had no other motive, but if you choose to interpret it any other way, it's up to you. But I don't like it and I won't take it. The show opens tomorrow and I guess my usefulness is ended. I resign as of now. I'll fly home in the morning."

"Please! Stop it—please!" Ingrid broke into tears. "I don't want to lose any of you."

At this, Lindstrom impulsively threw his brawny arms around me and started sobbing. The gesture sobered me and suddenly the temper-laden atmosphere cleared.

"I'm sorry, Peter. Let's forget it," I said. Ingrid put one hand on mine and with the other stroked her husband's head.

"You're like a couple of overgrown boys," said the always levelheaded Ruth Roberts. "You should be ashamed of yourselves."

Lindstrom and I disengaged and shook hands. Presently, emotions spent and tensions gone, we were on our way back to the hotel.

Late in the morning Polangin phoned, "I don't suppose you heard Sheilah Graham last night. She said Ingrid and her husband were having differences, that they were on the verge of a breakup. Anything to it?"

"Certainly not! Sheilah's crazy, hard up for an item, I guess. You've seen them together. Did you notice anything offbeat?"

No, he hadn't noticed anything, nor had I. Sheilah Graham was a syndicated movie columnist who also broadcast once a week over radio. We were good friends and it was her custom to check with me any questionable items regarding my clients. This time she had not done so. I wondered why.

As I reflected upon this initial intimation of gathering clouds, Dr. Lindstrom knocked and entered.

"Ah, good morning," he said affably. "You have a good night's sleep?"

"I sure did, Peter. Champagne is the best of all sleeping pills."

"I am flying back to Los Angeles tomorrow. Uh—there's something you can do for me," he said, hesitantly. "You know I haven't wanted any publicity, but I was thinking—it wouldn't be too bad—if you just kind of let it out—just a little—that I fly overnight so I can be with Ingrid for only one day. Yes?"

"Sure, Peter, sure. I'll be glad to."

As his tall, sturdy figure vanished through the door, Sheilah Graham's broadcast flashed through my mind. Was this the fire that underlay her smoke? What had happened between Ingrid and her husband? What or where was the fountainhead of this insidious rumor? Could it have begun with Greenwich Village? How much of his pride did it take for Lindstrom, this man of inner iron strength, to make the request?

I was suddenly very ashamed of my previous night's behavior.

Shortly after seven, dressed formally for the opening, Ruth Roberts and I rode to the Lisner Auditorium. I told her about the rumor.

"I don't believe it," she said. "You know how those columnists are. It'll all be forgotten tomorrow."

Crowds had already gathered before the auditorium, and there were portents of trouble. A score of uniformed police kept them moving. A picket line, entirely composed of whites, carried placards addressed to Ingrid, denouncing her local appearance.

Backstage, Ingrid restlessly awaited the curtain. Reports of the imminent disturbance reached her; several Negroes, holding tickets purchased for them by whites, were demanding admission. The management adamantly refused. Ingrid sent for me.

"Please, Joe, go out there and see what you can do," she said. "I get sick when I think someone might get hurt."

In the foyer, standing beside the ticket-taker, were four proud and good-looking Negroes, two men and two women, smartly garbed in evening clothes. They were quiet and impassive, but several white men and women were clamoring that they be admitted.

Addressing one of the two men, I identified myself and asked to speak with him for a minute. He politely responded and we moved to a quiet corner. His diction was cultured and manner impeccable. It flashed through my mind that these four had calculatedly been chosen to accentuate their cause.

"Have you heard about Miss Bergman's statement to the press today?" I said.

"Yes, sir, I did."

"The story was printed all over the country. Miss Bergman has a very big following; what she said is bound to exert a tremendous influence. It can do your people incalculable good. Our whole company is in sympathy with you. But if you persist in trying to gain admission, you'll only make serious trouble, and that kind of trouble can only undo whatever good Miss Bergman's statement might accomplish."

"Thank you, Mr. Steele," he said thoughtfully. "I see clearly that we have made a mistake. We shall leave immediately."

The tickets of the four Negroes were refunded, their spokesman prevailed upon the recalcitrant leader of the pickets, the mob dispersed, and peace reigned. Ruth Roberts rushed backstage to apprise Ingrid.

"Ingrid was so relieved," she said. "You should have seen her face."

At the conclusion of the premiere performance Ingrid and the cast took a dozen curtain calls to a standing ovation. Changing into black ties and formal gowns—those who had them—the entire company, including stagehands and all personnel, repaired to a private dining room at the 2400 Hotel for a celebration jointly hosted by Ingrid and the Playwrights' Company.

A buffet supper was served, a bar catered to every taste, and a small orchestra provided music. Spirits were high and all guards down. Since there were only seven women, including Mab Anderson, Margo Jones and Lillian Smith, Ingrid's maid, they were kept in perpetual motion on the dance floor by the overwhelming number of males.

One of Ingrid's two young brothers in the play was enacted by Kenneth Tobey, Irish as his surname, freckle-faced, carrot-topped, muscular, and mischievous as a terrier. As spirits soared and heads grew lighter Tobey elected to congratulate Lindstrom with a firm handshake. Before he knew it he was in a vise-like grip and pulled off balance.

The younger man quickly rose to the challenge and instantly the two, both in tuxedoes, were prostrate, fiercely absorbed in the ancient Indian game of arm bending. Dancers dodged the contestants as, right hands locked, elbows bent, they strained to floor the other's hand. Legs spread for leverage, they twisted and grunted and laughingly disparaged each other.

Presently, Lindstrom caught Tobey off balance and floored his hand. The actor demanded a rematch and the best two out of three downs was agreed upon. In a few minutes Lindstrom had won again.

The next morning Dr. Lindstrom woke up with a badly swollen hand. He went to a steam bath and had it massaged before taking off for California.

The play was well received by the critics, who considerately overlooked the faulty staging. Seats were sold out for the three-week run, and business-manager Samrock reported that the seven-month New York schedule was likewise nearing a sell-out.

In an effort to smooth out the rough spots Ingrid insisted upon rehearsals every afternoon when there were no matinees. In her otherwise free times she toured the landmarks with Max Anderson, who was well acquainted with the city. The Andersons were close friends of U.S. Supreme Court Justice Stanley Reed and his wife. Ingrid was introduced to them and as a guest of the Justice attended a session in which attorneys were sworn in to practice before the Court. She visited the great memorials, the Capitol, and Mt. Vernon, the quaint streets of Georgetown and the National Gallery. In the end her most vivid memory was of Daniel Chester French's awesome statue of Lincoln. Several times her sight-seeing was marred by individuals jeering "nigger lover," and each time she flushed a deep crimson but looked straight ahead and made no answer.

Letters streamed in from all over the country discussing her stand on racial discrimination, evenly divided between the pros and cons. And there also came letters about the marital rift rumor.

"Where did this start?" Ingrid wanted to know.

"I didn't want to worry you with it. Sheilah Graham had it on the air."

"Ugh. Why don't people mind their own business?"

"Is there anything to it, Ingrid?"

"Of course not. It's all so ridiculous. I wouldn't even bother to answer them."

Nevertheless, the name-calling and the rumor had their effect. An air of petulance infused her customary serenity, marked by a diffidence towards autograph-seekers and the adoring fans at the stage door. When leaving a shop or a restaurant, she dashed out ahead of me and was halfway down the street before I had paid the bill.

"Why all the hurry?" I once asked.

"Oh, I don't like standing there waiting for you. That's all," she said testily.

Leigh E. Ore of the Treasury Department, Fiscal Service, invited her to lend her name to the Community Chest drive, suggesting that she visit the White House and pin the Chest's emblematic red feather on the First Lady, Mrs. Harry Truman, who would be the first woman to receive it. Ingrid readily accepted the invitation, made the personal appearances and speeches that had been arranged, then went to the White House.

Mrs. Truman greeted her with neighborly simplicity and warmth, and expressed her regret that the President, who was out of the city, could not welcome her. They posed for pictures and talked like old friends, utterly devoid of formality. The First Lady served tea, then graciously guided her on a tour of the Executive Mansion, the while they discussed the problems of running "a big house like this."

"My, what a nice person she is," said Ingrid, as we drove away. "So natural and easy to be with. I was afraid it was all going to be pretty stuffy, but it was like visiting someone you've known a long time. Goodness, she must get awfully bored having to see people like us."

At the hotel we found that Bob Capa had come down from New York. That evening he sat in the front row and saw the play. In the morning he returned to New York. After his departure, Ingrid's manner became strained and edgy. In her dressing room, after the last curtain of the evening performance, I said, "How're you feeling, Ingrid?"

"Fine—fine! I feel just fine!"

"I thought you let down quite a bit tonight. You seemed to walk through the part."

"I don't care what kind of performance I gave," she said. "I gave my all last night. I had a special reason."

On termination of the second week there was no perceptible

improvement in the staging of the play. Palpably, it was carried along by the sheer weight of Ingrid's personality and talent. With only one week remaining before the crucial New York opening, nervous misgivings permeated the troupe.

In his role as director of the play-within-the-play Sam Wanamaker was required most of the time to sit down-stage at the extreme right wing. In this strategic position—after six weeks—he had had ample opportunity to observe and think about the production's defects. This fortuitous circumstance was our lifesaver.

On Sunday, November 10, an emergency council was held in the Bergman suite at the Carlton. Here it was decided to ask Miss Jones to relinquish her duties in favor of Wanamaker; she would, nevertheless, maintain program credit, plus a percentage of the receipts, in accordance with her contract.

Victor Samrock was given the unpleasant task of notifying Miss Jones, who shortly left the city. An adjustment was made in Wanamaker's salary, he took over the reins, and immediately instituted an exhaustive schedule of rehearsals.

"I keep thinking of Ingrid," said Maxwell Anderson. "As far as I know this is unprecedented. I know of no other actress who would agree to take completely new direction in so short a time before a New York opening."

"You needn't worry," I said. "She's made of granite. And besides, she's too stubborn to admit defeat. You'll see how quickly she'll switch to Wanamaker's naturalistic style."

On Sunday, November 17th, the *Lorraine* company moved bag and baggage to New York and we—Ingrid, Ruth Roberts, and I—took up residence at the Hampshire House.

Ingrid's apartment on the twenty-sixth floor—suite 2606—faced southward across the city, over the buildings, and down to the Brooklyn Bridge. She never tired of the wondrous vista, but it was the hour of dusk she loved most, when great walls of lights sprang up in the steel towers around us.

At ten o'clock Monday morning, November 18, 1946, by way of a dress rehearsal, a preview performance of *Joan of Lorraine* was given for a group of war veterans. At its end, Ingrid said, "I'm going to St. Patrick's Cathedral, Joe. I want to go alone."

"You want the limousine?"

"No, I want to walk," she said pensively.

That afternoon she wrote several messages which I was to distribute just before the 8:30 curtain of the premiere New York performance. They were paraphrases of actual Joan speeches:

(To Maxwell Anderson): "This man Maxwell Anderson came to me and said I must be Joan of Lorraine, and somehow or other it has come about. And now when I am about to be presented it is a little late to do anything about it. And if it was to do over I would do it again. I would follow my Max even to the New York critics. (signed) Ingrid."

(To Sam Wanamaker): "You Sam Wanamaker, who call yourself director, and if you don't do so I will raise such a hai-hai as the House of Alvin would never stand for it. I am only a girl. I knew nothing of falls, twists and writhings. I want to do everything you say, but tell me, please tell me how to get rid of stage fright. And if you do so I shall stand beside you. (signed) Joan, the Maid."

(To Alan Anderson, the playwright's son by his first wife who, as stage manager of the production, also acted as prompter): "Alan, stand by and read the part of Joan. Stand proudly and read well. I can depend on you as I can on Father Massieu. Because your voice is good. (signed) Joan, the Maid."

(To the cast): "Stand erect, Cast, we must make an entrance soon. Death by the critics is a horrible thing. But they can't hold you back. Nobody could hold you. Forward, my friends, they are falling by themselves. Strike them when they are dead. God will give us victory. (signed) Joan, the Maid."

On her dressing-room table, reflected in the mirror, was a bronze statuette of Joan, a memento from Wanamaker, on the base of which was engraved a line of his own dialogue: "You bring even my wry half-faith back to me."

Alongside the statuette were pictures of Pia, a leather triptych holding portraits of her parents, and a piggy bank for Pia. On a bedside table reposed an edition of George Bernard Shaw's *Saint Joan*, its title page inscribed: "Saint Joan for the consideration of Ingrid Bergman, submitted with great respect by Bernard Shaw."

"This is probably the greatest of all the Joan of Arc plays," I said. "How come you didn't want to do it?"

"I have read it several times. It is a fascinating play and many times I thought about doing it. But somehow I never liked Shaw's Joan. She was brazen. She called the Dauphin Charlie and hated to be a woman and wear skirts. She wanted to be with men and thought only of going to war. Max's Joan is truer; Joan of Arc was a simple country girl who liked babies and animals. She hated to see blood and she was frightened of the fire. Shaw's play is clever and wonderful to act, but I love the real Joan so much I want to be true to her."

In the wings of the Alvin Theater stood actors silently engrossed in going over their lines. Occasionally, Sam Wanamaker suited the gesture to the soundless word. The property man kept checking and rechecking his props. From behind the closed doors of some of the dressing rooms issued fragments of dialogue.

Two minutes before curtain, outwardly calm as Ingrid waited to make her entrance, I said, "How do you feel?"

"If they don't raise that curtain pretty soon," she said in an even tone, "I'll break into little pieces."

Lindstrom had arrived and was sitting in the third row. A large contingent from Hollywood had also come, and standees in formal attire packed the rear. Ingrid Bergman's vibrant instant was at hand.

The miracle of which Maxwell Anderson spoke—"a new living world set out on a bare stage"—took place in full view of the first-nighters. Ingrid Bergman and *Joan of Lorraine* made Broadway history.

Afterward, the author, cast, officials and associates repaired to a small private dining room at the Hotel St. Regis, there to await the morning's critiques. Sleep would not be possible for many hours.

Wearing the Valentina gown and a perpetual school-girl blush that matched her red shoes and red ribbon, Ingrid floated among the guests in a dreamy bliss.

Towering Robert E. Sherwood, one of America's greatest dramatists, declared to a small group, "Her radiance is indescribable. The moment she came on stage, before she uttered a word, something electric happened. You could feel it reach out and touch everyone. She is the greatest Joan I have ever seen. She *is* Joan."

Presently the morning papers were out and press agent William Fields came laden with a dozen copies of each. With nervous avidity each precious word was read. Without exception and with all-out acclaim the metropolitan critics embraced the new Joan.

Brooks Atkinson of the *New York Times*, dean of American critics, wrote, "Miss Bergman (gives) an exalting performance... Her part is wholly becoming, both as Maid of Orleans and as an actress brooding over the role... But that in no way impinges upon the rare qualities Miss Bergman brings to the part. Her appearance as Joan in New York is a theatrical event of major importance; and only professional cowardice prevents me from going off the deep end about her talents... She was excellent in *Liliom* six years ago. She is superb now in the much grander part of Joan. Anyone can see that she comes to the stage bearing gifts of extraordinary splendor.

"In the first place, she is beautiful, which is no handicap on the stage or anywhere else. She is also magnetic, which is also more essential than beauty on the stage... Miss Bergman endows Joan with a spiritual aura that is reflected in the audience as well as the play. It is a quality of sentience that among our younger actresses only Miss Bergman possesses—putting her in the category of Cornell and Hayes. To be less fastidious about the whole episode, the Gotham playgoers are now tossing their sweaty nightcaps in the air to celebrate Miss Bergman's transcendental portrayal of Saint Joan."

It was dawn when the celebrants dispersed. Ingrid, Dr. Lindstrom, Ruth Roberts and I walked leisurely to our hotel, and bade each other a weary good night. Late that afternoon Lindstrom left for California, there to resume negotiations on the projected William Wyler-Joan of Arc picture, the prospect of which was an added fillip to Ingrid's now-established Broadway ascendancy.

When we went to the theater for the evening performance there was a letter from Robert E. Sherwood. Penned in longhand on the Playwrights' Co. letterhead, it was dated November 19, 1946:

Dear Joe:

Would you be good enough to give the enclosed to Ingrid?

I hope she is pleased with the notices. That certainly was one of the supreme personal triumphs of all time.

We are all mighty grateful for the fine cooperation you have given us all the way through.

(signed) Bob Sherwood

The enclosure read:

Dear Ingrid:

This morning, at an exultant meeting of the Playwrights' Company, I said I was going to write you a fan letter, and all the others asked to be included in it. So this is official.

We feel that your performance of Joan is one of the great, historic achievements of the theater—that it will be praised forever—and we are proud and grateful to have been associated with it. It has taken five hundred years to find the person perfectly qualified for the role of Joan—but she has certainly been found in you. In short, we love you.

Yours,

(signed) Robert Sherwood

With the departure of Ruth Roberts the next day, Ingrid settled down to a life of rich and ceaseless activity, the more joyful and exciting because she was three thousand miles distant from domestic strictures. Her life was divided into three parts: (a) Suite 2606, where she slept and entertained and made home; (b) the theater, and the quasiluxurious dressing room whose walls were thumb-tacked with original sketches and illustrations of the Maid, the shelves peopled with her figurines—all sent by fans; and (c) the in-between hours of shopping, visiting the Metropolitan Museum or the Museum of Modern Art, seeing a movie or attending the matinee of some other play, lunching with Kay Brown at the Barberry Room, or somewhere else with someone else, or walking the teeming avenues or in Central Park, drinking great drafts of the heady wine of success and freedom.

In her passion to get out on that stage and lose herself in an imaginary world she frequently went to the theater half an hour to an hour too early. Having changed into costume and make-up, she would write letters on her little portable, go over fan letters of special significance which I would call to her attention, peruse a new Joan of Arc book that Ruth Roberts had unearthed, or make one of her many weekly calls to Pia, chatting for minutes on end.

In the beginning she wanted me to let her know if any notables or someone she knew was in the audience, and approximately where they would sit.

"It helps me," she explained. "I play to them, and it makes it easier for me. Otherwise, the audience is a big blank and I feel I'm playing to an empty house."

At her request press interviews were arranged for this precurtain period. One magazine writer asked when she planned to retire from professional life.

"My goodness," she said, "why should I think about when to retire? This country is very cruel to aging actresses. You think it is awful not to be young any more. You even make middle-age sound terrible. But I'm not frightened of age. Just think of the wonderful parts I can play when I'm seventy."

Ingrid's correspondence became so heavy that her husband insisted she have a secretary who also could assist me in many ways. Kay Brown recommended a highly efficient young woman named Mrs. Ellen Neuwald, who was given a leave of absence from Miss Brown's office for the duration of the play. Mrs. Neuwald was married and had a young son.

A close friend was Michel Bernheim, a young French director who had served as technical advisor on *Arch of Triumph.* He lived in an apartment on Central Park South, a short walk from the Hampshire House, with his widowed mother, Mrs. Helene Bernheim, and younger brother, Alain. Claude, an older brother, who was American agent for a large perfume house, lived in another section of the city.

A family of exceptional charm and culture, who spoke English as brilliantly as their native French, they endeared themselves to Ingrid. On occasion she would dine in their modest quarters and enjoy its warm informality and the interesting people she would meet there—among whom was violinist Jascha Heifetz.

Claude, who was taller and even thinner than I, was married but his attitude towards domesticity was rather loosely defined. His trenchant Paris sophistication held a curious attraction for Ingrid, and they often met before and after theater, dining in out-of-the-way bistros, or strolling in Central Park.

"When we were walking in the park yesterday," he once said to me, "there were hundreds of couples sitting on benches or lying on the grass. Every once in a while somebody recognized her and yelled out, 'That's her! That's Ingrid Bergman!' Right away Ingrid got self-conscious and began to walk so fast I could hardly keep up with her.

" 'Hey, slow down,' I said. 'What's the hurry?'

" 'Just look at them,' she said. 'See how happy they are. All I ask is that I am allowed to be happy too.'

"That woman's full of contradictions, Joe. She wants to be a star and at the same time wants to live like an ordinary person."

Another time, in my presence, Claude Bernheim said to Ingrid, "I'm not a bit impressed by what the critics have said. I have now watched your performance five or six times; each time you were different. But I noticed that there are certain tricks you always resort to. You're not as good as they say you are. You have yet to play your great part. Some day you will be a truly great actress."

I thought him flippant and awaited her quick resentment; instead, she beamed like a youngster who had just been given a shiny bauble.

"Thank you," she said. "Thank you, Claude. I hope so. I have so much to learn."

Her apartment refrigerator was stocked with champagne splits while other varieties of potations were available to guests. On nights when she had no after-theater plans she would change to a voluminous, tent-like robe, swallow a sleeping tablet (prescribed by her husband), recline on the big sofa, and sip champagne until sleep overcame her.

Sometimes she read a new novel or biography; sometimes she indicated she'd like me to come sit up and talk. The lights and shadows of Rockefeller Center painting a mural against the wide windows, I looked on as her tensions gradually dissolved, her blue-gray eyes grew heavy, and the gossamer wings of peace enfolded her.

"When I leave the theater I'm all keyed up," she once said. "When I come home the audience is still there in front of me, and the lights blaze in my eyes. It takes a long time before I can unwind and go to sleep."

The deluge of demands upon her precious spare time was overwhelming; declinations called for utmost tact and cajolery. Acceptances were made only after careful consideration and consultation with Lindstrom (by mail or phone) and Ingrid herself. Two or three times a week she appeared at some semipublic affair, or a radio broadcast, or a cocktail party in her honor, or to be photographed on behalf of some cause.

Despite the extremely formal Valentina gown and the courageous purchases of a year ago, her wardrobe was sadly skimpy and totally lacking in distinction, considering the multiplicity of her current activities. Soon it became evident she could not continue without augmenting her supply.

"What shall I wear, Joe?" became an oft-repeated question.

And so we went shopping; to Lord and Taylor, Bonwit Teller, to Bergdorf Goodman. She rummaged through racks and even asked if she might go into the storeroom—that mysterious place where saleswomen disappear and reappear with fineries.

At first she selected a couple of plain frocks, then felt she had done enough. It was hardly a beginning towards fulfilling her needs. I urged her to look at more. Her resistance was false. A little prodding did the trick.

In each store I asked that items be modeled by their tallest mannequin. Ingrid looked on with girlish anticipation.

"The models are so pretty," she said.

"The clothes are pretty, too. Why don't you try them on?"

"Oh, I can't wear anything like that," was her sing-song lament. "And besides I am tired of putting things on and taking them off. And it's getting late."

I asked that a dozen or so of the garments we had seen be sent to the Hampshire House for her trial and approval. By the middle of the afternoon they had been delivered to 2606. I found a note under my door, "Dear Joe: I want to hold a fashion show for you at six o'clock."

At six o'clock, martinis at hand, I sat in the living room as the little big girl paraded in and out of her bedroom, modeling one outfit after another. The third or fourth was a red satin suit, which heightened her coloring and looked gay yet chic. She glowed with pleasure.

"It's beautiful," she said, "but don't you think it's too loud for me?"

"No, it isn't too loud. We'll take it."

"They'll think I'm going to a fire." She peeked at the price tag. "Oh, it's one hundred and sixty-five dollars!"

"Stop looking at the prices!"

She changed into another and another; cocktail dresses, daytime frocks, tweed suits, in all kinds of fabrics and shades. Alterations were discussed, noted on a piece of paper and pinned to the particular item.

There was a suit she admired but felt she could not wear because of her broad shoulders. The skirt was a plain light gray wool, but the jacket, of lighter gray crisscrossed by red lines, with three large leather-covered buttons, barely reached her waist. It was the length that bothered her. Now she put it on and strutted around the room.

"Isn't it pretty," she said, then suddenly burst out, "Oh, how I like clothes!"

There were three or four we decided against. As to the others, I said I would have the stores call for those to be altered; any that fitted could remain in her closet.

"You think I should take all those?"

"Certainly. They're still not enough, but we'll go shopping again."

"You're ruining my family," she said, eyes twinkling. "Poor Pia. She'll have nothing when she grows up."

This from the biggest current attraction on Broadway, whose weekly income in minimum guarantee and percentage averaged around five thousand five hundred dollars. Untold wealth awaited her in future movies.

This Week magazine invited her to contribute an editorial for its "Words to Live By" feature. She chose a quotation from Carl Sandburg:

"Look out how you use proud words.
When you let proud words go, it is not easy to call them back.
They wear long boots, hard boots . . .
Look out how you use proud words." *

Then she added her own thoughts—with a little help in phraseology:

"There is in these words a primary lesson for individuals and classes and nations alike. All too often, we say the cruel and destructive things—because it is so much easier to be clever than to be kind. But in the long run, proud and angry words are the ones which cause trouble in our homes, our communities and among nations.

"Proud words are arrogant, intolerant and savagely ignorant of the great fundamental truths—simplicity, humility and ordinary decency. They are indeed rough-shod, and it is not easy to call them back."

As Christmas of 1946 approached I planned to fly home for the holidays. As a safety measure I engaged a private detective to escort Ingrid to and from the theater, and to remain outside her dressing room throughout all performances.

"But I don't want him following me everywhere I go," she said.

"I understand. Simply dismiss him whenever you feel like it. But he's got to be at the theater every minute you're there. All kinds of characters hang around the stage door."

I bought her a gift, attached a note and gave it to Ellen Neuwald

*Reprinted from *This Week Magazine*. Copyright 1947 by United Newspapers Magazine Corporation.

to deliver on Christmas Eve. The note was a paraphrase of one Ingrid had written me long before:

"Miss Bergman: Herewith instructions to be followed during my absence:

1: Don't catch cold.
2: Cut down on your smoking.
3: Don't drink too much.
4: Be careful whom you go out with.
5: No monkey business!!!

(signed) Papa."

She wanted her daughter for the holidays and Lindstrom sent Pia, now seven, in the custody of her governess.

The day after Christmas, in California, a letter arrived from Ingrid. On the back of the envelope she had scratched in ink a rough impression of Joan of Arc brandishing a sword:

"My dear guardian Joe: A big Christmas hug to 'father' and a big wish for a happy New Year. A wish that we'll be together, that you won't have too many telephone calls, and too many enemies due to me. I thank you for the 'instructions.' It gave me a good laugh, and I'll have stories when you return that will make you laugh too. We are struggling along quite beautifully on Broadway. I hope Beatrice [Mrs. Steele] can come here and hear the faith and see the glory while it lasts! Merry Christmas to you and your family. Ingrid."

Lindstrom informed me that the *Joan of Arc* film deal with Liberty Pictures had collapsed, saying only that satisfactory terms could not be reached. A day or two later Sam Briskin, one of the toughest business men in the industry, asked if I would come to see him.

"I guess you know we couldn't get together with Lindstrom," he said, in his office at the Paramount Studio.

"So I understand."

"The good doctor is a hard man to do business with. If he had his way there would be nothing left for us. Can you put in a word with Ingrid or help us in any way?"

"I'm afraid not, Sam. I'm only her public-relations man. If I put a bug in her ear, Lindstrom's sure to find out about it, then all hell will break loose."

There was a letter from Victor Samrock telling me that a telephone had been installed in the theater dressing room, and giving me the number. Among other things he wrote:

"Seats are now selling into April, and the demand continues unabated. All seems to be well backstage, and several rehearsals have been held to pep up the performance. To be quite frank about it, both Bill (Fields) and I are off balance—Miss Bergman makes too few demands to suit us and we are getting that plutocratic feeling that life is too easy. We'll probably both come down with the gout."

Irene Selznick, still determined to try her hand at play-producing, finally found one, *Heartsong* by Arthur Laurents. Ellen Neuwald wrote me, ". . . as Ingrid said yesterday, 'It's going to be a woman's world, what with Irene Selznick producing the play, and Phyllis Laughton and Ruth Roberts directing it.' "

Miss Laughton, who knew the theater and worked in Hollywood as a film dialogue director, was the wife of Ruth Roberts' brother, George Seaton, a leading writer-director. Both women put up at the Hampshire House, and there ensued neighborly visits back and forth with Ingrid.

When I returned to New York on January 7, 1947, I found Ingrid in a state of despondency over the Liberty Pictures *Joan of Arc* debacle.

"Oh, I don't know what goes on," she said despairingly. "I talked to Peter on the phone, but still I don't understand. Business, business, it's always business. How I feel doesn't matter."

Meanwhile, the demise of the Liberty Pictures deal and Ingrid's availability spawned a mish-mash of movie offers, none worth considering. George Stevens, a superlative director, flew in one day and asked me to get him a couple of seats for *Lorraine*. Though the show was sold out, there were always held out a few seats known in theater parlance as "house seats," which were obtainable in emergencies. Stevens got two of these.

"After the show," he said, "do you think I could see Ingrid for a few minutes? I want to talk to her about a story."

"She'll be delighted."

After she had changed into street clothes, Stevens, himself an Oscar winner, was cheerily welcomed into the dressing room.

"Ingrid," he said, "I came to New York for just one purpose—to talk to you about a story I want to make. But after seeing you in the show I've changed my mind. It's not good enough for you and I won't even tell you what it is."

Burgess Meredith, her costar in *Liliom* of six years before, was appearing at another theater in Synge's *Playboy of the Western World*. He sent Ingrid a telegram, "Congratulations. Please send some business over here."

British actor and playwright Noel Coward saw a performance and afterwards said, "Most exciting evening I have ever spent in the theater. When in the first scene she tried on the armor gloves, I knew she was an actress."

Producer Walter Wanger, now head of Ingrid's EN Corporation, secured rights to a story called "The Ballad and the Source," which he hoped was suitable for a Bergman production. Victor Fleming, having severed all ties with MGM Studio, joined hands with Wanger and came to New York to sell her on the project. Like George Stevens, he, too, attended a performance and planned to submit his proposal at a prearranged supper at 21 Restaurant.

Ingrid had no sooner taken her final bow, however, than the white-maned lion stormed backstage and clamored to see her now, instantly.

"Victor! Victor!" Ingrid cried out as they kissed and embraced with fervor.

Words gushed from him in a violent torrent, "God damn it, Angel, why do you want to make pictures? You should play Joan for two years, ten years, all your life!"

He grabbed her shoulders, held her off and gazed into her eyes. Tears streamed down the bronzed, part-Cherokee countenance.

"I came here to talk to you about 'The Ballad and the Source—' to hell with it, it's a lot of junk! I don't want to direct you or make pictures with you. God damn it, you belong here, out there on that stage!"

"Oh, Victor! Victor!" she said, and they cried together.

Next noon, Fleming and I lunched at 21. For two hours he spoke of nothing but Ingrid.

"To hell with 'Ballad,'" he said vehemently. "Even if she wanted to do it, I wouldn't let her. I was going to fly back today but I decided to stay a while. I want to see the show again tonight. And tomorrow night too, and maybe Saturday matinee. Can you get me seats?"

"Sure, Victor, sure."

In the late afternoon I took the elevator to 2606. "Listen, Ingrid," I said. "You're very fond of Victor. He's very fond of you. He'll do anything for you. He's a great director, and he is no longer under contract. He's free to make any picture he pleases. Walter Wanger is a producer, dying to make a picture with you. Why not let them set up a company to make *Joan of Arc?*"

She telephoned her husband and within a couple of weeks the project was under way. I proposed to Fleming that he set up headquarters at the Hampshire House to better facilitate conferences with Ingrid. The hotel manager escorted him on an inspection of available accommodations, including a lavish suite on the thirty-fourth floor renting for seventy-five dollars a day. Fleming, rated one of the wealthiest men in Hollywood, who always carried two thousand dollars in cash on his person because "it makes me feel good," balked at the price.

"That's too much, Joe," he said. "What do I want with all that space? Seventy-five dollars a day? That's a fortune, son!"

"Victor, you've got a big picture to work on. All kinds of conferences. Story and sets and costumes to worry over. You'll need all the room. Make your office there. The art director can use the dining room. It's got a kitchen and a bar. You never have to leave the place. Besides, don't you want a nice place for Ingrid to come to?"

"You're a bad influence, Joe," he grinned. "I guess you're right. Maybe I can make a monthly deal with them."

The hotel was happy to go along and presently art director Richard Day, another Oscar winner, arrived and set up his studio in the spacious dining room; a secretary was engaged; Noel Howard, a young artist, was enlisted to make sketches of armor and costumes of the period at the Metropolitan Museum; Maxwell Anderson dropped in and out for script conferences; the ample kitchen was stocked with food and refreshments; research publications were everywhere, and Joan of Arc in cinema was on the march.

Ingrid became a habitue of the Joan of Arc-Fleming headquarters, peering over shoulders at art work in progress, showing the writers a pertinent passage she had run across in some Joan of Arc book, or simply doing nothing but reveling in the activity of which she was the core.

Owing to the irregular hours and the accessory need for rest, the Hampshire switchboard was instructed not to put through any calls for me in the morning until I had notified them. Nevertheless, one morning, the phone rang about eight o'clock.

"Joe! Goddamn it, who are you that you shouldn't be disturbed in the morning?" Fleming's voice boomed against my ear like a trumpet blast.

"What's the matter? Can't you sleep?"

"Sleep hell! you turned out to be a fine friend . . ."

"Hey, wait a minute–What's eating you, Victor?"

"Why don't you let somebody know that Peter was coming?"

"Peter? What're you talking about?"

"Didn't you know that he was coming in last night?"

"No, I didn't."

"Well, damn it, he did. Ingrid didn't know he was coming, either. He went to her room and when he didn't find her there, he called me. It was damn near two o'clock. 'This is Peter,' he said. 'May I speak to Ingrid?' Damn embarrassing, that's what it was."

"Then what?"

"She got on the phone and told him she'd be right down. Pretty rough, my friend. Pretty rough."

Shortly after two, Dr. Lindstrom, voluble and exuberant, paid me a visit in my quarters. We discussed some business matters, then he left to catch a late-afternoon plane for Hollywood.

At seven o'clock, as we walked to the theater, Ingrid was uncommonly quiet. Obviously, she was not going to mention the incident. In her dressing room, as she applied her make-up, I said, "Victor called me this morning and told me what happened last night. I want you to know that I had no idea Peter was flying in."

"I'm just sorry for Victor," she said evenly. "He was terribly embarrassed. He came last night to see the show again, and afterward we went to 21. I guess we were there a couple of hours; I wasn't watching the time. When we came to the hotel we went directly to the elevator. I said, 'Let me come up for a little while. I don't feel a bit sleepy.'

"If five minutes after we came into the hotel someone had asked me if I saw anyone in the lobby, I would have said, 'Yes, I think so. I think there was a man sitting by himself, over at the far side. It seems to me he had his hat on.' That's all I could have said; that's all I would have remembered. Peter said he had been sitting there for hours, waiting for me. He said he saw us come in, but he didn't say anything because he didn't want to intrude."

One Sunday evening, when the Alvin Theater was dark, an impromptu cocktail party got under way at Ingrid's instigation. The elegant Fleming apartment sparkled with warmth and spirited chatter. Seated on the sofa, novelists John Steinbeck and Erich Maria Remarque engaged in a discussion of European politics. Listening absorbedly was balding, moonfaced, reticent but perceptive Richard Day.

Steinbeck, strictly a son of California's rugged Salinas County, was large and solid, tweed-attired, sunbrowned, with wiry brown hair and a thick brush moustache. Utterly without pose, he contrasted sharply with German-born Remarque's continental *savoir faire* and clipped Teutonic accent. Remarque also sported a moustache, trim and slick, and his barrel chest was contained in a finely tailored double-breasted herringbone suit.

Towards nine o'clock, Charles Boyer arrived.

"Alloo, Ingrid, alloo!" he said breezily, as he kissed her on both cheeks.

"You are late, Charles," she said. "I was afraid you weren't coming."

Boyer, rhapsody of gestures, charm and accent, waved a greeting to the assemblage, "I beg you to forgive me, I am so sorry, I was with friends at the Stork Club. It was so difficult to get away . . ."

"Everything's okay now," said Fleming. "Pour yourself a drink—what'll you have?"

"Scotch, please. With a little soda. I think maybe it is better I don't change."

"Joe!" commanded Fleming.

"Coming up!" When I returned from the kitchen-bar with Boyer's highball, Fleming was kidding him.

"Now don't give us that about being with friends. You're in New York without your wife . . ."

"Ah, no," said Boyer, "it is the truth." Then suddenly he plunged his hand into a coat pocket. "See! They gave me a souvenir!"

He pulled out a pair of dice etched with the restaurant's stork trademark. Taking them from his hand, I jokingly said, "Shoot you a dime, Charles."

Instantly, to my surprise, "You're faded," he responded, dropping a ten-cent piece on the carpet. He won the throw, rattled the cubes like an old-timer, and said, "Shoot all of it," meaning the twenty cents. He won the next roll and again doubled his bet.

"A dollar says you're wrong," interjected Fleming, as he, too, got down on his knees.

"You're covered," said Boyer, employing correct craps terminology.

In short order the silver disappeared and nothing but paper money bedecked the soft beige carpet. Ruth Roberts pulled up a chair and became an audience of one. Ingrid, attracted by exclamations of, "Come on, baby! Once more for papa! Ummmmah!" slid down beside Fleming.

"How do you play this game?" she wanted to know.

"Well, first, you need money," I said.

"But I would like to learn, and I have no money."

"Here, Angel," said Fleming as he handed her several bills. "Now you bet five dollars and I'll show you how to play."

Mild-mannered Richard Day deserted the two authors and joined us. "Is this a closed contest or can anyone get into it?" he said.

"We're not proud," Fleming said. "Charles' point is nine. Ten says he's coming out."

All bets were covered and presently sixty, eighty and one hundred dollars were changing hands. Each of us took turns explaining the rudiments of the game to Ingrid, who conservatively wagered one or two dollars. She never quite mastered the art of shaking the dice but her luck was beginner's, and she won steadily.

In a couple of hours Boyer lost the last of his cash, Fleming was out four or five hundred (he couldn't say exactly), Day was ahead about two hundred, and Ingrid counted a profit of sixty-two dollars. Which summing up would indicate that I fared well.

Boyer's withdrawal, due to his insolvency, put an end to the session. At the far end of the room, totally oblivious of the noisy gamblers, were Steinbeck and Remarque deeply immersed in some weighty discussion, just as they were in the beginning.

Around this time, in early February, Irene Selznick's maiden effort at play-producing aborted in tryouts at New Haven, Connecticut, and she abandoned the venture. Phyllis Laughton returned to California but Ruth Roberts was immediately put on Fleming's staff as research director for the *Joan of Arc* film.

Ingrid received a citation for excellence in diction from the National Teachers Association. "Ruth deserves all the credit for this," she said. "I'm going shopping this afternoon. I want to go alone."

She prowled the antique shops on Third Avenue and found something that suited her. Two days later she presented Ruth Roberts with a five-inch bisque figurine of a child whose hands were capped over both ears. Engraved on a brass plate on its wooden base was, "The Ingrid Bergman Award to Ruth Roberts—The Best Diction Teacher of 1946."

On February 17th a special performance of *Joan of Lorraine* was given for the Actors Relief Fund. In the audience were

Broadway stars Helen Hayes, Frederic March, Ina Claire, Jane Cowl, Ruth Gordon, Frank Fay, and many others.

"Ingrid, tonight was your greatest performance. Better than opening night—better than any you have given," said Maxwell Anderson, after the show.

"Thank you, Max. I had to, knowing all those wonderful actors were out there."

Chancing into my room one day, Victor Fleming spotted on the dresser a beautiful photographic study of Ingrid taken by Yousuf Karsh, the famous Canadian portraitist. Like a shot he grabbed it, "Marvelous! Just marvelous! I've got to have it—it's mine!"

"No you don't, Victor. That's the only one in existence. Karsh made it up especially for me."

"You can't have it, Joe. It belongs to me now." And with that he dashed out of the room. The portrait reposed on the mantelpiece of his living room, where Maxwell Anderson saw it and promptly declared he would also possess one. Bemoaning my own loss I got off a letter to Karsh, in which I blamed his genius and excellence for my troubles. I received the following letter in reply:

> Dear Mr. Steele: Both Mr. Karsh and I, as well as our staff, have been chuckling over your letter of February 22nd. We must admit that, for high-handed methods, we've never met its like before, but after your letter, what can we do?—except forgive you!!!
>
> Now, Mr. Karsh will finish two more and remember this time—but definitely—one is for you and the other is for Maxwell Anderson. Once more, these two will come with Mr. Karsh's compliments but let me warn you that any subsequent prints which are required because of highjacking will have to be paid for at the usual rate of $25.00 per print. I hope this will properly stagger you so that you will see the prints reach their rightful owners.
>
> Of course, there is nothing like blaming Mr. Karsh because he made particularly fine portraits of Miss Bergman, and Mr. Karsh thanks you for all the compliments. Everyone who has

seen the portrait seems to be of the same opinion that it is by far the finest portrait ever made of Miss Bergman's extraordinary personality.

Both Yousuf Karsh and I remember our meeting in Hollywood with a great deal of pleasure and send our best regards and warmest greetings.

Most sincerely yours,
(Madame) Solange Karsh
Business Manager

Throughout the seven-month run of the play, Ingrid saw much of Kay Brown, lunching at the Barberry Room or going to her home on East 86th Street.

"Ingrid is changing," Miss Brown once said to me. "Changing fast. She's growing away from everything she used to be. And she knows it. She said so herself."

In the spring of 1946, Ingrid had recorded an album for Decca Records of the Pied Piper of Hamelin, indulging her penchant for sound effects against the background music of conductor-composer Victor Young. She now proudly showed me a royalty check for $2,114.00.

"I am sending it to Peter," she said, "to open a special account for Pia. All the royalties will go into this account, and also on any other records I might make."

An outstanding radio show at that time was the United States Steel Hour produced by the Theater Guild, whose format consisted of adaptations of stage plays. Lawrence Langner, head of the Guild, put in a bid for Ingrid to headline one of the shows. Ingrid liked the idea, took it up with her husband, and it was decided that she would do one, providing the dramatic material appealed to her. For two brief rehearsals and the broadcast she would be paid five thousand dollars, which was the top radio fee of the period.

After several abortive story submissions, Langner became anxious that Ingrid might lose interest. An urgent meeting was held in Langner's office, with his wife, Theresa Helburn, and writer Eric Barnouw. Near the conclusion of the fruitless conference I recalled how much Ingrid had admired and enjoyed a

British motion picture called *Brief Encounter*, which was based upon Noel Coward's play, *Still Life*. I suggested that this might be the answer to the problem. When I proposed it to Ingrid she was delighted, and the radio production was put into motion. The broadcast was set for Easter Sunday, April 6th.

Sam Wanamaker, Romney Brent, and Broadway star, Peggy Wood, were cast in the other roles and the first rehearsal was held at the Vanderbilt Theater.

"Miss Bergman, the demand for seats is without precedent since these shows were inaugurated," said Langner, at the end of rehearsal. "We've decided to admit five hundred to the dress rehearsal on Sunday. All of us feel you're going to attract the biggest listening audience for a dramatic show in radio history."

Easter Sunday promised to be her busiest day yet: 1:00 to 3:00 P.M., preliminary rehearsal; 4:00 to 5:00 P.M., dress rehearsal; 6:00 P.M., going over her speech at her apartment for a Swedish Benefit at Carnegie Hall; 7:00 P.M., dinner; 8:30 P.M., Carnegie Hall; 10:00 P.M., the Theater Guild presentation over the air; and finally, the Antoinette Perry "Tony" Awards, Broadway's equivalent of the Academy Oscar, where performers were to be honored for "the finest performances of the year on Broadway."

Now, as we left the Vanderbilt Theater, Lawrence Langner's words fresh in her mind, Manhattan Island seemed uncommonly lustrous and tingling. We headed for Schrafft's on Fifth Avenue where she wanted to buy Easter eggs for the *Joan of Lorraine* cast and stagehands, the Alvin Theater employees, from the doorman out front to the doorman at the stage entrance, and for all those connected with the forthcoming broadcast of *Still Life*.

I could feel Ingrid's taut excitement.

"Oh, Joe," she sighed. "I often wonder how long this can keep up."

Came Sunday and Ingrid distributed the ninety-two Easter eggs she had bought. To the radio performance of *Still Life*, she wore an unflattering old black dress which she had had shortened according to the current fashion.

"Why are you wearing that old bag?"

"Because it's in keeping with the character," she said. "All my new things are too gay."

"But you're on the air; nobody's going to see you."

"Yes, yes, I know that," she said impatiently. "But *I* will know what I have on."

After the broadcast, en route to our hotel, she said, "I'm too tired to go to the Antoinette Perry—it's after eleven. You go and tell Kay Brown to accept the Award for me. They'll surely understand what a day I've had. I feel dead."

"You know very well that you're so hopped up now that you can't sleep. You'll get in your room and go through the same routine. Put on that red satin suit and pick up your own 'Tony.' "

"You are so right," she smiled wanly. And in twenty minutes she sat glowingly at Kay Brown's table in the Grand Ballroom of the Waldorf-Astoria, revivified and brand new. I was constantly rediscovering her.

In her mailbox at the Hampshire House was a letter from her husband. Folding it so as to conceal the main body, she showed me his signature, "The boy that made sure you had flowers at Oscar's Theater—he is still longing for you. (signed) P—." The occasion he referred to was her first professional stage appearance in Stockholm.

"Petter is so lonesome," she said, unconsciously pronouncing his name Swedish style.

In the same batch of mail was an invitation:

"The President and the Directors of the Drama League of New York request the pleasure of your company at a Spring Luncheon in celebration of the 37th anniversary of the Drama League of America, at one o'clock on Friday, May the Second, in the ballroom of the Hotel Pierre, Fifth Avenue and 61st Street."

Briefed that she was to be awarded with the League's Gold Medal for the most distinguished performance of the year, Ingrid prepared an acceptance speech with great pain. Helen Hayes, however, made the presentation and completely upset Ingrid's plan.

Said Miss Hayes: "... we of the theater are proud of Ingrid

Bergman . . . she has added to its dignity and lived up to its highest standards . . . not only of talent and beauty but also of graciousness . . . She is going back to Hollywood but we consider that we are lending her to Hollywood and that she will come back to us . . ."

Then Miss Hayes turned and faced Ingrid. "We thank you, Miss Bergman, for bringing the theater back to Broadway."

Ingrid's memorized speech dissolved in a flood of emotion. Her lips quivered, her eyes welled; finally she managed to stammer, "Thank you, Miss Hayes . . . thank you. . . . I don't know what to say . . . I can't think of anything . . . I just want to kiss you . . ."

Unashamed tears streamed down their cheeks as they hugged each other. And they were not alone.

Later, when Miss Hayes, Miss LeGallienne, Mrs. Samuel Newton (President of the Drama League), and Ingrid were in the rear vestibule posing for photographs, Miss Hayes said, "I cannot say enough, Miss Bergman. Your performance in *Joan of Lorraine* is a historical event in the history of the theater."

In accordance with the original contract the play was to end its run, with Ingrid, that is, on May 6th, which fell on a Tuesday. The Playwrights Company prevailed on Dr. Lindstrom and Ingrid to let her finish out the week with two final performances on Saturday, the 10th. Ingrid, now exceedingly fatigued, agreed, with the proviso that the entire cast be paid a bonus.

Lindstrom planed in on Saturday, the 3rd, with the announcement that he would remain until the play closed and fly back with Ingrid. Monday morning, Ingrid broke out with a bad cold, which progressively got worse until the Wednesday matinee had to be canceled. Nevertheless, she insisted on doing the night show, even though her throat was paining, nose running, and she felt weak and dispirited.

Dudley Digges, one of Broadway's outstanding stars, came backstage after the show to pay his respects. When told that she was too ill to see anyone, he said, "Tell her for me, that she was magnificent whether she was sick or not. And give her my best wishes. She's wonderful."

Ingrid was distressed about the people being turned away from the theater: "... and how about those poor people who bought tickets from scalpers. They'll only get back the regular seat price."

Thursday morning another doctor was called in and his diagnosis was grippe. The evening performance was canceled. Tokens of sympathy, telegrams, messages, candy, gifts, flowers poured to the hotel and the theater.

By Friday evening, Ingrid was well enough to carry on. The Saturday matinee witnessed a mass of fans jamming 52nd Street in front of the Alvin.

"So many of those people out there couldn't get tickets and many of them couldn't afford it," she said. "What do you think about letting them all in after the matinee, when the theater is emptied? The least I can do is to talk to them."

Victor Samrock said such a procedure was unheard of. He questioned its merit; they might become unruly, and besides, it was against police and fire regulations. Despite the doubts, when the last patron had left the theater I addressed the waiting fans, told them of Ingrid's plan, and put them on their honor to behave orderly and leave the theater promptly after her talk finished. The gesture came off without a hitch as Ingrid, still in costume, alternated her talk between thanking them for their loyalty and scolding them for the occasions when they overstepped their enthusiasm in the streets and public places.

After the final performance on the evening of Saturday, May 10th, languid and drooping from her illness and the rigors of the past eight months, she picked up her father's picture from the make-up table and kissed it. She then kissed me and kissed her husband.

"I'm glad its all over," she said, as she clung to her husband. "It's been wonderful, but I'm glad I'm going home."

The afternoon of the next day we got aboard an American Airlines plane and nosed westward. I sat directly behind Ingrid and Dr. Lindstrom. As the big ship became airborne and gained altitude, Lindstrom opened a *Time* magazine. Ingrid sat erect, looking ahead. Manhattan's cubist mountains receded beneath a silvery haze.

My thoughts were preoccupied with the man and wife before me. What had happened on that occasion when he flew in unexpectedly? What had they talked about after Ingrid came down from Victor Fleming's apartment? What now, this moment, was going on in their minds?

As I gazed at the back of Ingrid's lovely head she presently readjusted her body, rested her head on her husband's shoulder, and closed her eyes.

7.

Joan of Arc

THE triumphant conclusion of *Joan of Lorraine* was somewhat vitiated by the absence of triumph in the case of *Arch.* The lugubrious Remarque narrative, which cost four million dollars to put on film, achieved the sad status of being the biggest fiasco to date in Hollywood annals. Sadder still, its failure spelled the doom of budding Enterprise Pictures.

Nothwithstanding, whatever letdown Ingrid felt about *Arch of Triumph* was more than offset by her obsessive passion to get at the screen version of *Joan of Arc*. Immediately evident, too, was the radical change in her frame of mind. Gone was the latent rebellion against subconscious restrictions which had characterized the past year, and in its place appeared a curious kind of welcome surrender to subtler and stronger forces than hers.

Overnight, it seemed, she had once again become the bride, noticeably attentive to her husband, deferring to his wishes, indicating by little looks and little gestures her complete submission. It was a startling emotional about-face to witness, as though I were watching her play a new "role." I couldn't shake the notion that it was no less than a role, studiously enacted, written out of the recent yesterdays. And the dominating Lindstrom rejoiced in the revivified relationship, innocently trapped in a conflict over which neither he nor Ingrid had any control.

Not until two years later, in Rome, Italy, did I get an inkling of what had transpired in the domestic scene those last few days in New York.

"I felt guilty for not being satisfied with all I had," Ingrid told me. "Again and again I repeated to myself how fortunate I was—a faithful husband who loved me and did everything he could for me, a good child, a beautiful home. I had health and money and success in my work, but still I was in a constant struggle inside, looking for something I couldn't put my fingers on.

"Peter understood my restlessness, maybe better than I did. We had long talks about our lives, and I felt a great relief in leaning on him and letting him make the decisions. We decided to rebuild the house and make room for another member. I wanted to have another child, feeling that in that way my life would be filled and fulfilled. I thought that maybe in this was the true answer to all my restlessness.

"When I speak of restlessness, Joe, I don't mean only about my home life; I mean about my whole life, going back to my childhood and to my growing-up days. There were many, many times when I thought I would just burst if I didn't let go. But I didn't know how to let go, or I didn't have the courage. So, for a while it was easy to leave behind all the excitement of Broadway and go home again."

Victor Fleming and Walter Wanger established headquarters at the Hal Roach Studio in Culver City, a stone's throw from Ingrid's former home at Selznick. A corps of technicians went to work on the elaborate settings and hundreds of costumes. Decorators transformed an aged bungalow of four rooms into a modern cottage to serve as her dressing room. Day by day, costs mounted, with the hope that they could be retrieved through the magnetism of Ingrid Bergman. Her chief support—in the role of the vacillating Dauphin—was an actor named Jose Ferrer, whose portrayal of *Cyrano* on Broadway had brought him to the attention of critics.

Maxwell Anderson, collaborating with Andrew Solt, a Hollywood writer, worked with Fleming on the main structure of the story. Laurence Stallings, who co-authored the World War I drama, *What Price, Glory?* with Anderson, devoted himself exclusively to delineating the battle scenes. Producer Walter Wanger was chiefly preoccupied with the coordination of the film's complex practical aspects.

Dr. Lindstrom quit the County General Hospital and moved as an associate into the office of Dr. Tracy Putnam, noted Beverly Hills surgeon. Freed of the forty-minute journey to the hospital and its long, uncertain hours, he was enabled to oversee Ingrid's business affairs with greater facility. As the returns on *Arch* diminished with each quarterly statement, Lindstrom, mindful of Ingrid's 25 per cent partnership, requested an audit of Enterprise's books.

Said Charles Einfeld, "In due course, the doctor questioned several disbursements, including the salary we paid you. We explained that you had performed invaluable service on the picture, working closely with the publicity department and also as an assistant to David Lewis. But nothing we said seemed to allay his suspicion that we had made a deal with you. Why he should take that attitude I can't figure out. The picture cost too much, we know that, but we wanted to make a great picture, the best Ingrid ever made."

No doubt motivated by the fact that *Joan of Arc* was especially dear to Ingrid's heart, Lindstrom, in a protective zeal, began to manifest a broader interest in her professional attachments and activities. He frequented the studio and sat in on production, publicity and advertising conferences. He asked that the themes of magazine interviews be submitted beforehand, and wished to see press releases prior to their distribution.

Throughout the summer the housewife of Hillhaven Lodge played with Pia, swam in the pool, and occasionally went dancing with her husband. Several times a week she went to the studio to chat with Fleming and the writers about the script in progress, discuss costumes with designers Madame Karinska and Dorothy Jeakins, compare historical notes with researchers Ruth Roberts and Michel Bernheim and with Monsignor Paul Donceur, the little silver-haired Jesuit from Joan of Arc's village, Domremy, France, who acted as canonical consultant.

Meanwhile Lindstrom's expanded activity in her behalf unwittingly defeated his good intentions. By summer's end her new resolutions wavered.

"Peter tried so hard to watch everything," she said to me in

Rome. "He had no trust in anyone, although I must admit it is a hard thing to find in a place like Hollywood. Everything he did was for my best, but sometimes I got tired and angry at the endless business talks and turning our home into an office. When sometimes I ventured an opinion, it was usually wrong because I didn't understand the legal points. It made me feel small and embarrassed, so I decided to stick to my work while Peter took care of the rest. This submission on my part was not at all painful, for once I had decided to follow this course, I gave very little thought to it. Peter always thought he was in the right, but, for me, an easier-going character and weaker, the situation became more and more difficult as time went on."

Presently, the studio cottage, completely refurnished and redecorated at a cost of five thousand dollars, was ready, and Ingrid revelled in it. Here were volumes about Joan of Arc, or the latest books of fiction and biography, and quiet to read them in. Here she was free to invite whomever she pleased and entertain them from the well-stocked kitchenette. This she transformed into her own domain, her private, unique domain.

Film executives continued to try to get in touch with Ingrid through me. Johnny Meyer called several times to ask if a meeting could be arranged for Howard Hughes to talk over a picture deal with Ingrid. When I broached it to her, she said there was no point in seeing him; if he had a script to submit, he could send it to her. Then Hughes himself telephoned.

"Why won't she talk to me?" he said. "I only want to see her for a few minutes. I'll meet her anywhere, go to the studio, if she wants."

It struck me as childish and stupid for Ingrid to evade this important figure. I put it up to her, "Suppose he happened to come here to the studio. Suppose you ran into him on the lot. Would you refuse to say hello, or stop to speak a word?"

"All right," she said, "ask him to come tomorrow at six o'clock. You meet him and bring him to the bungalow."

Hughes was delighted, but as the zero hour approached Ingrid lost her nerve and informed her husband. At four o'clock she sent for me.

"You have to call off Howard Hughes," she said nervously. "I can't see him. I won't be here . . ."

"Shall I change it to another time?"

"No—no—just forget it."

"Why, what's happened?"

"Nothing—nothing!" she said irritably. "Peter says I can't see him."

After several weeks, Maxwell Anderson, at odds with Fleming's views about the screenplay, decided to return to New York. When ultimately the script was completed I expressed my disappointment to Ingrid.

"Oh, I don't know," she said resignedly. "I leave it all up to Victor."

Seeking general reactions, Fleming asked what I thought.

"Frankly, I am disappointed," I said. "It doesn't say any of the things it should say. After people have seen the picture they'll conclude that Joan was beatified only because she won a battle. It is pageantry and spectacle, but it has no heart, no comprehension of the low plight of the French masses whom Joan inspired back to self-respect and national unity."

"There you go!" he glowered. "You talk like a damn liberal. The picture's got to have a message, preach a sermon. We're making movies, son, entertainment!"

Mentally, I recalled a recent heated discussion in Ingrid's cottage, when Fleming declared, "I have no use for a poor man, because he hasn't got the guts or intelligence to make something of himself." That had abruptly terminated the discussion, after which he laughed uproariously, shook his finely chiseled head, put his arm around Ingrid, and said, "I need another drink, Angel."

On Halloween Day, Ingrid tapped members of the staff to come for cocktails at five. Once they had gathered in the cottage living room there issued from the adjoining make-up room the apparition of an evil-eyed witch, black-robed, hook-nosed, green-skinned, and snaggle-toothed. A mattress of flying black hair behind her, she leaped into their midst with a shriek.

"Aaoow! You are all under my spell!"

This was the first witch with a slight Swedish accent most of them had ever seen. After cavorting for a few minutes and posing for pictures, she asked me to drive her to Alfred Hitchcock's, where the director was bedridden with a cold.

"But you mustn't let him see you, or he'll know who I am," she said.

"Then wait a little while until I go home and get an old wig I used to wear to masquerade parties."

We presented a rather startling sight as we drove toward swank Bel-Air. At the busy intersection of Wilshire and Westwood Boulevards, several distracted motorists nearly tangled fenders. The traffic cop stepped over and took a look.

"Get going, you kids, before you cause an accident," he said. Ingrid bared her fangs and leered at him.

When we arrived, Mrs. Hitchcock answered the door and instinctively drew back. Quickly, before she could raise an alarm, Ingrid said, "Ssh, I want to surprise Hitch."

"Gracious, you did give me a fright," said Mrs. Hitchcock, leading us to the bedroom.

Hitchcock's eyes were closed in a half-sleep. Ingrid peered down and proceeded to emit eerie noises. The man whose business was frightening others slowly opened his eyes and calmly regarded the witch.

"Where did you find that getup, Ingrid?" he said quietly.

"Oh, you," she said, "you're no fun at all. Couldn't you be scared for just a little bit?"

After the turn of the year, early in January, 1948, *Joan of Arc* went before the cameras. During its nearly four months of shooting, Ingrid made the most of her cozy cottage. Virtually every evening Fleming's last command to "Cut!" was the signal for a soiree. Once again she lingered until the last possible minute before calling it quits and going home.

Several years later, when I saw Ingrid at her seaside villa in Italy, she spoke wistfully of these days, and revealed much about her state of mind at the time. "*Joan of Arc* was a very happy picture for me," she said. "I was especially fond of the little studio bungalow, which I used the way I would have liked to have used my own home. You remember, nearly every day, after we finished work, I would invite the people working on the picture, and we'd celebrate somebody's birthday or just have a party.

"Any excuse was good enough, because they were the people I liked; because there was laughter and stories and interesting arguments; because there were none of the inhibitions I felt at home. That little studio was full of friendship. We worked together, and when the work was over, we laughed together. I was very hungry for laughter in those days."

Ingrid appeared in practically every scene of the picture. Only an actress with her stamina could have withstood the long sultry days of riding broad-backed workhorses garbed in armor and heavy mail. But she gloried in the consummation of her childhood dream. She invited friends to come and watch the spectacle being filmed. Several times she brought Pia, held her on her lap, explained the action that was being shot, and had the still photographer take pictures for her private use.

On April 10th, the climactic scene of burning Joan at the stake was put on film and the prodigal production came to an end. More than any other picture, Ingrid experienced sadness at the production's conclusion. Her eyes welling with emotion, she embraced everyone, thanked them for their part in its making, and hoped they would work together again. A few days later the cottage was emptied of Ingrid's belongings and she retired behind the high steel fence of Hillhaven Lodge.

Once again, as happened after every picture, Ingrid faced the plaguing period of settling down to routine, the between-pictures round of prosaic existence. She resumed her French lessons with purposeful fervor, as though she anticipated their eventual importance in her life. Impulsively, she telephoned friends, hopped in her green two-year-old Ford coupe and went a-calling—to the Hitchcocks, or Ruth Roberts, or the Jean Renoirs, or to the Bernheim family, now transferred to Hollywood. When there was sufficient excuse, such as seeing the assembled segments of the picture, she dashed to the Hal Roach Studio to sit for hours in contentment in the projection room.

Almost immediately after the completion of *Joan of Arc* I sensed a nascent coolness in Dr. Lindstrom, until toward the end of the month he informed me that: (a) Ingrid was going to New York for a couple of weeks and it was not essential that she be shepherded; (b) she would be going to London in June to make *Under Capricorn* for Alfred Hitchcock, and that Hitchcock felt my presence there was unnecessary; (c) since under these conditions my duties were considerably curtailed, a readjustment in our business arrangement was in order.

Stunned by the peremptory decision, even though I could feel it coming on, I had no choice but to accept the "readjustment." As for Ingrid, she never brought up the subject–apparently under some kind of duress.

Soon after her return from New York, a business transaction took place in Hollywood, which was not only of special significance for the motion-picture industry, but, as time proved, was to be very meaningful for Ingrid Bergman. On May 11, 1948, Howard Hughes purchased the controlling interest in RKO Studios, one of the six major companies.

Shortly before her departure to London to make *Under Capricorn*, Ingrid called and suggested we have lunch at the Beachcomber's.

Sitting in an isolated booth, the artificial rain pouring, both of us nibbling on Cantonese spareribs, I said, "Are you excited about doing *Capricorn?*"

"Well, I can't say I'm crazy about the story," she said, "but the part is a good change of pace for me, it's a dipsomaniac. And you know how I like to work with Hitch, those wonderful little touches he puts in. But I guess I'm more excited about working in London than anything else. It'll be wonderful, Joe, to get away from here for a while. I'm sorry you're not coming with me."

In the course of our chat she told of a movie she had seen the day before. The leading man had had star ranking for many years, yet he somehow missed that electrical eminence symbolized by the Clark Gables, Gary Coopers and Cary Grants. "He's too nicey-nice," I said. "I can't stand him."

"That's right," said Ingrid. "That's exactly what's the matter with him. He has no secret vices."

"A very cogent observation. Did you make that up all by yourself?"

"Oh, no," she laughed. "Somebody said that once, and I thought it was pretty good. People like that are like a canvas that an artist has painted white, with no other colors."

Several weeks after her return from London, on October 20th, *Joan of Arc* was press previewed at the Beverly Theater in Beverly Hills. Ingrid sat between her husband and Victor Fleming, and her heart sank, and many other hearts sank as the audience gazed at the epic in stolid silence. The perfunctory applause at the picture's conclusion only emphasized its impotence. The reviews that followed echoed the same dirge.

Five million dollars and untold sweat and love had gone into *Joan of Arc*, all because artists and craftsmen and financial institutions believed in Bergman's drawing power. Deemed an ideal holiday attraction, it was released to theaters before Christmas, but its reception was not hearty enough to encourage its investors. The production would have to gross eight million dollars to recoup its cost. The outlook was dubious.

For the burning-at-the-stake scene, Ingrid had worn a drab monk's robe of coarse sackcloth, secured at the waist by a thick cord. During the week of shooting the scene several of the garments were actually burned in the process. For this reason a dozen emergency robes—each an exact duplicate—had been fabricated and were now of no further value.

With the imminence of Christmas, Ingrid conceived the idea of making gifts of these grave-digger habiliments to studio secretaries and other women employees. Where she got this ill-advised notion is beyond me. I first heard of it from a secretary over the telephone.

"For the love of God," she said, "does Miss Bergman expect *me* to go to the fire?"

"What are you talking about?"

"These robes—these burning robes she's handing out as Christmas presents. Gad, what ghastly taste! I couldn't get to the garbage can fast enough."

The reaction was typical and Ingrid heard of it. "My goodness, I don't understand," she said. "I thought it would be a nice souvenir of the picture, and they can be used as bathrobes."

On January 6, 1949, eleven weeks after the press preview of *Joan of Arc,* Victor Fleming succumbed to a heart attack. Soon thereafter, Joe Valentine, the cinematographer, followed him into death, to be shortly followed by Casey Roberts, the set decorator who had furnished Ingrid's studio cottage and built the massive Gothic props of the picture. *Joan of Arc* was a killer film.

While driving home on that January 6th I caught a glimpse of the Fleming headlines on the newsstands. I called Ingrid. Inconsolable and heartsick, she wept bitterly, "Victor's gone, Joe, he's gone—it's terrible—how could it happen? Dear, dear Victor..."

Three or four days passed and Dr. Lindstrom wanted to see me. Ingrid, he felt, had reached the point where she no longer needed public-relations guidance. Also, such matters as might require tending could be handled by John Vernon, a male secretary whom he had just employed to replace Doris Collup. He was "very sorry" to have to impart such news, but he was "grateful" for all past favors and wished me "luck" for the future.

"Does Ingrid know about this?"

"Yes, of course she knows," he said.

Taking twenty-four hours to reorient myself, I couldn't get Ingrid out of my mind. Her silence troubled me, and my inevitable conclusion was that she had been *told* the decision, not *consulted.* The inequity of meekly retiring from our extraordinary association was too burdensome. I called the doctor and requested an audience. "But I insist that Ingrid be present," I said.

"Yes, sure, that will be all right," he said. "Ingrid will be here. You want to come at three o'clock?"

When I entered the steel gate I found them seated on the lawn beside the swimming pool, he in bathing trunks, she in white shorts and halter. "Here," he called out, "we can talk here."

The summer playground setting induced a psychological block. It was awkward to get started. I sat on the grass facing them. Ingrid had not even said hello. She had looked up with the merest suggestion of a nod; her face an expressionless mask. I finally launched into an account of various behind-the-scenes clashes with the doctor.

"These are things Ingrid doesn't know about," I said. "I think it's only fair to her and to me that she does know. That's why I wanted her present when we talked."

Ingrid sat mutely, averting her eyes from mine. Lindstrom, cool, clinical and self-contained, merely nodded; a few times he denied my allegations. We spoke calmly, without rancor. The incongruity of our appearance continually intruded into my consciousness. The serious purpose of the session was embarrassed by the physical informality. Humiliation infused my being. It was poor judgment indeed to have asked for this meeting.

"You have insinuated, Peter," I said, "that I have done things for Enterprise against Ingrid's best interests, because I was on their payroll. You don't know the hundreds of times I told them that they couldn't do this or that. I protected her with such zeal that it was a common crack that Ingrid was surrounded by 'a Steele curtain.' "

Lindstrom started to reply, but Ingrid instantly—for the first and only time—spoke up. "What Joe says is true," she said, still betraying no emotion. She said no more. I quickly rose, said, "I thank you for listening," and bade them good-bye.

Of pertinence to this period of Ingrid's life, I should like to quote Laurence Stallings, who, when the Bergman-Rossellini scandal hit the headlines, said in a reminiscent mood, "I last saw Ingrid at Victor Fleming's funeral. I stood with the other pallbearers, the veteran stars like Clark Gable and Spencer Tracy, the old-line directors like King Vidor and Clarence Brown. Walking down the aisle of the church after the pall, grieving because no more would I see the great Fleming's lithe figure (his fierce eyes beneath the high forehead and the crest of silver hair) standing behind a camera to control the destiny of a movie set, I looked into Ingrid Bergman's eyes and thought of Fleming's judgment of her,

" 'Brother, she is bullet-proof. There never has been another figure like her before a camera; you can shoot her any angle, any position. It doesn't make any difference; you don't have to protect her. You can bother about the other actors on the set. But Ingrid's like a Notre Dame quarterback. An onlooker can't take his eyes off her!' "

Stallings paused a moment as recollection reached back into memory. Then he said, "I recall a day I spent with Ingrid and her family at Sam Wood's beach place at Malibu. I was writing a script with Sam, another great, lion-hearted director, and Ingrid would often come down for swimming and sunbathing. Like Victor Fleming, Sam Wood regarded her as bullet-proof.

"One day at the beach, she started swimming straight out into the Catalina channel. The surf is not too safe off Malibu, and she was swimming farther than ordinary caution would dictate. I asked Sam Wood if he did not think we should signal the lifeguard station.

" 'Ingrid wouldn't like it,' Sam said. Then he looked out over the Pacific, where we could barely see her brown arms flailing the rip.

" 'Some day,' Sam Wood said, 'Ingrid's going to start swimming straight out. She's going to start swimming, and never come back.' "

8.

Sicily

SPRING came, with no word from Ingrid. Not a sound since that sunny day beside the pool on Benedict Canyon Drive. I missed it, but I understood it; she dared not risk the commandant's dictum. Along with others, I, too, had become out-of-bounds. I put publicity behind me and embarked on an independent production venture.

Unable, however, to completely sever my sentimental attachment, I kept track of her every movement. Toward the end of March she flew to Italy to make a picture. A few days later, reports were rampant linking her with the Italian director.

In the spring of 1948, following the completion of *Joan of Arc*, when Ingrid went alone to New York for a two-week vacation, she had attended an afternoon showing of the most-discussed movie in town. It was called *Paisan* and was directed by the same Rossellini who had made *Open City*.

She had gazed enthralled at the six unrelated episodes that took place in the Allied advance up the Italian boot. Rossellini had evoked with terrific impact the feel of war and its effect on liberators and liberated. Like *Open City*, the film was a stark documentary, denuded of artifice. Implicit with the promise of new horizons, the two pictures were a stunning revelation to Ingrid. Her unresolved yearnings struggled for expression. She was a Galatea in search of a Pygmalion.

She returned to Hampshire House, where she stayed, and telephoned Irene Selznick, who was now the successful producer of Tennessee Williams' *A Streetcar Named Desire*, a drama of elemental passions played out in the seamiest section of New Orleans.

"I've got to see you, Irene," she said urgently. "I simply must talk with you."

They had dinner together in Mrs. Selznick's Hotel Pierre suite, and Ingrid talked of nothing but *Paisan* and *Open City* and the artist who had created them. Whenever the topic wandered off on another tangent, Ingrid obsessively brought it back on course again.

"How exciting it would be to make a picture with a director like that!" she said. "How can I do it, Irene? How could I let him know?"

"Why not just write him and tell him so?"

"I thought about that, but he's probably never even heard of me. He might get the wrong idea."

Irene Selznick smiled wisely. "You are probably the only actress in the world," she said, "who could write him without being misunderstood." Ingrid relaxed in gratitude and couldn't wait until she saw her husband.

A few evenings later, she poured her heart out to Dr. Lindstrom, who was very sympathetic.

"Why not?" he said. "I don't see anything wrong with writing a letter." So she took pen in hand and wrote:

Dear Mr. Rossellini–

I saw your films, *Open City* and *Paisan*, and enjoyed them very much. If you need a Swedish actress who speaks English very well, who has not forgotten her German, who is not very understandable in French, and who in Italian knows only 'ti amo,' I am ready to come and make a film with you.

Best regards,
Ingrid Bergman

This naïve but honest overture was inspired solely by the work of the man as she observed it on the screen. It was all that she knew of him.

What manner of man was this Rossellini? In his bailiwick of

Rome he was the object of all kinds of gossip, hearsay, and innuendo. His professional, personal, and motor-racing escapades were told and retold over many a glass of wine, and inevitably appeared in print. Where fact ended and fancy began is hard to say. But, as reconstructed by gathering the pieces here and there and splicing them together, the chronicle of this latter-day D'Annunzio went something like this:

Roberto Rossellini was born in Rome on May 8, 1905, the eldest of four children in a well-to-do family. His father, Giuseppe Rossellini, was a prominent architect.

As an adolescent, Rossellini first manifested the dual passions that were to dominate his life—automobiles and women. While still in his teens he designed and built a small car that, according to relatives, had on it many improvements over the best commercial models of the day.

Around the same time, young Rossellini became enamored of a pretty French girl named Titi Michelle, who was visiting Rome with her parents. When Titi returned to France, Rossellini followed, only to be severely rebuffed. Subsequent events, according to the record, would indicate that this was to be the first and the last of his amatory defeats.

In due time Rossellini succumbed to the charms of Liliana Castagnola, a singer from one of Rome's variety shows. He was said to have so lavished her with gifts that he soon ran through a legacy that had been left him.

Finding himself broke, the future film director turned briefly to automobile racing. He never finished in the money, but he somehow managed to leave the Rossellini imprint on that sport.

Rossellini's younger brother, Renzo—who later flourished as a composer of film scores, symphonies, and a ballet—functioned as his mechanic, riding with him. Renzo never forgot the day that Liliana sat in the stands as he and Rossellini flashed around the course.

Every time the car passed Liliana, Rossellini threw her a kiss with one hand, while he steered with the other. Toward the end of the race Rossellini abandoned the wheel altogether and started throwing kisses with both hands. After the last lap, when they came safely to a halt, Renzo, white and shaken, climbed out of the car and furiously pummeled his brother.

Nineteen hundred and thirty-one saw his father's passing and the dissolution of family ties. Some months later, Liliana Castagnola was found dead from an overdose of drugs; intentionally or accidentally, no one ever knew.

When motorcar racing and other odd jobs failed to pay off, Rossellini decided to give motion pictures a try. It was said that while working as a film cutter he became entangled with an exotic Russian girl named Asia Noris, who aspired to be an actress. This affair, however, endured only long enough for Asia to achieve her ambition; she got a leading part and married her director.

In 1935 Roberto Rossellini fell in love with Marcella de Marchis, a twenty-year-old university student, member of an old aristocratic family. On September of the following year, over the protests of her parents, he married Marcella in the seaport town of Civitavecchia, a stone's throw from Santa Marinella, where fourteen years later he and Ingrid Bergman were to have their summer villa.

Two sons, Romano and Renzo, appeared on the domestic scene, but after three years Rossellini began straining against the conjugal bond. The break came in the person of one Roswita Schmidt, a German nightclub dancer. Apparently, where women were concerned, Roberto Rossellini harbored no nationalistic prejudices. The Roswita liaison continued for the next several years, during which time Rossellini made rapid strides in the Italian movie field.

In 1942 Rossellini went to Hungary and filed a petition to have his marriage annulled, there being no divorce in Italy. It was said that in order to facilitate the action Mrs. Rossellini voluntarily testified that on their wedding day she "was not in her right mind," and, therefore, not responsible. This story was vehemently denied by Rossellini. In any case, the Italian courts refused to recognize the annulment.

The marital status remained *in quo;* he continued, as always, providing well for his family, and picked up his separate and private life where he had not left off.

As for his motion-picture activities, the end result of his efforts to date was strictly run-of-the-Italian-mill. It was not until after the Allies liberated Rome that his career took an upturn. It came in the person of a writer named Sergio Amidei, who expounded to Rossellini a story idea that could be filmed at low cost. The idea was based on Amidei's escape over Roman rooftops while SS troops cordoned the street, and the execution of a Catholic priest who had worked for the underground.

Sold on its dramatic possibilities, Rossellini proceeded to set up the production. He promoted a small sum of money, reportedly from an aging ballerina who had once been a friend of ex-King Farouk of Egypt. Then, hustling up a camera and a few lights, he went about casting the picture that was destined to bring him fame, fortune, and Ingrid Bergman.

In the summer of 1945 Rome's celluloid-set buzzed with the news that Roberto Rossellini had acquired a new leading lady—Anna Magnani, the firebrand Italian actress who had married his friend and fellow director, Geofreddo Alessandrini.

A short, pudgy woman, with moppy raven hair, Magnani was dynamite, given to profanity and violent outbursts. But whatever her outward appearance, none could match her sensitivity and power on the screen. Rossellini and Magnani made *Open City*, and *Open City* made history.

Photographed starkly—chiefly because of lack of equipment—*Open City* was conceived and directed with primitive veracity. Neorealism, American critics called it, and it crashed disconcertingly into Hollywood's wishful world of fantasy.

The tempestuous coupling of Rossellini and Magnani pursued its fitful course until Magnani got wind of Roswita Schmidt. "She goes or I go," was her ultimatum. And Roswita was gently exiled to the isle of Capri, where Roberto paid her bills for some time to come.

Following *Open City*, Rossellini embarked on a film titled, *The Machine That Kills Evildoers,* which he put into production in the hillside town of Maiori, a short distance from Amalfi, across the bay from Naples. Since working schedules never interfered with his unpredictable moods, he one day took off for Paris.

When he returned, close friends reported, it was in company

with Marilyn Buferd, Miss America of 1946. Though the film called for neither an American nor a pretty girl, Rossellini reshuffled the story to include his new "discovery." When Magnani in Rome heard about Buferd in Maiori the fireworks began. The picture was never released.

This, then, was the legend of Roberto Rossellini; a Renaissance figure, out of time and out of place.

Accustomed as he was to feminine conquest, Rossellini was staggered by the letter from the most sought-after actress on the globe. He proudly displayed it to everyone he knew. He could hardly be blamed; what director wouldn't?

But somehow the "ti amo" (I love you) in Ingrid's letter was wrenched from its context and became a source of leering gossip. I remembered "ti amo" as a fragment of dialogue she had spoken in *Arch of Triumph*, and her use of it in the simple, forthright note was meant lightly, an effort at gayety.

Rossellini received the unorthodox missive on May 8, 1948. With the help of friends he translated his Italian as best he could into English, and cabled a reply:

MRS. INGRID BERGMAN

I JUST RECEIVED WITH GREAT EMOTION YOUR LETTER WHICH HAPPENS TO ARRIVE ON THE ANNIVERSARY OF MY BIRTHDAY ON THE MOST PRECIOUS GIFT STOP IT IS ABSOLUTELY TRUE THAT I DREAMED TO MAKE A FILM WITH YOU AND FROM THIS VERY MOMENT I WILL DO EVERYTHING THAT SUCH DREAM BECOMES REALITY AS SOON AS POSSIBLE STOP I WILL WRITE YOU A LONG LETTER TO SUBMIT TO YOU MY IDEAS STOP WITH MY ADMIRATION PLEASE ACCEPT THE EXPRESSION OF MY GRATITUDE TOGETHER WITH MY BEST REGARDS

ROBERTO ROSSELLINI
HOTEL EXCELSIOR ROME

Subsequently, Ingrid showed me the "long letter" (four pages) he mentioned. The screen story it outlined was extremely sketchy and couched in makeshift English. Nevertheless, it blazed with dramatic promise.

She wrote Rossellini that his story sounded exciting; that she was leaving for London to make *Under Capricorn* for Alfred Hitchcock; and suggested that he prepare a script and send it to her in London.

Asking Rossellini to "prepare a script" was like commanding the Tower of Pisa to straighten up. Rossellini hardly knew what a script looked like. He always "wrote his stories with the camera," inventing scenes and dialogue from hour to hour. To side-step this potential pitfall, Rossellini asked that he meet Ingrid and be permitted to "tell" his story.

The site of the meeting was influenced by Ingrid's habits during the filming of *Under Capricorn* in London. It turned out that one of this production's chief attractions for her was London's aerial proximity to Paris, where Ingrid spent many weekends. The French metropolis exhilarated her as no other city save, possibly, New York. She knew no one in Paris, but she was content just to be there, to roam its avenues, gaze at the landmarks, browse through the Louvre, meander along the Seine. The conference with Rossellini was set, therefore, for a Sunday at the George V Hotel in Paris.

At this time Rossellini was in Amalfi in the midst of shooting *The Miracle*, which was to spark a censorship furor in America. His star was Anna Magnani. He abruptly quit the production and the lady, and bolted off to Paris.

Present at the story-"telling" conference were Dr. Lindstrom, Rudolph Solmsen (Rossellini's European representative), and Ilya Lopert, a distributor of foreign films in the United States, who was to arrange part of the financing. An agreement of sorts was arrived at, Ingrid returned to London to finish *Under Capricorn* and Lindstrom went back to Beverly Hills and his patients.

Ingrid's initial reaction to the man Rossellini, as she later tried to define it to me, was one she was hard put to express. She was nervous and awed and quivering with excitement, she said. He seemed so subjugated by the other men that she longed to throw her arms around him and assure him that she was on his side. She feared her husband would make too excessive demands, that the men of business would scuttle the union of artists. Her heart went out to the seemingly unarmored Rossellini in a joyous *simpatia*.

Rossellini returned to Rome, where Omar Garrison, writing in the Los Angeles *Evening Mirror*, quoted him as saying, "Swedish women are the easiest in the world to impress because they have such cold husbands. The love they get is an analgesic balm instead of a tonic." How he was received by the volcanic Magnani is not on record.

In January, 1949, the New York Film Critics voted *Paisan* the best foreign-language picture of the year. Leaving a raging Magnani behind, Rossellini—though he hates to fly—took a plane to New York. Reporter Garrison, who referred to Rossellini as "the Ace of Hearts," wrote, ". . . when he was leaving for the United States, the Ace of Hearts announced: 'I'm going to put the horns on Mr. Bergman.' "

In New York, Rossellini accepted the Critics' Award, and the next day took a train for California.

While he was en route, came the first intimation that the Bergman-Rossellini combine was something more than cinematic. Over the radio Walter Winchell rattled, "Ingrid Bergman's one and only love is coming to Hollywood to see her!"

Producer Samuel Goldwyn showed interest in the projected enterprise. He held several rather foggy meetings with Ingrid, Rossellini, Lindstrom and Lopert, during which conflicting and capricious viewpoints gave Goldwyn an uneasy premonition.

One evening Goldwyn gave a small party at his home and showed two of Rossellini's films, *Germany, Year Zero*, and *The Miracle*. When the pictures ended, Goldwyn's guests sat quietly, cool and visibly unimpressed. Ingrid suffered for Rossellini. Impulsively, she brushed his cheek with her lips in a spontaneous gesture of sympathy. Those who saw it did a double-take.

Despite the cool reception of these two films at the Goldwyn party, Rossellini's fame inspired the top people in Hollywood to compete for him as a guest. The film executives also began to keep his phone busy on business as well. Finally, David Selznick made him an offer.

But in the midst of all the hoopla, Rossellini remained aloof and indifferent. He had already captured filmdom's most precious commodity; all else was anticlimactic.

"Hollywood is like a factory that turns out fine sausages," he pontificated. "I cannot work here. I go back to Italy where I have freedom."

By the middle of February, Goldwyn, unable to rationalize his involvement, withdrew from the project. Rossellini broke with Lopert and presently found himself without funds, since he could not draw any money out of Italy. He could no longer stay at the expensive Beverly Hills Hotel.

The Lindstroms invited him to move into their small guesthouse, to bide his time until the doctor dug up some other source of financing and distribution for their picture. Now, however, the Italian director's daily proximity served only to aggravate Ingrid's unuttered torments. The situation eluded her grasp or comprehension. A lifetime of discipline and straight-laced living had ill-prepared her for anything else. Even her straining-at-the-leash of recent years had not conditioned her for the total, all-consuming moment of emotional crisis.

With her husband's knowledge and acquiescence, Ingrid took Rossellini on coast and mountain drives, to lunch at the Beachcomber's or the Farmer's Market, and even to drive-ins. She listened in hypnotic fascination to ideas and anecdotes, to descriptions of Rome and Capri and the island of Stromboli, where they would work. They spoke in French, the most melodious of romance languages.

Meanwhile, Ingrid's doctor-manager-husband did not want for long in his quest for backing for the projected Rossellini-Bergman production. Dr. Lindstrom turned to Howard Hughes, who had recently purchased control of RKO Studio.

Hughes agreed to furnish the money for and distribute the Bergman-Rossellini opus, stipulating that camera work must begin ten weeks hence, by April 1, 1949. Ingrid's EN Corporation was written into the contract for 40 per cent of the net profits, Rossellini for 20 per cent.

At the end of February, Rossellini returned to Italy. On March 20th, Ingrid landed at Rome's Ciampino airport a little past midnight. As all other passengers filed out, Ingrid remained behind, trembling and feverish. Rossellini, rarely punctual, hurried into the plane, and saw her standing, irresolute. He kissed her on both cheeks, European style, and whispered, "*Je t'aime.*"

He led her through an unruly mob, whisked her into his red sport-model Cisitalia, and roared for Rome. He put her up at the swank Excelsior Hotel. Overzealous reporters and hordes of fans created bedlam.

Early next morning they checked out and, escaping through a service entrance, sped towards the Sorrentine Peninsula.

They strolled through the ancient ruins of Paestum, with Rossellini describing the sights in French. They lingered at the picture post card resorts of Capri, Sorrento and Amalfi, and hourly, Ingrid's course became clearer and sharper—she was in total love with Roberto Rossellini, and there was no turning back.

The two decided then that Ingrid should immediately write her husband, explain what had happened to her, and ask for a divorce. Close friends of the director said that Ingrid wrote the letter but could not bring herself to mail it; that on learning this, Roberto became furious and insisted that it be dispatched forthwith.

Ingrid then gave him the letter to mail, but before doing so, Rossellini reportedly allowed his closest friends to see its contents. In any case, soon afterward, Italian newspapers quoted from it.

The letter was the tragic confession Dr. Lindstrom submitted so tellingly as Exhibit A during the court trial in 1952 over Ingrid's petition to have Pia visit her in the summer:

> Petter lilla [little]—
>
> It will be very difficult for you to read this letter and it is difficult for me to write it. But I believe it is the only way. I would like to explain everything from the beginning, but you already know enough. And I would like to ask forgiveness, but that seems ridiculous.
>
> It is not altogether my fault, and how can you forgive that I went to stay with Roberto. I know he has also written you and told you all that there is to tell.
>
> It was not my intention to fall in love and go to Italy forever. After all our plans and dreams, you know that is true.

But how can I help it or change it? You saw in Hollywood how my enthusiasm for Roberto grew and grew, and you know how much alike we are, with the same desire for the same kind of work and the same understanding of life.

I thought maybe I could conquer the feeling I had for him when I saw him in his own milieu, so different from mine. But it turned out just the opposite. The people, the life, the country is not strange. It is what I always wanted.

I had not the courage to talk more about him at home than I did with you as it all seemed so incredible, like an adventure, and at the time I didn't realize the depth of his feelings.

Min [my] Petter, I know how this letter falls like a bomb on our house, our Pelle [the name they had planned for their next child], our future, our past so filled with sacrifice and help on your part.

And now you stand alone in the ruins and I am unable to help you. Stackars lilla pappa men also stackars lilla mama [poor little papa, but also poor little mama].

Mama

In their meandering tour down the Italian boot to Messina, jumping-off point for Stromboli, there were two photographs taken, both significantly showing them holding hands or otherwise looking more like lovers than director and star. Discretion was something they had left behind in their impetuous flight.

The photographer's handiwork was avidly grabbed by the press, published throughout the world, and readers looked twice at what they saw.

Twenty-four days after Ingrid's arrival in Rome, on April 13, Hearst society columnist, Cholly Knickerbocker, mentioned in the New York *Journal-American* the "rumors" of a Bergman-Rossellini romance. Newspapermen surged into the breach, and by the time the two principals were immersed in their movie-making on Stromboli, the world was being regaled with juicy tidbits of the idyll, garnished with scandal.

My initial shock was tempered with disbelief. I decided to mark time until I heard from Ingrid herself, even though the incriminating photos gave me pause.

A tidal wave of condemnation swept the nation. The airwaves clattered with backfence prattle. Columnists and newscasters were miraculously transfigured into moral arbiters; fan magazines mourned over the fallen idol; editorials discoursed on their favorite scapegoat, Hollywood. PTA's and sewing circles and beauty-salon clients fumed in frustration and self-assumed betrayal, vowing a Bergman boycott; and theater chains played along, proclaiming they'd ban her films. The Philistines and Pharisees had a field day.

Not since the Teapot Dome oil scandal had the American people been so outraged.

From the beleaguered lovers themselves there issued only vexations and ambiguities. No forthright denial was heard; no affirmation; no clarification. Only half-statements. The truth lurked darkly on the lava slopes of Stromboli.

One day I went to Paramount Studio on a luncheon date. As usual I was met with questions on every side: what did I know? had I heard from Ingrid? was it all true? what did I think? ad infinitum. And then I ran into a director who had made one of Ingrid's most successful pictures, and an actors' agent who represented several top players.

They drew me aside and smirked that Rossellini had made certain boasts soon after his arrival in the film city, that it was now apparent that he had made good his boast. The locker-room story nauseated me, particularly coming from the director whose piety was well advertised.

I wrote Ingrid, "... for God's sake, tell me what's going on! Is there anything I can do?"

She replied,

> Stromboli, 12 of May—'49. Dear Joe: How nice it was to hear from you. On this God-forsaken island we receive very few letters, no newspapers, no telephone calls. We have cable service, but no electricity, no bathrooms, no cars. It is not a place for you! Though your earmuffs might come in handy! Never in the Sicilian summer history has it been so cold and rainy. This picture surely is a problem. I thought we had trouble on "Arch," "Joan" and "Capricorn." This way of making a realistic picture leaves you dead by the realistic road-

side. And to only have amateurs to play with when you have as little patience as I have! But all the hardships and bad weather, you know, I take gladly when I work with somebody that really is remarkable. Never has RR [Rossellini] hesitated one second in front of a setup. He writes the dialogue just before the scene. He chooses his people a couple of hours before the work. He is full of new ideas, unafraid and with an authority that makes the whole crew adore him. His violence, if something goes wrong, can only be compared to the volcano in the background. His tenderness and humor come like a surprise immediately after. I understand well that people call him crazy. But so are all people called, if they dare to be different, and those are the people I always loved, isn't that so?

I have seen nothing but bad press from all over the world. My God, Joe, how awful it has been. And I still haven't read the Swedish press, which, I understand, is, as usual, the worst ... You know how the talk was in Hollywood about us, long before there was any truth to it. It has often amused me how the columnists were smart and right for a change ... Here we have been continually hunted. The photographers have been everywhere ... As the island is free, nobody had the courage to throw the newspaper people in the sea when they arrived to snoop around. Now we have a "closed set," and nobody is allowed near us. And after the Messina meeting [with Peter] RKO sent a publicity man from England to "protect us."

I hope the papers will soon give up their persecution, but at the same time I understand how much more fun it is for them to write these things about me. However, I am afraid my hope is in vain. It makes me so terribly unhappy that Petter [sic!] and Pia must suffer for my sins. And also that the people involved in "Joan of Arc" may suffer. I can't imagine that "Capricorn" will, because I'm not a saint in it.

I worry about RR's future. It will not be easy. He has been praised as Italy's foremost director, but now there are newspapers that steadily attack and insult him. He is unable to defend himself, for every time he does, they come back with more dirt and insults.

I am very worried about the future and what can happen when we get back to civilization again. Therefore, when I received your letter I thought I might ask you what your plans are toward the end of June—we're way behind schedule—and if you would be interested to come to Rome at that time and help me. We should be finished shooting here in two weeks, but the terrible weather will make it four, I am afraid. Also, I don't know what more can happen that has not already appeared in the press. Oh, Joe, remember how I used to suffer when someone wrote just one little word against me?

I don't know where Ruth [Roberts] is. If still in California, give her my love. I haven't written much to anyone, as I felt the newspapers gave much more news than my letters could. And the letters and cables I have received floor me and upset me so, I cannot possibly answer them.

Let me hear from you as soon as you can. I hope this letter reaches you before Christmas. But, who knows?—the way this picture is going we might still be here by then!

Love,

Ingrid

P.S.: Be sure not to talk about your coming here, because it might easily be prevented. Cable me and we'll see how we can arrange your trip.

The postscript puzzled me. Could she have meant Dr. Lindstrom? Howard Hughes? How could they have prevented me from going anywhere I pleased? But, whatever the reasons, I entered into the cloak-and-dagger spirit.

Temporarily shelving my production plans, I immediately wrote Ingrid, saying I would be happy and ready at any time to join her. I reminded her that telegrams pass through many hands, that sometimes their contents are divulged to the wrong people. I recalled her fondness for my special brand of whiskey sour, and because it would be easy to remember and identify, I suggested we both sign our cables "Scotch Sour."

Several such messages passed between us, until the following letter from Ingrid, dated May 30, 1949:

Dear Joe—

Your letter came yesterday—nine days en route. Even if that is a long time you'll receive this still in time to be in Rome before us. I believe we will be here [in Stromboli] three more weeks. Last week I thought it would be two more weeks; so you can see we are going backwards. We have had such enormous difficulties with the weather and shooting conditions in general. Also the crew is hard to handle because of the friction between the Americans and the Italians.

They don't like to see their boss [Rossellini], with whom they worked for years, during the war, during hardships with no pay, so distraught. They have stood by him. Now RKO tries in every possible way to kill him.

The newspapers are filled with lies and RR is not able to defend himself. But all these stories and the outrageous way the Rome office of RKO behaves have broken RR's spirit, and I am really worried about him. The way he works he needs his peace. We have been commanded to finish the picture, and fast! Nobody has any concern that they might finish a man and artist who is too sensitive to both take all the abuse and also work like a machine.

Kay Brown is not very sympathetic but she did suggest your coming. But I hesitated as I didn't know Petter's opinion. [Ingrid spelled her husband's name the Swedish way. She has done so ever since in a voluminous correspondence which continues to this moment of writing. Hereafter, in conversation also, Ingrid pronounced Petter the Swedish way.] I guess I am doing so much already contrary to Petter's wishes, that I can just as well ask you to come. Petter sits in England waiting for us to leave Stromboli, and I am full of fear for what is going to happen when we get to Rome. I believe that we'll end up with another "Messina meeting," which I fear greatly.

I feel very, very sorry for Petter and I don't want to do anything to hurt him, but I cannot go back home with him. In spite of what he is going through, he is still able to look beyond his grief and think only about my professional reputation and my pictures, especially "Joan." Tell me if it is true that that picture is falling off [in business] because of my scandal. To me it seems such hypocrisy to go against your true feelings for business reasons. In the end, people would hate me even more because I was afraid the truth would hurt my career.

We give no interviews, but the press keep coming to the island. And they don't have to ask any questions of us; too many people around us will gladly talk.

I think it is very important to keep everything quiet until you reach Rome. Say hello to Ruth. Ask her to forgive me for not writing. I just can't. She wrote me that she wishes I had you with me, but I had already asked you to come. Tell her about it, but she must be silent. Maybe you shouldn't even tell Ruth. I am getting so that soon I shall be afraid of my own shadow!

I'll hear from you then by wire, and I'll wire you when I think we'll leave this volcanic place. Have a good trip, and let us hope the ship—I mean mine here—won't sink. Thanks for your encouraging words. I don't worry about myself, but the future of Pia and Petter alone, and the work of RR and the films already made. That is enough to make me afraid.

Love,
Ingrid

This letter reached me on June 8th. I immediately made plans to be in Rome a day or two ahead of Ingrid so as to familiarize myself with the city, the papers, and wire services.

I sent off a "Scotch Sour" cable to Ingrid, naming the hour of my arrival. She replied with the same signature, saying that one Enrico Donati would meet me at the airport.

I left Hollywood on June 11th with my wife, Beatrice, who was planning to visit her sister in Philadelphia and to join me in Italy later.

Once I was serenely suspended over the Atlantic in a plane I reflected on the public-relations enigma that confronted me: how to clean up a situation that was inherently a mess to start with and that was getting messier as time went on.

I thought of *Arch of Triumph*, costing over four million; *Joan of Arc* at more than five, and *Under Capricorn*. Judging by their public reception, it was glaringly evident that Ingrid would never collect a nickel on her percentage participations.

Her current production was ironically titled by Rossellini *Against the Storm.* He later changed it to *God's Earth*, and eventually it was released as *Stromboli*, named so by Howard Hughes in a smart move to cash in on the word's by then special connotation.

Like all the film industry, I was convinced that *Stromboli* spelled money in the bank for Ingrid—lots of it. Money she could well use. No picture in the annals of Hollywood had had such prerelease publicity, the brand of titillating ballyhoo that always lures the pious as well as the prurient. The notion of somehow protecting Ingrid's financial interest in this film dominated my thinking as the plane winged toward Italy.

Going through customs at Rome's Ciampino airport, I scanned the faces outside the guardrail, wondering which was Ingrid's emissary. A tall, handsome man, taller than the average Italian, trim in well-cut gray, made a tentative gesture. I nodded back and he quickly pressed through the crowd to my side.

"You are Mr. Steele? I am Enrico Donati." His English was impeccable. Donati led me to a chauffeured Cadillac, one of Rossellini's half-dozen cars, and we were off to the Eternal City.

En route I was curious as to how he had singled me out so readily. "Ingrid described you just so," he said. " 'He is very thin,' she said. 'Too thin. He is dark and distinguished looking.' She was very worried I might miss you."

Donati explained that I would spend the night in Rome and the next morning entrain for Sicily. The work on Stromboli was way behind schedule. Rossellini had transferred his operations to a Sicilian location to take advantage of a certain seasonal spectacle of tuna fishing.

When Donati called for me in the morning, he introduced me to a striking, patrician lady of quiet dignity, who occupied the back seat of the car.

"This is Marcella," he said, "Roberto's sister." She nodded and spoke in fairly good English: "We are so happy you are here."

We boarded the train; I went into a compartment shared with a male stranger; Donati and Marcella into one of their own. Throughout the long tedious journey, and for several days afterward, I automatically referred to them as "your husband" or "your wife." Since they always occupied the same quarters wherever they were, and because their manner towards each other was marked by connubial respect and attentiveness, my assumption was understandable. Moreover, these two fine people volunteered no correction.

It was Ingrid who later enlightened me, explaining that Marcella, whose married name was Mariani, had been legally separated from her husband for several years; that she had a ten-year-old son and a thirteen-year-old daughter. In time I was to encounter many such liaisons among Italy's upper classes, a condition imposed by the country's stringent no-divorce laws.

There was one thing about Donati that particularly interested me. When he had called for me at the hotel he was clutching a crude package, perhaps eight by twelve inches, carelessly wrapped in newspaper and tied with an ordinary piece of string. This object never left his sight. He carried it with him constantly. He held it on his lap when he talked; he took it to the dining car and laid it on the table beside his plate. Funny people, these Italians, I thought.

We talked all the time, I doing most of the listening. Donati and Marcella briefed me on how matters stood. Roberto and Ingrid, they said, were surrounded by sycophants and toadies capitalizing on their chance connection with world figures, advising them badly, humoring their headstrong whims.

The cumulative gist of their account, however, was a masterpiece of confusion, with allusions to "the press garbles their statements," "they're persecuted on every side," "Dr. Lindstrom makes unreasonable demands," "RKO harasses Roberto to finish the picture," "no one has any consideration for their personal feelings," "they must be protected from the backslappers," etcetera.

One note characterized the word-picture painted by my cicerones—Marcella's brother, Roberto Rossellini, was their chief concern; the Swedish woman from America was secondary. "Poor Roberto" was the theme.

At Reggio, in Calabria, the passenger cars rolled onto the biggest ferry in the world, crossed the Straits within sight of Scylla and

Charybdis, and we were in Messina. Squeezed into a midget Fiat, my bulging suitcase shoehorned against my knees, we headed south along the coast. The Sicilian sun blazed hot and dry.

The mysterious newspaper bundle lay on Donati's lap. I couldn't stand it any longer. "What the devil is that thing about?" I said.

"Oh, that is money," he laughed. "Thirteen million lire (roughly $21,000). It is for Roberto's expenses and payroll. I carry it this way because it looks like nothing. If I put it in my bag it may be stolen. If I put it in my briefcase—thieves are always looking for briefcases. This way they pay no attention. See?"

After forty miles of narrow, tortuous roads, and a thousand near-misses of peasants, sheep and sundry fowl, we drew into the deserted courtyard of the Albergo [hotel] Bianchi in Castroreale, a minor sulphur-bath resort.

It was two o'clock and the movie makers were busy at sea. Eager to see Ingrid, I disposed of my luggage and was driven a short distance to the fishing port of Oliveri. There, about six hundred yards out, was a ring of manned boats, perhaps twenty, encircling a huge submerged net. In the center of this trap floated a small plaster Madonna, bobbing up and down in a curious rhythmic dance.

Perceiving no camera activity, I was informed that the tuna had not yet begun their run. Two days had already been lost, but Rossellini had no choice but to wait, crew and cast in readiness, for that climactic once-a-year moment when hundreds of the great creatures would enter a mile-long avenue of nets that would lead them to their death; with, of course, the blessing of the bobbing Madonna.

As the sun edged near the horizon Rossellini called it another day, and he and Ingrid were rowed shoreward. As they approached the frail landing dock I clamped on the Minnesota headlights—my red earmuffs. The natives stared skeptically and began mumbling to each other. Came a ringing shout from Ingrid, "Joe! Hallooo, Joe! Those e-a-r-muffs!"

Embraces and tears and a jumble of incoherence from both of us followed. Rossellini stood silently by, taking in the sentimental reunion. I held her shoulders and gazed into her face. Her skin was pastel-browned by the Mediterranean sun; her eyes crimson from much weeping.

I turned to Rossellini and he welcomed me with genuine warmth: "I am happy you here. You have a good trip?"

I felt an instant impact; this was no ordinary man. His wide brown eyes were inquisitive yet uninformative. His smallish mouth curled enigmatically like mouths I had seen in Florentine paintings. His chin was pointed and slightly receding. His hair thinned backward over a well-formed head. His skin was white, not swarthy. He was no taller than Ingrid, and his midriff showed signs of middle-age softness and expansion. No maiden's dream of Don Juan, this "other man," but he exuded charm from every flaw.

I recalled tales I had heard of his mercurial temperament; how, for example, in a restaurant he had once beaten a news photographer in a blind rage, held him for the police, paid his fine at the police station, then embraced him with an apology and taken him back to join his table.

"When you are with him you feel that you're at the edge of a spiritual whirlwind," was a description offered by Anna Magnani. "He isn't just a man. He is a hurricane."

While Rossellini aided in the unloading of camera equipment, Ingrid and I sat on the edge of the dock.

"Tell me about Pia," was the first thing she said. "Have you seen her?"

"No, I haven't. But I understand she's all right."

"Does Ruth see her?"

"Yes, she keeps in touch. But mostly it seems that John Vernon [Lindstrom's secretary] and his wife look after her."

"Does Pia know anything about this? Has she heard? I am more worried about her than anything else."

"Ruth says she doesn't know anything yet."

"I worry about what she might hear at school. I know how cruel children can be."

That evening we had a fish dinner, including octopus and the ubiquitous spaghetti. At the large table sat Donati, Marcella, Art Cohn (a Hollywood writer, who, on March 22, 1958, met a tragic death with film producer Michael Todd in a plane crash near

Grants, New Mexico), his wife Marta, and Ellen Neuwald, Ingrid's temporary secretary.

Ingrid hungrily pumped me for news, but the presence of strangers made me loath to talk until we were alone.

Rossellini, sensing my indisposition, changed the subject. "How you like Italy?"

"Very beautiful. You say *bellissimo?*"

He smiled agreeably. "Ah, you have learn Italian!"

An atmosphere of distrust and self-consciousness pervaded the assembly, however, and throughout my entire stay in Italy I was constantly aware of this.

When dinner was over, Ingrid, Rossellini and I repaired to their quarters, which consisted of two adjoining bedrooms on the ground floor of the two-story structure. The room we sat in had two screenless windows facing a bare cemented court. The door, which led to an unlighted, uncarpeted hallway, was opened wide in a vain attempt to get some air. For a resort hotel, the furnishings were singularly drab.

Ingrid upended a pillow against the bed headboard, stretched out her legs, and lit a cigarette. The first of our protracted talks got under way.

Ingrid related that immediately upon her arrival in Italy she was overwhelmed by the realization that she was in love with Rossellini; that her life was irresistibly bound up in his; and that she had to make the break with her past, now or never.

"There surely have been many times, Joe," she said, "when you must have noticed how restless and unhappy I was."

"Yes, I thought so at the time. But then you would change, and I would decide they were transient moods, such as we all have. You never really opened up to me, you know."

"I know. I was always holding it inside of me, until sometimes I felt I would burst. I think that if I had been able to put it into words, I would have talked to you. But I couldn't have explained my feelings even if I had tried. I was pretty mixed up."

"When did it all begin?"

"It's awfully hard to say." She stared down at the cigarette in her hand, groping around the maze of her memory. "Maybe it started when the war was over and there were no more trips to distract me. I began to get bored with Hollywood, and bored with my home life.

"Three years ago I asked Petter for a divorce. But when I tried to explain to him why, I couldn't find the right words, and he talked me out of it. About a week after I came to Italy I wrote him a letter and told him about Roberto, and how I felt, and that I wasn't coming back. But still he wouldn't give in. He insisted it was just an infatuation and would pass away."

The room became a stifling box, humid and smoke-laden. As the evening wore on I fixed a Scotch and mineral water. I proffered one to Rossellini, but he shook his head, "Thank you, no. I do not drink." The only drink I ever saw him take was a little wine with dinner. As for cigarettes, he smoked but moderately.

Under the spell of this strangely confessional session, the step-by-step recounting of their tribulations, the two lovers became increasingly emotional. Ingrid told how in the past three months she had again and again pleaded with her husband for a divorce, on any grounds he chose. But he remained adamant that all such talk be deferred until the picture was completed and she was back home in Beverly Hills. She was equally adamant that she would never return home. It was Swede against Swede.

Throughout Ingrid's tearful recital Rossellini kept exclaiming that if she left him, it would be his death! Fidgeting nervously, thwarted by the alien language we spoke, he sat twisting a lock of hair behind his left ear. Fitfully gesticulating and fumbling for the right English words, he several times vowed melodramatically that, "If Ingrid she go back to that man, I kill myself!"

Then Ingrid picked up the threads again: "Petter then went to London, and we wrote letters back and forth, and sometimes talked on the telephone. He wanted me to meet him anywhere in Europe, but Roberto didn't want me to. Petter refused to come to Stromboli. I begged him to tell Pia what had happened, but he said I should be the one to tell the child why her mother wasn't coming home."

She told how the doctor, who seemed unwilling to accept the glaring facts, paradoxically had been willing enough to let his wife remain on a remote island with his rival for the many weeks it takes to make a movie. And how he had finally capitulated and agreed to meet her in Messina. That had been in April.

Then the sordid and tangled story of the parley at the Albergo Reale—the "Messina meeting"—with Ingrid abjectly begging for understanding, crying for a divorce; with Dr. Lindstrom unbendingly holding that their motion picture must first be finished, then Ingrid must come home, and only then would he discuss their future.

"Petter had sent for Kay Brown, and she was there," said Ingrid. "Some of the people you met tonight at the table were there, too." Then somberly, "Everybody had their own advice to give. It was impossible to talk with Petter with so many people saying what should be done. Petter insisted it was his right to see me alone . . ."

"Ahh!" interjected Rossellini, tugging fretfully at the lock of hair behind his left ear. "Ingrid is lost if she stay alone with him. That cold man—he is *dominante* (dominating) Ingrid. She have no will when he look at her!"

Ingrid turned to Rossellini beseechingly, "But that is not right, Roberto. I had to see him alone. It was the only way we could have talked . . ."

"Ahh, it is *stupido*," he pouted.

"So I went into Petter's room," Ingrid continued, "and he quickly locked the door. Then Roberto went crazy."

At this point Rossellini jumped to his feet, declared, "I don' listen more!" and stalked into the other room. Ingrid, with a sudden look of fear, instantly followed him. From the room their voices issued in a jumble of French; one petulant, the other conciliatory. So far, the evidence—both visual and verbal—was a bizarre manifestation of high romance.

What transpired next in the Messina drama I later gathered from Kay Brown and one of Rossellini's hangers-on. Their first-hand account was that the moment Dr. Lindstrom turned the lock on Ingrid, Rossellini was fit to be tied. He promptly summoned the police and told them that Ingrid was being held against her will. "But, Signor Rossellini," they said, "she is his wife. You cannot prevent it." Then the frantic Lothario posted guards from among his courtiers at each of the three exits of the Reale and, leaping into his flashy Ferrari, raced furiously round and round the hotel, raging that the doctor was bent on abducting his own spouse.

In a few minutes, Ingrid and Rossellini, now somewhat calmer, returned to resume our talk. This time they sat together on the edge of the bed.

"Well, I got nowhere with Petter," said Ingrid. "I got awfully tired of arguing, so I gave up. We decided to give out a statement to the press. Here is a copy of it. Everybody had a finger in it."

The statement, released on May 4, 1949, under Ingrid's name, was as ambiguous an arrangement of words as ever saw the light of print:

> "It has been necessary with respect to the picture I am making with Mr. Rossellini to issue a statement for the protection of my family.
>
> "I have met my husband here [in Sicily] and have clarified our situation. I am returning to Stromboli today to continue work on my picture.
>
> "On its conclusion I will leave Italy and meet my husband either in Sweden or the United States.
>
> "Beyond this there will be no further statements about our personal life. It has been quoted in the press that I will not make future pictures with any director except Mr. Rossellini. This is untrue and I so informed my representative, Lew Wasserman [head of MCA Agency].
>
> "I sincerely trust this statement will now allow me to proceed on my picture without further interruption."

I looked up at a worn, drooping Bergman. "It's no wonder the press haven't let up on you," I said. "This is nothing but double-talk. It says nothing, yet says much because it's evasive."

"I know," she said with great weariness. "I wanted to tell the truth, and announce that we were going to be divorced. But this is what they cooked up. They were more worried about finishing the picture, and about my reputation, and how it might affect the business on my pictures than they were about the truth—or me. We could make decisions after the picture was released—when *Arch* and *Joan* and *Capricorn* had made some money. Oh, Joe, that's all I can tell you about Messina. It was late at night when the meeting broke up and we started back for Stromboli."

I looked at my watch; 2:20 A.M. I said, "Good night," and went to my room. Musing over what I had just heard, I could only conclude that when finally the classic triangle had dispersed, the "meeting" had added up to a total impasse, compounded of passion, pride, hysteria, self-interest, and just plain bullheadedness.

Dr. Lindstrom's version of the Messina episode was something else again: "I went there," he testified in the custody trial for Pia in 1952, "to plead with Ingrid to consider our child, and to desist from her public display of affection for Roberto Rossellini, who was a married man."

Lindstrom further stated that the Messina police had been called to arrest him on a charge that he was holding a woman against her will in a hotel room.

His arrest was prevented, he said, "only when it was established that the woman was my own wife, that I was not holding her against her will, and that we both were Swedish citizens in a hotel room just above the Swedish consulate."

Somewhere between these phrenetic viewpoints lay the truth. It appears certain that if that truth could somehow be extricated it still would emerge as an amalgam of confusion and contradictions.

Throughout the draining Castroreale nights Ingrid's narration of these events was imbued with declarations of concern and consideration for her husband, painfully sensitive to his hurt. These avowals, tinged with apologia, invariably elicited angry outbursts from Rossellini, declaiming that Lindstrom was "unreasonable," "made of stone," "thought only of himself," "had no appreciation of Ingrid as a great star," "never bought her a decent jewel," and "acted like a father, not a husband."

Rossellini's attitude then, and throughout my whole Italian sojourn, was that of "the injured party." And in this he was loudly yessed by a formidable coterie of lap-lickers, from lackeys to lawyers.

One day, the tardy tuna put a period to our nocturnal confabs by deporting themselves according to habit. They scrambled into the monster trap and were swiftly slaughtered by the fishermen, who meanwhile chanted a haunting and taunting obbligato about "the stupid fish."

The blue Mediterranean turned a bloody red, and Rossellini, the realist, got his scene; a scene of savage violence, which, in the finished picture, ran for half a minute, and signified nothing.

The technical staff was ordered back to Stromboli, and Rossellini announced that the rest of us—Donati, Marcella, the Cohns, Mrs. Neuwald, myself and, of course, Ingrid—would be off to Taormina, the justly famed resort lying midway between Messina and that other well-known volcano, Mt. Etna.

"But why do we go there?" I asked.

"Ah, it is beautiful!" said Rossellini. "You will like. We rest a few days, yes?" He gently curled the little lock of hair behind his left ear.

Rest from what? Sitting around for a week, waiting for the tuna to make up their minds? And what of the motion picture Howard Hughes and the world were itching to see? Had he meant the emotional flagellation he and Ingrid were suffering? Or was it a stalling for time—time for Dr. Lindstrom to act upon that desperately needed divorce?

One thing was certain: Rossellini didn't give a damn whether or not the picture was made on schedule.

I questioned no further. I was delighted at the opportunity to see Taormina.

In a few hours Rossellini's "vacationers" ascended the step-laddered streets of the historic town to our hotel, the San Domenico, a one-time monastery. Our rooms had once been austere cells, but now were furnished as well as the Ritz. Ingrid and Roberto took over a suite overlooking the gardens that terraced down to the sea.

Once we were comfortably ensconced, we each went our own way enjoying the beautiful surroundings. We shopped, visited the remains of a pre-Christian theater, and never tired of gazing at snow-covered Etna. Ingrid and Rossellini stayed mostly in their quarters; I had yet to have a free moment alone with her.

One mid-afternoon, Rossellini conducted his guests down to a rockstrewn cove so that those who wished could swim or boat. Once there, however, he blossomed out in skin-diving gear and set out to demonstrate his favorite sport—spearfishing.

The water was too cold for most of us. Ingrid swam a little, then dried in the sun and sat with the rest of us watching Rossellini's antics. Pursuing his quarry deep and far, he would submerge for as long as two minutes, often diving to a depth of thirty feet. We admired his skill.

We watched him an hour, two hours. Shadows vanished with the sun, the air chilled our lightly clad flesh, and we who sat and waited began muttering about something to drink and something to eat.

Some yelled for him to come in, but there was no response. No doubt he could not hear. We waved our arms, but he did not seem to see. I was witnessing the first of many instances of Rossellini's almost rude preoccupation with himself. I say "almost" because eventually I became convinced that it was not conscious or intentional. This pronounced absorption in the mood of the moment was but one facet of a many-sided personality.

Finally, it got too dark even for our submarine huntsman. He gave up the elusive contest.

"If only he had caught one little fish, he would have come," said Ingrid. "He hates to give in."

What does he want with one little fish? I thought. He's already snared the biggest.

Towards noon of the following day Ingrid suggested a stroll in the gardens. At last I could talk with her freely, without fear of tempers and tantrums inhibiting her.

"There are things I must know, Ingrid. Questions I must know the answers to, so that I can answer them when they are put to me. What about Roberto's wife?"

"He has been separated from her for many years," she said. "I love Roberto very much, but I don't imagine he is an easy man to live with. She is a very fine woman. She respects and understands him. And Roberto has always provided well for her and their two young sons.

"After they separated she took the boys and settled in Barcelona. She still lives there with Renzo, the younger son. Several years ago Romano got an appendix attack and died of peritonitis. It almost killed Roberto. He felt guilty because he was on Capri with Magnani when he got the news. He speaks of Romano all the time. He'll never get over it.

"He has tried and tried to get an annulment of the marriage, but it is very difficult in Italy. His wife has cooperated in every way. Now he thinks he can get it in Austria."

(Rossellini had only recently petitioned an Austrian court for an annulment of his marriage. This time, it was reported in the Rome press, he had stated that "he was under the influence of drugs when he signed the marriage vows." This was categorically denied by Rossellini. Whatever the facts, at the time we were enjoying Taormina's sunshine, it looked as if the Austrian courts would grant the decree. How this second try for annulment would be received by the Italian courts remained to be seen.)

Ingrid and I came to the four-foot stonewall that rimmed the far side of the gardens. We rested our elbows and gazed down the sheer precipice to the sea, seven hundred feet below.

"Somewhere out there in that mist are Scylla and Charybdis," I said.

"What are they?"

"One is a rock and the other is a whirlpool. In Greek mythology they are personified as monsters, and to say that someone is between Scylla and Charybdis means that they are between two dangers or two evils."

"I must remember that," she said, almost in a whisper. Then, after a wordless minute or two, "It's too bad. I wish we could have settled all this quietly."

"I know, Ingrid, but that's the way it is. You never could get used to the fact that you're public domain. That's why it's important that you both be discreet; that you keep your private life private."

"What can I do, Joe?"

"Well, for example, staying together here at the hotel is not too bad, because it's out of the way and the press don't know you're here. But I understand that on Stromboli you are in the same house—out in the open, where everybody can see."

"But we are not alone," she said, with slight irritation. "Marcella and Enrico and Helena, my maid, live there too."

"Okay. Anyhow, we'll stop taking pictures and stop issuing statements until you and Peter come to some kind of sensible agreement."

We turned and walked in silence for two or three minutes. Then, "What about Pia?" I said.

"Why? What about Pia?"

"Are you prepared to give her up?"

"What do you mean?" she stared at me in muted anger. "Certainly not! Petter wouldn't do anything to keep her from me! I wouldn't want to take her from school, but there's no reason why she couldn't spend her summer vacation with me. She's too young now to know what this is all about; when she grows up, she'll understand."

Early the next morning, when the mood was finally upon him, Rossellini gathered his guests and informed us that we were pushing off for Stromboli.

At Messina we boarded the "San Lorenzo," a weathered but sturdy-looking auxiliary schooner, which normally plied the fishing trade. Roughly forty feet in length, it boasted no cabins or deck awnings. Nothing resembled a chair. The July heat was stifling and mucky.

We scattered our luggage all over the deck and, staking out positions of comparative comfort, we settled down for the estimated eight-hour run to our destination.

Soon we were out of the harbor and in the Tyrrhenian Sea, heading towards the distant gray flecks of the Lipari Islands, of which Stromboli is the northernmost. A veil of silence hung over the polyglot passengers (Italian, Swedish, Jewish, Hungarian, and American). What conversation there was, was guarded and *non sequitur*. Attempts at humor fizzled and sputtered. A few tried sleeping, while others leaned back and scanned the surrounding arena of the Odyssey.

At midday Donati brought out the store of provisions for our lunch: bread, cheese, salami, oranges, figs, and tiny but succulent pears. We ate hungrily, washing it down with bottled mineral water. The leather-skinned skipper and his crew of one ate their share and shortly our supply was gone. No one gave this any thought at the moment, since we looked forward to a hot dinner at Stromboli.

The toilet facility was not only primitive, but foul and flyblown. It appeared not to have been scoured since the ship was launched.

The "San Lorenzo" had been chartered for the duration of the filming on Stromboli. It was used to ferry the personnel between the island and Sicily. These passengers had ridden it only a few days ago to Messina, or perhaps to Castroreale; didn't anyone complain at the time? Couldn't the filth have been removed while we were lolling at Taormina? Apparently, complaints were useless.

About five hours out of Messina the motor developed an ominous coughing spell, then quietly expired. For half an hour, the skipper and Rossellini, who is an expert on racing motors, tinkered and swore and cajoled, but the frazzled mechanism refused to respond. All sails were raised, but they drooped listlessly. The Tyrrhenian Sea was as unruffled as a California swimming pool. The "San Lorenzo" was becalmed.

Then it started to rain, and we scrambled for any kind of shelter. The mainsail, being otherwise useless, was hauled down and fixed into a canopy, under which we all huddled. Throughout, Ingrid remained unperturbed, while Rossellini tugged and twisted the little lock of hair behind his left ear. The sky cleared, but no flicker of air came our way. We drifted, willy-nilly, for another two hours.

There was no radio aboard, no distress signals, nor any means of sounding an S.O.S. After a bit we sighted a fishing vessel about a mile off. We waved our shirts, jumped up and down, shouted in unison, fired a pistol, and burned a pile of papers on the deck.

But all in vain. Seemingly, such shenanigans aroused no curiosity in these myth-storied waters.

Toward the middle of the afternoon Rossellini stirred into action. The solitary rowboat, a flat-bottom, was lowered into the languid pond. Rossellini announced that he and Ingrid would be rowed to Stromboli, and that he would send us help from there. They climbed into the small boat; the crew of one took over the oars, and the headliners rowed serenely towards a black cone jutting out of the sea.

For a few minutes we watched their diminishing figures, then we looked at each other, saying nothing.

Evening came, darkness fell, our stomachs rumbled, but there was nothing to eat. It turned cold and we dug into our bags for warmer clothing. We covered ourselves as best we could, then tried to sleep.

Shortly after midnight, a motor fishing smack, dispatched by Rossellini, hooked a towline onto the intrepid "San Lorenzo," and we resumed our witching journey.

Dawn was yet in the future as we neared the fire-spitting speckle that is Stromboli. Our craft was beached, we clambered through the fringe of the surf, stumbled up pitch-dark paths of rubble, and went to bed.

9.

Stromboli

ON JUNE 25, 1949, I was awakened at noon by the most tenacious, truculent and heavy-booted flies I had ever beheld; they were thick as a storm cloud. The screenless window was wide open and the bare floor felt like a frying pan.

I flailed at the monsters, but to no effect. They remobilized and returned to the attack. Swinging the bedsheet in circles I managed to drive most of them out the window, then slammed it shut. Stalking the gamier laggards one by one, I finished them off.

Having by now acquired a smattering of basic Italian I sought out the maid and inquired about a lavatory. She showed me to a room equipped with a toilet, a washbasin, but no bath. Gesturing that I wished to bathe my whole body, she led me to a small open-air balcony that was an extension of the second-floor corridor. Overhead had been rigged a shower that was piped to a gasoline drum which was perched on the roof.

The maid said an hour's notice would be necessary to heat the water. This was done in the kitchen. When the water was hot enough a boy would fetch it up in buckets, fill the gasoline drum and, *pronto!* you would have your bath. I put in my order for an hour hence.

Enrico Donati dropped in to see how I was getting along. He pointed out that my temporary residence was the parish house of the sole church in the village: that it was through the kindness of the young priest that I was privileged to have this luxury.

He said breakfast was now being served in a dining room especially set up for the film folk; I could eat while my bath was being readied.

The "dining room," in a house otherwise untenanted, consisted of an oblong table covered by a tattered oil-cloth that bore the petrified remains of many previous feasts. There was no kitchen door to stem the tide of fishy odors and grease-laden heat that permeated the atmosphere. The flies were ecstatic. If the windows were closed we couldn't breathe; if opened they charged in. There was nothing to do but eat with one hand and brush them aside with the other.

Donati introduced me to the new faces, among them an Italo-American from Hollywood named Renzo Cesana and his freshly arrived companion, an attractive young woman aptly addressed as "Redsie." I doubt any of us ever remembered her surname.

Amenities done with, Donati said he would see me "at Roberto's." This, I learned, was the designation in general use; never "at Ingrid's." My guide withdrew without eating and, as it turned out, with good reason—he fared infinitely better "at Roberto's."

Cesana, a tall Romanesque figure with an impressively resonant voice, had a dual function on the film. As a writer he translated Rossellini's Italian dialogue into English; as an actor he essayed the role of a priest. American television was to hear much of Cesana following his return to Hollywood.

Shortly after three, having breakfasted on eggs fried in olive oil, and taken my public shower, I went down the town's main street, a narrow, walled lane to the single-storied four-room house that Ingrid and Rossellini shared with Donati and Marcella. The dwelling, one of the few decent habitations on Stromboli, had been rented from a schoolteacher named Maria Russo.

Ingrid, looking unrested, gave me a letter from my daughter, Olivia, in which were enclosed some hysterical newspaper clippings, including the statesmanlike injunction of Colorado's Senator Edwin C. Johnson that Ingrid be forever barred from the United States for "moral turpitude," and that "from the ashes of Ingrid Bergman, a better Hollywood will rise . . ."

In the comparative cool of a bare living-dining room, which was furnished with a plain square table, six wooden chairs, with an open doorway shielded from sun and insects by a flapping divided curtain, Ingrid said, "What time did you get in last night?"

"A little after midnight. How did you make out?"

"Ugh, it was awful, just awful," she frowned. "I thought we would never get here. It took five hours. That poor man who rowed and rowed; his hands must feel broken. After a while big black sharks started following us. Then they came right up to our little boat. They were so close I could have touched them. It's a miracle we weren't turned over. Roberto sat there hitting at them with an oar, but they paid no attention. They kept following us until we got almost to Stromboli. It was like a a nightmare."

Ingrid then spoke of Rossellini's and her own apprehensions regarding Michael Wilson, the publicity man from London whom she had mentioned in her letter to me of May 12th. In support of her contention that Wilson was not sympathetic to their cause, she gave me a carbon copy of an interoffice memorandum that had been sent her and Rossellini at the time of its issuance by Phil Reisman, then head of all RKO operations in Europe.

Dated May 7, 1949, it was addressed to Ed Killy, a veteran production manager from the studio who had come here at the very outset of camera work:

Hotel George V, Paris
Dear Killy:

Michael Wilson has been appointed by RKO to be in complete charge of public relations for the picture presently being made at Stromboli and to remain with you until its completion.

It was agreed upon during the meetings at Messina by the principals concerned that such a man be placed on the picture with complete authority to:

1–Approve all press releases.
2–Approve all future still pictures.

3–Arrange and supervise all press interviews with either Miss Bergman or Mr. Rossellini.

To ensure cooperation and to carry out instructions Mr. Wilson has been told of the agreement reached between Miss Bergman, Mr. Rossellini and Dr. Lindstrom at Messina, which includes the following:

1–Private and separate living quarters for Miss Bergman and her secretary, Mrs. Ellen Neuwald, at Stromboli.

2–No further public appearance of Miss Bergman and Mr. Rossellini unless in connection with the picture.

3–No stills of Miss Bergman and Mr. Rossellini without inclusion of other members of the cast and crew.

4–Separate living quarters, if obtainable on locations, in different hotels.

5–In Rome, separate hotels.

6–No social appearances together whatsoever.

(signed) Phil Reisman

The memorandum had been in Ingrid's and Rossellini's possession for nearly two months. It was now more than three months since Ingrid came down out of the sky at Ciampino and raced off in the red Cisitalia. What sophistry and irony were contained in Mr. Reisman's mandate!

As for Ed Killy, who had for many years successfully withstood the ravages of his calling, the Italian assignment was short-lived. Unable to cope with Rossellini's capricious habits of work plus island conditions, much less enforce Reisman's ingenuous instructions, Killy became a nervous wreck, and was recalled. In his stead was sent Harold Lewis, who was tough, six-foot-four, with nerves to match, and with whom I was acquainted.

Shortly, the inner circle–Donati and Rossellini's sister Marcella, Art Cohn and his wife, Ellen Neuwald, myself, and now augmented by Cesana and Redsie–gathered in conclave.

Out on the terrace of the schoolteacher's house the conversation turned to Anna Magnani and a picture she was making on the neighboring isle of Vulcano. It was bruited that the film's story was based upon Magnani's rift with Rossellini, which piece of intelligence was received with a titter of counterfeit amusement.

Truly knowledgeable, glib, and unencumbered by modesty, Rossellini discoursed on a wide range of subjects, never wanting for anecdotes. An oracular air characterized his pronouncements. His audience converged upon him as the polestar and made frequent allusions to his "genius." Sycophancy was rampant, and he loved it. Ingrid listened quietly, never laughed, occasionally smiled, and seldom spoke.

Harold Lewis, who, it seemed, was the object of a certain ostracism, as was Michael Wilson, dropped by to ask Rossellini when he planned to resume shooting, reminding the director that the picture was weeks behind schedule, and that the studio was "beating his brains out."

Rossellini blandly admonished him not to worry so much, asserting the delays were wholly due to the whims of nature; how could he help it if the tuna wouldn't run and if Stromboli got too hot to handle.

Wearing a blank look of utter bafflement, Lewis ambled off in the direction of the primitive telegraph office, doubtless to try to put some logic in a report to his superior.

A little, wiry wisp of a man, quivering with nervous energy, appeared on the scene, briefly exchanged a few words in Italian with Rossellini, then hurried off. He, it proved, was Alberto Manni, chief flunkey of the Rossellini entourage, with whom I would have some dealings in Rome.

The siesta hour crept upon us and the group dispersed. I called upon the Michael Wilsons, who occupied a distant house overlooking a craggy cove, and found them affable and eager to be friendly. Undisturbed by the dubiety of his employment, Wilson, a stoutish man of about forty, had philosophically settled down to making the most of his prepaid sojourn. They swam in the warm waters, read British papers, played cards, and concocted tolerably good drinks of gin and lemon juice. They stayed away from the embattled lovers and desired nothing so much as to be let alone. After a congenial half hour I set out to explore the island.

Stromboli was in constant ferment, a crimson glow illuminating the peak day and night. Ships were said to use it as a beacon. Once the island boasted a population of 6000, now there were less than 500, composed mostly of the aged waiting to die. When youngsters attained the late teens they migrated to wherever they would be welcomed—North Africa, Australia, or the Americas. Many of the children were stunted, their dark eyes full of sadness. They were the best-behaved and most courteous children I had ever seen.

The clothing most people wore there was black, aged and young alike. There was no electricity, no telephones, no theaters, no bars, no radio, no ice, no running water, no newspapers; few pets, save a few cats and a few mangy dogs. Nowhere was there a sign of early man's prize invention—the wheel. The black-green vegetation consisted of ragged patches of caper shrubs and a handful of scrawny grapevines.

At the peak of his Caesarian glory, Mussolini offered to move the entire population to new homesteads in Ethiopia and Tripoli, but they preferred to stay. Those who chose to stay were born here and they intended to die here. Virtually all of them subsisted on the bounty of sons and daughters who had long since escaped this wretchedness.

Once a week, a steam packet, fourteen hours out of Naples, would anchor off-shore and deliver food and mail, with an occasional rare passenger, come to pay homage to his parents after many years in a foreign land.

Spasmodically, a decrepit maniac sitting at an open window, pathetically moaning and wailing, would suddenly burst out with a hoarse cry, as if he were defying the burning mountain.

This, then, was the melancholy wasteland on which blossomed the love that shocked the world. And yet, beneath this sullen, Stygian surface lay a majestic spirit straining at its thralldom—a kind of cosmic rebellion, storing up its fury for the day of deliverance.

Perhaps this was Ingrid Bergman's story.

As twilight merged into night and night fused into the black land, the ground underfoot gave a nervous shudder. Then again and again it came, as subterranean pressures heaved upward. The symptoms were familiar, for I was from California. But this was no mere earthquake.

Stragglers paused and gazed up at the 3000-foot turret. Incandescent puffs of vapor and dust poured from the crater's mouth.

"*Si, signor*. She come," said a white-haired man, casually. On his bent shoulders he carried a bundle of brushwood to build a fire to cook his supper. "*Buena sera*," he said, and started for home.

Then "she come." Stromboli exploded in a violent convulsion. Flames and molten rock disgorged in a fantastic display. The black cone trembled in labor. I hurried down to Ingrid's.

The others were already there. Rossellini had sent for his cameraman. Donati explained that the volcanic gullet tilted towards the other side of the island; there was no danger to the village. The cameraman arrived, toting a 16 mm. camera.

It was nearing nine o'clock when we climbed aboard the "San Lorenzo," its engine now in working order. In about an hour we had rounded the island to a position in full view of the cascading lava. The ship moved within several hundred yards of where the crimson tentacles of liquid rock crashed into the sea. Stupendous chunks of Stromboli's innards hurtled into the sky, then joined the boiling torrents.

Rossellini took over the camera and proceeded to photograph the cosmic spectacle. To what purpose only he knew. When eventually we saw the film of the explosion, photographed in black and white, it looked like nothing. And no frame of it ever found a place in the finished picture.

For three hours this went on, as the rest of us huddled in discomfort, inadequately dressed for the cold night air. After the first hour Stromboli's big show became a bore. There was some mumbling about having had enough, but no one questioned the maestro. The cameraman lazed idly, seemingly having come along for the ride. Ingrid, crouched in a corner, mutely stared ahead.

Stromboli kept up its fireworks for several days, precluding any activity near the crater. Since the "screenplay" was wholly in Rossellini's mind, I was not aware that this interim could well have been devoted to shooting scenes in the village. The tedious, workless hours were consumed by the nagging issue—whether or not Ingrid should rendezvous with her husband on the mainland and resolve, once for all, the question of an immediate divorce.

Ingrid would emerge from the back room of the house, dressed in a blouse, peasant skirt, sandals on her bare feet, looking as though she had not slept all night. And the unsettled arguments would start all over again.

"I cannot help it," she would reiterate. "I think it is unfair to Petter not to see him. Roberto is afraid that if I meet him he will make me change my mind. But this is not true; I'll never go back. But I've got to convince Petter to his face. That's the only way he'll ever believe it."

"No!" Rossellini would cry. "She has no will when she with him. He treat her like child!"

And I would side with Ingrid only to come up hard against Rossellini's vehement objections, climaxed by histrionic threats to kill himself if she carried out her notion. Throughout these highly charged sessions her face was a depressing sight to behold. Had I had an inkling of her biological condition at the time, I would better have understood her desperate urgency.

In faraway places the flamboyant headlines had begun to have their effect on two innocent children—eleven-year-old Pia Lindstrom and Rossellini's eight-year-old son, Renzino. Cruelly taunted by her schoolmates, Pia had been withdrawn by her father and placed in the San Fernando Valley home of his male secretary, John Vernon and his wife; Renzino got into a fight, was struck on the head by a stone and required a delicate operation.

Dr. Lindstrom was now in London, waiting for Ingrid to meet him anywhere in Europe. Early in July the Vernons took Pia to the Swenson farm in Minnesota for three weeks and Hank Swenson penned Ingrid a lengthy letter beseeching her to reconsider her actions.

One morning the volcano spluttered out and lay quiescent. Rossellini announced that shooting would be resumed at dawn. He outlined the action and dialogue of the scene as he conceived it to the two writers. Whatever suggestions they ventured were ignored.

Owing to the withering sun and deadly sulphur fumes, filming was endurable only in the morning hours. At 3:30 A.M. that night a caravan of eight mules—the first ever seen on Stromboli—halted by the house. Ingrid, wearing masculine pants and sturdy boots, perceptibly haggard, mounted one, Rossellini another, and with the other beasts bearing equipment and crew, they commenced the two-hour trek to the top of the volcano.

I watched them disappear up an invisible tenebrous trail, wondering what was going on in Ingrid's head. There went the incomparable Bergman, up the grimy mountainside, without benefit of a hairdresser, make-up man, a stand-in, or any of the accouterments she had become accustomed to. Not even a medical man in the event of an accident.

At noon day Ingrid and Rossellini and their colleagues returned from their labors, all on foot. Black-faced, black-clothed, beaten, they dragged themselves along the wall-lined pavement, each to his abode. As I gazed at this indefensible sight I was minded of newsreels I had seen of rescued coal miners emerging from their moment of hell.

It seemed there was a "short cut" for the descent from the summit. Tucking their pants inside their boots, they would slide down on their backsides—down the more than 2000 feet of sandy, gravelly blackness. Ingrid's Nordic constitution survived these rigors, but one day Rossellini's production executive, Lodovici Muratori, a former general of engineers in Mussolini's army, was overcome by the poisonous fumes and died of a heart attack. His body was taken to Messina aboard the "San Lorenzo," placed in a coffin, and services were held on the ship as we all bowed ceremoniously around the casket.

The steam packet from Naples brought a cargo of mail, some with clippings from Italian, British, American and Swedish papers, teeming with wild quotations and reportorial fantasies. Present, too, was the stench of obscene missives embellished with crude hand-drawn erotica, significantly, every one from the U.S.A.

But rummaging through this offal there was here and there a note of compassion. Witness: on the letterhead of The Film Guild, 117 West 48th St., New York City:

> My dear Miss Bergman:
>
> Twenty-five years ago the Film Guild was the first to uphold the sacred right of the artist in matters that concerned his intimate self . . . We pleaded for this inalienable right . . . Now that you are faced with the same unreasoning hostility, we wish to add our humble support and confirm again our unqualified belief that an artist in any medium should not and cannot be criticized for any act which may be dictated by his inner conscience.
>
> . . . an artist pays his debt to society in creating and society has no further demand upon the artist. . . . Incontestably you are an artist as you have proven by your creations on stage and screen . . . The public or that part of it which always designates itself as the mentors or moralists of society, should not seek to interpose their decisions on your personal life which should be . . . something sacredly personal and apart.
>
> . . . Let us hope that there will be a return to a sane appreciation of the circumstances involved and that you will go on to greater heights . . .
>
> Sincerely yours,
> (signed) Simon Gould, Director.

One more breath of humanity, initialed by a secretary, written on the letterhead of the law office of Chambliss, Chambliss & Brown, Provident Building, Chattanooga, Tennessee:

> Dear Miss Bergman:
>
> I am sure that most people have known at least some of the tragedy that shadows the footsteps of true happiness. Just as there are two sides to the moon, so there must be the dark as well as the lighted half of man's life. The birth, or death, of an emotion is truly as moving as the birth or death of a body . . .

... the real reason why I am writing is that statement of yours in which you said that because of your role in *Joan of Arc* some people seemed to feel that you were a saint, and to resent your being otherwise, but that you were merely a person ... a statement that is one of the most powerful and poignant I ever heard.

... There is always hope for man so long as he realizes that he is merely man ... There was in it a strange admixture of dignity, pathos, hope and despair—an admixture that was truly as human as are those pathetic folk who hunger for saints to worship ...

Sincerely,
(signed) Jac Chambliss

P.S.: And remember always the truth of Santayana's statement that:

> 'To possess goods and persons in idea is the only pure good to be got out of them; to possess them physically or legally is a burden and a snare.'

Ingrid was distressed that Lindstrom would believe some of the misstatements attributed to her and to Rossellini. I too was concerned lest the doctor place some of the blame on me. I wrote him:

Dear Peter:

This note is written at my own suggestion, without any prompting on Ingrid's part. You will understand, I am sure, why I emphasize this point.

I ventured here, into the middle of a nasty situation, with the sole desire and aim of helping Ingrid. I firmly believe that I can help her best by making every effort to keep the press from publishing recriminations, name-calling or anything derogatory to the three principals involved. Towards achieving this mutually desirable result, it is my earnest hope that this whole affair will be settled in a civilized manner, with maturity and intelligence.

With this policy in mind, I wanted you to know that I shall write nothing or say nothing that will put you in a bad light. However, because the press, as you well know, is unpredictable and beyond control, if anything unpleasant does appear, be assured that it did not come from me.

Being a fatalist I cannot but feel that this entire matter was inevitable though painful, far beyond the will of those concerned. I deeply regret you and I had differences, but I want you to know that there is no reproach left in my heart.

Very sincerely,
(signed) Joseph H. Steele

I expected no reply and received none.

A cousin of Ingrid's, named Britt Engstrom, arrived from Stockholm to spend a week of her vacation as Ingrid's guest.

"We grew up together," Ingrid told me. "I think of Britt as my dearest friend in Sweden. She's never been out of the country, and for a long time I've planned to give her a trip as a present. She works and has not much money. When she wrote me here and said she was going on a vacation, I thought it would be interesting for her to come and spend it with me. So I sent her all her expenses for the trip."

Tall, slim and fair, strongly reminiscent of Ruth Roberts, Britt was deeply perturbed over "the situation." En route from Stockholm she had paused in London to see Lindstrom. She said he had lost considerable weight and appeared like a broken man. This tragic report only served to heighten Ingrid's depression.

When we chanced to be alone, Britt tearfully pleaded that somehow there must be a less harsh solution to the three-cornered riddle, since she did not believe that Ingrid's was more than a passing infatuation.

"Make no mistake about it," I said. "Ingrid is head over heels in love with Roberto, and her mind's made up that she's not going back to Peter no matter what happens. There's nothing to be done."

"But it isn't right that she won't see Peter."

"It isn't that she won't; she wants to very much. She cries all the time. I've backed her up all I can, but we get nowhere. Roberto's dead set against it."

Yachts began to anchor off the island; and the pleasure-bent paraded past the little house, eager to glimpse the celebrities. Reporters and photographers popped up under various guises, one cloaked as a monk. Not since Homer had Stromboli boasted such glory.

I soon learned the reason for Harold Lewis's extravagant gladhand when first he spotted me. Every time our paths crossed he wailed, "For Christ's sake, Joe! Can't you do something about getting this picture going?"

Rossellini's menage was run by Helena, Ingrid's maid, who, until recently, had worked for Anna Magnani, and a cook and his wife, brought from Messina. The kitchen was stocked with food, good wine, and blocks of ice, periodically fetched from the Sicilian city by the "San Lorenzo." The provisions included bread, butter, eggs, veal, chicken, sardines, canned tuna, fresh fruit and vegetables.

Cesana and I groused so much about our own fare that Rossellini was finally moved to invite us to an occasional luncheon or dinner. These mealtimes presented welcome opportunities to talk of matters other than the onerous Lindstrom stalemate. Income tax, for example. How was it in Italy?

"Aah," shrugged Rossellini, "it is nothing. We pay what we want. They have no system. You tell them how much your income, how much your expenses, how much you can pay. They take what you pay. It is big foolishness."

Ingrid's leading man was a twenty-one-year-old fisherman named Mario Vitale, whom Rossellini picked off the beach at Salerno, paying him seventy-five dollars a week for his starring role. Not having met him formally, I remarked that it was odd that he had never so much as made one appearance in our social circle.

"Aah, he is not important," said Rossellini, contemptuously.

Though Vitale courted and married Ingrid in the picture, Rossellini never permitted him to embrace or kiss her.

Work on the film progressed by fits and starts, depending on the director's moods. And when the sterile hours dragged on, flagging energies took up the same old arguments.

When I did catch Ingrid alone for a fleeting second, I said, "Ingrid, this can't go on this way. There's no sense to it. The only way you can stop all this is to see Peter and settle this damned business."

"I am so worried," she said. "Roberto says he will leave the picture—go away—do anything—kill himself. What can I do?"

"Let him go," I said. "He's bluffing. He won't do anything."

Then suddenly Rossellini appeared and demanded to know what we were talking about.

Ingrid looked at him beseechingly: "We were talking about Petter. Joe thinks like I do. I must see Petter . . ."

"Okay," he said, with dramatic resignation. He walked away petulantly and we did not see him for several hours, when Alberto Manni came to tell us that his master had taken the "San Lorenzo" to Messina.

Ingrid was distraught and convinced that Rossellini would do something rash. The next day, however, Rossellini showed up, slightly subdued but offering no explanation. But he had made his grand gesture, soon became his former self, and the incident was tacitly forgotten.

The steam packet brought an addition to our group in the person of Rossellini's composer-brother, Renzo, a placid, flaccid gentleman of soft voice and manner. At the same time Alberto Manni took off for Rome bent on some errand.

Meanwhile, studio executives—insensitive to the emotional turbulence surrounding the production—kept hammering at Rossellini, Ingrid and Harold Lewis to be done with the work on Stromboli. On July 24th I was one of several in the group who framed the following cablegram to Ingrid's Beverly Hills attorney, Mendel Silverberg:

HAROLD LEWIS YESTERDAY DELIVERED ULTIMATUM THAT UNLESS WE END SHOOTING ON STROMBOLI TOMORROW HE IS INSTRUCTED TO TAKE DRASTIC STEPS, INCLUDING HALTING OF PRODUCTION. THIS IS CLIMACTIC INCIDENT OF MANY UNWARRANTED INDIGNITIES WHICH HAVE ADDED TO TREMENDOUS DIFFICULTIES UNDER WHICH WE HAVE WORKED. INCLEMENT WEATHER, ILLNESSES

AND INJURIES HAVE INCREASED THE PROBLEMS ON THIS PRIMITIVE ISLAND. IMPOSSIBLE TO BELIEVE RKO HAS BEEN INFORMED OF THESE DIFFICULTIES, OTHERWISE IT WOULD NOT HARASS US AT A TIME WHEN WE ARE WORKING NIGHT AND DAY TO FINISH QUICKLY AS HUMANLY POSSIBLE. NO ONE REALIZES WHAT SACRIFICES WE HAVE MADE EXCEPT THOSE WHO HAVE HAD TO LIVE ON THIS ISLAND, AND NO ONE ELSE KNOWS HOW MUCH WE WANT TO LEAVE. BUT WE CAME HERE TO MAKE THE BEST PICTURE OF WHICH WE ARE CAPABLE. DESPITE MANY DELAYS WE HAVE HARDLY EXCEEDED THE ITALIAN BUDGET, ALTHOUGH WE HAVE BEEN OBLIGATED TO MAKE TWO COMPLETE VERSIONS OF THE PICTURE AT GREATLY ADDED COST IN TIME AND MONEY. WE HAVE NEVER BEEN GIVEN AN ACCOUNTING OF THE AMERICAN BUDGET NOR EVEN CONSULTED ABOUT SEVERAL COSTLY EXPENDITURES, INCLUDING MICHAEL WILSON, ALTHOUGH ROSSELLINI AND I ARE PARTICIPANTS IN PICTURE AND HE IS FINANCIALLY RESPONSIBLE FOR ALL COSTS OVER THE BUDGET. SUGGEST YOU PROCURE COPY OF PHIL REISMAN'S LETTER TO ED KILLY REGARDING WILSON. ENTIRE TROUPE HAS UNDERGONE MANY PRIVATIONS. ONE OF OUR MEN DIED OF SULPHUR FUMES ON VOLCANO. ROSSELLINI SUFFERED SEVERE INJURIES IN FALL AT CRATER AND IS NOW WORKING DESPITE DOCTOR'S ORDERS TO REST FOR TEN DAYS. NEVER IN MY EXPERIENCE HAS A COMPANY UNDERGONE SUCH HARDSHIPS. NONE OF US EXPECT ANY PRAISE FOR THIS, BUT NEITHER DO WE EXPECT THE DEFAMATORY STATEMENTS THAT HAVE COME FROM THE RKO ROME REPRESENTATIVES NOR THE RKO ROME LAWYER WHO ALSO REPRESENTS THE COMPANY SHOOTING THE ANNA MAGNANI PICTURE ON A NEARBY ISLAND. NOR DO WE EXPECT RKO TO THREATEN TO SUSPEND PAYMENTS TO US IN VIOLATION OF OUR CONTRACT WITHOUT CONSULTING WITH US ABOUT OUR PROBLEMS. THIS IS THE MOST IMPORTANT PICTURE I HAVE EVER MADE. THAT IS WHY I STRONGLY RESENT THE IMPLICATION OF HAROLD LEWIS'S ULTIMATUM. PLEASE APPRISE LEW WASSERMAN [Head of MCA Agency, Ingrid's representatives in Beverly Hills] OF THIS CABLE, AND ADVISE ME IMMEDIATELY WHETHER I SHOULD SEND A COPY TO HOWARD HUGHES. REGARDS. INGRID BERGMAN.

This expensive, wordy cablegram, reduced by half from the original, was typical of Rossellini to whom money was merely something to be spent. He had an aversion to writing letters and a passion for sending voluminous telegrams and cablegrams. As to the reference to his injury atop the volcano, it was apparently so minor that I had not heard of it. The "doctor" who prescribed a ten-day rest existed solely in the imagination, since there was none on the island. The message was phrased as coming from Ingrid at my suggestion that it would thereby exert a more telling impact on studio powers. Its first immediate effect was the recall of Michael Wilson to London, thus cutting short his holiday.

Rossellini's Rome attorney, Signor Verdozzi, arrived at his bidding, and weighty sessions ensued. The dignified, professorial lawyer reported that Rossellini's Austrian annulment was now at the mercy of an Italian court; its decision must be awaited with patience.

Inescapably the moot question of a Bergman-Lindstrom meeting was rehashed, with law-minded Verdozzi vainly arguing from an ethical and tactical standpoint that it was a wise thing to do. Nevertheless, Rossellini tugged at the lock of hair behind his left ear and pettishly held his ground.

A man of fierce contradictions, this Rossellini was an amalgam of poet and sensualist; spasmodically tender, brutal, profound, and crass; at once selfish and generous. Horse-sense, however, was an alien virtue; his emotional moat was an impregnable barrier.

Since my vocal arguments were incessantly disjointed by his outbursts of contrariness, I thought it best to put my feelings on paper for both him and Ingrid to study at leisure; he wouldn't find it too easy to bark back at the written word.

Half the night of July 27, 1949, I sat up and wrote the following:

My dear Ingrid and Roberto:

I have made abortive efforts to speak my mind, to act as a balance wheel in your essentially confused struggles to find a way out. But Roberto overwhelms me and it is almost impossible to maintain a proper perspective, to see the over-all picture, to consider the consequences. I wish I could say "to hell with the world, with the press and the public, with the motion-picture business. Nothing matters but the love of these two people."

But the truth is that the love of these two people is dependent on their mutual admiration and respect for each other. When that goes, everything else will go with it. Your individual work is the foundation of your mutual happiness, and it is my very profound feeling that that work is now, in this crisis, in dire jeopardy. Oh, I know that Ingrid told me she didn't care if she ever worked again, that she would be content only to be near Roberto's work. I want to remind her of the time I asked if she would give up her career if it interfered with her home. She set her jaw firmly, looked straight into my eyes, and shook her head in a positive "Never!"

One day all this will pass away, as all things do. A year from now Ingrid will become restive and yearn to be doing the thing God created her for. I don't believe she has the will to cast away her career, nor do I believe she has the right to do so. She belongs to the world and it would be shameful and criminal to take her from it. Thus, I think it nonsense for Ingrid to reiterate that she doesn't care. She'll care like hell, one day.

Roberto's life, too, is this same world—his work. Without it he will perish. He, too, belongs to the world, with obligations and responsibilities he can never deny. He is no king willing to give up his throne to spend the rest of his life in empty pursuits on some dull island. Neither is Ingrid a nonentity who marries the king. Roberto is no international playboy, independently wealthy for life, contributing nothing more important than a race horse to the Derby. Who cares what these people do?

The papers made a field day of their escapades, but in your case it is different. The clippings about you both prove it. True, some revel in the scandalous aspects, but there are many who try to explain it away, deplore it and demonstrate their unwillingness to believe it. Where there is disillusionment it is bitter, bitter as the hurt we feel when someone we love and trust deceives us.

I am constrained to say all this to you because most of the time I have a frustrated feeling that neither of you quite comprehends the magnitude and far-reaching impact of this situation. It is not lightly that some of the press refer to Ingrid as 'Fallen Idol.'

After all these months of blunders and unrestrained exhibitionism, which has only mired you deeper and deeper into a situation pregnant with self-destruction, it is time you both employed some calm reflection and unimpassioned judgment.

I beg of you, let us have done with recriminations; you are both equally guilty. This is not the age of Cellini; it is the age of press, radio, churches and sundry organizations into whose eyes you cannot spit with impunity. Whether you agree with them or not, they are an indisputable fact, and when they are aroused they'll cut you to pieces and eat you.

Roberto is fully aware that he has been vilified and condemned as the culprit in this drama. Both of you have told me that the reaction in America was duplicated in European countries, including Italy. It is vital that you recognize the wide spread of this antagonism. It is of exceeding significance. Ingrid asked me last night if I knew of a precedent for this case—where a wife and mother remained in another country and made no effort to see her home and child again. No, I never heard of a similar case. So far as I know there is no precedent for the whole mess. But what I am fearful of is the immediate future, and it is that which concerns me now. We need all the wisdom we can bring to bear. All is now quiet on the Stromboli front, but don't let the lull deceive you; a hell of a storm may follow.

I hold no brief for the press but, whether you like it or not, they are the watchdogs of public opinion. Rant and denounce them all you wish, but the fact remains that you are, in the final analysis, minor figures in the contest—two individuals defying an armory of such journalistic weapons as can destroy you. Let us not again fall flat on our face with such a statement as "We had hoped to keep it quiet."

Permit me, then, to bring up the major question that has harassed us for weeks: should Ingrid have another meeting with Peter or not? Let us weigh this carefully from every angle:

Ingrid has had only one meeting with her husband since she left America, the one at Messina. True, it was a meeting that lasted a very long time, but it is also true that that meeting was muddied with the presence of too many people and too many conflicting interests: you, Roberto, Kay Brown, Enrico Donati, Schiffrin [a friend of Rossellini], Ellen Neuwald, Marcella, the Art Cohns, and I don't know who else; I wasn't there. Studio interests and MCA Agency interests were there also.

The auspices of that meeting were bad and the results were inevitable. I've heard the details a hundred times but still it persists in my mind as a complete bedlam. Roberto's argument that a second meeting for a final irrevocable conclusion will achieve no better results than the Messina muddle does not hold water because the then existent conditions defeated its aims. The conclusion reached there—if it can be called a conclusion—was unhappy and indecisive, resulting in that other blundering statement, 'I will meet with my husband either in London or Sweden when the picture is finished.'

A second meeting, with only Ingrid and Peter present, could and should result in a definite, unalterable conclusion. However we may look at it, it was not unnatural for him to refuse to recognize the true state of affairs at Messina. Peter is not accustomed to being opposed; no one has ever said no to him, and therefore it was difficult for his bull-headed, Nordic nature, wearing blinders and seeing only a limited area, to accept this initial onslaught upon his will. But time has passed; he has had letters from Ingrid, he knows she brought me here without consulting him, he has talked with Britt [on her return to Sweden] and other of Ingrid's emissaries. He cannot ignore all that has happened since Messina. He is infinitely better conditioned for the showdown.

A vital element is Ingrid's conscience in this matter of seeing Peter once again. She feels it keenly and we all know it. The truth is that deep in her heart she knows the injustice of not having it out with him, face to face, though I am sure she would give anything if the meeting wasn't necessary. That's the way she has felt ever since I arrived at Castroreale, and nothing can change it. Pressure may force her against this action but it will not eradicate the dictates of her conscience.

As for you, Roberto, if you will stop to envisage your future together, then you too will not want it on your conscience that you prevented Ingrid from doing what her heart says is right at this crucial moment. And, too, Ingrid shall never have reason to accuse you of it.

I cannot believe, as you keep insisting, that Peter can hold Ingrid against her will, once the meeting is held. There is no law on earth that compels a wife to stay with her husband against her wishes. Besides, it is my thought that instead of a hotel or villa the meeting be held in an office or place of business which would have a closing hour. The office could belong to some friend who would willingly stay away that day. Perhaps Verdozzi could arrange it in Naples or Rome. Ingrid and Peter could arrive singly, not together, so as not to attract attention, entering the office as if on ordinary business. I'm confident this could be maneuvered in such a way as to circumvent reporters or any snoopers.

Regarding another of your fears—if the meeting was set up in this manner—Peter couldn't very conveniently manage to spend the night with Ingrid in an office, could he?

The meeting will necessarily be painful for Ingrid. She is aware of that and is ready to face it. It is possible that Peter will not yield to a single point at such a meeting; that he may refuse a divorce; and that he may persist in his demand that all decisions be deferred until the picture is finished and Ingrid has returned home.

If it turns out that way, then there is nothing left for Ingrid but to file the papers herself and issue a statement that she has met with her husband, that their differences are of long standing, that he denies her a divorce, and that she had hoped and strived for an amicable separation, but that his attitude has left her no choice.

When she talks with Peter she should make it clear and positive that if he did not cooperate she would follow this course. She should tell him that she had wanted to protect him and accomplish the parting in a civilized manner, with dignity and decency. But if he remains adamant her conscience is in the clear and there is nothing left but to act and act quickly.

I have been sorely troubled by the thought of what Peter might do if we issue any kind of an announcement without Ingrid's having had it out with him in person. He could make a statement in rebuttal, in which he could vent all his hatred and bitterness, declaring that his wife was not acting freely and voluntarily, that she has been kept a prisoner, etc., etc., ad nauseam. More stink, more front-page headlines of the sort that will be most difficult to recover from. Therein lies the underlying danger if you persist in the present course. Our defense will be pitifully weak and all the sympathy will go to him, particularly if he meets the press personally and presents the physical appearance which Britt and others have described. And you can be sure that the Messina statement about "meet with my husband" will be branded a lie.

Peter will drag in the home, the child, everything he can think of. It will not only be very damaging, it can be irreparable.

I think Ingrid can very well say to Peter: "You know I have been unhappy and restless for a long time, long before I ever heard of Rossellini. Once before I asked you for a divorce. Now more than ever I can never live with you again. And do not accuse Roberto; he is far less at fault than I am. This thing is of my own doing. As to my own future I cannot predict what will happen. A divorce takes time, and I shall have plenty of time to think."

I don't presume to write the dialogue, but that is the essence of what she can say to him. And when she leaves that office she has left Peter forever. And she will cry, cry a lot, but tears are an integral part of this story and nothing we can devise will prevent them. It is a period of anguish for all three of you; it cannot be resolved in tranquillity.

Ingrid's behavior in this entire matter is far from admirable, but beyond question it is a tribute to the woman in her that she cannot make this final break in cold blood. It is, I think, acid irony that she has been forced into this position.

If you agree upon holding this meeting I earnestly hope that you arrive at it without threats and insinuations. It seems to me that wisdom indicates the meeting should be held *immediately after* we have finished our work on Stromboli.

Here, then, are the best arguments I am able to muster for

both sides. I plead with you to weigh them carefully, come to a decision, and abide by it in good faith. God bless you.

I embrace you.
(signed) Joe

I delivered it to Rossellini in Ingrid's presence. "Please read this together," I said, "when you are alone and quiet; maybe after dinner."

That was the last I heard of my honest try. The only reaction I got was a stretch of strained silence from Rossellini.

Whether or not my epistle brought matters to a head, they presently came to a decision–Ingrid would *not* meet with her husband, and a statement would be issued that, despite Lindstrom's resistance, she would immediately institute divorce proceedings in any country where it could be effectuated.

Though I deplored the ultimate resolution, it nevertheless had some salutary effect: the weepings ceased and the tensions relaxed. Under Verdozzi's legal eye I drafted an announcement for release to the press upon our arrival in Rome, purportedly several days hence. The closing paragraph kicked the props from under the pressure groups who threatened to ban Ingrid's pictures–"It is my intention to retire from the screen."

Verdozzi departed, a spurious peace pervaded the group, and the motion-picture camera moved into the outskirts of the village.

The burdensome shadows vanished from Ingrid's face. Between scenes, seated amidst the charred ruins of an old house, we talked.

"Ingrid, I'm curious about how Peter got together with Howard Hughes on the picture. I was amazed when I first heard of it."

"Oh, that's a very amusing story," she nodded with a grin. "One day Hughes telephoned me and said, 'I have just bought RKO Studio for you. You can have anything you want. May I come and talk with you and the doctor?'

"When I told Petter about it, he thought it was all very funny. You remember what trouble he made for you about Hughes. So now he just laughed and laughed, and said, 'See how far they will go to win you over?'

"When Sam Goldwyn pulled out of the deal, Petter had a hard time finding someone else to back the picture. Then one day he said he was going to talk with Hughes. 'But I thought you were always against Hughes,' I said.

" 'Ah, this is business,' he said. 'As to the other, I'm sure you can handle any situation that comes up. You don't *have* to get social.' "

"Very amusing indeed. Tell me," I said, "now that you have determined on the next step, what about Pia?"

"I already told you," she said with some impatience. "Petter would not keep her from me. She can be with me in the summertime."

"What of your community property?"

"Oh, I don't care about that. He can take the house, the money, everything. All I want is my freedom."

Through my memory flashed the vision of a draftsman I had known, who had abruptly quit his lifetime trade to become a painter. "I just got damned sick of straight lines," he had said.

"With Roberto," continued Ingrid, "I don't feel shy or afraid or lonely for the first time in my life." She threw back her head and gazed at the sky. "I feel free for the first time."

"Let's face it, Ingrid, you may never make another picture. What will you do with your life?"

"I love Roberto," she said, quietly, thoughtfully. "One day, when I am free, we shall be married. He is a great artist, and it is exciting and full of wonder to watch him work. I shall be content to be near him and, in a way, make his career my career. If he will let me I shall be happy to work as one of the crew—help cut his pictures—anything."

The Stromboli chapter and the month of July neared an end. I cabled my wife to take a flight that would bring her to Rome on the 30th, so that we could be together on her birthday, the 31st.

Apprising Rossellini of my plan to leave ahead of them, he assured me the island sequences would soon be completed and they would see me in Rome.

I packed my things, said the good-byes, and boarded the steam packet that would poke its lazy way among these Aeolian isles until it reached Messina.

As the ship pulled away there was one final desolating sound from the bleak, black boil that is Stromboli: the defiant madman of the open window cried out in a long, echoing, wounded howl of agony—cursing the volcano that was his home.

10.

Rome

ONE of Europe's famous hostelries, Rome's Excelsior Hotel is situated on the sidewalk-cafe-lined Via Veneto, across the street from the American Embassy. A small bedroom on its top floor was the quarters to which newspapers referred as "Rossellini's year-round apartment," a cheerless, inside cubicle where Alberto Manni had temporarily installed my wife.

I arrived long after midnight, worn by the tedious train ride from Messina. It was late morning when we went down for breakfast. Harold Lewis was in the lobby.

"Manni told me you were here," he said. "When is the troupe getting in?"

"Roberto said he'd be sure to finish today. So I imagine they'll be in sometime tomorrow."

A young, heavy-set man came up. "Pardon me, are you Mr. Steele?"

"Yes."

"I'm Michael Chinigo, Rome correspondent for I.N.S. (International News Service). When are Miss Bergman and Rossellini due in?"

"I expect them tomorrow."

"Got anything I can use?"

"No, I haven't. Miss Bergman will issue a statement when she arrives."

After breakfast I picked up the accumulated mail.

From Stromboli I had written Ruth Roberts a description of the existing situation. In the mail was her reply; among other sage observations, saying: "... I am not so sure what happiness Ingrid wants, or rather if she knows what she wants of happiness. Rossellini is an artist; he makes good pictures and I feel that she wanted to work for him because his pictures had the 'reality' she is searching for, but I feel a bit wry about this. Ingrid's 'reality' is still on the screen. I wonder if she has found any true realities to hold to—some basic ones. I hope so.

"She has to find these for herself and this is what I want for her more than anything. The minute she starts thinking about it she is near to finding them. That is the wonderful thing about it. Ingrid has always had a strong sense of honesty. This is the first thing she has to start on, and that is a good deal."

At precisely 7:17 of the next morning my wife and I were wrenched out of deep sleep by loud banging on the door. It was Manni, puffing breathlessly from having run the five flights upstairs. Rome had not fully recovered from the war and periodically there were no lights or elevators owing to the power shortage.

"You must come—no time—Roberto *telegramma* you go Amalfi," he sputtered. "Train go *subito*—quick—now—no time."

Plainly, it was a matter of life and death. His bursting urgency was overwhelming. I threw some things into a bag, assured my bewildered spouse I'd be back in the evening, joined Manni in the lobby, and we were off in a cloud of confusion.

After four uncomfortable hours on the train we arrived at Salerno on the tip of the Sorrentine Peninsula, and were met by a Cadillac sedan chauffeured by a swarthy fellow named Pietro. Rolling along the precipitous, winding road, high above the Mediterranean, I said, "Seems funny seeing a Cadillac here. How come?"

"Belong Roberto," said Manni. "He have Cisitalia here too. *Molto bellissimo* (very beautiful)."

In twenty minutes we arrived at the Albergo Luna Convento, a former convent balanced on the edge of a rocky promontory. Signor Barbaro, the proprietor, informed us that the Rossellini entourage would be in early next morning.

"Get me the Excelsior porter on the phone," I said to my *cicerone.* I instructed him to immediately secure a ticket on the earliest train, to notify my wife to pack all her things, and that I would meet her at Salerno.

When in the morning we entered the pergolaed garden for breakfast, Ingrid and Rossellini were already there, having come by chartered boat. Present, too, were the Cohns and Mrs. Neuwald; other members of the Stromboli coterie had returned to Rome by train from Messina.

Ingrid, dressed in a flowered peasant skirt and white blouse, shod in sandals, looked hearty and happy. Rossellini's lips curled in a satisfied smile. "Nice here, yes?" he said.

"Beautiful. I've never seen such beauty."

"That is good. I think maybe you like. We stay here three, four day for rest."

After a breakfast of figs, scrambled eggs and *prosciutto,* Ingrid showed us the small suite they occupied. Overlooking the cliff-side crescent that hugged the tiny bay, it contained mementos of Henrik Ibsen, the Norwegian dramatist who in the 1870's lived in it while he wrote *A Doll's House,* the story of Nora Helmer, who found herself squashed by the strictures of a rigid society and an overbearing husband.

"What a lovely place to write such a gloomy play," she observed.

"Have you ever thought about doing *A Doll's House?*"

"Oh, no, I wouldn't want to," she said. "Its truth is too depressing."

Then followed two days of sight-seeing, sun-bathing, swimming, and just sitting. The world could go hang. Ingrid bloomed by the minute. Gone were the tear-red eyes and the harassed look of the haunted. Rightly or wrongly, a decision had been made and with it came serenity.

One day, we strolled along the twisting roadway that hung above the rocks that held the azure sea. She stopped and pointed toward the Bay of Naples.

"See that island? That's Capri. It is so beautiful, like a comic opera stage set." She paused in meditation. "I have heard all those things they say about Roberto and his women. He has told me about them. One of them is on Capri—a German girl. He continues to send her money because she is unable to work."

Around a sharp bend we came upon the step-like remains of an ancient house, which reached twenty or thirty yards down to the lapping water. We stopped and Ingrid peered downward.

"Do you recognize this?" she said.

"Yes. It looks like the picture in *Life*—of you and Roberto."

"I thought you would know," she laughed.

The reference was to a full-page picture published in *Life* magazine in the very incipience of the Italian idyll, showing the two lovers holding hands as they climbed the mossy steps. It was this photograph, perhaps more than any other single agent, which had triggered the scandal that encircled the world.

In the morning of the following day—August 4th—further discussions were held anent the forthcoming press statement. Here and there a word was changed but the main issue centered around the "retirement" angle.

"Unless I am forced to, I wouldn't think of retiring," said Ingrid. "Why must I say so?"

"I thought you already understood why. You and Roberto own a big piece of this picture. You'll need all the American dollars you can get. But if it is boycotted in the United States, you'll get nothing. However, if they think this is your last picture such talk is sure to die down. Again, I remind you that nothing prevents your changing your mind a year from now. Sarah Bernhardt made fourteen farewell tours of the United States before she finally gave up."

"Joe is right," said Rossellini, with finality. "We do that way. Now we talk no more about it."

"Oh, all right," she said submissively. "But still I don't feel good about saying something I don't mean. And, Joe, I want you to wire Petter about the announcement as soon as you write it. He must hear it first from me."

When Rossellini telephoned Enrico Donati, in Rome, to apprise him of our coming, he was given the news that Rome papers had three days ago carried a London dateline story that Dr. Lindstrom, upon reading of Ingrid's impending announcement, had abandoned his two months' European vigil and returned to California. There, with admirable restraint, the doctor had refused to make a public statement.

"I am glad," said Ingrid. "This means that he has finally given up. And it would have been terrible if you had sent the wire to London and he wasn't there."

I immediately went to the telegraph office in Amalfi's marketplace, and sent the following cablegram to the Benedict Canyon address:

> RESPECTFULLY WISH TO INFORM YOU INGRID WILL TONIGHT MAKE THE FOLLOWING STATEMENT TO THE PRESS: QUOTE IT WAS MY DESIRE NOT TO MAKE ANY DECLARATION UNTIL THE CONCLUSION OF THE PICTURE I AM NOW MAKING. BUT PERSISTENT MALICIOUS GOSSIP, THAT HAS EVEN REACHED THE POINT WHERE I AM MADE TO APPEAR AS A PRISONER, HAS OBLIGED ME TO BREAK MY SILENCE AND DEMONSTRATE MY FREE WILL. I HAVE INSTRUCTED MY LAWYER TO INSTITUTE DIVORCE PROCEEDINGS IMMEDIATELY. ALSO, WITH THE CONCLUSION OF MY PRESENT PICTURE, IT IS MY INTENTION TO RETIRE INTO PRIVATE LIFE UNQUOTE. (signed) JOSEPH H. STEELE.

Tragically, as it turned out, Dr. Lindstrom immediately upon his return had taken Pia from the John Vernon home in San Fernando Valley, and both had vanished into some unidentified "nearby ranch." The cablegram lay undelivered in the Beverly Hills telegraph office, and Dr. Lindstrom first learned of it in the headlines.

After luncheon, Ingrid and Rossellini donned windbreakers and racing-drivers' headgear, then, settling in the Cisitalia, they streaked down the narrow road like a hotrod. The rest of us piled into the Cadillac and followed, to meet later in the two-thousand-year-old ruins of Pompeii for some sight-seeing.

Like any tourists on a holiday we wandered in the shadow of Mt. Vesuvius, whose ashes of pumice had hidden the city until a century ago. Inevitably, our hired guide led us through the bagnio district and finally to one of Pompeii's best-preserved domiciles.

Four unchaperoned American girls in their early teens were already there, piloted by another guide. Presently, their guide unlocked the only door we had seen and the girls followed him inside.

"We must wait for them to come out," said our guide, cryptically. "Room is too small."

Shortly, the young things came out tittering and fluttering, and nervously hurried away. Then we entered.

The windowless chamber was about the size of an average bathroom. To one side was a running fountain, formed of a three-foot statue of a lusty naked youth standing erect. Opposite stood a marble couch surrounded on three sides by murals of classic erotica. Awkwardly, self-consciously, we listened to the guide's mechanical spiel. Once or twice I glanced at Ingrid, but noted no reaction one way or another. The guide locked the door after us. Obviously, this was a tourist attraction to be treasured.

It was dusk when we finished a meal of *pasta* in a little restaurant outside the confines of the ruins. Leaving behind the *sans souci* allurements of Amalfi, the stark remnants and pornography of Pompeii, we raced towards the Eternal City and the eternal violences of human kinship.

As Rossellini's scarlet beetle flashed out of sight, I could still see Ingrid's regal image, incongruously encased in goggles and helmet, plunging headlong into the unknowable, irresistibly drawn by disaster. The distant rumble of thunder sounded through the moonless night as somewhere midway to Rome we approached the blinking tail lights of a car.

"*E Roberto*," said Pietro, pulling up behind the Cisitalia.

Ingrid wished to take another look at the press release. I'm sure she reread it two or three times. Gone from her countenance was the light-hearted serenity of the past several days. "Thank you," she said, soberly handing it back.

"Joe, I have a very good friend write for American papers," said Rossellini. "His name Michael Chinigo."

"Yes, I've met him."

"You take care him, yes?"

"Of course. I'm going to give the story to all the wire services."

"Tonight?"

"Soon as I can get them all together. Then all the morning papers will be able to have it at the same time."

Arriving in Rome a few minutes past ten, Ingrid and Rossellini went directly to a furnished apartment on Via Antonelli, rented for them by Donati.

A telephone call came through from Perry Lieber, publicity director of Howard Hughes' RKO Studios. I went to my room to talk.

"Louella Parsons has been running me ragged to get hold of you," he said. "For the love of Mike—and I mean Mike Chinigo—give her a break, will you?"

"He'll get the story, Perry, same as the other wires."

"I don't mean exclusive. Give her a little start, if you can. I know you're in a tough spot, but do what you can, Joe."

I phoned the American and European news services and called a press conference at 12:30 A.M. in a small room off the downstairs bar. In ten minutes, Chinigo knocked on my door.

"My chief in New York has been after me," he said, "and so has Louella Parsons. Say an hour, that's all I need."

The pressure was on and, shamefully, I succumbed.

"I'll give you half an hour, Mike, but you'll have to do it on my terms. You come to my room at 12 o'clock and I'll give you the release. But you must attend the conference at 12:30 and accept a handout along with the others."

Chinigo readily agreed. At 12:30 he entered the conference room, took his second copy of the release, perused it along with the rest of the correspondents, said "Thank you," and immediately left. His abrupt departure had no effect; they remained to dawdle with their drinks and ask further questions.

"I'm sorry, gentlemen," I said, "there is absolutely nothing else to add." Mentally I was saying, "For Lord's sake, get out and put your story on the wire. Chinigo's already beat you to it." It was ten minutes past one when they finally dispersed.

The Los Angeles *Morning Examiner*—one of the Hearst chain of papers—was on the streets with the story two hours ahead of the local *Times*. When ultimately I returned home, my very good friends, Edwin Schallert, drama editor of the *Times* and Bud Lewis, city editor, questioned me about the Hearst beat. I denied that I had given them two hours or even *one* hour. It was the wretched truth, but scarcely solace for my conscience.

In the morning, August 5th, Rossellini phoned to say that Chinigo was coming to the apartment at eleven to interview Ingrid, saying she wanted me present. Ingrid walked quietly into the antique-filled living room, holding her head high with a hint of defiance.

She had on blue Capri rope-soled shoes, a navy blue cardigan sweater and a bright red beach skirt with a vertical row of blue buttons in front. A red, white and blue sash girdled her waist. She wore no jewelry.

She greeted Chinigo, then sat in a stiff, high-backed chair. As she spoke she kept clutching and unclutching the arms of the chair. She seemed wilted and depleted.

"Now I pray my husband will give me a quick divorce," she said.

In Los Angeles the press tried to contact Dr. Lindstrom through John Vernon, but the secretary would not reveal his whereabouts. "Miss Bergman's statement was a shocking and stunning surprise for the Doctor," he said. "I, myself, feel very sad, because I never believed for a minute all the stories connecting her with the Italian director. Dr. Lindstrom does not wish to make any public statement."

Louella Parsons wrote in her column, "The most surprised man in Hollywood when Ingrid Bergman announced that she would retire from the screen was Howard Hughes. He just couldn't believe it, because their understanding (no contract actually signed) was that there would be a second Bergman-Rossellini picture to follow *Stromboli* and RKO would finance it. I have a hunch Hughes need not worry. Those wise to publicity ways believe there was a reason for the 'retirement' angle. It takes the heat off any possible bleat about banning Bergman's pictures. How can you ban somebody who is quitting?—until she should change her mind later on."

Ingrid showed me some clippings from Stockholm. "How horrible the Swedish press is! They are the worst. They say I have made such a scandal that I am a blot on the Swedish flag, so I guess if I do retire I'd better not go back to my own country."

"Ingrid, you look awfully tired. Are you all right?"

"No, I'm all right, Joe. Just run-down, that's all."

"You should see a doctor."

"I did. I went to the hospital and had a check-up. They gave me medicine and said I must rest."

The morning of August 6th I was roused by American correspondents conveying the shocking news of a Rome paper's (the *Giornale della Sera*) allegation that Ingrid was pregnant; did we have a statement to make? Vehemently denying it, I hastened to Via Antonelli. Italian libel laws are among the most stringent in the world. Even actors have been known to win suits against drama critics who have treated them too roughly. With a naïveté rather curious in a public-relations man, it never occurred to me that there might be truth in the report; this assumption was based chiefly on the premise that I was in Ingrid's confidence and if it were true she would have told me so.

"This is outrageous, Roberto. You should file suit immediately —today—scotch it before it gets out of hand."

"Yes—yes," he said, with puzzling diffidence. "I have talk with Verdozzi. He take care right away. Do not worry."

"It is terrible—just terrible," said Ingrid, her expression betraying nothing. "What next will they do?"

On the 9th, as forecast in a Louella Parsons' cablegram to me, Hedda Hopper, her then bitterest competitor, arrived on the field of battle. A former actress, of Ingrid's height, comely and stylish, acid-tongued, Miss Hopper had achieved her journalistic eminence by sheer dint of persistence. Registering at the Excelsior, she demanded an audience with Ingrid Bergman forthwith.

Panic instantly pervaded the Antonelli residence. Rossellini was dead set against the interview, and Ingrid expressed dire apprehensions of the outcome.

"I urge you to weigh this carefully," I said. "You are not in Hollywood. Hedda has flown the ocean for the sole purpose of seeing you. See her, be courteous, and she'll be sympathetic. Reject her and you'll never hear the end of it."

"But I do not see her," said Rossellini.

"She didn't ask to see you."

"Okay. I send Pietro with car—he bring you."

Riding in the Cadillac, Miss Hopper, an equal distillation of nerve and nerves, said, "Well, you've had a time of it."

"It hasn't been easy."

"What do you think of this Rossellini person?"

"Doesn't matter what I think of him. Can anybody explain why a woman falls in love with any given man?"

Pietro drove up a strange street and pulled up between two large apartment buildings. Here Enrico Donati waited. Following introductions, he said, "If you please, Miss Hopper, I will show the way."

With that, he led us down the walk that divided the two buildings, came to a crosswalk, changed direction for a few yards, then entered a long, dark passageway into the *rear* of a six-story structure. At its end we climbed a short staircase and emerged in the elevator vestibule. What machinations to thwart Miss Hopper's learning Ingrid's address!

On the fifth floor, Donati unlocked a door and showed us into —his apartment! "I will tell Miss Bergman you are here," he said.

Ingrid came into the room with hands extended and a warm greeting for the columnist. Wearing a white blouse speckled with dots of red and blue, a billowing red skirt with white vertical stripes, and stockingless feet in red slippers, she presented a sprightly picture. Red is bright and gay; it is also the color of danger.

I detected a touch of rouge on her pale lips. Ingrid was giving one of the greatest performances of her life, playing to an audience of one.

Asked about her daughter, Pia, Ingrid said, "It is only right that she should finish her education in America, but surely Petter would not want to keep her from me during summer vacation. All my husband wants is to be let alone so he can do his work, and all

I want is the same thing. But I am afraid as long as some reporters have to write stories, they will make up their own. This only makes it worse for Petter and for me."

They chatted amicably for close to an hour; then, Miss Hopper —herself the mother of a son long since grown to manhood—popped the key question.

"One more question, then I'll go, Ingrid. What's all this about you being pregnant?"

"Oh, my goodness, Hedda," Ingrid laughed lightheartedly. "Do I look it?"

One good question deserves another. Ingrid had skillfully dodged an outright denial. Her face reflected the miracle of innocence.

"That's all I wanted to know," said Miss Hopper.

On her return to the Excelsior Miss Hopper cabled a long story to her syndicate, in which she stated:

"Ingrid declares she will bring suit against the Italian papers which said she was going to have a baby. *I don't blame her; there is not a word of truth in it.*" (The italics are mine.)

A flood of mail poured in deploring Ingrid's "retirement." Of a sudden, outrage and disillusionment became subordinate to "losing a great artist."

The press habitually alluded to "their" apartment, thus metaphorically affirming the actual state of affairs. Even an ostrich would have acknowledged the *status in quo* from since before Stromboli. Yet an obstinate, dog-in-the-mangerish attitude persisted in letting it continue, defining the involvement as "a passing infatuation," waiting with open arms for the moment it had run its course. No facet of this tragic triangle was more ironic.

From Hollywood came Frank Sundstrom, a Swedish actor who had married a wealthy American divorcée. A fairly close friend of Lindstrom's, denying he had come as the doctor's envoy, he was bent on talking with Ingrid.

"She must be out of her mind," he said. "She needs to talk to someone who has no selfish motive. She must be made to understand. I cannot leave here without seeing her."

"I doubt she'll want to see you. And even if you do, you'll get nowhere."

Correctly concluding that a meeting could only result in upsetting her, Ingrid finally consented to speak with him on the telephone. The lengthy and gainless conversation apparently satisfied Sundstrom's sense of duty, for he promptly dropped the matter, and stepped into the role of tourist.

Ingrid, still a Swedish citizen, tried to file for divorce in her native land, but the technicalities were insuperable. As of record she had already applied for American naturalization; currently she was a resident of Italy; and her husband—avowedly awaiting final American citizenship papers—was six thousand miles away from Stockholm.

The mystic maze of these complications, plus the uncertainties of his Austrian annulment, brought Rossellini into querulous conflict with attorney Verdozzi. What if the situation was messy—what were lawyers for, anyhow?

Hardly a week went by that Rossellini didn't purchase Ingrid some expensive trinket. "A woman in her position have no jewelry!" he declared. "It is disgrace. Never Lindstrom give her a ring—nothing!"

For the first time since I had known her Ingrid regularly appeared wearing a jewel in one shape or another: a pearl necklace, pearl earrings, gold bracelets, an emerald-and-diamond ring. She wore them proudly and happily.

How Rossellini managed these romantic luxuries posed a mystery, for he was currently hard put to it for money. Our business arrangement included the payment of living expenses, yet the Excelsior exchequer was perpetually compelled to hound him about his bills. His resourcefulness, however, was a wonder to behold. Owning certain European release rights in his films, he would restore solvency by selling the French rights, the German, and so on. And because *Stromboli* was generally deemed a gold mine, he had no difficulty in cashing in sizable hunks of his Italian rights.

One day, to the joy of Harold Lewis and RKO Studios, he decided to resume shooting. Having secured special permission from the government, he moved personnel and equipment to Farfa Sabina, a displaced-persons camp about fifty miles from Rome. Farfa, which once housed more than 3000 men and women of many nationalities, now billeted about 500 women.

These inmates remained in the stockade because they were unwanted and unemployable, the pitiful, melancholy residue of war. The camp consisted of several rows of unpainted, one-story huts, each housing fifty or sixty women. Bare floors were crowded with army cots, the walls festooned with magazine cutouts. A high steel fence enclosed the barren, drab area. Pervading everything here was a stench that hung over all like a tent.

The filming at Farfa was entirely restricted to night work, using naturalistic light only. The finished scenes offered no visual justification for dragging Ingrid or anyone else out there for eleven nights of all-night shooting. The only thing about Farfa which could not have been more sensibly duplicated on a studio stage, or in the environs of Rome, was the camp's distinctive odor.

On August 22nd the shooting ended at Farfa Sabina, and *Stromboli* was at long last completed except for redubbing of unintelligible dialogue.

Presently, two members of our family group bade Rome goodbye, to return to the United States. The first was Renzo Cesana, actor-writer and *savoir faire* personified.

"Joe, I have something big coming up in television," he said. "When you get back I'd like to talk to you about handling my publicity."

"Thanks very much, but I have other plans."

The second to leave was Ellen Neuwald.

Under Capricorn, Ingrid's Alfred Hitchcock picture, had been released to theaters in May. Now the first reports of its public reception trickled in from Hollywood—another Bergman failure. Hollywood nurtures a superstition that everything happens in threes. Here it was *Arch of Triumph*, *Joan of Arc*, and now the cryptic third, *Under Capricorn*.

The news distressed Ingrid, not because of herself or the profits she would never draw, but because of others whose money and careers were inextricably involved. Inescapable was her feeling of guilt that the failure of these pictures, whose combined cost was more than eleven million dollars, was due to the scandal and not to their quality.

On August 29th she celebrated her thirty-fourth birthday at Nino's Restaurant, favorite hangout of Rossellini and the local movie colony. He presented her with a diamond scorpion brooch, but the occasion was strained. Conversation lagged, and what gayety there was, was hollow and forced. Palpably, there wasn't much to cheer about.

Ingrid had little to say, but once she leaned close to me and said, "This is where Roberto and Magnani would always come. He told me how they used to fight all the time; people out on the street could hear them." Then she chuckled quietly at the mental picture.

Dubbing dialogue for a motion picture is a tedious undertaking. A clip of film containing three or four lines of dialogue is glued at the ends into what is called a "loop." This loop is then projected onto a screen while the actor, wearing earphones, watches the action and listens to the articulated timing. The loop is run over and over again until the actor feels ready to record the fresh sound track. When he is ready the original sound is turned off and the actor—speaking into a microphone—dubs the new dialogue. The whole process requires the utmost patience and concentration.

The contract with Howard Hughes stipulated that the picture would be edited and dubbed at RKO Studios, but under the existing unforeseen circumstances this now was out of the question. Having no screenplay to go by, the studio was hard put to piece together the filmic jigsaw.

Howard Hughes offered them a private plane if they would come to Hollywood and finish their work, but Rossellini rejected it and immediately commenced dubbing in a Rome studio.

Throughout this normally arduous work Ingrid looked ill and said she "had a bad cold." Much of the time she had a fever, and a doctor was often in attendance.

September came, but still no word from Lindstrom, no move in the direction of a divorce. A Damoclean burden hung over Ingrid, and Rossellini became increasingly solicitous, fondling her hand, stroking her head, kissing her cheeks. It was thought a trip away from the city would be a palliative and Florence was agreed upon. But at the last minute Rossellini changed his mind, leaving my wife and me to make the trip without them. On our return it was apparent that Ingrid's condition was worsened. Like me, my wife suspected nothing. It was as if Ingrid had survived the knowledge of evil and emerged sharp and clear and clean, leaving no telltale trace.

I wrote an article for an American magazine in which I said, "A Rossellini was inevitable. Nothing could have altered the course of Ingrid's destiny. And if there is any blame to be heaped upon anyone (blame for what?) it cannot, in all justice, be placed upon the shoulders of Ingrid Bergman, nor of Roberto Rossellini, nor of Dr. Peter A. Lindstrom. This could have happened three years ago, before a Rossellini appeared on the scene; it would have happened a year from now, Rossellini or no Rossellini."

Ingrid read and approved the story. "You should have been here when Roberto read it," she laughed. "When he came to where you say 'A Rossellini was inevitable' he said, 'What does he mean? What Rossellini? There is only one Rossellini!' "

Having completed his assignment, writer Art Cohn and his wife, Marta, made ready to depart for Hollywood. Ingrid went shopping on smart and expensive Via Condotti, purchasing pretties for Marta to take back with her to Pia—hand-embroidered linen dresses, a Tyrolean sweater, a dainty child's wristwatch, and a large stuffed monkey, because "I always called her 'my little monkey.' "

Ingrid's sister-in-law, Karaste Anna-Britta, had written her several times from Stöde, Sweden; sympathetic letters of counsel and caution. Ingrid, hardly knowing how to answer them, finally decided to present her side. From her handwritten Swedish she read her reply to me, translating into English as she went along. This is the letter as closely as I can remember it—dated September 3, 1949:

Dearest Anna-Britta:

If I suddenly woke up and found myself in Beverly Hills, and I had only dreamed these months of tears and scandal, I would probably continue as before. Petter and Pia are constantly in my mind, but at the same time I tell myself that it is impossible for me to go back. Petter is a good man and a settled man, I know that well, but I am a *flyttfågel* [bird of passage]. Ever since I was a little girl I have hungered for something new, something different. Much as I saw and experienced, it was never enough. I tried very hard to get through the daily *tristesse*, looking for happiness and satisfaction. But I didn't understand what kind of happiness and peace I wanted.

I was constantly searching, searching for new roles to play, new people to work with, people who could help me towards my need of fulfillment. That was my goal—fulfillment. Perhaps I came closest to my goal with *Joan of Lorraine* on the stage.

At home with Petter everything was all right. During the years when we were separated while he was studying to be a doctor, I longed for a home with a pool and everything, like other stars have. Finally, we got a home, fixed it up the way we wanted, then the *flyttfågel* began to spread its wings again. I should have been satisfied with all that I had, but, instead, I began to feel everything closing in on me. I knew so few people and saw so little of the world, that I felt as if I could not develop any further.

Then I started to travel on War Bond tours, entertained soldiers, and visited military hospitals. I was very happy doing that, although the work was hard. Petter knew how restless my soul was. He tried to help me, gave me freedom to go to New York whenever I wanted, and tried not to burden me with all the business problems. After *Joan of Lorraine* I told Petter how happy I had been during the past year. I said I wanted another child, thinking that would cure my restlessness.

Then I met Roberto Rossellini and in him I found another *flyttfågel*. He had a great curiosity about life and people and the world, and tried to make the most of his own life. He has seen much and knows the good and bad sides of life, because he has lived them both—poverty and riches, hunger and luxury. He has deep understanding, broad knowledge, immense sympathy, and a great generosity toward his fellowman.

Roberto had a rich father who was probably too kind and easy, giving him anything he wanted. He grew up doing anything he felt like doing. He was wild and temperamental, and never satisfied with what he had or with what he was accomplishing.

You mention his women. I don't know what you have heard or read in the Swedish press, but I guess most of it is not exaggerated. But now he has met someone who, in spite of her totally different background, understands him, maybe because I see in him a reflection of my true self. If this is my true self. Anyway, right now I feel as if I have found what I have been inarticulately searching for for a long time.

How do I know, dear Anna-Britta, if this is the real happiness? I understand well that I have taken the big step. But who knows the end?

I am sad about Petter, but the truth is that far inside of us we had grown apart. Still, we have happy memories. Petter took me as a young girl and taught me much, but I hunger for more life, and Petter does not fly where I want to fly. Petter with his hardheadedness, uprightness, and stubbornness cannot understand it. I guess nobody really understands. But I hope that you understand one thing, that I will never hate Petter. If I hate anyone, it is myself, who has ruined a home and made a worldwide scandal.

To appease my bad conscience I keep telling myself: Petter is better off without me, without being the husband of a movie star and living in Hollywood. Now he is on his own, with a great career ahead of him. He has always wisely said that work is the most important thing to a person, and comes first in life.

You worry about Pia, but I am sure that when she gets over the first shock, she will grow up into a stronger, richer woman. Life in Hollywood is not good for a child, where they have everything, and only have friends who have everything. Now she can go to a school with normal children, in normal circumstances, and she can come to see me and see what life is like in other parts of the world. Maybe, one day, she can go to school in Switzerland. By seeing different sides of the world she will get a wider view and understand more.

With all my heart, I embrace you.

Ingrid.

The demoralizing inaction and silence from Beverly Hills determined Rossellini and Ingrid to send a legal deputy to California in an effort to resolve the impasse. Attorney Verdozzi was resought for counsel, and upon his recommendation they employed an American lawyer named Monroe MacDonald, who had served in the Judge Advocate's division of the American occupation forces.

Around forty years of age, of average build and appearance, MacDonald was well versed in Italian, had an Italian wife, and had settled to practice in Rome. With enthusiasm he grabbed the opportunity to play an important role in the *cause célèbre*. On the surface, MacDonald seemed like an ideal choice for the delicate mission.

MacDonald's function, it was understood, was to go directly to Beverly Hills, select a lawyer of repute and one experienced in similar matters, engage his services, and remain only long enough to effect an amicable agreement with Dr. Lindstrom regarding the divorce and a property settlement in which Ingrid stipulated that her share be placed in trust for Pia.

Since the young lawyer was entering the case in total ignorance of its complex background, Ingrid reasoned that he should be thoroughly briefed and armed for his talks with Lindstrom and the as yet unnamed California lawyer. After introducing me to MacDonald and acquainting me with the new strategy, Ingrid showed me a typewritten account she had drafted for his private and confidential edification, which I took back to my hotel and copied.

A candid self-revelation, the document ran more than three thousand words. A composite of biography, credo and confession, it began: "I was born on August 29, 1915," and told of her mother's death, her father's death, about Aunt Ellen, and the uncle who assumed her charge.

She told of her school days, her shyness and awkwardness, of play-acting in private and dreams of becoming an actress; of dramatic school, and how Peter Lindstrom came into her life; of their marriage and the birth of a daughter, and of going to Hollywood.

When it came to telling of her life with Lindstrom in Hollywood, a sudden note of restraint entered her narrative. As always, she was reluctant to say anything against him.

Ingrid wrote of her husband's conduct of her business, how he was regarded as "too hard" and "too difficult." But he was "too smart for them," she said. "He was just and demanding and very stubborn. I wanted to be free from big studios and was glad when my contract ended, though I regretted to leave with hatred behind me, because it (the Selznick studio) was my 'mother' studio in America."

She related how Lindstrom "worked like a madman" at the hospital, at the same time persisting in "taking care of my business matters"; of his reluctance to let her agent function, or to let her attorney act freely; that many of her friends were alienated "because of these business dealings." She told of her embarrassments and resentments; her gradual submission and withdrawal, and of finding a modicum of peace in her work.

"Four and a half years ago," she said, "I started to go overseas to entertain soldiers. This was my husband's idea. I was far too shy to be with so many men, and I had no idea how to entertain them. But a program was finally worked out and I left for Alaska. There I discovered that I was not so helpless as I was in my own home, that I could express myself freely and people would listen. No doubt, I sometimes said the wrong things, but so did many others."

She told of going alone to parties when Lindstrom was detained at the hospital, of her pleasure in these occasions. But in the same breath she pointed out that in the beginning it was not easy for him to mingle with the movie set: "In Hollywood nobody is anybody who isn't in the business and Petter didn't enjoy his position as Mr. Bergman. But after some years he had many friends, too, and he was gay and loved to dance."

She said her husband knew that she enjoyed the company of other men, but paid little attention to it, knowing they were fleeting enthusiasms. "Deep down in my heart I was still the wife of Petter, and he knew it. He often said no man ever gave his wife more freedom. That is true, but I was always free *away* from him and not *with* him."

She told of her eight months on Broadway in *Joan of Lorraine*, and three months in London, for *Under Capricorn*, and how little she saw of him; of how during these last years she became "even more restless and difficult," that her work had soured, and she had become "bored with the ways of Hollywood."

Presently, she found herself "bored with my home. I felt as if it was the end of growing. I was searching for something, I knew not what." She wanted to travel, but after the war there were no more trips. She longed to meet new people—"artists with the same desire to accomplish something, to live to the utmost." Peter Lindstrom's occupation and circle of medical friends presented no easy solution to the dysphoria that enveloped her. Skiing at Sun Valley, Idaho, or at Aspen, Colorado, was the extent of their trips and vacations. "When I felt like traveling all over the world," she said, "it was in freedom I wanted to go."

She wrote of the corrosive feeling of guilt for not being satisfied with all that she had. "I kept working. Despite not being in on the business side its difficulties came through to me. The independent pictures I made were made under very trying conditions. And they turned out mediocre. Maybe the biggest blow to me was *Joan of Arc*, which I loved more than anything."

She had hoped her interest and enthusiasm would be revitalized by *Under Capricorn*, that it would turn out "different and better," and that during the making of it she was happy to be back in Europe again.

She wrote of her excitement at the prospect of doing her next picture in Italy. "I had seen *Open City* and *Paisan* and admired their boldness, integrity, artistry and newness. When I wrote Mr. Rossellini it was with my husband's permission, because he understood my desire to do new, different things. I was excited like a school girl in love, my husband said. And so I met Mr. Rossellini."

Thus ended Ingrid Bergman's confessional.

During this period there ensued a comparative lull in newspaper stories. They seemed to have exhausted every possible angle, and Ingrid hoped the waning hullabaloo would lessen her husband's resistance. Since MacDonald's identity was unknown in the United States it was logically presumed that Lindstrom and lawyers could meet and negotiate without the glare of prejudicial publicity. Aware of all this and with the clear understanding that Ingrid's epistle was solely for his eyes, MacDonald took off for America.

That afternoon Ingrid gave me a message to cable to Ruth Roberts, "Please send Pia on September 20 [her 11th birthday] from Hahn's [a florist] a bouquet of small flowers, signed, from Mama, Love to you."

On Pia's birthday, ostensibly en route to California, Monroe MacDonald arrived in New York and inexplicably decided to stay overnight. He must have slept fitfully, impatient for the glories that morning would bring.

The sun had hardly pierced the morning fog when screeching headlines in red ink shattered Ingrid's prayers for an early and peaceful settlement—

NOW, FOR THE FIRST TIME!
INGRID'S REAL LOVE STORY!

The New York *Journal-American* and all the other Hearst papers from coast to coast blared and bared the confidences placed in MacDonald's trust. By a curious coincidence, Cholly Knickerbocker, who in April was the first to print the romance, had another scoop.

"Ingrid is determined to secure a divorce from her husband, Dr. Peter Lindstrom," he wrote, "and she will not return to America until she is Mrs. Rossellini.

"This I learned yesterday exclusively from her friend and

attorney, Monroe E. MacDonald, who just landed in New York from Rome with full power of attorney from Bergman and Rossellini to negotiate with Dr. Lindstrom for Ingrid's freedom and to present before the American public the real facts behind this great love story.

" 'Her first and last words before I left,' said MacDonald, 'were, "Don't do anything to hurt Peter." '

"So far, however, MacDonald points out, it is Ingrid Bergman and Roberto Rossellini who have been hurt."

The society columnist then cited at length those intimate items which could only have been obtained by someone given access to Ingrid's confidential memorandum to MacDonald: that "the doctor dominated her completely ... many years her senior ... never let her make a decision by herself ... felt so guilty for not being satisfied with all that she had ... in Hollywood she felt stifled ..."

Knickerbocker then launched into matters known only to the tightly knit clique which surrounded her in Italy, matters which he could only have secured from a source exceedingly close to Ingrid.

He said that Ingrid had been a faithful and devoted wife since her marriage ... that "Lindstrom controlled all the money, although his salary as a resident surgeon was only eighty dollars a month" ... that "Ingrid never owned a single piece of jewelry except her wedding ring since they were married" ... that "when she left for Europe last March he gave her three hundred dollars, and that's all she has received from home since" ... that "from the first he impressed his powerful, domineering personality on her" ... that "Ingrid's love for Dr. Lindstrom was more that of a daughter for her father than that of a grown woman in love with her husband" ... that she had asked for a divorce three years ago, "but Dr. Lindstrom cried, said he had sacrificed everything for her, and Ingrid gave in ..."

Knickerbocker went on to further quote from MacDonald: Rossellini was the first man Ingrid had ever been really in love with, but that Lindstrom refused to accept the fact of a divorce ... that a violent scene occurred during the Messina meeting in which "Dr. Lindstrom insulted Rossellini, telling him he had stolen his wife"

... that Lindstrom "finally made Ingrid sign a statement in which she promised that she would not discuss her divorce plans until after she had completed her picture and returned to America"... that Ingrid was in a state of near collapse then, and says "she doesn't even remember what the document said, and that she would have signed anything just not to have a scene"... that "even today she is deathly afraid of what her husband might do"... that she would never return to America "because she is too afraid that she would fall under her husband's influence again..."

This, then, was the dynamite that exploded in Ingrid's face and churned the quieting waters.

"Who told him these things?" raged Ingrid. "Who? Here I've been doing my best not to say anything to hurt Petter, and now all these terrible things are said." She waved her clenched fists. "Who said these things? Who? Who? Who?"

Rossellini, curiously undisturbed by the uproar, spoke soothingly, and said he would subdue the impetuous envoy. He called MacDonald by radiophone and talked at length in Italian. At the end, he reported that the lawyer had decided on the Knickerbocker interview in good faith, thinking that "it would put the fear of God in Lindstrom," and that henceforth he would refrain from further contacts with the press.

Every newspaper in both hemispheres carried the story. And if Lindstrom retreated farther into the manger, who could have blamed him?

As Ingrid smoldered over this, MacDonald landed in Hollywood and presently announced the appointment of lawyer Gregson Bautzer as her and Rossellini's attorney in California.

Neither Ingrid nor I had ever met Bautzer. We knew of him only by reputation. His clients numbered Louella Parsons, Howard Hughes, producers, directors, and many of the biggest stars in the film industry. Owing to these newsworthy connections Bautzer was one of the most publicized lawyers in the West. Also, he was well known as the escort of such famous actresses as Joan Crawford, Lana Turner, Ginger Rogers, Mari Blanchard, and others.

On the face of it Bautzer appeared to be the antithesis of the type of lawyer Ingrid had discussed with MacDonald; indeed, she had even said she preferred someone who was in no way connected with the motion-picture business. The appointment of Bautzer further aggravated Ingrid's feeling of futility with regard to a decisive conclusion of the domestic muddle.

From Beverly Hills, however, MacDonald continued to issue statements: "Ingrid Bergman is prepared to offer Dr. Lindstrom half of their community property, the remaining half to be put in trust for the use and benefit of their daughter, Pia . . . she will also ask for part-time custody of her daughter . . . she is even willing for the doctor to go to Reno (Nevada) to obtain the divorce . . . This is no sudden decision. He was informed by letter on March 30. He is adamant in refusing to believe this is any more than a wild infatuation. He replied and said, 'When you are over this nonsense, come home' . . . Mr. Rossellini has authorized me to say that he wants absolutely no property from Ingrid Bergman. Said Mr. Rossellini, 'I have never yet lived by any woman's earnings and I do not intend to start now . . .' "

More MacDonald quotations were front-paged. "Miss Bergman has absolutely no idea of what community property there is. She never wrote a check. All money went to the doctor, who completely dominated her . . . Miss Bergman has done everything to avoid bitterness, but she was deeply hurt when Dr. Lindstrom tried to send a psychiatrist to examine her. Naturally, she refused because it wasn't Rossellini's influence that caused her to fall in love, nor was she sick . . ."

To one reporter MacDonald said that he hoped to reach an amicable settlement with the doctor, "However, I am fully prepared to take off the gloves, if necessary."

Attorney Mendel Silverberg, who had for several years been the family lawyer, felt that he could not honestly sever his loyalty and fondness from one litigant in order to defend the other. Advising Lindstrom to get another attorney to represent him in the impending dispute, Silverberg said, "I don't know what Dr. Lindstrom intends to do at this time. I do know that since the doctor has committed no offense against his marriage, if he refuses to allow Miss Bergman to get a divorce, there is no way in the world that she can get one."

Ingrid's offer to divide the community property, and give her share to Pia, was unconscionably twisted by some newspapers into melodramatic headlines:

INGRID OFFERS HER FORTUNE
AS DIVORCE LOVE SACRIFICE

Ingrid could stomach no more; she demanded of Rossellini that he put a stop to the mounting clamor.

Unable to reach Dr. Lindstrom for a statement, newspapers contacted John Vernon. Said the doctor's spokesman, "This method of offering Dr. Lindstrom a 'fortune' in exchange for his wife places him in a position for refusing a divorce on this point alone. I do not think he would ever consider 'selling' his wife."

Asked about Ingrid's attitude toward Pia, Vernon said, "I firmly believe that she became too deeply involved in romantic and professional problems before she realized her daughter is in a most unhappy situation. However, now that Pia knows of her mother's decision, she is accepting her fate with sadness but with reality. I believe that Miss Bergman will try her best to make amends to the child."

Simultaneously, Vernon announced his resignation as Dr. Lindstrom's secretary, giving no reason for doing so.

On hearing of Vernon's exit, Ingrid wrote Ruth Roberts, "It is too bad about John Vernon . . . I'm sorry about all this trouble . . . Now that he is gone, please, Ruth, I hope you can find time to visit with Pia, and take her out, do what you can . . ."

Piling one on top of another, the agonizing events took their toll. The seeming standstill between lawyers and Lindstrom rankled deep in the core of her heart. Ingrid's eyes bespoke of tears and sleepless nights.

Her "cold" persisted and she looked palpably unwell. Lawyers paraded in and out of the apartment, voluminous cables were dispatched daily, and Ingrid seldom ventured outdoors.

Rossellini grew less and less communicative, receiving my inquiries with monosyllables and a faraway look. Slowly I became imbued with a feeling that I was deliberately being left out of things. It troubled and perplexed me, but neither my wife nor I could wholly penetrate the situation.

My hotel bills fell behind as much as two or three weeks. And despite Rossellini's proprietary attitude towards the Excelsior, the cashier treated the delinquency as any other defaulter. "Aahh," Rossellini would shrug, "I take care." And lost little Alberto Manni moped in and out of the lobby, bereft of his former bounce and ebullience.

As October neared its end, I found myself being discouraged—on one pretext or another—from coming to the residence on Via Antonelli. It even became difficult to get Ingrid on the phone. "She is sleeping" was the recurrent answer from Rossellini or his sister, Marcella.

Contemplating these unaccountable circumstances, I wondered what the purpose of my presence in Rome was as of now. Indeed, as I reflected on the events of the past five months, beginning with Sicily, it seemed that I had accomplished nothing of real value. The runaway situation was beyond any influence. My dubious usefulness had run out.

In their somber living room one evening, Ingrid and Rossellini sat across from me on a high-backed medieval sofa. "There doesn't seem to be anything more I can do here," I said. "I think I should go home. I'll meet Greg Bautzer and see what help I can be there."

"I understand," said Rossellini quickly, evidently welcoming the decision.

"But why must you go right away?" said Ingrid, with undisguised concern.

"Well, it's not exactly 'right away,' Ingrid. I've been here five months. From now on, whatever remains to be done is up to your lawyers."

Then we talked for thirty or forty minutes, during which Rossellini never once left her side—caressing her solicitously, brushing her cheek with his, whispering inaudible tendernesses. She gave me verbal messages to take back to Ruth Roberts, Cary Grant, and Alfred Hitchcock—"and tell Ruth to forgive me for not writing."

The blue of her eyes had faded, her lips were colorless. Her pale cheeks sagged, and her voice issued in a tremulous murmur. She looked haggard and sick—and stranded.

"Will you take back some things for Pia?" said Ingrid. "I'll get them this afternoon."

"Of course. There's plenty of time. We were planning on leaving day after tomorrow."

Doing some last-minute shopping of our own, my wife and I ran into Ingrid as she came out of a store on the Piazza di Spagna. "Oh, my goodness!" she laughed brightly. "Isn't this nice! I'm all finished for Pia, now I wanted to get something for myself. Why don't you come with me?"

In the chill of the late afternoon she was hatless and wore a light wrap-around coat of a dark beige fabric. Her slippers were black. She stepped along energetically, dodged a motorcyclist, and crossed over to Via Condotti. Glancing at the window displays as she walked, she suddenly stopped short, took my wife by the hand, drew her back a couple of shops, and paused before an array of infants' wear.

"Look, Beatrice. Aren't they sweet?" she said. "They make such pretty things . . ."

One by one, she pointed out the different items, from baby bonnets to an exquisite christening dress, each article evoking exclamations.

Farther down Rome's main shopping street, Ingrid led us inside a shop dealing in sundry merchandise. "They have so many interesting things," she said, indicating baskets, ceramics, leather goods, and racks of multicolored fabrics. "It is all handmade. Aren't they lovely?"

Greeted like an old customer, she asked to be shown some scarves. Her eyes caught a striking hand-loomed stole of fine wool, black with gold and purple metallic stripes running across its ends. She draped it over her shoulders, observed the effect in the mirror, then said, "How do you like it?"

"Oh, my, that's very handsome," my wife said.

"Oh, I don't know," Ingrid said doubtfully. "Try it on and let me see how it looks on you." She looked at my wife as she modeled the stole, then said, "Maybe you're right. I'll take it."

We walked back with Ingrid to the Piazza, where Pietro waited for her with the Cadillac. Mindful that we were taking off for California at midnight of the next day, she said, "I want you to come for dinner tomorrow night. There will be just the four of us."

The farewell gathering devolved into a self-conscious tableau. Conversation was sporadic, strained, and forced. No one said what he wanted to say. Eyes evaded eyes. Rossellini barely uttered a sound. Beatrice also fell under the spell of the circumscribed atmosphere. Once in a while Ingrid and I ventured a word.

"I don't imagine Petter will let you see Pia," she said.

"It's doubtful."

"But if you do, please write me right away and tell me how she is."

"I will." Then an interval of silence; then I made a try. "We're going to stop over in Paris for a couple of days."

"Oh, I'm glad," she said. "It would be a pity to come to Europe and not visit Paris. Such a beautiful city. I love Paris."

It was a relief when dinner was over and we retired to the cheerless living room. We sipped an Italian liqueur with *espresso* coffee and again groped for things to say. Then suddenly there was a knock on the door. Rossellini instantly leaped up and opened it. Donati, Marcella, lawyer Verdozzi, and a Miss Liana Ferri, said to be a writer—all obviously invited—were volubly welcomed by the host.

I glanced at Ingrid's downcast face. "I didn't know they were coming," she said in a hushed tone.

The new arrivals promptly exchanged greetings in high spirits, as if the occasion were a celebration. Rossellini now became talkative. I gazed at Ingrid's drooping figure as she receded into the background.

After a few minutes of this, Ingrid gave a meaningful nod and went into an anteroom. I followed. She turned and started to speak when Rossellini stepped in.

"You want talk with Joe by himself?" he said sternly.

"Yes!" she flared. "Why did you have to invite all those people?"

"You cannot do this while you have guests," he said evenly, then stepped aside to indicate our retreat. Ingrid lifted her chin and strode back into the now quieted living room.

"Here are the things for Pia," said Ingrid, opening a flat cardboard box. In it were a crocheted red-and-blue bonnet, a white sweater with tiny red and green figures, three or four embroidered linen dresses, and a pair of handknit bedroom slippers. On top lay a sealed envelope with a note for her daughter.

"I hope it isn't too big for your luggage," she said.

"No. It'll fit just fine."

"And, oh, Beatrice, I almost forgot," she said. "Here's something for you to remember Rome by." It was the black stole with gold and purple stripes.

"As if I needed something to remember it by," said my wife, as they embraced.

Rossellini's lips curled in the kind of enigmatic smile Da Vinci painted so well. The muted group shifted uneasily. The air was leaden with anguish. I rose, picked up the box for Pia, and started for the door. "Well, I guess we better push off." Ingrid got up and walked with me.

"I will take you back to the hotel," said Rossellini, as he, too, joined us. "Pietro will come for you ten o'clock to take you to Ciampino."

At the door Ingrid and I faced each other and for an eternal moment said nothing. What was it that she had wanted to say to me? Her lips quivered from whatever it was that she would say. Then impulsively she threw her arms around me and cried. We both cried.

Neither of us said good-bye.

11.

Three Cities

BEVERLY HILLS

IN the fall of 1948, while engaged in some medical research, Dr. Lindstrom chanced across an account of one Dr. Peter Weger, a Czechoslovakian discovered in a Nazi concentration camp. Profoundly affected by the story, he told Ingrid about it, then enlisted the aid of friends and colleagues, prevailed upon the Bureau of Immigration, provided the necessary funds, and had Weger brought to Beverly Hills. Until such time as he had established himself in the new land, Weger was made a house guest and lived in the small comfortable apartment over the garage. Of less than medium height, slight in build, smooth-shaven, Dr. Weger was gentle-mannered, unassuming, and basically good-humored.

On November 3rd, two days after my return from Rome, I mailed Ingrid a lengthy report, which contained the following items:

"I got Peter's new phone number from Ruth and called him. Pia answered the phone but, of course, didn't recognize my voice. I asked for Dr. Lindstrom and he answered. He was surprisingly cordial. I told him I had a package from you for Pia, and asked whether I might bring it over. He said that I could. I went over immediately and found him in his shirtsleeves working in the garden with Dr. Weger. He came forward, smiling amiably, unlocked the gate and admitted me. He never ceased smiling, giving me the impression that he was determined not to let me know what he was thinking. He looks well and in the pink of health, despite how he might have looked in London. No mistake about it, he appears as robust as he ever did.

"We stood on the lawn, Peter smiling, the pretty box under my arm, Weger staring at me. Our conversation was conspicuously forced. I said I was glad to see him looking so well. He was glad I looked well; how was my trip? how was my family? etc., etc. Then I tried to break the ice. I said to Weger, 'The last time I saw you you were working in the garden. Do you get paid for this?' Without an inkling of humor, he said, 'No, I just live in the guesthouse.' I said, 'I think I'll report you to the gardeners' union.' But Weger ignored my feeble effort to ease the tension, and suddenly blurted out, 'Yes, I live in the guesthouse. I live there for a long time and I see many things. When the time comes I shall testify to what I saw!'

"Peter instantly lost his composure and, pushing him aside, said, 'Now—now! That's enough!'

" 'Well, Peter,' I said, 'I just wanted to deliver this for Ingrid.' He took the package and rested it against the stonewall, then stood there silently, waiting for me to make the next move. It was now obvious that he was not going to call Pia out or let me see her. I thanked him for letting me deliver the package, and left . . .

"The next day I delivered the blouse and shawl to Ruth, which pleased her very much. I mentioned my experience with Peter, and she told me that she saw Pia after she got the clothes, that Pia was overjoyed, and that they fitted her perfectly. Ruth said, too, that Pia was in fine health, growing rapidly, and loving her role as lady of the house. She sits at the head of the table and play-acts at being grown-up.

"Because Mendel Silverberg is unwilling to take sides between you and Peter, it seems that Peter has engaged a New York attorney named Lawrence Brinn, who represents monasteries and sundry Catholic organizations. In particular, Brinn is said to be an authority on international divorce laws.

"Several papers have called to ask why Peter 'hired' a New York lawyer? Of course, I didn't know the answer. However, Sheilah

Graham got on the air and expounded her own theory: 'Lindstrom will file suit for divorce in New York, where the only ground for divorce is infidelity.' Then Hedda called and posed the same question, but I said, 'How can he bring suit there since he is not a resident of New York?' Which seemed to give her pause. In any case, she's made no comment in her column.

"That splendid gentleman, Silverberg, received me very cordially and spoke frankly. He reiterated his determination not to get in the middle of any controversy between you and Peter. 'I'm too fond of Ingrid to do that,' he said. A little angrily I brought up the matter of your need for cash and why wasn't a reasonable amount being transmitted to you. He said, 'Now don't take it out on me. That is the situation with Peter. He won't release one penny unless it goes into litigation in court. And that will take weeks.'

"Mendel then remarked that matters had been progressing nicely, with Peter prepared to yield without making too much trouble—until Cholly Knickerbocker broke his big story from New York, whereupon Peter promptly froze up.

"... On the more cheerful side, the feeling at RKO is very excellent about the picture. As to the general feeling about you, personally, it is imbued with a sincere wish that your tribulations are settled peaceably and swiftly, and that all is forgiven if only you will not quit the screen. Including the press, the general reaction is: 'There is still only one Bergman.' ... *a rivederci* ..."

I called attorney Gregson (Greg) Bautzer and made an appointment. A weatherproof figure, over six feet, athletic in bearing, a mite too well tailored, he presented a far more impressive personality than the glamor boys he represented. Brown, curly hair clung close to his head, and his skin was dark from plenty of sun. In his middle forties, and unmarried, he naturally was the target of just about every predatory female in Hollywood. He spoke in a modulated baritone invested with quiet authority.

"When I heard you were back I hoped we could get together," he said.

"Thank you. Please forgive me, but I feel I must be very frank with you. Ingrid and I knew of you only by what we read in the columns—that you were dating this or that star, at some party or nightclub. She emphasized to MacDonald that he find a lawyer of dignity and standing, preferably an older man—someone not connected with the picture business. MacDonald himself never suggested anyone or indicated whom he had in mind. I think you should know that Ingrid was bitterly disappointed when he settled on you."

Bautzer received it gracefully, in no wise bristling or betraying resentment. "I appreciate your frankness," he said. "I'm sorry Ingrid feels that way, but I can understand it. I wish I could stop this kind of publicity, but what can I do? If I went to some out-of-the-way places the columnists would make even more out of it. The only alternative would be to stay home and not go out at all.

"And that wouldn't be fair, Joe. I've worked hard all my life. I worked my way through S.C. (University of Southern California) doing all kinds of mean jobs. I'd hate to tell you some of the things I had to do. Then when I started out on my own the going wasn't too easy. I don't mean to say I had it tougher than a lot of other men. It's not that. It's just that I feel I'm now entitled to have a little fun. What's wrong with that?"

"Nothing. Now let's drop all that and talk about the main subject. Ingrid's anxious to hear from me and I want to make as comprehensive a report as possible."

"It's a relief to be able to talk about it openly," he said. "I had had no previous correspondence with MacDonald. Not even a phone call or a wire. He called the office one day and made an appointment; that was the first I knew of him. It was the most unorthodox arrangement I ever got into. He said Miss Bergman was prepared to get a divorce in a foreign country, whether Dr. Lindstrom agreed to it or not. I told him that a foreign divorce without the doctor's cooperation wouldn't be recognized in this country, but MacDonald said it didn't matter; she was never coming back here anyhow.

"I asked him about her little girl. He said she was so determined on a quick divorce that she would relinquish her rights to Pia. I said this was shocking and highly damaging. Does she realize the effect this would have on her future—a year from now—five years—ten years from now? He said it was too bad but that's the way it was. It was hard for me to believe.

"We had a meeting with Mendel Silverberg and MacDonald repeated all this in his presence—here in this office. We pointed out to him that this matter should be settled quietly, out of court. If it went into litigation a public hearing could well wreck Miss Bergman's career, and Lindstrom's, and possibly ruin Pia's life. But he was for tearing the roof down—if Dr. Lindstrom refused to come to an immediate agreement, they were going to blast the case wide open.

"Mendel told him that Dr. Lindstrom was on the verge of giving in when MacDonald's statement from New York stirred the whole mess up again. After that the doctor sat back and decided to wait it out.

"MacDonald gave me to understand that I was to deal only through him. He was my only contact. I've had no correspondence with Miss Bergman or Rossellini; I don't even have their address. I have no idea how much Miss Bergman knows about the true situation as it exists here. And certainly, my only impression of her attitude is what MacDonald chose to tell me.

"Dr. Lindstrom is still waiting it out, and I'm making no headway."

Igor Cassini wrote in the Los Angeles *Examiner*, "Though everyone from the humble gent who rents out rowboats on the volcanic isle of Stromboli to the Hollywood hierarchy have been discussing l'affair Rossellini-Bergman, they haven't even scratched the surface. A most intimate pal of this gr-r-reat romance informs the column that right now there is more eruption to it than meets the eye or ear."

I dispatched a report to Rome of my meeting with Bautzer, and included a clipping of the foregoing, "The Knickerbocker item baffles me utterly. What the hell does he mean?" I also noted that, "Charles Boyer called . . . very anxious to hear about you . . . very relieved that you were well and happy. 'Good,' he said. 'That's all I wanted to hear. That's all that matters.' Said he'll write you."

Ingrid replied:

I was so sad after you left that I became desperately ill. I have not had a worse cold since Alaska. I managed in no time to infect Roberto who came down with a cough. In the middle of this we moved into a new apartment (49 Bruno Buozzi). It is big as the ocean with lovely old antiques that three people must keep dusting all the time. It is cold as the ocean, too. We have an open fireplace but we also have all the smoke. Despite it all, it is better than the other one. I'm the only one who wishes there were a few functional things around, but I guess that idea will wear off with time.

Petter's attitude is funny, but I was surprised he saw you at all. But Weger; he is superfunny. You know, aside from Art Cohn, I have never seen a man love Roberto as much as Weger did those weeks in Hollywood. And Roberto liked him, too. He is intelligent and has read everything, so they talked and talked way into the night. Weger said to me so often, "What a wonderful man! I am so glad you have met him and will work with him." Often when I had a dispute with Roberto, Weger said, "Ingrid, you should not question Roberto. You should always do what he says. He is right." I laughed and answered that maybe that was a little too much to ask. Now what is it he could have seen from the guest-house? Well . . . some people are very funny.

Saturday night I had a fit of unhappiness that lasted until Monday. I cried and cried; poor Roberto with his solitaire and helplessness. I had not heard from Pia in six weeks. I thought of that little creature, so lonely, maybe, with so many questions and problems and no answers. Well, I finally got through on the telephone. I was choking with emotion and could hardly speak. But she seemed O.K. and still *knows nothing*. "When are you through with the picture? When are you coming home?" She had read an article about us, but it must have made a very small impression. Petter was not at home.

If only that divorce would get under way. But Petter demands that he will settle in peace only in the following way: I can see Pia as much as I like, but *only* in America. (That means rarely, if ever.) He wants fifty per cent of *Stromboli*. (That means no future security for me.) He offers me one-third of what we now have in the United States. (As he figures it—the house, $75,000, and the rest, insurance, bonds and cash at $80,000.) I don't want to give in on these points, especially about Pia, so that means more arguments and maybe going to court. Oh, God, how dreadful!

I was happy to hear all the good things you said about Bautzer. Now I feel much better and look forward to hearing from him directly. After that Rome *Daily American* story I told Verdozzi how mad I was, and told him I would like to see MacDonald once more, just to be able to throw him out!!

With lots of love,
Your Ingrid.

In a postscript she said:

I have no idea what [Cholly] Knickerbocker means. Nor do I understand a wire that came for you today from *Photoplay*, which I opened, "Please cable regarding rumor Bergman leaving Rossellini to return home." I ask you, what is cooking on the columnists' stoves now? They must be desperate for something new. I am sincerely happy to hear that some people in Hollywood are still "for me," and I was very glad to hear about Charles Boyer's call. Give him my best.

I wrote, "Last night Walter Winchell on his broadcast said: 'Ingrid Bergman may return to the United States in six weeks—done with Roberto.' . . . All this is very curious . . . Knickerbocker was the first to print the rumor about you and Roberto way back in April . . . soon afterward it was Winchell who on the air said, 'A top European star is in love with her European director and her husband knows all about it' . . . both are I.N.S. men (International News Service) . . . so is Michael Chinigo . . . and it was Knickerbocker whom MacDonald chose for that New York blast . . .

"Sometimes a thing like the Winchell item stems from a scene in a public place, such as an argument or quarrel in a restaurant. Many couples in Hollywood have been said to be 'rifting' because somebody was present in a restaurant and witnessed the quarrel. The fact that many married couples have fights at one time or another in a public place without serious consequences doesn't stop such rumors. Therefore, I wonder if you and Roberto did have such a scene somewhere . . ."

Ingrid replied:

Winchell is wrong. Now he should say "the romance is hotter than ever" instead of as he did when we were on Stromboli and arguing every day. I don't know what their source is, but he and Knickerbocker manage to dig something up all the time. We have not seen or heard from Chinigo. And we have not had a fight in a restaurant, God forbid! I would never, was I ever so mad, have a public brawl. We have not even had a small private one. I am unhappy and cry, and you know how that affects Roberto, because we don't get anywhere with the divorce, and I don't hear from Pia . . .

I don't understand what goes on with the mail. I have not heard from Petter for a long while. I talked with Pia two weeks ago, who said, "I sent you a letter yesterday and I'll write you again right away." But I have had nothing. I sent a wire yesterday, and if no reaction, I'll call again. I'm also anxious to hear from Bautzer. There can't be anything wrong with our mail service because your letters arrive in good time.

We looked at a house on the coast Sunday [referring to Santa Marinella] . . . waves come right up to the windows . . . cost the same as these expensive apartments in Rome. Roberto is crazy about it . . . wants to use an old house at the far end of the grounds for cutting and working on his films. It reminded me of Selznick who said that actors should not go home. They should stay at the studio and work all the time, sleep there, be comfortable, but never leave!

Roberto wants to build a studio on the ground. (It has seven acres.) I can just see the whole crew running in and out of the house. It is thirty minutes from Rome in the Cisitalia, and by train or bus about an hour. Maybe it will be lonely for me, but I'll start driving again, and, after all, it is no farther than from Beverly to Warner Brothers studio. The summers must be lovely by the sea . . . It is nearly midnight and Roberto should soon be back from the studio. I'll get his coffee ready, and good night to you.

On November 9, 1949, Dr. Peter A. Lindstrom issued forth from behind his citadel of silence to appear in Federal Court and receive from Judge J. M. Carter his final naturalization papers. Ingrid Bergman, a Swedish citizen, currently a resident of Italy, had now to deal with an American-citizen husband.

Presently, in a variety of shapes and forms, there appeared intimations in the press that "reports from Rome persist that the famous screen star so prominent in the news is with child." The city desks called, the wire services called, columnists called. One by one, day after day, they called. "We have it on good authority that Bergman is pregnant. Is she or isn't she?"

"I don't know. I don't think so, but, of course, anything's possible. So far as I know it isn't true. This rumor first started in an Italian paper a couple of months ago. But Rossellini threatened suit and they stopped printing it. My wife and I saw her three weeks ago and there was no sign of it then. My wife is a mother–surely if Ingrid is that long pregnant she would have noticed or suspected . . ."

At studios, in restaurants, on the streets, I was besieged by the mounting queries. Finally I put it up to Ingrid: ". . . and that's the situation here. It's damn well irritating, but they deserve an answer, and I don't know how to make that answer since I am in fact not in possession of the truth. Only by knowing the truth can we cope with the problem, whereas under the circumstances I can only fumble and grope in the dark, praying I have said the right thing . . ."

In the midst of this commotion there were three arrivals from Rome–Rossellini's brother Renzo, his wife, Anita, and Marcello Girosi. Renzo had come to write the music for *Stromboli* in accordance with the RKO contract. This was a first visit to the United States for both him and his wife. Girosi, a balding, swarthy former lawyer, now an American citizen, was an associate of Rossellini's and sometime producer of films. His presence was as Rossellini's personal representative, to oversee the local opening of *Germany, Year Zero*, and to conclude the Lindstrom-Bergman litigation as best he could. Renzo and his wife moved into the Garden of Allah, a cluster of hotel-bungalows on Sunset Boulevard in Hollywood, while Girosi checked into the fashionable Bel-Air Hotel, in Stone Canyon outside Beverly Hills.

> Dear Joe: Just received your big letter with the clippings and the carbon copy of your answer to Herb Stein. [Stein conducted a column on the Hollywood *Reporter*.] He surely gets things mixed up. Remember when he wrote that I had said: "I realize I have been a very foolish woman." Maybe I have been very foolish, but I never *said* it. The truth is that I have never said any of the things he has ever printed. He has always been terrible about Roberto, little hints and hurts. Your letter to him was too kind, but maybe it's better that way. I think it is fine when you answer them now and then, when they go too far . . . I still have had no word from Pia. I sent a wire four days ago, but no response. I do think Petter could at least send a wire that all is well . . . It is two months now that they are both silent. Marta Cohn wrote that she talked with John Vernon on the phone . . . he was very courteous . . . said Pia probably never wrote because he was not there to tell her and force her, as she does not like writing letters on her own. It seems that Pia still sees the Vernons . . . she had told them I telephoned. As long as she is well and happy I am satisfied. Marta also said that Pia doesn't know yet that I am not coming home . . . So long, dear Joe, and don't worry about what the papers say—I still love Roberto and he loves me. That's what the man says . . .

Her signature—"Ingrid"—at the end of the long missive indicated that this was all she had intended to write. The other letter was headed: "The day after—November 27, '49." She led off by saying that after finishing the first letter she had talked it over with Roberto, and had decided

> I must write you more, but this is for your eyes alone. I want your family and friends and everybody, except your God, kept outside . . .
>
> You want to know how to answer the columnists . . . There is only one thing I have to warn you about . . . if again somebody prints that I am pregnant, don't sue them, as you so

bravely wanted to here in Rome, because you will be sure to lose your case .... that's all in a nutshell .... [The blank spaces are Ingrid's] .... I give you a little time to recover.

Dearest Joe, maybe you suspected it toward the end. The question was always in your eyes, but I couldn't bring myself to tell you the truth. Maybe it was a mistake, but I simply couldn't talk about it. I knew it would upset you so, and we would end up in a terribly emotional scene, with tears all over the floor. I couldn't bear it.

I had to tell Marcella about it two weeks ago, because I wanted her to buy me some clothes. She said that many people had asked if it was true or not, but that was all earlier, right after we left Stromboli. I trust Marcella, and I am sure she says nothing. She got very upset, the poor thing. The doctor (remember him?) naturally knows, but he is such an old friend of Roberto, and he wants so desperately to help me and keep it out of the papers that I feel safe. Also, Verdozzi was informed some time ago. He closed his mouth even tighter. If anyone else says anything, they are only guessing, and that goes for Renzo and Anita, too. But I know the time is very short, and then, whether they guess or not, all they'll need is a pair of eyes. Nevertheless, as long as it is possible, I will try to avoid the storm.

It has not been an easy time, as you now can understand better. All our problems were doubled because of my condition. In the beginning I did not have the courage to go through with it, to face worse scandal, more insults, more dirty talk, more stones thrown. I didn't feel capable of standing it. But slowly, through Roberto, I gained the strength and the courage, and now I am not afraid any longer. As a matter of fact, I am curious to see who throws the first stone.

It would have been possible, when I had regained my health after Stromboli, to do something about it. But, after all, what a poor, miserable way out.

When all this hits your shores, what will you say? What can you say to all those people who ask you? I guess your answer will have to be as in your letter to the columnist: "I don't know. All is possible." I guess that's the safest answer for you to make. Anyway, you didn't know when you left Italy. As for Roberto, he is going to say, "It's none of your damn business," if he is asked. That is about as smart as he can get around this time.

Don't worry about me. I feel so much better, since I have left all in God's hands. Roberto will be by my side, and no storm will be strong enough to wash us away.

This addendum was also signed—this time: "Your Ingrid."

Slowly, I reread it. It was like having your leg blown off and having no sensation of it at first, then the feeling that something hit you, but it's dark and you can't see, and your hands go up and down your body trying to find out what happened. There was no bite or sting or sense of pain.

I called my wife and read it to her aloud.

She was stunned by the revelation. "There I was, seeing her practically every day, and never a suspicion. Just before we left I was with her in a shop while she was buying some lingerie—and she stood there straight as an arrow."

The next day, having partially recovered my equilibrium, I got off a letter to Rome:

... it should be very apparent to you and Roberto that sooner or later your condition will get out. If the story breaks in the United States it will spell the end of your picture. Nothing can possibly ameliorate the situation except a quick divorce and your marriage before the birth. But judging by Peter's do-nothingness that possibility looks unlikely.

No major releasing company will be permitted to release or show the picture. Such organizations as the Legion of Decency, women's clubs, church groups, etc., will rise up in all their fury. The press will editorialize, there'll be speeches, and Senator Edwin Johnson will froth in outrage. The picture will not make a nickel in this country, and you will thus be deprived of the money you need so badly and on which you count so much. Indeed, it is not exaggerating to envision that Roberto's future pictures, with or without you, will also be banned in this country.

These are brutal facts which must be faced. This matter must be kept quiet. Don't trust anyone. Make some arrangement, damned quick, to be off by yourselves somewhere where you'll have no visitors, no snoopers. Get out of Rome. Play for Time–Time, that great dimmer of ugly memories. . . .

On December 1st, she wrote:

. . . I will surely fight for Pia, because as time goes by I am losing a bit of that big guilt complex I had. I don't know what goes on between Petter and Pia, but I finally received a letter yesterday. It made me as unhappy as Petter could have wished. She said, she couldn't look at the map at school any more because she didn't want to see Italy. . . . She asked me why I was doing the dialogue dubbing over here, when it was supposed to have been done in Hollywood. As if Pia knows anything about such things! She said, 'No picture has ever taken so long. Something very funny going on over there.'

How can I be sure that these are Pia's own thoughts? She has always hid her emotions. And now I am stuck. How can I go on writing her my silly letters, saying nothing? And how can I give her straight answers, when Petter does not help to explain? I'll write a letter to Pia in an envelope to Petter and tell the truth. I hate to do it without letting him know. I might telephone, also. I have not made up my mind yet. You mentioned that I should telephone more often to Pia. I would, Joe, if it were not so difficult to lie.

Three days later, I received the following from Ingrid, postmarked Amalfi, and dated December 5th:

Dear Joe–Here we go again! Remember this place? In this place overlooking the sea and expanding mountains I wrote my first letter to Petter, asking for a divorce, exactly eight months ago.

Roberto is going to make a film about St. Francis, and the Vatican has been most helpful and very enthusiastic about it. All those holy men seem to have adopted Roberto as their favorite sinner. In Rome we had priests coming and going all the time, and very often some priest joined us for dinner at Nino's. My Lutheran reputation is shot to pieces.

Roberto wants to work fast now and make a lot of pictures. He wants to get rich, and I guess he had better, with so many penniless people around him waiting with open hands! He wants a real monk to play the part of St. Francis, and he is here looking for the right one. Today he is at one of the many monasteries in the mountains. He is so happy about the picture, it makes me happy, too, because I recognize that wonderful feeling in front of a new job.

I wrote Petter about the letter Pia sent me. I again implored him to tell her the truth, and I sent her a two-page typewritten letter to try to explain as well as I could from here. If he does not give it to her, really, I don't know what next to do. She will end up by hating me. She might do that anyway, but to hide the truth from her for so long, while Mama stays in Italy for Christmas, for no reason—that is even more difficult for her to understand than the divorce, I think.

This will kill you: A Mr. Ajo, Roberto's friend who lives in New York, sent me a letter from Cholly Knickerbocker. It began "My dear Ingrid:" He is *such* a friend now, he said, and suffers *so*, because so many *wrong* things are said about me. He wants to *help*, so would we please *wire* answers to his questions. And the questions were: What did Roberto think about the whole situation? What would I do if Petter didn't give me the divorce? What were my acting plans? And so on. I'll answer Mr. Ajo by slow pigeon to beg Mr. Knickerbocker to drop dead.

Now I'll run to the post office before I get some more ideas to write down.

Love,
Ingrid.

The fact that Ingrid could be humorous at this time seemed very reassuring to me; this was ample proof of her indestructibility.

The knowledge I now possessed bore down on me like a ten-ton die. Rossellini, I knew, was sunk in debt; Ingrid had no money and access to none; their expenses were tremendous; and a baby was on the way. Their sole potential asset was their joint sixty per cent ownership of *Stromboli*. I could foresee nothing but financial and economic disaster if the baby was born before the public release of the picture. If, according to my calculation, the baby was due in March, there was still time to get the picture out and do enough business to give them some benefit.

On Sunday, December 11th, columnist Sheilah Graham called before her weekly broadcast, "Before I go on the air, what do you know about Bergman being pregnant?"

I repeated what I had said a hundred times—that it was certainly possible, but that when we left Rome neither my wife nor I knew or even suspected anything, etcetera.

"Well, you've always played straight with me, Joe," she said. "I'll take your word for it. Would you rather I say nothing?"

"Please."

Two similar calls followed and suddenly all the queries of the past two or three weeks merged into one mountainous question mark—this thing's about to break wide open—nothing can stop it—maybe my calculations are wrong; maybe Ingrid's in her seventh or eighth month—what is the answer?

I telephoned Johnny Meyer. "I've got to talk to Howard, Johnny. It's terribly important. I must see him personally." Meyer said Hughes was living in a bungalow of the Beverly Hills Hotel and gave me his private phone number. I called Hughes and arranged to go right over and see him.

Looking like anything but an industrial monarch, he opened the door and let me in. He wore no jacket, his belted trousers hung loosely and looked in need of pressing, his tieless white shirt was open at the collar and bulged untidily at the waist; his feet were shod in white sneakers.

"Howard, I have something extremely confidential to tell you . . ." He indicated a sofa to me, then drew up a chair and faced me. "What I have to say is intended solely for your information." He drew his chair closer. "This is strictly between us." He nodded in acknowledgment and drew closer. His knees now touched mine. He leaned his head slightly to favor his good ear.

"Ingrid is in serious trouble. I've come to you because I think it's the only way I can help her." His head was now inches from mine. "If this gets out there'll be hell to pay. I'm doing it only for Ingrid, but if she knew about it, she'd never forgive me..." Hughes sat taut and motionless, straining to hear.

"Ingrid is going to have a baby..."

"What did you say?"

"Ingrid is pregnant—she's going to have a baby."

"How do you know?"

"She wrote me. I've known it for nine days." There was no visible reaction. It might have been news that TWA stock had fallen half a point.

"When is it expected?" he asked.

"I can't be sure; I figure probably around March. That's three months away. Now look, Howard, Ingrid and Roberto need money desperately. They're broke and deep in debt. The picture is their only hope for a long time to come, but if this story gets out in the open, *Stromboli* won't be worth a dime. I think you should rush it out as fast as you can—give it a saturation booking; maybe five hundred theaters—before anybody starts banning it. Give Ingrid a break, Howard."

Hughes expressed his gratitude and assured me that he would follow the suggestion. I left with mixed emotions, trusting I hadn't blundered.

At 11:30 in the morning of the next day, December 12th, the telephone rang. It was my friend, George Halasz, owner of the Mercury Bookshop in Beverly Hills.

"My Gawd, Joe, what is this?" he said.

"What is what, George?"

"Haven't you seen the *Examiner*? In big headlines it says Bergman's going to have a baby!"

"No, I haven't seen the *Examiner*. Call you later—"

I half-ran three blocks to a newsstand, swearing every oath I could think of.

"You're lucky," said the crippled newsboy. "Sold out the first batch quicker'n anything. Boy, they're going like hotcakes!"

INGRID BERGMAN BABY DUE
IN THREE MONTHS AT ROME

This shrill, back-fence headline—how could it have happened? How? Obviously, through me.

By the time I reached home I had read the account several times. Under her by-line, Louella Parsons wrote, ". . . this news comes straight from the Italian city, where Ingrid has made her home since she finished her picture, *Stromboli*, with the suave, dark-eyed Italian movie maestro . . . Few women in history, or men either, have made the sacrifice the Swedish star has made for love . . . Mary Queen of Scots gave up her throne because of her love for the Earl of Bothwell . . . Lady Hamilton gave up her position in the London social world to bear a child out of wedlock to Lord Nelson . . . King Edward VIII renounced his throne to marry the woman he loved, Wallis Simpson . . .

"Now the question is, Will Dr. Lindstrom grant her request for a divorce so that her child may be born in wedlock? . . . He will have to act quickly, for the days are going quickly . . . and three months does not allow for very much time to obtain a divorce and for her to marry the man she loves, apparently above all else in the world."

Three months? That would make it March, which I had merely guessed at. Louella seemed positive. I swallowed a tablet of phenobarbital and got Louella Parsons on the phone. "I just saw the *Examiner*, Louella. How could you do it?"

"I had to, Joe, I had to. I'm awful sorry, but I just had to. You understand that . . ."

"Where'd you get the story, Louella? Who gave it to you? Howard Hughes?"

"Oh, honey, you know better than that. You know I can't reveal my sources . . ."

"I know—I know. But that's the only place you could have got it . . ."

"Now, Joe, I know how you feel about Ingrid. I just feel terrible about it—just awful. But, honey, you understand, I couldn't do anything else. It's a big story—I couldn't pass it up—I just had to do it . . ."

"Well, it stinks—a rotten, dirty shame . . ."

Back and forth, we interrupted each other. The zealous reporter dominated the woman in her. "What did she say in her letter? (her letter? How did she know about a letter?) . . . does Dr. Lindstrom know? . . . what about Pia? . . . did she say anything about Pia? . . . do you want to make a statement?"

Fishing, fishing. "No, I have no statement to make. Thank you, Louella," I said.

Marcello Girosi called next to say that he and Renzo Rossellini had talked with Ingrid and Roberto by radiophone. (The Atlantic cable had not as yet been relaid.) "It was hard to make out what they were saying," he said. "The interference was pretty bad. The Parsons story was printed in Rome and Ingrid's very sick about it. It's simply outrageous—not true, you know . . ."

"What did Ingrid say? Did she have anything to say at all?"

"She said, 'Tell Joe I'll phone him tomorrow at 12 o'clock.'"

"Midnight or what?"

"She meant at noon."

I doused my cigarette in an ashtray piled with stubs and lit another. I stared at a color photo of Ingrid as the nun in *The Bells of St. Mary's*, which hung above the desk.

My wife stood by helplessly. Then she said, "Why don't you have some lunch, Joe?"

"I can't eat."

"A glass of milk?"

"No."

"How about some tea?"

"No! I said no!"

"Why don't you lie down for a while?"

"My mind won't lie down, that's why!"

Toward five o'clock I went over to see Miss Parsons at her Maple Drive home in Beverly Hills. We sat in a room designed for entertaining, equipped with a large well-stocked bar and overlooking the garden. Of medium height, maternal and housewifely, there was nothing to suggest the indomitable, enterprising veteran of thirty-five years of movie gossip columning. In conversation, it was her nervous habit to turn her head and gaze off into space. Dressed in a white-collared black frock, she welcomed me with solicitude.

"This is a terribly cruel thing you have done, Louella."

"I had to, honey. I had to," she said, breathing fitfully. "I've felt awful about it ever since. Just awful. I couldn't sleep last night for thinking about it. I went to church today and prayed. It was big news—you know that—the biggest story I ever got . . ."

Why was I here? What was the point in my coming to see Louella Parsons? Conscience? Scene of the crime?

"Will you have a drink, honey?"

I poured one. She tried to pump me for a follow-up story, but the well was dry. The burning sensation around my eyes increased. I loosened my tie and refilled the glass.

"I'm awfully sorry, Joe," she said with genuine feeling. "I know how much this means to you . . ."

"No you don't, Louella. I feel like a heel, as if I've betrayed my dearest friend."

"Listen, honey, the *Examiner* told me they'll pay you five thousand dollars for your own story about Ingrid. You can write anything you want to. Will you do it?"

"No, thank you. I'm not interested. I've done enough damage already." I mopped my brow. "Do you mind if I just sit here a while?"

" 'Course not, honey. You shouldn't go home this way. Why don't you take a little nap?"

"I think I will."

She called to her husband, Dr. Harry (Doc) Martin, a genial, well-liked physician employed by 20th Century-Fox studios. "Joe's not feeling very well, Doc. Take him upstairs and let him sleep for a bit."

Showing me into a beautifully furnished bedroom, Martin said, "Why don't you take your clothes off and be comfortable. Here—here's a pair of my pajamas."

It was nearly nine o'clock when I awoke. I got dressed, ate some poached eggs, thanked my hosts, and went home.

The strange and wondrous ways of modern journalism! Two years later this episode found its way into an article about Miss Parsons, published in a September, 1950, issue of *Look* magazine:

"Trained in the old tough school of newspaper reporting, shc still resorts to a little refined kidnapping if necessary. When Louella's big scoop on Ingrid Bergman's expected baby appeared, every newspaper and every columnist in Hollywood was hunting Joe Steele, Ingrid's press agent and close friend. They didn't find him, for Joe was sound asleep at Louella's house, in a pair of Doctor Martin's best pajamas. Louella had convinced Joe he was in bad nervous shape, fed him poached eggs she cooked herself, and tucked him in bed, safe from all her competitors."

Around eleven of the next day Girosi phoned to say there had been a change in plans; Ingrid had put in a call for three o'clock to Renzo's Garden of Allah apartment and wanted me to be there.

Apprised by Girosi of the three-o'clock rendezvous, Bautzer called and asked me to give Ingrid a message about the divorce and accounting of the community property. I suggested he join the conclave and talk to Ingrid himself.

"Also, Greg, there's something I must discuss with you and the others, and I need your moral support. Let's get there early so we can talk before Ingrid's call comes through."

On arriving at the Garden of Allah I was confronted by a dozen men and women of the press. Mingling with them was a man named Levy, press agent for the local showing of *Germany, Year Zero*.

"How did you know about this?" I asked, noting that Levy quickly scurried away.

"Levy called the papers," said a woman reporter. "He said Rossellini and Bergman were phoning you at three o'clock."

While a bald, round-bellied man and a bikinied blonde—oblivious of the headlines the press was waiting for—splashed in the swimming pool outside the sitting room, we talked.

"The reporters say the press agent at the theater, Levy, called the papers about this," I said to Girosi.

"Bad business. He should not have done it," said Girosi.

"Who told Levy?"

Girosi shrugged.

"Well, anyhow, there they are—their ears are glued to the door and the windows. When the call comes through, let's use the bedroom phone."

Renzo's wife, Anita, who spoke English, said, "This is disgraceful, the way they wait out there. It's not decent, not human..."

"Oh, yes it is. It's human as hell. They're after news that their readers want—and Ingrid's news. Italian reporters are no better, or the Swedes, or what have you. What we must face is that Parsons' story is true."

"What are you saying?" said Girosi.

"I said it is true. Ingrid is pregnant..."

Anita whirled on her husband and translated. His face signified indignation and disbelief as he replied in Italian. "Renzo said, 'Roberto is my brother,'" Anita said, "'and he would not have kept it secret from me.'"

"Nevertheless, he did. I got a letter from Ingrid almost two weeks ago and she told me the truth."

"No—no, I don't believe," said Anita. "I am a woman, I would know. I see her two weeks ago—no, no, no..."

"Obviously, Ingrid can't sue Louella, and if she doesn't sue, it's an admission that it's true. It's futile and foolish to try to evade the fact. She should grant me permission to say that it is so, and that we have no other statement to make. Otherwise, the papers will cook up stories and rumors and all kinds of angles that'll keep running from now until the baby's born. I'd like to tell Ingrid that we have discussed this and that we're all in agreement."

Renzo kept shaking his head incredulously. Anita kept muttering, "Tch-tch-tch." Girosi gravely nodded approval. Bautzer said, "I think Joe's right..."

The telephone jangled harshly. We rushed into the bedroom.

"Rome calling Mr. Rossellini..."

"They're asking for you, Renzo."

He grasped the receiver with trembling hands: "Roberto—Roberto—" The rest was in excited Italian. After two or three minutes, pale and perspiring, Renzo held out the receiver to me: "Ingrid—you—"

"Hello—Ingrid!—I don't know—no, I don't know how she got the story—" Her voice faded in and out. At times it was smothered in rasping, abrasive static. Her words came across in spurts and snatches: "—here it is terrible—reporters everywhere—we cannot step out—my God!—what more can they do to me—?"

"Listen, Ingrid," I shouted above the aerial din, "listen carefully. We're all here—Girosi and Greg Bautzer—we have agreed that it's best you tell the truth—"

"I can't understand you," came her voice. "I can't understand you—"

Thinking she meant the bad transmission of sound, I repeated myself. But it wasn't that at all; what she meant was that she couldn't understand how I could advocate such a thing.

"No—no—no!" she cried.

"But, Ingrid, I've got to say something to the press. If I say nothing, it's the same as saying it's true—"

"No—no! You say I am writing you—you have to wait for my letter—let me talk with Bautzer."

I was left holding a bag of confusion and interrogation marks. Nothing had been accomplished. When, finally, Girosi had finished talking with Rossellini and hung up, we looked at each other emptily. "Let's call the reporters in," I said.

When they were inside, I said, "I'm afraid there's nothing to tell you. The static noises were so loud I could hardly make out what Miss Bergman was saying. And the reception in Rome must have been bad; she kept saying, 'I can't understand you.' We all tried to talk but the result was the same, very frustrating. Finally, I did manage to hear Miss Bergman say that she would write me. So, there you have it; I can't be of much help to you until I get that letter."

Sheilah Graham got on the air and quoted an unnamed RKO producer as saying, "If this is true about Bergman then you might as well throw *Stromboli* out the window. It isn't worth the film it's printed on."

Dr. Lindstrom promptly packed himself and Pia off to Gary Cooper's winter lodge in Aspen, Colorado. He changed her name to Jenny Ann, but Ingrid and I continued to refer to her as Pia.

The *New York Times*, in a Rome dispatch from correspondent Camille Cianfarra, quoted Rossellini in an interview, which Ingrid confirmed to me as having been authorized, "... because Cianfarra is our very good friend and wrote only what we told him."

Cianfarra cabled that Rossellini said Miss Bergman "explained things quite clearly to Dr. Lindstrom" when they met in Messina last May (sic!); that Rossellini said, 'at that time the relationship between Ingrid and myself was absolutely correct. It is not our fault, is it, if we cannot get married because Ingrid has been unable so far to obtain a divorce?' "

Anent the Parsons story, the dispatch further quoted Rossellini, "Whether she is or is not pregnant is nobody's affair. I think that report deserves neither denial nor confirmation because it is an attempt to pry into the private life of a woman who, to assert her right to her own life, has given up her career—which is what an artist regards as the most important thing in life."

Florabel Muir, Hollywood correspondent for the New York *Daily News*, wrote, "Hollywood philosophy concerning sin has long been in accord with that of the ancient Chinese teachings: the sin of sin is being caught at it... In a community where the Mary Magdalenes abound I haven't encountered one person who had the courage to publicly defend Ingrid Bergman or even to ask for mercy from those who are judging her.

"One of her fellow countrywomen, a film actress, did give me some quotes about the tragic events which have caught up with the gal, but as soon as they appeared in print the bosses at her studio jumped on her and ordered her to clam up and deny she ever said it in the first place.

"The girl quickly ran over on the other side of the road to join those who are pointing the finger of shame at Ingrid because that is the popular thing to do now..."

Meanwhile, the press waited in vain for the promised "letter."

So far as I was concerned, it was coming by Ingrid's "slow pigeon." The letter that did arrive was not disclosed to the press nor to anyone. It was dated December 13th:

Dear Old Man:

I have so much to say, I don't know where to begin. It is the day *after the first day of turmoil*, the day after our telephone conversation. We will talk to you again tonight, if your telephone is in order. They told us that your phone was broken. I had to laugh; so many people had called you that your phone broke down! Also, your letter arrived this morning. I wish I had had it last night, so I could have calmed you better. I realized from your letter that you were in a terrible state.

I probably made a mistake not to have told you everything when you were here. You would have had more time to figure out what to do and say. I thought I wrote to you in good time, but Louella is smart. Where in God's little green pastures does she get her information? "Direct from Rome!" she says.

As I told you on the phone, I was very calm. I have thought about this for a long time. I have made my decision and I am not afraid. For that reason I moved around calmly yesterday, while everybody else fell on top of each other. I must tell you how funny Roberto was. His hair standing on end in a thousand curls, his clothes in a kind of upside-down fashion. All day he screamed at me to take something for my nerves. Which I did just to please him. A long time after we talked with you, he shouted at the top of his voice, "I beg you, take something for your nerves. You are driving me crazy. I can't stand to see you hysterical. Do you hear what I'm telling you? Do something about it!" I told him very quietly that I felt calm, and I am sure by that time I looked like a kind cow grazing in the sun. All dishevelled, he fell in bed and slept, woke up with a horrible headache, has been sick all day, rushing around in his robe, screaming and yelling, then falling back in bed to be served some food because he was too weak to sit up. Now, finally, he has gone to the studio, at seven in the evening, and *all* is calm.

The first we heard about the story was a phone call from a friend who lives at the Excelsior. He said Mike Chinigo called him and wanted to know how to reach Roberto. When our friend asked why, Chinigo said he wanted to get more news about the baby. Well, all hell broke loose. Our friend almost tore the receiver out of the wall. Right after that, Art Cohn phoned. We had hardly time to get our breath. Roberto kept telling him that he couldn't hear or couldn't understand. Art kept saying, "But is it true?" and Roberto kept saying, "Merry Christmas!" Then brother Renzo called. He was quite calm, but was sick and mad because, he said, his phone at the hotel was ringing all the time. Then we talked with Verdozzi and he advised we say nothing to anybody.

I refuse to deny. I would like to say yes and be direct, instead of beating around that same Messina bush. But, as I have been instructed, it is better to say nothing, so I'll say nothing along with the rest. But, really, that tactic didn't help any in Messina! However, Verdozzi argues some good legal points, so I'll shut up. I know how you feel, Joe, but, please don't surprise me on Via Veneto, even if I would be ever so happy to see you again.

Now to your letter. You fear that this may be the end for me, with the Legion of Decency, Senator Johnson, women's clubs, churches, even the Immigration Bureau, all against me. As you know, I heard that same thing from Petter. Yet, *Joan of Arc*, which didn't do well in the U.S., has made more money in Europe than any other picture since *Ben Hur!* I say that to show you that you may possibly exaggerate the situation. You think that because an actress has a *private* life, her public film will not sell? How come then, that all the world is so anxiously waiting for *Stromboli?*

What is it these individuals and organizations want of me? An abortion? Would that have pleased all the women in all those clubs? As Helena [her maid] put it: "Don't worry, Madame, you are not the first nor the last woman in such a predicament." But, because I am a public figure, my "predicament" becomes different. Nevertheless, I am not afraid. I am glad that all those other women, in small and big towns all over the world, who suffer because of their "sins," will take on a little more courage because of me.

Your anger as you write is not too much for me, and you don't have to retire to your mental tower. I only want you to try to think a little bit closer to a man here, who said, "Why do they talk about a scandal, when God has been so good and blessed their union with a child?"

Now because of what I have written don't think I intend to go out and shout the truth in the streets. I am careful and we have talked about leaving town, first for a week, then for Christmas. But Roberto must begin to work and I am very safe at home. I won't go out. I'll try my best not to "offend" people.

Roberto just called from the studio to find out how I felt and asked me again to take something soothing! That is all, Joe. What else can we do? Go mad? No, it makes you old, and we can't afford that. I'll close with our motto: Don't worry.

Your Ingrid.

She signed it clearly and firmly; the "I" in Ingrid a bold, sky-written loop.

Sympathetic letters and cablegrams, flowers, gifts, and all manner of good-luck symbols streamed into the apartment at 49 Bruno Buozzi. Cary Grant called and asked where he could address a wire. It read, "Ingrid dearest: It would not be possible in a single cablegram to tell you of all your friends who send you love and affection." "When I received it I was so happy I cried," said Ingrid. Actor Van Johnson and his wife, Evie, sent a simple, "God bless you."

Attorney Verdozzi cautioned Ingrid and Rossellini to issue no statements nor make any move which might complicate the divorce proceedings; that under Italian law a child born while a marriage is still legally in force belongs to the husband.

During the shooting of a bedroom scene for *Stromboli* on the island, Rossellini had sat on the edge of the bed and illustrated to Mario Vitale, the fisherman-leading man, how he wanted the scene played. The company still photographer snapped a picture which in movie parlance is known as an "offstage publicity shot." In some devious manner this picture appeared in *Tempo*, a weekly Italian magazine, captioned as actually having been photographed in their own Rome bedroom. The picture was transmitted to the United States and was widely published. Such journalistic abasements served only to heighten Ingrid's distress.

Dr. Lindstrom flew to New York to confer with lawyer Brinn. "It is now my hope," said Bautzer, "that the doctor will quickly agree on a settlement of the issues involved." But Dr. Lindstrom returned with no tangible progress.

Casey Shawhan, city editor of the Los Angeles *Evening Mirror*, phoned to say that Renzo Rossellini had proposed that he write his brother's life story for the paper, because the truth had not been told about him. "He wanted five thousand dollars to do it," said Shawhan, "but we told him we weren't interested."

Rossellini's Austrian annulment of his own marriage, to be valid in Italy, had to be submitted to an Italian court for *deliberazione* or review. Gino Sotis, another Rossellini attorney, submitted the case to the Turin Court of Appeals for a ruling. The court upheld the annulment, in spite of strong opposition from Catholic circles, which termed the action a violation of the Lateran Pacts, whereby only the Church was held competent to judge the validity of a Church marriage.

On Christmas Day there was a cable from Ingrid. "Please find where Pia has gone. Have tried to telephone her in vain." Those who might have known refused to give me the information. Several days too late, I learned that Lindstrom had taken her to Aspen for the holidays, leaving strict instructions not to make their whereabouts known.

Soon after New Year, 1950, Bautzer flew to New York to meet with Brinn in an effort to speed the stalemated negotiations. He returned empty-handed, however, saying that Brinn reported that Lindstrom wouldn't change his position.

Having exhausted every possibility of instituting divorce proceedings in a European country, Rossellini instructed Girosi to file in Mexico.

On January 22nd Ingrid wrote: "...I have not been out of

the house for weeks. Yesterday was a lovely day and Roberto was going to take me out for an airing by the sea. I went down to meet the car. It was Sunday, and I thought after all these weeks of waiting outside in cars the photographers had given up, and all the good men had gone to church. I took three steps outside the house, and up from nowhere jumped a man with his camera. I burst out crying in the street and ran back to the house. He followed and took another photo. I screamed, 'Stop it, you devil!' Afterwards, I had to smile when I recalled his satisfied, joyful expression. You can imagine, he has probably waited since before Christmas when they started to hang around the house for a 'baby photo.' You can imagine his happiness! I had my long black overcoat on, in which I would look pregnant at any time."

She said she was calling Bautzer that night, agonized that no progress was being made. She spoke of having received a five-page letter from her husband, which "gives me no hope for a friendly settlement."

"I have defended him like a lion," she wrote, "but it is surprising what a human being can arrive at. He writes that all my divorce talks have been money, money! That my lack of concern about Pia is frightful! That Bautzer talks about her in the lightest manner! That as an adulteress I have no rights to anything and no court would grant me anything!"

She ended by saying, "I am feeling fine and all is well otherwise. I don't sleep too well, because I spend my nights arguing with Petter, Sotis, Verdozzi, Hughes and the press and the judges and God and everybody that will listen. And so many listen when you talk alone!"

Louella Parsons, in New York for a short visit, called me and asked if there were any new developments. I suggested she get hold of Lawrence Brinn, who might have some news. Miss Parsons said she already had contacted Brinn and that he could contribute nothing new.

"Why doesn't he settle this thing quickly?" she said. "Doesn't he realize that it is best for Pia?"

"I wouldn't presume to analyze Peter's thinking processes."

As soon as Miss Parsons hung up I called Bautzer and told him what she had said. He laughed. "No wonder Brinn can't contribute anything. He's no longer Lindstrom's attorney."

The Vatican's Holy Year was thirty days old when Ingrid again set paper to typewriter–forty-nine days after Louella Parsons had made known Ingrid's condition:

> Dear Joe: It is some time since I have written, but the days go by, and even though I don't accomplish anything, I still seem to be very busy.
>
> There is no special news; only the same old stuff, the same old fights and trouble. I am sure you know more about what is happening with the divorce than I do. What a mess it continues to remain. We will end up in court, I am sure. How I have tried to avoid it, because if I had wanted to take that course, I would have done so long ago, and I would be married to Roberto by now.
>
> Do you know, Joe, that Petter asked for fifty per cent of *Stromboli?* When I refused and threatened to go to court, he said, "All right. I'll give up my part, but Pia should have fifty per cent. Now I'd like to see you go to court against your own daughter." How do you like that? I am so tired, so exhausted. When is he going to give up? Tonight's paper here says he will let me get the Mexican divorce, then he will go against me in a California court when he also has *proof* of my adultery. I don't know if this is true, but I know enough Italian to read the papers. They write something every day. Today we have been bothered by constant phone calls, because Winchell said on the radio that I was having my baby now. I am sure that I shall have this baby in the presence of Chinigo, Forte, Clarke, Weller [all reporters], the Pope, and an uncountable number of photographers. I am sure the hospital walls will break down. I will have the entire Italian population in my room. Wait a minute–I forgot a part about Petter; he first demanded fifty per cent for Pia out of my forty per cent and of the remaining twenty per cent he wanted half. Oh, what a hell! I am too tired tonight. I'll write you in the morning."

The continuation of her letter was subdated January 31st:

I don't feel too hot today, either, but I'll try to get this letter off. You know why we finally decided on a Mexican divorce? Bautzer said it was hopeless to fight against the fifty per cent for Pia, if I wanted a quick divorce, because only that way would Petter sign the necessary agreements. So, I finally gave in, but when the papers went back from here with my signature, he still refused to sign. At the last minute he demanded full custody of Pia. If I gave him that, he would sign immediately. I said no, and so we decided on Mexico.

In Petter's last letter he again accuses me of being such a casual mother; at least I can pretend to love my child, he says. Then when I try to fight for my child, he is against me. It all makes no sense.

I hear nothing from many people I used to think were good friends . . . After Petter's circular letter to all the relatives and friends in Sweden, they have not written me, either. Well, I have enough consolation in the correspondence from the Alvin Gang!!! They send you greetings, too. And I hear from a few others who strengthen my faith in human nature—the English painter, Poor; my piano teacher whom I haven't seen since I was thirteen; the singing teacher I had when I was twenty; my old Swedish director, Molander; and Ernest Hemingway, who wrote me so beautifully that I could have cried. Milly [Milestone] and Kendall [his wife] were here and we saw them several times. Sidney Bernstein [the British producer] is here now; I see him almost everyday. He is so comforting and thoughtful.

Roberto is very busy and full of ideas. He is interested in the big problems of today. He wants a message in his stories, even if it isn't too apparent, as in *St. Francis*, which has a great lesson for all men. Roberto's already working out his next picture in his mind, and it, too, will have something to say about today's struggle to find life and peace.

You ask, "How much time before the big event?" So you worry about that. I don't. If the Mexican divorce goes through fast, and the papers come here fast, and we quickly send a man to Sweden to register them, then it is possible for us to marry before it is too late. But, knowing that the father is always late himself, the baby may be late, too, and we may be able to marry in time. There is always the possibility that the baby will be a bridesmaid! If the divorce comes in time so that I don't have to sign the name Lindstrom, that will be good enough for me. After all, the rest is only paper, and the world knows I am an adulteress. If they don't, I guess Petter will see to it that it becomes well known.

Love,
Ingrid.

Los Angeles papers presently announced that Dr. Lindstrom had engaged new legal counsel in the person of Howard F. Shepherd of the law firm of Shepherd and Shepherd.

ROME

At noon, on February 2, 1950, a transatlantic call came through to the Bruno Buozzi residence. It was from Mrs. John Vernon. At first Ingrid was "terror-stricken," she wrote me in pencil from her hospital bed at the Villa Margherita Clinic.

I was horrified, thinking something had happened to Pia. And at the same time my labor pains began.

How she found out our number I don't know, but it meant that even Petter could phone me if he wanted to. She told me she wanted to meet me in Mexico with Pia, because Pia wanted to see me. Mrs. Vernon had read somewhere that I was going to Mexico. She said that Pia cried so because all the papers said such bad things about her father. I promised to write Pia and explain as much as I could.

After the phone call, I wrote Pia a two-and-a-half-page letter on the typewriter. It took me three hours, because after each three or four lines I had to stop, crawl on the floor, chew up a chair, climb up the wall, then go back and write a little more. When the letter was finished, I called the doctor.

It was four o'clock when Dr. Pier Luigi Guidotti arrived. Ingrid —bulging heavily in her big black overcoat—crowded herself into his small Italian car and they hastened to the hospital, three kilometers distant. Fortuitously, no photographers were on the prowl. The press was caught off guard attending the gala premiere of *Volcano,* which Anna Magnani had filmed on the island near *Stromboli.*

Five hours later, with obstetrician Dr. Giuseppe Sannicandro in attendance, Robertino—weighing 7 pounds, 14 ounces—joined the troubled world. An hour later, the Italian news agency, *Ansa,* informed its subscribers of the event. Within minutes there was a mass assault on the now-locked iron gates of the clinic—every reporter and photographer within reach of Rome.

In their competitive zeal, unable to gain entrance to the hospital or talk with someone in on the know, they concocted a torrent of imaginary descriptions and quotations. As though they had been eye-witnesses of the event, they wrote of Ingrid's "tears and laughter" following the baby's birth. Actually, on hearing the infant's first cry, Ingrid wrote that she had said, "What time is it?"

Hospital attendants, nuns, nurses, janitors were besieged for newsy morsels; Rossellini's relatives were hounded. One man was caught shinnying up a rain pipe to Ingrid's balcony. A nun was offered a bribe of a million lire. One Italian cameraman had his conveniently pregnant wife installed in a nearby room, until the staff learned that her time was many weeks off. There were attempts to scale the gates and the walls surrounding the clinic. And as the hours grew chillier they collected wood, built a fire, and settled down for an all-night vigil.

"Roberto looked at his son," Ingrid wrote, "and he said, 'He certainly is Swedish. They always arrive ahead of their appointment.' Everything went well with the birth, and everybody talks of how beautiful my baby is. And I think it is true; he is perfect, not a scratch or mark, with a little round head, and bald like his father!

"Much love from Mama, Papa, and their little Robertino [diminutive for Roberto]. Ingrid."

In the afternoon of the next day, the clinic director, in a moment of institutional pride, decided there was no harm in letting the press come in to see what a fine hospital it was. Then bedlam broke out; photographers with hidden cameras raced up and down the corridors, peering into every room. One photographer was intercepted as he tried the locked door of No. 34, Ingrid's room. Armed *carabinieri* were hastily summoned and the press ejected. Some hired a room across the street and aimed their cameras at Ingrid's window.

A few days later, Ingrid wrote from her hospital bed, "This madhouse went on for days. The police were constantly outside my door; they were stationed at the desk, on the stairs, and in the halls. The guards at the gates directed the crowds like a Hollywood premiere."

They climbed the trees and the walls armed with telephoto lens, but the Venetian blinds of No. 34 were perpetually closed. "One man pretended he was sick and was assigned a room, but his camera was discovered under the bed, and he was taken off to jail . . ."

The first three or four days she "was drowned in telegrams and flowers." About two hundred were from America, from strangers and friends, proffering courage and compassion. There were avowals of admiration and endearment from Helen Hayes, from authors John Steinbeck and Ernest Hemingway; from Cary Grant, Gary Cooper; the actress, Elizabeth Bergner; Van Johnson; Leonard Lyons, the columnist; David Selznick and Jennifer Jones; songstress Ella Logan; the French author, Georges Simenon; Phil Baker, the comedian, and Broadway producer Billy Rose.

"The first wire I received," she wrote, "was from Marion Davies. Yesterday she sent a huge basket of flowers, and another loving note."

A small but vociferous percentage of the messages were drenched in obscenities, some bristled with threats. And her own native land observed the event with invectives as harsh as their press.

La Settimana Incom, an Italian weekly, bypassed the impregnable medical fortress and published a photomontage with posed models presumably photographed in a hospital room but with the faces of Ingrid, Rossellini and the doctors pasted on. The enterprising paper, however, evaded the stringent libel laws by frankly admitting the hoax.

Despite the savagery of all these antics, here and there a compassionate voice was raised. On the third day of Ingrid's accouchement, Walter Winchell addressed his vast radio audience:

"Mr. and Mrs. United States: The only thing more brutal than a firing squad pointing its rifles at a man is the world pointing its finger at a woman. Tens of thousands of American girls in 1949 experienced the same ordeal that Ingrid Bergman faces tonight—with this exception; they, like Ingrid Bergman, were pelted with the traditional stone, but not with the heart-stabbing headline. Every major newspaper knows that this social problem happens so frequently that it isn't even news. Ingrid Bergman comes from Hollywood instead of Main Street, but that does not change her from an unfortunate girl into a wicked woman. If she weren't talented, she wouldn't be famous, and if she hadn't been famous, the world wouldn't even have stopped to sneer.

"Ingrid Bergman, I think, is a great moving-picture star; but even public figures have a right to personal tragedy. The very moral code she is supposed to have offended is her greatest defense. There are few who can cast the first stone. And there are even fewer who can afford to throw mud.

"I remain, your New York correspondent, Walter Winchell, who has this to say about the Ingrid Bergman story: All of us should be able to forgive sinners because none of us are saints. Good night."

The days-old son of Bergman-Rossellini was unaware that his advent stirred up a roar of anger across the Atlantic. Ministerial groups, religious bodies, women's organizations, legislative representatives and private citizens passed resolutions, bombarded Hollywood and wrote letters to their newspapers protesting the planned release of *Stromboli*. Civic groups and even theater owners arranged to forbid its showing.

"Let he among you who is without sin cast the first stone," declared *Il Popolo*, official organ of Premier Alcide de Gasperi's Christian Democrats (Catholic) party.

Il Popolo called the attacks on Ingrid a "plan of cannibalistic aggression. If an American actor goes to jail for using narcotics none of them bats an eye; if an actress, advised by her publicity agent, marries and divorces innumerable times in the course of a year nobody finds anything to say, but the Bergman case is indeed game for such delicate sensibilities."

On February 9th the petition for a Mexican divorce was heard by Judge Eugenio Calzada Flores of the First Civil Court of the Juarez District. Grounds of cruelty, incompatibility and non-support were set forth in ten pages of documentary evidence. After studying the petition for nearly an hour, Judge Flores granted the decree. Arturo Gomez Trevino, a Mexican lawyer, signed the decree for Ingrid, who had forwarded him her power of attorney.

The proceedings were ignored by Dr. Lindstrom, whose spokesmen stated he would himself file for divorce in California, where one year is required for a final decree.

The following day, Ingrid wrote:

> Dear Giuseppe [Italian for my name]
>
> Today all the papers print that I am a "divorcée." By "mail order," they say. Well, at least that's something, and will help in making out the baby's registration papers... We didn't much like the idea of having to name him Roberto Lindstrom! ...
>
> Well, the little fellow has finally been named. First, he couldn't be called Roberto because Italian law forbids the same first name as a living parent. I wanted to call him Robin, a combination of our first names, but again the law says no foreign names. This also ruled out Ingmar, which is the Swedish masculine for Ingrid. We therefore decided on Renato, which is not after any special person. Then we were told that we could use Roberto as long as it wasn't the first name. That gave us two names—Renato Roberto, but we still could have two more names. His third name became Giusto, which is Italian for Justus, my father. And the fourth became Giuseppe, after Roberto's father. But, for me, who did not know the old man, Giuseppe is after Papa Joe!! We were only going to use my father's name, but when Roberto told me his father's name, I immediately wanted it. I am so terribly happy, because I now have both my father's and also Mama Roberts and Papa Joe.

> So, you see, the little thing is full of big names. Dear old Giuseppe, tomorrow is the baptism here in the Villa Margherita's chapel. I know your thoughts and good wishes are with us.

Italian civil code requires registration within ten days of birth. Ingrid waited until the last moment, hoping the divorce papers would arrive from Juarez in time for them to marry. But the papers were late in coming.

Precisely one minute before the deadline another Rossellini lawyer, Signor Mormino, dashed into the registry office in Rome's City Hall and duly recorded the baby's birth. Ironic and galling, however, was the manner in which the registration had to be phrased: "Father, Roberto Rossellini; mother, unknown." Italian law regarding an unmarried mother was complied with.

"Isn't that funny," Ingrid wrote, "now I am unknown. But at least they changed that to '*temporarily* unknown,' so when we get married we can tell them who the real mother is."

The infant Robertino beat the film *Stromboli* into the world by thirteen days. On February 15th, Howard Hughes belatedly flashed the picture on the screens of four hundred theaters. The reviews were generally negative. At first, the attendance was heavy.

Three days before the public opening of *Stromboli*, John Vernon got into the car Lindstrom had loaned him—a 1948 convertible Pontiac, which had been Ingrid's, and still was registered in her name—and left his home in San Fernando Valley, telling his wife, Lydia, that he was going to see some man on Seventh Street near the Ambassador Hotel on business. That was the last she heard of her husband until three days later when he was found in San Francisco suffering from a "type of amnesia."

Vernon carried with him a portfolio containing papers pertaining to the divorce suit contemplated by Lindstrom. He was taken to St. Luke's Hospital, where his physician reported that he was "extremely upset" and could remember nothing except his name.

At the same time, Greg Bautzer revealed that he had "for a long time been asking for a detailed accounting of funds," but that he was offered only general information and nothing in detail.

"Finally, last week," he said, "at a meeting with Dr. Lindstrom's attorneys, Shepherd and Shepherd, an attorney from Mendel Silverberg's office, and John Vernon, I insisted on a detailed accounting by Monday or I would file a suit demanding an accounting.

"Tuesday there was another meeting, the first time I had talked to Dr. Lindstrom. The doctor told me that Vernon had been handling his accounts since last May."

Vernon's unfortunate state further impeded Bautzer's efforts to bring the litigation to a head. Weeks later, by his own investigations, Ingrid's lawyer unearthed some startling facts as to the family funds.

Meanwhile, the press pack had deserted the Villa Margherita Clinic, and Ingrid was taken home. On February 16th she returned to the hospital in company with the Rossellini clan, and had her son baptized in its chapel.

"I see in the *Weekly Variety* of February 8," wrote Ingrid, "that most exhibitors would ban *Stromboli* because of me as *a person*, if the picture did not make money in its first days' run. If it *made* money then they would not ban it! . . . I think I am living in a bad dream. How can they openly and without shame express such hypocrisy? And they call me a person of low morals! Robertino joins me in a big scream against human stupidity . . ."

The law firm of Shepherd and Shepherd, unable to cope with Dr. Lindstrom's resistance and procrastinations, tendered its resignation as counsel. Rome lawyers encountered insurmountable regulations wherever they probed the possibility of marriage for Ingrid and Rossellini. Sweden did not recognize the Mexican divorce, and Italy would not authorize a civil wedding unless Sweden certified that Ingrid Bergman was free to marry. As the weeks went by it appeared that the only alternative, albeit an undesirable one, was a marriage by proxy in Mexico. Once again, Marcello Girosi was dispatched to California to collaborate with Bautzer in setting up such a ceremony.

On March 2nd, Ingrid picked up her portable and sat in the

sun on the veranda. She asked for addresses of persons she wanted to send thank-you notes to and lamented the now sing-song lag in marriage plans and settlement with Lindstrom:

> ... almost every day we talk to Bautzer. I don't know how we are ever going to pay the telephone bills, or pay Bautzer. He is so patient with us and keeps saying, "Don't worry about the money; all I want is to settle your affairs to your satisfaction." ... Bills, bills, bills! We eat them, we sleep with them ...
>
> This is a lousy letter, but I feel lousy. The whole day I have been fighting with the nurse and Helena [her maid]. They keep getting in each other's way and the nurse can't stand her ... we have so many servants and they are fighting with each other all the time. Pietro and Manni, the cook and the other maid, the nurse and Helena. What can I do? I never was a hausfrau and I don't know how to manage them. I believe the best thing is to move to Hampshire House. I was never so happy as I was there.
>
> [Throughout the letter all the y's were inked in] My "y" is broken and won't move. This is the third time it has collapsed. Manni fixed it??? Damn all y's! ...
>
> Robertino is fine, eats like an ox and grows too fast for his age. He looks just like me, says everybody. His eyes are blue, and I thought his hair would be black, but it is coming out blonde. Papa doesn't like it ...

The day the letter arrived I had luncheon with Greg Bautzer, who told me of having uncovered a deposit of $80,000 in an obscure Los Angeles bank to the credit of John Vernon, plus the discovery of a $10,000 cashier's check made out by Vernon to Dr. Lindstrom. The negotiations, he felt, would now accelerate.

The initial box-office stampede to *Stromboli* dwindled to nothing under the impact of negative reactions to the picture itself. In show-business parlance it was a "flop," and the fondest expectations of Ingrid and Rossellini to cash in on their percentage grew dimmer by the day.

Bautzer and I met with Marcello Girosi in his Beverly Hills

Hotel suite. The chief topic was the picture's failure and its corollary, the worsening financial status of its two principals.

"The irony of this situation," said Bautzer, "is that long before the baby's birth, Howard Hughes offered to buy out Ingrid and Roberto's American rights for $250,000 and $350,000 in European currency for the European rights exclusive of Italy, Albania, Jugoslavia, and Turkey. Ned Depinet (RKO's sales chief) pleaded with Hughes, 'For God's sake let's get hold of their interest (60%)! This picture will make as much money as *Gone With the Wind.*' "

But Bergman and Rossellini rejected the offer, said Bautzer. Then soon afterward Hughes proposed that Ingrid costar with Cary Grant in a film version of *O Mistress Mine*, based on the Lynn Fontanne-Alfred Lunt Broadway success. For this, Hughes dangled a $250,000 bait, but Ingrid refused to bite.

"Hughes said, 'I'll even change the title,' " averred Bautzer.

Bautzer filed suit for an accounting and thereby forced a meeting between himself, Dr. Lindstrom, and the latter's new attorney, Isaac Pacht. The points agreed upon were set forth in legal form and presented to Lindstrom for his signature.

"He took up the pen five times," said Bautzer, "and laid it down five times."

Bautzer reached across his desk, took the pen from Lindstrom's hand, set it in the holder, and said, "Oh, I'm tired of all this. Let's call the whole thing off. You be at my office on Friday and make out the deposition. Let's cut out the horsing around." Whereupon, Lindstrom retrieved the pen and scrawled his name.

I wrote Ingrid, "Greg Bautzer spoke about his telephone talk with you yesterday, and how he expressed his opposition to a proxy marriage. You already know how I feel about it; now I can add Girosi's concurrence. 'Proxy' has a spurious ring to it and I plead with you and Roberto to renounce it. Now that the property settlement is *un fait accompli*, surely it is no longer a desperate last resort. Please, why can't you fly to Mexico and be married in person?

"Also, Ingrid, my thought is that you could go to Juarez, which is just across the bridge from El Paso, Texas. Pia could be brought to El Paso and it would be a simple matter for you to visit with her. I'm sure Peter would have no objection to such an arrangement."

She replied:

Dear Joe: yyyyyyyyyyyyyyyyyyyyyyyy! Surprise, eh?

You have a right to scold me for not writing. Getting ready for a trip and having so many visitors have kept me busy. And the typewriter wasn't fixed until yesterday.

Yesterday I went to the Swedish Legation and the Minister told me Sweden would probably never recognize the Mexican divorce. That is what is holding us up. I am Swedish and cannot marry anywhere unless Sweden recognizes my divorce; this our lawyers found out in all the countries they have looked into.

It makes me very unhappy that you feel so strongly against a proxy marriage, but now you can see there is no other way for us. The only reason I would consider going to Mexico would be to see Pia, but it will surely be horrible what with all the press following Roberto and me around, and Pia witnessing all the to-do. No, Joe, I have waited such a long time to see her; I can wait a little longer. And when I do, I want to feel calm and at home, with my arms open, and without people peeking. I have a strong hunch that Petter will go to Sweden this summer and leave Pia with me for a short time. I talked with him on the phone and he said that if there was no war this summer, there was a chance I might see Pia. It must be only in America that they speak of war. You never hear of it here.

I feel very low today and don't know what to do with myself. I would really like to get away from Rome for a while. Not that I can leave my troubles behind, but Ruth [Roberts] is in Paris, Irene [Selznick] in London. How good it would be to talk with them! I try to talk on the typewriter with you, but most of the time I stare out of the window, and smoke and smoke and smoke. It isn't good for the milk, you know.

I am thinner than I have been in years. All my dresses have to be taken in. I never thought you could lose weight on spaghetti. Roberto complains that I am too thin. Petter used to complain I was too fat. I don't ever seem to find a man who thinks I am of perfect flesh!

Robertino is fine and has NO troubles. He has started to talk—"grrrrgnugu . . ." The nurse is fine for him but awful for the household. I am trying to collect enough courage to fire her. Never did such a thing in my life. I'm scared stiff.

She enclosed a twenty-dollar bill (black market, no doubt) and an Easter card, instructing me to purchase some appropriate confections and have them delivered to Pia. The card read, "For my little Pia girl—lots of Egg kisses and Rabbit hugs—Love, Mama." On the margin she had drawn a cluster of four-petalled flowers.

"*A rivederci*, Joe," she signed off. "Lots of love and yyyyyyyyyyys, Ingrid."

During these hectic months, while Ingrid and Rossellini were grappling with their dilemmas, urbane Renzo Cesana, the actor-writer of *Stromboli*, who played the priest in the picture, was making ready to scale the heights of television fame. With great fanfare he made his debut as "The Continental," a glib, oleaginous boulevardier, whose undisguised appeal was to love-starved feminine fans. Cesana's electronic charm, however, brought down an avalanche of criticism on the national network and was soon taken off the air.

On April 12, 1950, Ingrid wrote:

Dear Joe: You must have bought a wonderful Easter gift for Pia! Thank you, thank you. I spoke to her on the phone and she was so happy. She talked on and on cheerfully, though I had a hard time to keep from crying. It had been so long since I heard her voice.

She spoke of all the things she was doing, and finally, she said, "And what do you do?" I said, "I play with the dog, and I—I—play with the baby." She couldn't hear too well, and a few times, she said, "What? What?" I tried to repeat myself, but didn't succeed. My God, how difficult it all is . . .

Yesterday was Easter Sunday. The town was so filled with pilgrims you could hardly move through the streets. Long processions were everywhere. It was a beautiful day and we went out in the country to look for a house again.

Some day I hope Bautzer will take a trip to Rome. I would like very much to meet him. I think he has done one very remarkable thing; he has handled himself so fine with the press. What he has said in the press he has done with great taste.

Marcella was here and gave me a letter from you. I tore it open and read it. Afterward, we discussed it and talked about you. It was nice, as if you really had also dropped in for a drink. Your letters are always welcome. And even if you haven't much to say, it is as if you had just come by for a brief visit.

And so, good night.
Ingrid.

In the meantime, while Ingrid walked the treadmill of legal processes awaiting her proxy marriage, what was the shape and color of life in the Eternal City? She wrote on May 20, 1950:

...Last night we had dinner with Artur Rubinstein [the pianist], his wife, and Leonard Lyons ... after a few minutes at the table a photographer popped up and snapped a picture and rushed out ... Roberto got so pale we thought he was sick. He rushed out, grabbed the man, and called for the police ... People eating outside joined in, people inside rushed out ... Sirens were blowing, jeeps coming, police on bicycles, everybody yelling and shouting and waving their arms. Roberto was there in the middle of everything ...

By now, out of nowhere, more photographers arrived ... Rubinstein—oh, what a noble Roman he is!—joined the fight, screaming in Italian, Spanish and Russian. The photographers didn't mind; they kept taking pictures until they were put in the police wagon ... When this little war was over, Roberto left with the two Rubinsteins, and Lyons and I got in a taxi. The street was full of people, everyone delighted with the excitement ...

But the police had missed one photographer. He jumped in another car and followed us home. When I stepped out of the car he started taking some more pictures. Roberto and Rubinstein, who were waiting for me, flew upon him and a fine fist fight began—Rubinstein brandishing his cane, his wife screaming ... My goodness, never a dull moment ...

JUAREZ

A cryptic cablegram from Ingrid read: "Champagne at eleven P.M. May twenty-four." I knew its meaning.

In the salon-living room on Bruno Buozzi, attended by a few friends and relatives, Ingrid and Rossellini awaited an overseas telephone call with nervous expectancy. She looked youthful with her unruly, new short hair-bob. She wore a simple blue and white striped seersucker suit and cloth-soled sandals. The room was banked in flowers, and on some of the antique Venetian chairs were a few fine old paintings they had recently purchased to go into a new house.

The chambers of Judge Raul Orozco in the border town of Juarez, Mexico, was situated on its main thoroughfare, El Commercio, an avenue solid with saloons. The general aspect is that of a movie Western. It seemed appropriate, therefore, that the leading actors in this drama have stand-ins.

At 10:50 A.M. on May 24, 1950—when Robertino was nearly four months old—lawyers Javier Alvarez, representing Roberto Rossellini, and Arturo Gomez Trevino, representing Ingrid Bergman, stood before Judge Orozco and took the oath of marriage. Marcello Girosi was witness to the ritual.

In Rome, timing themselves to coincide with the Mexican ceremony, Ingrid and Rossellini went quietly and alone to the Chiesa della Navicella, a small church near the Colosseum.

"At the same time as our vows were read in Mexico," wrote Ingrid, "Roberto and I were in the church. It was a lovely old church that neither of us had visited before. I was on my knees on the hard stone floor, and cried buckets! The people were singing, and I was thinking, thinking, thinking, while Roberto pressed my hand . . ."

The devotees were still singing, all unknowing what had just taken place, when the two exchanged plain gold wedding bands and wordlessly left the church. They returned home and joined their guests, and there was much laughter and tears. And then Girosi's transatlantic call came through and they felt that now, in truth, they were wedded in the eyes of the world.

From Beverly Hills Dr. Lindstrom's attorney, Isaac Pacht, issued a statement: "Dr. Lindstrom has never recognized the legality of the Mexican divorce. So far as the doctor is concerned, she is still his wife until they are divorced in California . . . He is proceeding with his divorce suit just as if the proxy marriage had never taken place. The divorce action is expected to reach a Los Angeles court in several months."

12.

Santa Marinella

THOUGH Ingrid was now Signora Rossellini, the phrenetic tangle of events left one lacerating obsession—the longing to see her daughter. School had closed for summer vacation; surely, Pia could spend a portion of it with her mother, or if Lindstrom would not permit her to come to Italy, her mother was ready to visit with her anywhere in Europe. The thought of the inevitable press invasion, if she went to the United States, appalled her.

Time and again she wrote her ex-husband or spoke to him by telephone, pleading, trying to reason, even threatening to take the matter into court. But the results were exasperatingly the same—"He always says he hasn't made up his mind. He may take her to Sweden later in the summer, and maybe I can see her then . . ."

On June 20, 1950, now married twenty-seven days, Ingrid telephoned from Rome: "I wrote you last night, but I thought I'd call you anyway. We have bought a place on the seashore at Santa Marinella, not too far from here. It has big grounds—about seven acres—and we have our own beach. It's a lovely little house and quite new, with lots of gardens. The water comes right up to the window. If only now Pia could come to me.

"I wish you would talk to Greg Bautzer, or maybe Petter's lawyer—see what you can do. What's wrong with Pia coming here for a little while?

"I've had a room especially fixed up for Pia. It's Pia's room—

where she will sleep when she comes. Petter says maybe he'll let her come near the end of summer. There is a room in our Rome place that is also Pia's, and, Joe, in any new house I ever live in there will be a Pia's room. Her furniture, her bed, and her things will always be there . . ."

A few days later, her letter arrived:

> I had hoped that my next letter to you would be from a different city, preferably Paris, where we had planned to spend our honeymoon, as I wanted. But I guess it is hopeless. I might just as well unpack my typewriter and go on from where we left off.
>
> The day before we were ready to leave for Paris, we got a message from Anna Magnani. She was also going to Paris and would we please not stop at the same hotel as she—the Raphael! Well, we tried to make reservations at another hotel, but it was difficult. And besides, Roberto was too disappointed because he always likes to stop at the Raphael, where they treat him like a little king.
>
> So we packed and went to Capri for a week. There, Roberto got a little too enthusiastic with his spear-fishing, dived too deep, and the pressure hurt his ears. He became quite deaf and had pains, and lost what little equilibrium he had left. We stayed on a couple of more days then went back to Rome, to the doctors, the lawyers, all the other people, and the heat. I won't make any more bets on when we'll ever get to Paris.
>
> The day before we went to Capri, little Robertino left for Fiuggi, which is in the mountains outside Rome. That's where the famous medicinal water comes from. His grandmother and new nurse went with him. He was so sweet I cried. Roberto drove one car and Renzo another, because he has so much luggage it wouldn't fit into one car. Getting already like Papa!
>
> After we came back from Capri we went to see how Robertino was getting along, then we drove through Florence and Pisa to Portofino, where we spent a little time with Alexander Korda [the British producer] on his yacht.
>
> And still no Paris! Magnani upset my honeymoon, but I think it was only fair. After all, I ruined her premiere of *Volcano* by giving birth to Robertino the same evening.

It is too hot to write, Joe. I'm beginning to feel faint. I wish I had a lake to jump into.

Love,
Ingrid.

On July 2nd she wrote from Amalfi:

I console myself by thinking maybe Paris is not pleasant at this time of year. Must be so hot there. Here, at least, I can go barefooted in sandals, but in Paris I would have to wear shoes!

What a pity—all those clothes I bought for Paris! They're definitely not Amalfi clothes. But, if we ever get to Paris within the next two years, I don't think I'll be too much out of the fashion. I have big hems on the dresses, and can let them up or down!

Roberto has come here to finish up that picture called *The Machine That Kills Evildoers!* Surprise, eh? But after a year-and-a-half being on the shelf, it's time he did something about it. When he finishes we go back to Rome for some more dubbing of *Stromboli* in Italian, and also *St. Francis* in Italian and English. Quite a life for a newly married gal!

But I guess it's better this way. If we had gone to Paris and spent a lot of money, with Roberto's head full of troubles, and his ear constantly on the phone to Rome, it wouldn't have been much fun. Now I don't ask any more when are we going to Paris. It becomes an embarrassing question, and so as soon as we go back to Rome I'm going to move out to our new house on the sea. I'm so happy we have a place called our own.

[Then the recurrent theme] I am becoming quite lunatic on the subject of Pia. I can't think of anything but her, and if she doesn't come to see me this summer, I'll go to America or any place, come hell or high water! It doesn't matter if Petter has his own way; I will not let anything separate Pia and me any longer . . .

Love from Amalfi and
Ingrid.

But Dr. Lindstrom remained unmoved, summer ended, and Pia went back to school. Attorney Isaac Pacht quoted the surgeon as saying that he would not even consider permitting the girl to leave the country until after a settlement had been approved in his forthcoming divorce action.

From Fiuggi came a letter, dated August 1st, written in Ingrid's long-hand and signed "Robertino."

Dear Mr. Steele:

I have been told that the blown-up mattress I use every day is a present from you. I want to thank you. It is a marvelous mattress. My nurse, who is French and has taken care of many French and Italian children, says America must be a wonderful country to have invented such a mattress. It is fine to wet on . . .

I am here with my grandmother, who always says to my parents, "Don't worry about anything. I am here. I never leave the child (that's me) a moment." It is quite amusing because she can't hear a thing. Even when I scream she doesn't hear. She has decided to get an earphone now, because she has, after many years, realized her shortcoming. I don't think she really knows what I look like, either. It might be just as well; I am embarrassingly un-Italian looking.

My parents come pretty often. My father is a lot of fun. He takes me out of bed at any hour. Sometimes I yell because in my sleepiness I think it is a newspaper man. But then I see it's the old man and we'll have fun. I ride on his stomach, and what a stomach! He talks and sings and throws me in the air. I love to play airplane. I go through the air with the greatest of speed and I land on his nose, sometimes on my mother's nose, because she comes to see what the racket is. I talk and laugh out loud, though I'm not supposed to be doing that yet for a couple of more months . . .

My father hugs and kisses me a lot. He says there are going to be headlines in the newspapers, "SON EATEN BY FATHER." Then my mother takes me away and just holds me in her lap. She is always chewing on my hair. I didn't have any hair for a long time. I guess she thinks it might grow faster if she licks at the few straws I have. I don't mind being without hair. Have you seen my father?

When, subsequently, I paid a visit to Santa Marinella, Ingrid spoke of her brief sojourn at Fiuggi. In particular, she recalled Fiorella, daughter of Rossellini's sister, Marcella, by her estranged husband. About fifteen or sixteen years of age, Fiorella was a shy, gentle, sensitive girl, who accepted Enrico Donati with affectionate respect.

"Many times, when I was lonely for Pia, Fiorella's presence was very consoling," said Ingrid. "She came and stayed with us at Fiuggi, and I got to know her well. There were long, quiet days with nothing to do but sit and talk.

"Because of her mother's own marital difficulties her attitudes were of special interest to me. Through her I got a pretty good understanding of Pia's point of view. I felt that Fiorella loved me very much—as a person, as the wife of her uncle, and as the mother of Robertino, whom she adored. But beyond that, she loved Pia, whom she had never met.

"We used to talk about Pia for hours. She put many difficult questions to me, but these questions gave me an insight into what must have gone on in Pia's mind.

"Often I would think, one day Pia will also talk to someone in the same way, like another link in the chain of human experience."

Toward the end of August, the Rossellinis went to Venice to present the films of *St. Francis* and *Stromboli* at the annual Film Festival. On their return to Santa Marinella, Ingrid wrote:

Dear Joseph-Giuseppe:

We went to the Festival, and it is a pity to try to put down on paper all that I would like to tell you in person. At this moment the day is ending, I hear the sea under my windows, and all is peaceful. I don't even have a telephone, and I am alone. Roberto has gone back to Venice to attend a reunion of movie clubs. I have a drink in front of me and my typewriter, but if you were here instead of the typewriter, it would be better.

Venice is first of all so beautiful. To say it is "out of this world" is most fitting. There are no sidewalks, and I imagine many drunks must have been quickly sobered when they stepped outside, because when you open a door, you step right into a canal.

Oh, what a big success we had with our films! You know how good it feels right after a success. While you sit with the audience and watch your film, you are still a bit numb. But afterward, what a nice feeling it is! Roberto was so nervous, so sick to his stomach, we thought he would never make it.

The theater where they showed the pictures was half-empty most of the time, which was a great surprise to me. It seems that most people go to the Festivals, not to see the films, but to see each other, dance, drink, and gamble. It was a hot, hot afternoon when Roberto showed *St. Francis,* but the theater was packed to the ceiling. I cannot describe with what warmth the picture was received. The applause *during* the running was like that in a theater when you expect the actor to take a bow. You sensed that everybody knew what a brave picture it was, and how difficult to make, and what it meant for Roberto.

In the evening we ran *Stromboli,* and again the theater was packed. They stood in the back and sat on the balcony steps. Tickets had been sold on the black market for 5000 lire! When my name appeared, I thought the house would fall down. After all that has happened, it was a very heart-warming sound to hear. Many times during the running there was applause, but I must say, and I say that gladly, the applause was even stronger for *St. Francis.*

We were dead tired after all the excitement in Venice, so Roberto and I went away alone, which is really something rare. We spent two days in the mountains in Cortina, and slept and slept. Poor Roberto, what a grind he has had. We were in Cortina on my birthday, and being alone with Roberto was the best present of all!

When we went back home I went to Fiuggi, got the baby and brought him here. We have had a lot of fun organizing the house, and for the first time I feel we are at home.

I saw Jack Benny and his wife in Rome. We had a good time together. Roberto took them on a night tour of Rome. They are so friendly and nice, it was a real pleasure to be with them.

Walter Winchell carried an item to the effect that Ingrid would soon come out of her retirement and make a picture. I sent it to her. She responded:

> Regarding Winchell, it is not too unfounded. I have mentioned to several people that I might do something in the future, but, naturally, I would not do anything without Roberto. I have long thought it silly for me to just sit. I hardly ever see Roberto. If I worked with him, I would at least see more of him. It also seems foolish that he should bear all the expenses, while I, perfectly healthy and capable, could easily help him carry the enormous load.
>
> Of course, all this is a secret between us. Roberto would not want my help, but he might be convinced of my restlessness and desire to be active. While in Venice the press wanted to know why I did not work. I explained that my films had been thrown out of theaters, the recordings I had made for the Salvation Army and for charity had all been destroyed. "Why should I offend people with my work?" I said. One journalist said very quietly, "Do you want to make pictures only for America? There are other countries in the world, and the Italians surely would be happy and appreciative if you made a picture for them. In Italy everybody has loved you and still loves you." I was very impressed. I was very quiet for a minute, then I said, "You are right. I'll make a picture for Italy." But what that picture will be, Joe, I don't know, nor when it will be.

On November 1st, Dr. Lindstrom brought suit for divorce in the Los Angeles Superior Court of Judge Thurmond Clarke. At Greg Bautzer's request I attended as a possible witness in Ingrid's behalf.

Lindstrom, trimly tailored in a pin-striped gray suit, appeared completely relaxed and self-possessed on the witness stand, as he responded to questions put to him by his attorney, Isaac Pacht.

Q. Mrs. Lindstrom left Los Angeles for New York on or about March 15, 1949, did she not?

A. Yes.

Q. Before she left for Rome, had the relationship between

you and Ingrid been a happy one? Had you and she been on a holiday to Aspen, Colorado, before her departure to Rome?

A. Yes. We decided to meet two months later in Italy.

Q. Did you make any plans for your future life while in Colorado?

A. Yes. On the basis of her drawings and suggestions, we started building a new nursery on the house. Previously, she had seemed to take the attitude that her career would interfere with her having a second child. About that time (at Aspen, Colo.) she changed her mind and then planned for a second child.

Q. That was about two weeks before her departure for Rome? Then, when she left for Italy, your relationship was one of affection and matrimonial bliss?

A. Yes, one of the last things she did was select wallpaper for the new nursery.

Q. What occurred about two weeks after she arrived in Rome that led you to believe your relationship with Mrs. Lindstrom was not all that could be desired?

A. I read in the newspapers that she had taken up a certain other relationship.

Q. This was a surprise?

A. Yes, it was. I read about it in several papers. I remember especially the Cholly Knickerbocker column in the New York *Journal American*.

Q. What happened after that?

A. I received a letter a few weeks after she arrived in Italy—she said she planned to stay in Italy forever.

Q. Did you go to Italy to try to dissuade her?

A. Yes.

Q. You left about April 17, 1949, and arrived in Messina, Italy, did you not?

A. Yes.

Q. Did you have an interview in Messina?

A. Yes, we did. We talked things over on May 3, 1949. She referred to her previous behavior. She said she would have to change, that she would stop. She also promised she would discontinue the relationship she had started—that she would have nothing more to do with the Italian director outside their professional relations. We made an arrangement for a meeting outside of Italy after she completed her picture.

Q. But she did not return to you?

A. No.

Q. You begged her to come back, did you not?

A. Yes.

Q. Did you know at that time that she was pregnant?

A. No.

Q. When did you first learn?

A. I first learned about it in the newspapers.

Q. Did you try to reach her by telephone on numerous occasions?

A. Yes—when her spokesman denied these rumors publicly, I tried to reach her. Her spokesman said he had been instructed not to give me her telephone number in Rome.

Q. Do you have any bitterness in your heart as far as Mrs. Lindstrom is concerned?

A. No, I have no bitterness. I feel sorry for the awkward predicament she has placed herself in. I think she has many good qualities besides being very beautiful.

Q. And she is a very fine actress?

A. That's right.

Q. Would you like to take your daughter to see her mother?

A. Yes, I would be glad to take my daughter to Europe to see her mother. But I have no intention of taking my daughter to Italy.

Q. It is agreed that for the present best interests of the child, she shall reside and receive her education in the state of California; that the child's parents shall have joint legal custody, but it is agreed that Dr. Lindstrom shall have physical custody. Mrs. Lindstrom may have the child for one-half of her school vacation and Dr. Lindstrom shall have the child the other half.

A. That is correct.

Q. Did you have anything to do with the Mexican divorce suit Mrs. Lindstrom started?

A. No.

Q. All this conduct on the part of your wife—has it caused you any mental pain, suffering and embarrassment?

A. Oh, I would say—you could say that—yes.

Since obviously the belated divorce was not contested, Judge Clarke granted the decree by default. The trial lasted but one hour. In sixty minutes was consummated what Ingrid had begged for nineteen months ago.

I mailed Ingrid a copy of the proceedings and she commented that she would like to have shown Judge Clarke the letter she wrote to Lindstrom "dated *before* the scandal hit the newspapers." She wrote that the holiday in Aspen was "hell" and that she "pestered" him until they cut their holiday short, after which she promptly went to New York, "where I stayed more than a week, just to be alone before leaving for Italy."

Nine days after Lindstrom's divorce, twelve-year-old Pia appeared in Federal Court, with Judge James M. Carter presiding, and gained American citizenship on the basis of a petition by her naturalized father. Looking very pretty—as her mother might have looked at her age—she was clad in a checkered wool jumper dress and wore ribbons in her hair.

The Los Angeles *Mirror* printed, "Dr. Lindstrom, previously coy or cold with the press, was most cooperative today. When photographers spotted the honey-haired little girl, Dr. Lindstrom proved helpful. He took his daughter to a nearby empty room for the picture-taking."

On December 12th Ingrid sent me money with instructions to buy "a big toy monkey and a couple of new children's books" for Pia's Christmas. She also said that director Mervyn LeRoy had been in Rome and she had given him a wristwatch to deliver to Pia. But hearing nothing from Lindstrom or Pia—"they did not even send me a Christmas card"—she asked Bautzer if he would check with LeRoy. Bautzer reported back that Lindstrom had taken Pia to some mountain resort for the holidays, and that when Mervyn LeRoy found no one at home, he had left the watch inside the doghouse.

By January 3, 1951, Dr. Lindstrom and Pia had returned to Beverly Hills and Ingrid managed to get them on the telephone.

No, they knew nothing about the watch; and it was never heard of again. "...so the dogs know what time it is, but no one knows where the watch is!"

Now her passion for professional activity began to assert itself, but she was determined to make pictures solely with her husband. Rossellini initiated plans for a spring production, but summer came with nothing tangible, and they moved to Santa Marinella.

"It is so peaceful here," she wrote. "I have cleaned the house in the Swedish manner—you can eat from the floors. I do all the shopping, and I fight with the butcher's wife about the best fish. Robertino is happy, always outdoors, and today for the first time he put his little feet in the sea. He screamed for joy. Roberto is taking it easier, too. It is going to do him a lot of good. So many of us live in the shadow of his moods; if he is worried or burdened by things, we are sunk.

"Never do I have any news from Petter or Pia. If I didn't telephone now and then, I wouldn't know if they were still alive. I still think they will come this summer, but not to Italy."

A few days later, "Bautzer came to see us and has left for Capri and Amalfi. I look forward to talking with him some more when he returns. Roberto has started to work on the script again. He didn't like the writer's work. He will never like anyone's words but his own!"

In August, Lindstrom took Pia to Sweden. On their way, he stopped in London and notified Ingrid that if she wished she could now come and see her daughter. Ingrid flew to London, and upon her return to Rome, wrote me,

"My visit with Pia was wonderful and sorrowful at the same time. It is hard to write about it all. Pia was very bewildered by the whole episode. It was good for all concerned, though, that we met again. I think it will help Pia to have a little better understanding of what has happened these past years.

"I saw her three times at Sidney Bernstein's farm outside London; another day we went to see a movie; one night she slept with me in Ann Todd's house. On the last day we saw each other briefly just to say good-bye. That was all, and that was always with Petter present. He never left her alone with me."

One year later, when I visited with Ingrid at Santa Marinella, she recounted her experience on the night she spent with Pia at the London home of British actress Ann Todd and her husband, director David Lean.

"When I saw Ann in the morning," said Ingrid, "she told me that she had got up early, and on her way downstairs, she saw Petter sitting in a chair outside my door–sound asleep. He was sure that I was going to steal her or something."

On October 26th, John Vernon, who had been in and out of hospitals since the day he was found wandering around San Francisco, came to a tragic end at the age of forty-one. He was found dead from an overdose of sleeping pills in a downtown hotel of the Bay City. He left a long virulent note, concluding with, "I no longer blame Ingrid and Peter for my breakdown. Lydia [his wife] must take the responsibility. I sincerely hope the memory of me will haunt her always..."

As the year ebbed, Ingrid and Rossellini embarked on a new film, with Alexander Knox as her leading man. At first it bore a typical Rossellini tag–*Europe: '51*–but this underwent several metamorphoses until it eventually was titled *The Greatest Love*. Simultaneously, Ingrid was again with child.

Because of the Roman heat, "We shoot at night and sleep in the day. Except that I can't sleep; I'm too nervous and excited about going to work again. I caught a cold and have been in very poor health ever since. We work at the studio from one in the afternoon until nine or ten at night. Then we see the rushes, eat dinner around eleven or twelve, then to bed."

Aside from her physical condition, she said the picture was going well. "Roberto is in good form, writes fast and in the last minute. Which drives Knox a wee bit mad..."

Tragedy seemed to beget tragedy. Seven weeks following John Vernon's suicide, on the afternoon of December 13, 1951, cultured Walter Wanger, now fifty-seven, parked his car on a lot directly across the street from the Beverly Hills police station. There he waited for the arrival of his actress wife, Joan Bennett, and her agent of twelve years, Jennings Lang. Two hours later they drove onto the lot and for a moment stood discussing business, as she later testified. Wanger drew a 38-caliber pistol and deliberately shot Lang in the groin.

"I shot him because he broke up my home," Wanger told Police Chief Clinton Anderson of Beverly Hills. Miss Bennett stated that her husband had been distraught because of recent financial reverses and was on the verge of a nervous breakdown. Wanger blamed his "reverses" on the loss of his investment in *Joan of Arc*.

"After that Stromboli incident," he was quoted, "Bergman was no longer looked upon as the saintly girl who saved France with her spiritual strength. *Joan of Arc* should have gone on grossing big at the box office for years, but that extramarital love affair virtually killed it."

Lang, the victim, apparently innocent, refused to prosecute. Wanger was tried, sentenced to a county prison farm and, with exemplary behavior, was discharged after a few months. For a time he had a hard time of it in the film industry but, eventually, regained his former status.

Ingrid, by now inured to the bizarre and the sudden shock, received the news with objective detachment. If his accusations are true, she observed, how dreadful it will be if he airs the details in court. "I suppose people will call that love," she wrote. "What was it you once said, 'What nobility lack of temptation engenders.' "

Unwilling to suffer another ordeal such as the visit with her daughter in London, Ingrid instructed Bautzer to file a petition to permit Pia to visit her in Italy during the coming summer. The case was brought to trial on April 15, 1952, in the Los Angeles Superior Court of Judge Mildred L. Lillie. On this occasion Dr. Lindstrom's twenty-one-page affidavit opposing the petition was made public; this time he submitted in toto the "Petter lilla" letter of April, 1949, wherein Ingrid confessed her love for Rossellini.

"I am curious to know about the reaction to Petter's making my letter public," she wrote. "I have lost all patience . . . how many, many times I have had newspaper men change their stories, so that nothing was said against him. What can he gain by showing what I wrote out of my heart?"

The trial dragged on with heated clashes between attorneys

Bautzer for Bergman, and Isaac Pacht for Lindstrom. Dr. Charles O. Sturdevant, a psychiatrist testifying for the defense, stated that after four sessions with Pia he had come to the conclusion that a trip to Italy at this time could prove very harmful to the young girl.

Dr. Sturdevant also testified that he had made a recording of a three-way conversation between himself, Lindstrom, and Dr. Robert Lumsden, a dentist and friend of Lindstrom. "I used it to help me appraise this whole situation," he said. Lumsden, in turn, testified that Lindstrom told him, "If Pia were asked, he would see to it she would say she did not want to go to Italy."

In the course of the proceedings Dr. Lindstrom announced that he had accepted a post as neurosurgeon at the Veterans Hospital in Pittsburgh, Pennsylvania, and that he planned moving there at an early date. Pia, now thirteen, had just received her graduation diploma from junior high school, the Hawthorne Public School in Beverly Hills.

Three days after her graduation, on June 13, 1952, at 2:15 P.M., Pia was called as a witness. The next morning headlines blared: I DON'T LOVE MY MOTHER, PIA SAYS. Following is the reason—an excerpt from her long testimony:

Bautzer: "Have you ever written your mother telling her in the letter that you love her?"

Pia: "I always sign my name, 'Love, Pia.' "

Bautzer: "And does that express the way you feel about her?"

Pia: "No; it is just an ending for a letter."

Bautzer: "Did you say it to her to be pleasant?"

Pia: "No, it is in my letters. I always say in my letters, 'Love, Pia," to my mother. To my father I say, 'Love, Pia.' "

Bautzer: "But the meaning to you in each case is different, is it not?"

Pia: "I think so."

Bautzer: "So I take it to mean that you actually, when you sign the letter saying 'Love, Pia,' that you don't love your mother?"

Pia: "I don't love her. I like her."

Bautzer: "And you don't miss her, do you?"

Pia: "No."

Bautzer: "And you don't have any desire to see her?"

Pia: "No. I would rather live with my father."

Seven thousand miles from the courthouse, Ingrid, heavy with twins, entered Rome's International Hospital. From her bed she wrote:

> I was told twins come fast, twins come ahead of time. Now the suspense is killing us all. Each time I ring the bell, the nurses run like hell; then all I want is a glass of water. The press are suffering too . . . first they thought the babies had already come . . . some made the expensive mistake of sending me flowers . . . Now they phone and phone, they print I have checked in the hospital, then they print I have checked out . . .
>
> As nothing happens, Chinigo thinks up ideas, asking me to pose for pictures for the Hearst papers: me running towards a car with a small bag in my hand and a painful expression on my face! When I finished telling him what I thought of his tasteless photo he was in pain, too, believe me . . .
>
> When you were here you saw the Italian wet nurses—huge, fat women in colorful dresses. Well, we are going to need one for the newcomers . . . she's already living in the apartment with her two-month-old baby, which Robertino thinks is the baby we're waiting for . . . I hardly sleep at all . . . I have been up all night . . . Now I feel fine, but after a while I'll fold . . . I throw up everything I eat . . .
>
> Willie Wyler [the director] is in Rome. I am so pleased, he came for dinner before I went to the hospital, and I think we'll see a lot of him and his wife . . . Now Roberto says he wants to go to India and to Japan to make pictures . . . Oh, brother! With a caravan of women and children! . . . It is five o'clock in the morning . . . I am so hungry I wish they would bring my breakfast so I'll have something to throw up . . . Top of the morning to you!

For a time it appeared that she might require a Cesarean section, but on June 18th, Ingrid, thanks to skillful care and her own robust constitution, gave natural birth to a pair of girls, each weighing close to seven pounds.

Five days later the legal struggle in Los Angeles came to an end. Judge Lillie pronounced in favor of the defendant, Dr. Peter A. Lindstrom.

Four weeks after the birth of the twins, on July 17th, I arrived in Santa Marinella on special assignment for *The American Weekly*. There was nothing in Ingrid's manner or appearance to suggest her recent mental and physical tribulations. She was dressed in blue denim shorts, a flowered white blouse knotted at her bare midriff, and rope-soled Capri slippers. Her waist was slim and unmarked; her movements lithe and youthful.

Situated on a crescent shore line of the Mediterranean, fifty-nine kilometers from Rome, the estate comprised a fairly new main house of eight rooms, a caretaker's lodge at the iron gates which fronted the Via Aurelia, and at the far end of the extensive gardens was an abandoned, two-story house, badly in disrepair and pocked with wartime shellfire. Since the main house was already filled to capacity, Ingrid had hastily furnished for me a room in the lodge with a cot, a bureau, and loose-hanging draperies to ward off the ever-present flies. I promptly dubbed my abode Palazzo Steele.

"Come," Ingrid said. "First, you must see my little giants."

She led me down a graveled walk to a shaded clearing. Here was a huge, oblong table, whose top was a single slab of black marble. On this lay two portable cribs, each containing a pink, fat infant. Hovering over them was the *balia*, an Amazon with fierce black eyes and a hands-off mien.

"That is Isabella Fiorella Elettra Giovanna," she said, "and that is Isotta Ingrid Freida Giuliana."

"How do you tell them apart?"

"It's easy," she laughed. "Ingrid sleeps all the time—see? But Isabella is wide awake, full of curiosity. See how she follows you with her eyes? I can almost hear her thinking."

"Why all those names? Just plain Ingrid was good enough for you."

"It's an old Italian custom," she said. After showing me where I was to sleep and work, we went to the main house. Furnished rather plainly, its chief feature was a spacious veranda looking out on the sea. Going through the house, Ingrid opened the door of a charmingly arranged bedroom, done in a pink-white-and-blue motif.

"This is Pia's room," she said. "You remember, I told you about it."

In the stifling summer heat, Rossellini slept by day and worked by night, editing and dubbing *The Greatest Love*. During my six-week stay, Ingrid and I sat out on the veranda after the late dinners and talked till long after midnight, while her husband was busy with his film.

"I can't get over Robertino," I said. "I have never seen such a handsome male child."

"Oh, thank you," she said. Then, gathering the threads of a memory, her face clouded. "I never told you what happened after he was born. He was about six weeks old, and Roberto and I weren't married yet.

"I got a telephone call from Rome. It was Father K. . . .—you surely remember him?"

"Yes, I do."

"He had made a special trip just to see me. I was happy to invite him. When he came we sat out here, and he started right in. 'You have already made one terrible mistake,' he said. 'Now you mustn't make another mistake by marrying this man.'

"I turned on my Swedish coolness. 'What would you advise?' I said.

" 'You should return to your husband in California.'

" 'But, Father, even if I wanted to go back, I'm sure Dr. Lindstrom wouldn't want me after all that has happened.'

"He said, 'You must go back home. If it is necessary, you must crawl on your hands and knees, and beg his forgiveness. Because—you must understand this—if our women see that you are not punished, that you are not properly remorseful, it will make them think that they can get away with the same kind of behavior.'

"I said, 'You mean I should make an example of myself as a lesson for American women?'

" 'And why not?' he said. 'You can redeem yourself by returning to your home and letting them see you in your humility.'

" 'But what about Roberto? I love him, and he loves me.'

"He brushed his hand like this," and she demonstrated. "He said, 'Love is not important. Only duty is important. It is your duty to go home.'

"I said, 'But what about my baby, Robertino? I can't take *him* to Dr. Lindstrom. What will I do with him?'

"You can't imagine what his answer was. 'He can be placed in an orphanage,' he said. 'He'll be quite happy not knowing who his parents are.'

"I got so angry I started to cry. I said, 'If I had wanted to get rid of Robertino I wouldn't have had him.'

"My crying didn't stop him. He said, 'Oh, such arrangements are not unusual. I know many of the best families in America who do this. They have a child—perhaps by the chauffeur—they go quietly into the country. When the child is born, it is placed in an orphanage. And everything's all right . . .'

"I couldn't take any more. I stood up and said, 'I have heard enough. Please—now you must go!' "

She lit a fresh cigarette and took a puff. Then, more to herself, she murmured softly, "My beautiful son . . ."

The Santa Marinella establishment was overrun with help. Not counting the coming-and-goings of chauffeur Pietro, flunkey Alberto Manni, and Ingrid's part-time secretary, Miss Thorssen, there were the wet nurse for the twins, a nurse for Robertino, a housekeeper, a general maid, a cook-butler and his cook wife; there was the caretaker's family—a wife, two small children, and a grown son who assisted him.

And there were dogs everywhere; three belonged to the caretaker, and three belonged to Ingrid and Rossellini, a Labrador retriever, a cocker spaniel, and a bulldog named Stromboli. A score or more of chickens roamed the grounds, and outside the front entrance of the main house was a large cage full of doves.

Four cars reposed in the big garage: a Fiat coupe, a Fiat station wagon, an Alfa-Romeo sedan, which was for Ingrid's own use, and Rossellini's sleek, new racing Ferrari, painted his favorite red. Alongside the Alfa-Romeo was a tiny play-car for Robertino, equipped with a one-goat power motor which enabled the blond youngster (now two-and-a-half) to whiz around the winding walks at a snail's pace.

Visitors from far and near came and went, and Sundays saw the veranda humming with many voices and many languages. Among them would be actors Gregory Peck and Joseph Cotten, directors William Wyler and Billy Wilder, Tennessee Williams, Alexander Korda, French director Marcel Pagnol, authors Richard Wright, John Steinbeck, Ernest Hemingway, Swedish sculptor Carl Milles, Jean Renoir, Artur Rubinstein, Italian novelist Alberto Moravia, actor Eddie Albert and his wife, Margo, photographer David Seymour (a colleague of Bob Capa famed as "Chim"), and countless others.

Throughout my visit I automatically took over the bartending. "The butler claimed that he was a bartender in an American officers' club all during the war," said Ingrid. "Why, he can't even fix a Scotch and soda."

Over a whiskey sour one evening she became reminiscent. "Isabella was the first to be born. We had prayed for a girl and as soon as she came into the world, I said to the nurse, 'Tell my husband I love him and he has a daughter.'

"His sister, Marcella, was with him when he got the news. She said that he turned white as a sheet and she thought he was going to faint. Then he wept like a baby.

"While I was fighting to give birth to my twins, I was fighting for my Pia in a California court. But the wind was blowing against me—I was losing her. What a strange Providence—while I was losing one child, I was given two . . .

"You know, Joe, in Hollywood, on days when I wasn't working I used to call for Pia at school. One day she asked me to please not come any more. When I asked her why, she stammered that she felt embarrassed at her schoolmates' curiosity in her actress-mother.

"A certain amount of curiosity in movie people is natural, specially by the press. Petter was very stubborn about permitting the press to photograph Pia. I always wanted to take Pia to the studio wherever I was working, but Petter wouldn't allow it because he was afraid somebody would take her picture. I realize now that this created more trouble than it prevented. Roberto and I have learned that the simplest solution was to invite the whole press to come and take all the pictures they want. Then they would leave very happy, and we would have wonderful peace.

"Pia has always been a very observing child. And also she had great fun teasing me. When she was very small—about seven—we had a dialogue that went something like this:

" 'You always do what Papa wants you to do?' Pia said.

" 'Certainly I do. Papa is very intelligent, and he is head of the house.'

" 'All right. But does Papa ever do anything *you* want him to do?'

" 'Of course he does.'

" 'For example?'

"I hesitated while I searched like mad for an example. Pia watched me quietly and, before I could find an answer, she said:

" 'I know. When you say dinner is ready and you tell Papa to come, he comes.'

"Another time, Pia caught me eating some chocolate. 'Oh, you're eating chocolate,' she said. 'Does Papa know about it?'

" 'No, he doesn't,' I answered. 'Because he's not here.'

" 'Are you going to tell him about it?'

" 'Of course,' I said.

"Later that evening Petter came home and I said nothing about the chocolate because I knew that he wouldn't like it. You see, sweets were my weakness and dieting was my cross.

"Well, Petter and I talked of many things and I carefully avoided the candy subject. Pia kept watching me, waiting for my confession. Then she couldn't stand it any more, and said:

" 'You haven't told him yet!'

"So, just to show Pia how brave I was, I had to tell Petter.

"One day I told Pia she could go to the movies. She looked up at me with a twinkle in her eye.

" 'What's the use of *you* telling me?' she said. 'You know very well that I have to wait for *Papa's* permission.'

"Yes, Pia was a very observing child. And she made a very smart observation in court, when she said that her mama was always bored at home, that Mama would get tired of sitting by the pool, and be very glad when she was going away.

"She was right. I was bored and I was tired. I had to make a break. I felt that I had reached the end of growing.

"I never fully realized how observing she was. I always played with Pia as an equal, as a friend. I never put myself on a pedestal as a perfect mother. Petter used to say, 'It is not good, the way you play with her—like another child. The child should have respect for you.'

"And I would answer, 'I don't want her to respect me. I want her to love me.' "

13.

Paris and Bombay

THEIR cumulative tribulations seemingly spent, the Rossellinis took a deep breath and bent all energies toward a happier future.

The Italian version of *The Greatest Love* was released in Italy and did an enormous business. But, alas, its local success accrued no profit, for Rossellini had long since sold out their Italian interest in order to defray current bills.

On December 13, 1952, Rossellini opened the San Carlo Opera season in Naples with his staging of *Otello*, his first theatrical effort outside of films. The following day, Ingrid wrote on the stationery of the Hotel Continentale, Naples:

> It was all so thrilling. I wish you had been there. Roberto has done very well, and I am so proud of him. I never saw the opera before, but those who have say there is no comparison. Roberto has caught the stage bug and talks of nothing else but what to do next in the theater or the opera. I am delighted, as right now I feel quite fed up with pictures.
>
> Everybody loves him at the opera. He is so *calm*, they say. I almost died! That he could make all those singers move around and act like normal people is a miracle.
>
> Roberto is going to start a new picture in January and George Sanders will play in it with me. He will be here on the 4th, but so far we have no script, not even an outline, just an idea with no ending.

It seems I always have a million things to do, certainly there is never a dull moment—relatives, visitors, servants. But it has been worse than ever lately, until I got to the point where I could scream. I had no time even to go to the bathroom. I am, nevertheless, stealing these few minutes to write you a Christmas greeting, with Renzo and Anita impatiently waiting downstairs to go to the opera.

We have once again redubbed the dialogue for *The Greatest Love*—I hope, the last time! David [Selznick] saw it a few nights ago and said it was wonderful. It is doing a tremendous business in Italy, but, dear Joe, we don't get a cent of it!

Belatedly, Rossellini started the film on February 5, 1953, shooting scenes inside the marble halls of the National Museum in Naples.

We have finally started *A Trip to Italy*, the picture I was telling you about. It started with a lot of titles, but Roberto came out with *Viaggio in Italy*. Although I don't think it's too good, there's always a certain style to all of Roberto's titles, and I think this fits the story very well. Sanders suggested "Such Is My Love," which I thought pretty good, but it was too sentimental for Roberto.

We are shooting in Naples' National Museum at the present. Sanders has had several nervous breakdowns due to not even seeing *one* word on paper. He has been quite a problem, even though he hasn't yet begun to work in the picture. I hope he'll feel better when he finally gets into scenes. But, who knows, it might be even worse for him then!

We have brought the children here with us and we almost take up a whole floor at the Continentale. It gives the hotel problems, but Roberto and I had to have them with us. The thought of leaving them for two months was too much.

Sanders saw *The Great Love*, and didn't like it—so what can you do? Chaplin and Selznick love it—so what can you do? Humphrey Bogart says he dislikes everything Roberto does—even without looking at it—so what can you do? God, this museum is cold! My hands are numb.

From the Albergo Luna Convento in Amalfi, Ingrid wrote on April 10th that the picture was nearing completion: "Sanders relaxed his unhappy nerves a bit while we were shooting on Capri, but it didn't last long. Not even Zsa Zsa [Miss Gabor, Sanders' wife at the time] seems to be able to make him a happy man. In Ravello [a nearby resort] John Huston was shooting with Jennifer Jones, Humphrey Bogart, Peter Lorre and Robert Morley. I went up every night for dinner and laughs, as we don't have many laughs on our set . . . Capa was here with Chim. We had a wonderful time. They are both crazy, wonderful people."

The Rossellinis made a down payment on a ten-room apartment at Via Bruno Buozzi 62, in the heart of Rome's fashionable Parioli district. Towards the end of April they moved in with a housekeeper, a cook, Robertino's governess, the *balia* for the twins, and Helena, the maid.

In June they drove in the red Ferrari to Stockholm, where she spent several days with relatives and friends:

> Roberto drove thirty-one hours without sleeping. Then we rested five hours, and he drove from five in the morning until three that night. It took three days to make the trip, but it was worth it. Seeing all those people I hadn't seen in years made my heart warm with happiness.
>
> You remember that record album of Honegger and Claudel's oratorio, *Joan at the Stake*, which you and Ruth gave me? As you know, the Joan part does not sing; she recites against a background of chorus and orchestra. I'm going to do it in opera, and La Scala in Milan have already said they want it. Who would have thought that one day I would appear on the Scala stage! Will I tremble!
>
> I'm delighted to be doing it, because it brings you and Ruth back to me. I have the album here with me, as Petter sent it along with some other of my personal belongings. Inside the cover you and Ruth have written, "from Mama Roberts and Papa Joe."
>
> On his way to Sweden Roberto will stop at Milan to discuss it, and then he has business in Germany and in Belgium. He is so busy. You know how hard he always works, but the way he has been going these last few weeks is incredible. Sometimes it is hard for him to make ends meet. And the somersaults he has to go through! Well, we hope that in another year we won't have any more of these worries.

I talked with Pia on the telephone and she made me promise not to go to court about her. I promised because she said that she is not being prevented from coming to see me. She can whenever she wants to, only *she doesn't want to!* In June we will move to Santa Marinella. I have made no plans for the summer, because I want to keep myself free in case Pia comes.

We have had many visitors, both in Santa Marinella and the apartment: Lillian Hellman [the dramatist], Jed Harris [the play producer], Gabriel Pascal [the film producer], Irene Selznick, Dorothy Thompson [the columnist], Sidney Bernstein [British film producer], Robert Sherwood, John Steinbeck, Larry Adler [the harmonica virtuoso], Sam Spiegel [the film producer], Leonard Lyons [the columnist], Gary Cooper and Rockie [his wife], and, of course, Chim, Prinzmetal, and a lot of the old dear friends. My goodness, how I enjoyed them all!

In November, the press and public acclaimed Ingrid's operatic debut in *Joan at the Stake*, at the San Carlos in Naples. She played it in Italian. *A Trip to Italy* was released and dismissed as second rate. In the United States, *The Greatest Love* registered a dismal failure.

The Bruno Buozzi apartment still lacked rugs and necessities and minor luxuries. "When we'll ever have enough money to rebuild Santa Marinella, or do all the other things we plan to do, I don't know. Too bad opera doesn't pay like a movie. Damn it, nothing pays like the movies. But one day I hope we don't have to think about money! Oh, is *that* a joke!"

In Beverly Hills, I lunched with Cary Grant at Romanoff's. Inevitably, we spoke of Ingrid. "I wish she would come here and do a picture," Cary said. "Hollywood has been empty ever since she left. There has never been anything like her."

When January, 1954, came around, the Rossellinis decided to put *Joan at the Stake* on film. "No one wants to invest money in it," Ingrid said, "because it is opera. But we are stubborn and will do it anyway. We love it and believe in it. You just have to do things that way; not what other people think you should do. If you make a mistake, that's too bad. But, surely, that is the only way to live."

On May 25, 1954, Bob Capa, at the age of forty, wearing the uniform of a correspondent, was killed by a land mine on a battlefield near Phuly, Indo-China, thirty miles south of Hanoi. Three days later Ingrid wrote me, "How terrible about Bob Capa. I have felt so depressed ever since the news. He was one of the people I liked most in the world. Do you remember how often we said those are the kind of people that make life interesting and worth living? And now he is gone!

"He was in Rome just before we left for Milan. He had been sick during the winter; one of those disc troubles that so many people have. But now he was well. He had gotten gray at the temples, which was such a surprise. Otherwise, he was just the same as in the old days. Chim, his best friend, was with me the evening before. Chim had some kind of premonition that something was wrong. Both of us felt terrible. Then in the morning Chim phoned to give me the awful news. Why did it have to end this way? Or was it the only way?"

In April she repeated her Neapolitan triumph at La Scala in Milan, then boned up on her French and did it in Paris. Still rejecting outside offers, she agreed to do Stefan Zweig's *Fear* in Munich, Germany, with her husband.

Rossellini encountered great difficulty in selling the film version of the operatic *Joan*, and this, together with the ultimate failure of *Fear*—his fifth picture with Ingrid—found their finances steadily worsening.

From Santa Marinella, on September 5th, Ingrid faced her typewriter:

> Heavens! Just as I wrote down the date I remembered that your birthday is tomorrow. How could I forget? Well, it takes a Swedish chicken head, I suppose.
>
> I loved your comic birthday card. That horrible looking fat woman who had passed out under the table! And they called her "Sweetie Pie"! I laughed and laughed when I opened it, and believe me, I can use a good laugh these days. The card is still standing on my desk and I think I'll just have to frame it.
>
> How maddening that I have no funny card to send you, or

anything else, for that matter. But, as you see, I am a little late with my Happy Returns. However, there must be magic in the air as I sit down to write you, just you, this evening. It is midnight and your birthday has just begun, at least in Italy. Many good wishes to you, dear old friend. And think what an old friend you have in me. I am sure you think of me as you saw me two years ago, but I assure you I feel ten years younger. The passing of years never frightened me. Each year I know more of life, and that makes the year special and worthwhile.

Roberto left yesterday for Sweden. I smile when I think he's going back to the country he thought he would hate so much. Of course, his pleasure lies in the thought of what a fine race he is going to make in the Grand Prix of Stockholm. Although I don't like the idea of him racing again, specially without me being close to him, I still feel it's better for him to go alone. For me to have gone back so soon after that wonderful trip in June would surely be an anticlimax. I want to remember Sweden as it was then.

On September 9, 1954, Dr. Peter A. Lindstrom married a professional colleague, Dr. Agnes Ronanek, in Pittsburgh. Ten days later, Ingrid wrote from Munich, in the midst of shooting *Fear*.

Isn't it wonderful news about Petter's wedding! I am so happy for him. Maybe he won't have so much time to hate me any more. I received a very sweet letter from Pia for my birthday. She said she has sent me a gift. It hasn't arrived yet, so I can't tell you what it is.

After this picture we'll be going off to London, then Spain, back to Munich, then Sweden in February and probably Belgium in April—all with *Joan*. Terribly busy, but not much money, and all those travelling expenses! If a good picture comes up, it might be better to do that so as to buy the children new shoes.

Well, we'll see what is in the cards. I am looking forward to all these trips, but I can't help worrying about our places in Rome and in Santa Marinella, and five servants who'll have nothing to do while we are gone. Oh, well, Roberto just shrugs his shoulders.

I replied, "Do I smell in your 'If a good picture comes up' a little hope that you would do a picture without Roberto? That you might now condescend to reach for some of that big money which would set you up forever, and wipe out all those financial worries that constantly beset you? One picture would do it, Ingrid. A few weeks of your time, and after that you and Roberto could go back to making 'artistic' flops. It's a pity, and makes no sense whatsoever, that you insist on enduring your precarious economic existence, when there is a fortune waiting for you to say yes.

"The children are growing rapidly. Before too long you will face the problem of their education. You'll probably want them to go to school in Switzerland or some fine private schools. This takes money. May I spread the word that all artistic elements being equal you would consider making a picture for someone else?"

Promptly came the not unexpected reaction. "No–no–no! I did not mean I would do a picture without Roberto! He got awfully sore when he saw your letter, so for God's sake . . . You know that he is too curious to let a letter go by without reading it. So please remember. I probably would do a picture without Roberto, but it would have to be so wonderful that he would understand my wish to do it. However, nothing like that has yet come along."

Later in the month, Kay Brown, now a vice-president of MCA Agency, flew to Europe and tried to interest Ingrid in a couple of scripts. Though Ingrid rejected them on their merits, she for the first time openly evinced a desire to make non-Rossellini films. Barely discernible was a slight fissure in the Stromboli idyll.

On October 20th she opened with an English version of *Joan at the Stake* in London's Stall Theater. To a *Daily Express* reporter she said, "When I met and fell in love with my husband, things were not easy. But two years ago the people who kicked me began to change. They rallied round, tried to pick me up. I am happy, content and patient and relaxed. When you are young you put your ambition first and your children second. When you grow older, ambition comes second. I still want to act well, but my children have first place."

Four-year-old Robertino and the year-and-a-half-old twins, plus their two nurses, traveled with them on these continental jaunts. Neither Ingrid nor Rossellini could stand being away from them for long. "The children had a picnic wherever they went—Paris, Munich, London. We were advised not to take them with us, that we shouldn't make them suffer because of our profession. Well, I had heard that kind of advice before. I never took Pia anywhere with me. This time I want my children with me.

"Moving around from city to city doesn't give children a feeling of insecurity. Security isn't a place—it's a person."

After thirty performances of *Joan* in London the Rossellini caravan returned to Rome for a brief respite. When next I heard from Ingrid, it was from the Hotel Arycasa, Barcelona, Spain, where she was presenting the oratorio in French.

> Last day of 1954: . . . In a few hours this year is gone, too. I get very sentimental on New Year's Eve and would like to cry in *all* my friends' arms. The time goes so fast, and year after year one says Happy New Year, and sometimes they are happy, sometimes not. But one thing is sure, they pass fast, and I always feel I haven't accomplished enough with the year that went. So this new year I want to do so much more!
>
> In each city we use their orchestra, and now again a different one. It is dreary to rehearse *Joan* again. I have already given at least sixty performances, and now I have to begin from the beginning. I was so bored with the rehearsals here, how bored am I not going to be in Palermo and then Stockholm! Well, there is no out until this tour is finished. Certainly, it is all very lovely, but, like every coin, it has its other side.

Late in January, 1955, one of Italy's best-known movie critics, Angelo Solmi, writing in the big Italian weekly *Oggi,* said Ingrid and Rossellini "would either have to change their style of work radically—or retire into dignified silence."

It was the first sharp criticism to be directed at the pair since *Stromboli*.

"The abyss into which Bergman and Rossellini have plunged can be measured by *Fear*," said Solmi. "This is not because this picture is any worse than their other recent films together, but because after half-a-dozen tries with negative results it confirms the inability of the couple to create anything acceptable to the public or the critics. Once the world's indisputable No. 1 star and successor to Greta Garbo, Miss Bergman in recent pictures has been only a shadow of herself."

The Rossellini entourage arrived in Stockholm the last week of February. In contrast to their previous visit, for some unaccountable reason, all the newspapers launched into an attack, raking up the past, criticizing her low-heeled shoes, their recently acquired Rolls-Royce, their meanderings all over Europe. One said they were nothing but gypsies, and that the only reason the children were brought along was to get free publicity.

"Even on the radio they made up nasty songs," wrote Ingrid. "After the opening night, the critics tore me to pieces. But apparently a lot of people don't read the critics. We had agreed to give only ten performances, but we ended with twenty-two."

Ironically, one of the dailies asked Ingrid if she would appear at a Sunday benefit to help raise polio funds. She quickly agreed, but on Sunday morning she read still another scathing attack upon herself. This time it was printed in the very newspaper that was sponsoring the benefit!

That night, standing before the charity audience, she said, "Please forgive me, but there is something I must speak out about. It is the only way I can defend myself against the newspaper attacks which have welcomed me home. Everything I say to them is twisted; everything I do is wrong. They say I bring my children with me for publicity. If I had not brought them, they would accuse me of neglecting them. If I permit photographers to take pictures, I am publicity mad. If I protect our privacy, they shout that I am uncooperative.

"They print lies—lies which I cannot answer!" she cried passionately. "They make statements about things they know nothing about. Maybe there is truth in Hans Christian Andersen's story of the town where anyone whose head is a little higher than the others must be cut down to others' level."

The audience sat spellbound as Ingrid paused a moment to compose herself. "Please forgive me," she concluded, "but this was my only chance to tell you how I feel, you who have been such wonderful audiences at our opera. No matter what they print about me, please believe what I say to you now."

Ingrid stopped and, for a moment, gazed at the hushed audience grimly, as if to say, "There, I have said it!" She turned to leave the stage and instantly the hall reverberated with bravos and applause.

Admiring her courage, the press reversed themselves and rallied to her side. When eventually Ingrid bade her native city farewell, it was in triumph.

Upon her return to Rome, she reported:

> Sweden was great fun. I had a hunch that the papers would pick on me, but I never dreamed to what an extent. It was great fun when war was declared and I answered back.
>
> Petter came to Stockholm while I was there, but he didn't call me. He didn't even call his friends. Too bad he wouldn't give me an opportunity to give Pia a direct message from me through him. So happy it would have made her to know that we don't quarrel any more.
>
> We still have not been able to rebuild Palazzo Steele. We were sure that with *Trip to Italy*, *Joan at the Stake*, and *Fear* we would be rolling in money. But all three turned out badly in Italy, where the theaters were empty.

Apparently, Ingrid's loyalty to her talented but misguided mate had by now been strained to the utmost; she now boldly stepped out on her own. With Rossellini's acquiescence, she flew to Paris, conferred with their mutual friend, Jean Renoir, and signed to do a picture with him during the coming winter. While there, she was approached by Miss Elvire Popesco, a play producer of Rumanian descent, about doing either *Tea and Sympathy* or *Cat on a Hot Tin Roof* on the Paris stage in French. She turned down *Cat* as not right for her, but she was attracted by *Tea and Sympathy*, the story of a preparatory-school student who is considered a sissy by his schoolmates, but is initiated into manhood by the headmaster's wife. Ingrid agreed to play the role of the headmaster's wife a year hence. This done, she rejoined her family at Santa Marinella.

Of *Tea and Sympathy*, Rossellini said, "It is trash."

In the meantime, Rossellini dreamed and schemed all manner of ambitious projects. He planned a five-month tour of Mexico and South America with *Joan at the Stake*. He held conversations about joint productions with English, French, German and Italian producers. He planned to make *Carmen* in Spain. He talked of doing a film in China, and one in Japan. Nothing jelled. He languished in confusion.

From Santa Marinella, Ingrid wrote, "Yesterday the roof over your room in the Palazzo Steele collapsed and crashed to the floor."

Finally, Rossellini galvanized into action, accepted an offer to make some documentaries in India, and announced he would be leaving for Calcutta around the end of the month, September, 1955.

For Ingrid, the prospect of doing a full-length play in a strange language presented a formidable challenge. She plunged into the manuscript of *Tea and Sympathy* with grim determination.

> It will be one year before I do it, and I hope that by then my French will be—good! I dare not say perfect!
>
> Thanks for the birthday cable. One isn't a young girl any more. I am beginning to feel a little embarrassed at the thought of playing Joan of Arc, I must say! All our friends were here by the sea, and we feasted for twenty-four hours. We even had fireworks at midnight, which pleased me no end.
>
> In a few days I am moving back to Rome. I must begin to think about the children's wardrobes for the winter. Roberto will leave for India at the end of the month. Here are a few snapshots for you. You can see how the children are growing.

Their Papa gets more and more overcome by their beauty, and has not yet been able to say no to anything they ask for!

The summer by the sea came to an end with the acute disappointment that "Pia's room" was still untenanted. Letters and cablegrams to Dr. Lindstrom and her first-born received scant attention. With bitter resignation, Ingrid decided "it is now up to Pia to make up her own mind."

By the end of November, Robertino and the twins with her, she was in the French capital, filming Jean Renoir's *Paris Does Strange Things*, a satirical lark concerning an exiled princess who schemes to help the careers of three men. Her costars were Mel Ferrer and French actor Jean Marais. Rossellini had not yet put off for India.

During the shooting of the picture, Kay Brown arrived from New York with an offer from 20th Century-Fox for Ingrid to appear in *Anastasia*, a story based on the life of a woman still living in Germany, who was persuaded to proclaim herself daughter of the last czar of Russia and claim a Romanov fortune.

Sharp intramural disputes ensued between Darryl Zanuck, its producer, and the sales department. Buddy Adler, head of all studio production, sided with Zanuck, while Spyros Skouras, president of the company, backed the sales experts. "Americans have never forgiven Miss Bergman and she will not be received at the box office," maintained the latter. But Zanuck, contending that "the Bergman case was inflated and publicized out of all proportion," held that Ingrid should be judged solely by her work as an artist. Zanuck persisted and Ingrid signed.

Of *Anastasia*, Rossellini remarked, "It is junk."

From Paris, on February 20, 1956, Ingrid wrote:

> We are now in the final week of the Renoir picture. It's the same old story—the picture finished, you leave new friends behind and start out with strangers again. Mel Ferrer and Jean Marais have been so wonderful to work with, and Jean Renoir is adorable as he always is.
>
> Roberto is still here. He is going to drive to India, and he wants to take pictures in the countries he passes through. It has taken him a long time to arrange for visas and permits in

the different countries. I worry for him when I think of the deserts and mountains he must cross. Now, I think, he'll be leaving in March.

Ruth wrote that she'll be coming to Europe in March. I'll be back in Rome by then and I hope she'll be able to come there. How good it will be to see her again!

The March and April rains of India forced Rossellini once again to postpone the venture. While he marked time he accepted an offer by producer André Hakim to direct British stars Richard Burton and Joan Collins in *The Seawife*, the story of a woman and two shipwrecked men, neither of whom knows that she is a nun. However, after several days of shooting on location in Jamaica, Rossellini quarreled about the interpretation of the script, quit the picture, and returned to Europe.

The end of May saw Ingrid established at the Savoy Hotel in London and busily occupied with *Anastasia*, which was directed by Anatole Litvak and costarred Helen Hayes and Yul Brynner. Because the picture would be filmed in both London and Paris studios she felt it best for the children that they remain in Santa Marinella.

They are with Marcella, Fiorella, and Roberto's mother, and having a great time. It is kind of restful for me too, as coming home after work I'm pretty exhausted. I have to get up at 6:30 every morning, and on weekends I work on *Tea and Sympathy*, which goes into rehearsals around the first of October.

We finally got a director for *Tea*. He is Jean Mercure. The others thought the theme was too naïve for France, and so were afraid of it. But I like it and will stick with it. It is a gamble, I know, and all my friends are against it. But you know a Swede; I'll go right against their advice, even if I fall flat on my face . . . Looking at your letter I see you ask about Pia. You know, it is now seven months she does not write. I have written and written . . .

Helen Hayes came on the set for the first time today. I almost burst out crying. She is such a great woman, and all the suffering she has gone through just breaks my heart. There is no one I would rather see as my grandmother in the picture than her. Can you imagine, she is worried about playing the part! The bigger they are, the humbler. How wonderful!

Early in July, Ed Sullivan, whom Ingrid and I had known for more than ten years, flew to London and made some film of Ingrid on the set of *Anastasia*, to be used on his television program. On his return he announced that he would show this film on a forthcoming Sunday night, and at the same time Ingrid would make a "live" appearance.

On the 29th of July, 1956, at the end of his show, Sullivan announced that the event would take place on the following Sunday. Then, inexplicably, he solicited an expression of his viewers' approval or disapproval of the appearance of "this controversial figure," reminding them that, "after all, Miss Bergman has had seven years' time for penance."

Sitting in my living room, watching the show, I was stunned by the inept, ill-advised invitation to the stone throwers. "Time for penance" resounded like the sanctimonious dogmatism of a modern-day Pharisee. I picked up the phone and dictated a radiogram to Ingrid, telling her what had gone on and suggesting that she cancel all commitments she had made to Sullivan.

20th Century-Fox studio promptly canceled the film from Sullivan's program. Ingrid denied that she had also promised a personal appearance. An avalanche of protests in the press and on the airwaves rose in her defense. Affection for Bergman, the woman, crushed the carpers and the cavilers.

On August 2nd, from the Savoy in London, Ingrid wrote:

Thanks for the wire. I think it outrageous, too. I raised hell here after your message came and the studio sent Sullivan many wires. Sullivan himself sent me *two* wires, telling me that he did it thinking it was for my own benefit. I am told he is really a nice person and that he made this error in good faith.

Now another picture draws to an end and I am quite sad, as always. Just when we are all so happy together the picture ends and we say good-bye. I have had the French director of

Tea and Sympathy here working with me on my French. I am quite uneasy, as I am not very good. I had thought it would be as easy as conquering English, but it has been far from it.

Around this time rumors emanated from Swedish papers that all was not harmonious in the Rossellini menage. Both issued vehement denials and the reports petered out in short order. In an interview, Ingrid said, "I am happy in my work and in my personal life. And I also want the world to know that I am not doing penance for anything."

On November 17, 1956, from the American Hospital in Paris, where she had gone for an appendix operation, she wrote:

This was an unexpected and welcome rest! You have no idea how I've worked lately. It was much tougher than I thought to learn *Tea* in French. Then with the Hungarian trouble and threat of a war next door, you can imagine in what a state we were. Roberto was leaving with the children for Italy, where he thought they'd be safer, when I became sick. He has been frantic lately, first because now he *is* going to India, and second, he fears there might be a war while he's away from the family.

Tea will open on December 1st. I hope I'll be in condition to do it. The way I feel today—two days after the Big Cut—I am not too sure. But, at least I have a few more days to study my lines.

Did you notice how Walter Winchell stood up for me after that Sullivan business? He even sent me flowers here at the hospital. How precious a little kindness can be!

I have no more interesting news for you—only Tea, Sympathy, and Appendix. No future plans as yet, but, then, I hope to play *Tea* the whole season. Roberto thinks it will run one week!

Her recuperation complete, on December 1st, as scheduled, she made her bow in *Tea and Sympathy* at the Théâtre de Paris. For this moment she had studied, prepared and rehearsed for more than one year, a feat of theatrical dedication which is truly remarkable.

Her success was instantaneous. Throughout the entire performance Rossellini sat in her dressing room, pouting, refusing to glimpse his wife on the stage. When the curtain fell after the last act, Paris was Ingrid Bergman's, and the first-night audience called her back fifteen times. Rossellini turned livid with fury. The wild applause still mocked him as he stalked out of the stage door into the rain-hushed street.

Thirteen days later there were omens of more honors to come. 20th Century-Fox held a press and industry preview of *Anastasia,* in the Beverly Hills theater of the Academy of Motion Picture Arts and Sciences. The instant Ingrid's name appeared (the first time in seven years that it had occurred in an American picture), the hard-boiled spectators burst into crashing applause. It was their way of saying hello and welcome back. And again, at the conclusion of several of her big scenes, they responded in like manner.

A few days later, the New York film critics voted her "best actress of the year." Bosley Crowther, motion-picture critic of the *New York Times,* said, "Miss Bergman's performance as the heroine is nothing short of superb. It is a beautifully molded performance worthy of an Academy Award."

Archer Winston of the *New York Post* said, "*Anastasia* is a royal pudding of grand quality and Ingrid Bergman is the priceless plum in it." Alton Cook of the New York *World-Telegram* said, "Miss Bergman is the same torrent of passionate and impulsive ardor that she was before leaving American films."

Three weeks before Christmas of 1956, Ingrid kissed her India-bound husband good-bye. He had yet to see a performance of *Tea and Sympathy*. The parting was perfunctory, the emotions dulled.

"We knew then that it was over," Ingrid told me, when next I saw her. "If only Roberto had accomplished something successfully, the marriage might have been saved. I understood him, but I was powerless to alter the way things were. Roberto's pride was hurt. Everything seemed to go against him—very hard for a man of his talent and ability to swallow. And *Anastasia* and *Tea and Sympathy* didn't help any."

On January eighth of the new year, 1957, Ingrid wrote of her projected trip to New York to personally receive the Film Critics' Award.

> Roberto does not want me to go, but then, he didn't want me to do *Tea and Sympathy*, either. So I am assuming my own responsibilities for a change. It is going to be a very tiring trip, but I look forward to it and feel quite emotional about seeing my beloved New York again.
>
> I feel sad that I won't be able to see Pia, because I will be there such a short time, and every moment is so busy with the schedule the studio people have arranged that it is impossible. Anyway, I prefer to see her under quieter circumstances, when we can be alone. You know what a field day the press would make of it, and that wouldn't be good for Pia. But, nevertheless, I look forward to phoning her from New York. Then we'll have no trouble hearing each other and we can have a nice, long, quiet talk. It'll be wonderful to hear her real voice and not that awful sound that comes over the radiophone.

On the 18th, as Ingrid prepared to wing across the Atlantic, she said in an interview, "I regret nothing in my life. Whichever way the wind blows, you have to take what life gives you. The press have implied that I am a bitter, beaten woman. This is not true. Dr. Albert Schweitzer has said that happiness is good health and a bad memory. I'm lucky in having both. I easily forget and forgive."

Ernest Hemingway was in Paris. "Why don't you let me fly with you to New York?" he said. "If anyone is mean to you, I'll fight them."

"No, thanks," Ingrid laughed. "I can take care of myself."

An Associated Press dispatch from Boulder, Colorado, reported, "Jenny Ann (Pia) Lindstrom said today mid-term examinations in her classes at the University of Colorado will keep her from visiting her mother, actress Ingrid Bergman, in New York this weekend. Miss Lindstrom said her mother had also written that 'this would not be a good time' to get together because Miss Bergman will be in New York for only a very short time. She added her mother told her most of the time would be given to press interviews and other affairs in connection with the Film Critics' Award.

"Miss Lindstrom said that her approaching exams and the fact that her mother's time in New York was mostly taken were the only reasons for not going to New York. She said her personal feelings for her mother were not involved in the decision . . . that she would meet her mother some other time when they would not be under so much pressure."

On the morning of Saturday, January 19, 1957—nearly eight years since her flight to Italy—a radiant Ingrid Bergman landed at Idlewild Airport to be met by warm, cheering welcomes from the show world and from hundreds of plain citizens. She was attired in flat-heeled shoes, a full-length mink coat over a black woolen suit and a white kerchief round her throat. The Alvin Gang teenagers of *Joan of Lorraine* memory, now grown into men and women, were there en masse, greeting her with banners and placards.

Everywhere she went crowds gathered, friendly crowds, asking for autographs, cheering and jostling police lines by the hundreds to see her. Scores of stage and screen notables turned out to greet her at the Award presentation ceremonies at Sardi's Restaurant.

Buddy Adler, production chief of 20th Century-Fox, had arranged for his studio to purchase outright three performances of *Tea and Sympathy* so that Ingrid could be free of her theater commitment to make the trip. He met her in New York and squired her through the many ceremonies and appearances. On his return to Hollywood he was interviewed by Dick Williams, entertainment editor of the Los Angeles *Mirror-News*.

"The public's acclaim for Miss Bergman in New York," said Adler, "was amazing and a source of great gratification to her. She never turned down a single autograph. She went on signing until the police asked her to stop and leave to avoid a riot." He took her to lunch at the Colony, at her request for a quiet place.

"Within minutes," Adler said, "there were at least fifty photographers from every wire service, syndicate and magazine surrounding us. She posed for their pictures throughout lunch." When they got up to leave, a crowd of more than a thousand persons had gathered on the street. Adler enlisted police aid, and eight officers moved with them after that.

Ingrid wanted to see *My Fair Lady*, the big hit musical version of Bernard Shaw's *Pygmalion*, so arrangements were made for her to attend the matinee performance. She first went backstage to pay her respects to the show's stars, Rex Harrison and Julie Andrews, then slipped quietly through the side door to the orchestra. Within minutes of her entrance, the word swept through the audience. When the show was over and the cast had taken its bows, the audience remained seated. Then as Ingrid got up to leave, they all arose and gave her a standing ovation.

She was escorted backstage again, and in Julie Andrews' dressing room she changed into a cocktail dress of black satin with an oval neckline, pinned a diamond brooch over her heart, circled a black velvet ribbon around her hair, and dashed over to the sixth floor of the Roxy Theater. There she was presented with another "best actress" award by Joan Crawford for *Look* magazine.

During her crowded thirty-six hours in New York Ingrid stayed in Irene Selznick's private suite at the Hotel Pierre. She planned a visit to the famous Fifth Avenue toy shop of F. A. O. Schwartz, but the store management volunteered to bring an assortment to her suite for her convenience. "Ingrid was amazed that they would do this," said Adler. "She told me, 'I once saw a picture of Mrs. Vanderbilt making a jewel selection at her home. I never dreamed you could do the same thing with toys.' "

She made only one selection, but it was the equivalent of a score—a "jungle gymnasium" consisting of many mechanical animals. Too large for the current nursery at the Hotel Raphael in Paris, she had it shipped directly to Santa Marinella, where it would be set up on the spacious lawn.

Wearied by Saturday's events, Ingrid slept late on Sunday. Waking fresh and exhilarated, she had morning coffee with Robert Anderson, author of *Tea and Sympathy*. Afterward, she put in a phone call to Boulder, Colorado, and talked with Pia for more than half an hour. This done, she called me in Los Angeles and with girlish exuberance recounted the thrills and joys of the past twenty-four hours. "I have just talked with Pia," she said. "We talked a long time. I hated to hang up. She sounds wonderful, and she said she'd come over and visit me this summer. The days until then will be long, but, then, these past years seem like forever."

After lunching with Irene Selznick and Kay Brown, she received a few old friends—actor Walter Pidgeon, actress Audrey Hepburn, Anatole Litvak, Mel Ferrer, Buddy Adler and his wife, Anita. At five P.M. an Air France plane bore her back to Paris.

The following morning a movie trade publication, the *Hollywood Reporter,* stated, "The No. 1 lady of the screen today is again Ingrid Bergman, judging by the tremendous press coverage and public reception that greeted her triumphant return . . . No other star, visiting potentate or returning hero received nearly as much space in the metropolitan press and on TV and radio as that accorded Miss Bergman for her 36-hour trip to New York."

A few days later, Lloyd Shearer, writing for *Parade* magazine, interviewed Pia at the University of Colorado. "When I was very young," she explained, "I went to court and they asked me how I felt about my mother. I said things I felt at the time. Now that I'm older I know I have no right to pass judgment on anything my mother's done. I just accept it. I never think about it. To me she's a fine, talented woman, and I love her.

"Naturally when it first happened I was self-conscious, but then we moved to Pittsburgh and my name was changed, and I forgot all about it. My mother used to call me on the transatlantic phone, but the connections were so bad we never could understand each other, so she stopped that. She has her family and her work to think about, and I have mine. My father's remarried, you know, and I have a new stepbrother (sic) in Salt Lake City, where we live now. His name is Peter Michael.

"The thing is that I haven't seen my mother in almost six years. When I was very little, she was very busy making movies. I didn't see her nearly as much as ordinary children get to see their parents. When she was working in a picture, she'd be gone before I got up. When she came home it was late, and I was already finished with dinner. At other times she was away on location or acting in a play on Broadway.

"The plain truth is that I don't really know my mother very well. That's why it's difficult for me to gush about her or get emotional every time someone asks me a question. Stories to the effect that I don't like my mother are not true. Will you please write that? I'm very proud of her. She's been through a lot, and she's shown a great deal of courage."

On February second, I had a long chat with Ingrid via transatlantic telephone. Some of the conversation went like this:

"What were you doing when this call came through?"

"I was sitting here with the children and the nurse. It's Robertino's birthday—he's seven years old today. We're going to have a big party for him. I've engaged two clowns from the circus, and there will be fifteen other children. The apartment at the Raphael is too small, so we've taken over a large room to entertain the children. It's a happy day, Joe."

In regard to her work, she indicated that she felt she was maturing in it, and added, "I think I would just quit if I didn't believe I was going to get better."

We discussed the five languages she speaks and the one in which she does most of her thinking.

"English, strangely enough, much more than Swedish," Ingrid mentioned. "English is the language which comes easiest for me. When I write letters, for example, I prefer to write them in English."

Then we talked about the memory she cherished most out of her quick triumphal return to New York.

"When I talked with Pia," she told me simply.

When we touched on her feelings about this country's reception of her, she remarked that the people in ". . . New York were very kind and I didn't expect them to be that kind. You know, I think it would be silly for me to say that they have forgiven me," she added. "That's kind of presumptuous. I mean, it's kind of presumptuous for one human being to forgive another one. I am not asking forgiveness. All I ask is: Look at her work; do you like the actress or not? And let me live in peace and don't bother about forgiving me. Because, you know, I'm not forgiving anything. That's just ridiculous. Should I forgive because people were nasty to me, too? Let's not talk about such things. Let's talk about the work we are doing."

On March 27th, Ingrid won Hollywood's supreme tribute, the Academy Award Oscar, at the Pantages Theater on Hollywood Boulevard. Cary Grant accepted the statuette in her behalf, saying, "It is a privilege to accept this award for so fine an actress." And then he directed his remarks to the microphone and to Ingrid in Paris, "Dear Ingrid–If you can hear me via radio, all your friends here send you congratulations, love, admiration and every affectionate thought."

But Ingrid did not hear it; she was sound asleep. In the morning she held a press conference in English, French and Italian. "I was so nervous and excited," she said, "as to whether I'd get the award or not, that I knew I couldn't sleep all night. So I took a sleeping pill. This award was much easier than the one I got for *Gaslight*, because I slept all through it. At the *Gaslight* award I was there in the audience and sweating it out, a most exhausting experience."

Seven weeks later, on May 17th, Rossellini telephoned Ingrid from Bombay, India, at 3:27 A.M. He was tremulous and incoherent. "There's going to be a scandal," he said, speaking now in Italian, now in French. "You must not believe one word you read–it is all blackmail–please don't let it upset you–blackmail–rumors–nothing but blackmail–they make trouble for me–blackmail–blackmail–blackmail . . ."

Two days later, the story broke concerning Rossellini's love affair with twenty-seven-year-old Sonali Das Gupta, mother of one- and five-year-old sons, wife of an Indian film director, Hari Das Gupta, age thirty-three. A fair, slim native of West Bengal, Mrs. Das Gupta was a writer working on Rossellini's scripts.

The last thread that held their marriage together, Ingrid's respect for the head of the family, suddenly snapped. But, confronting the world, Ingrid put on another face. To reporters she said, "I think someone is trying to hurt my husband."

From Bombay, the United Press reported that Rossellini termed the rumor as "absolute nonsense" and "humbug." "It's not the first time a newspaperman has indulged in fantasy," he was quoted.

Sonali added her own denials. And when asked if she was expecting a child, said, "I refuse to talk about it. It's all too absurd."

The New York *News*, which first broke the story of the romance, stated that Rossellini was trying to book steamship passage to Italy for both himself and Sonali, that "Sonali remained under heavy guard and in seclusion in her hotel room, adjoining Rossellini's, in the Taj Mahal Hotel. She has been confined to her bed for days while six guards stood outside expressly to keep her husband's relatives from rescuing her or wreaking vengeance upon her . . . A doctor called upon her. The nature of her illness is still undisclosed."

His six-month visa to remain in India having expired, Rossellini faced official resistance securing an extension. Efforts to obtain a passport for Sonali met with the same results.

Meanwhile, Ingrid Bergman Rossellini continued to play to packed houses at the Théâtre de Paris, and continued to defend her husband. On May 27th, in answer to a cable asking if she'd like me to come over and "hold her hand," she replied,

"Take it easy—I am not in need of any consolation, no hand to hold, not in the sense you meant it, anyway! The Indian hoopla is made-up stuff (or at least part of it; what does a wife ever *really* know!). Roberto told me on the telephone that all this started with a journalist whom he threw out of his room. The man promised to get even with him. That's all—he got even! I am terribly sorry for Roberto and the poor girl, but what can one do? It'll blow over."

The Bergman bravado had a hollow sound. Her defenses were tottering. It was good that she had her play to do, and audiences, responding to her lone predicament, applauded her performances louder than ever.

Around this time, Kay Brown hopped the Atlantic to submit the script of a story called *Indiscreet*, to be made with Cary Grant.

Ingrid liked it and signed a contract. Miss Brown also had business to transact with a Swedish impresario named Lars Schmidt, who had successfully invaded the French capital with several plays.

"You and Lars are the two nicest Swedes I know," Miss Brown said to Ingrid. "I think you should know each other." And forthwith, she arranged a dinner party.

The initial meeting was in an atmosphere of casualness, marked by Nordic reserve. They talked theater-talk, the plays Schmidt was currently presenting, about *Tea and Sympathy*, and Ingrid's cherished memory of *Joan of Lorraine* on Broadway. She related her adventure with *Joan at the Stake* in Stockholm, and joked about her "war" with the Swedish press. He made some good-humored observations of his own; then they both laughed and found a common ground in jesting about the foibles of their countrymen.

It was a good dinner, the conversation light, the evening pleasant. But no bells rang.

I wrote a friend in Paris and, among other things, asked him if by chance he had met Lars Schmidt. "Yes," he replied. He had. "To paraphrase an old cliché, Schmidt is tall, blond and handsome. In appearance, deportment and presence, he is a gentleman to the manor born. We would say he is *très distingué*. If he carried a briefcase, he could be the diplomatic hero of a movie."

The Indian government was finally persuaded to give Rossellini leave to stay long enough to complete the job he had half finished, and for which it had advanced him $25,000. At the same time, the central office of the Home Ministry reversed itself and issued Sonali Das Gupta a passport on the grounds that further delay would "infringe the private liberty of the individual."

Three weeks passed uneventfully for Ingrid, until toward the end of June when Lars Schmidt telephoned and asked her to dine with him. She welcomed the break in her routine and, after her evening performance, he called at the theater and took her to La Tour D'Argent, most famous of restaurants.

They chatted amiably, said nothing serious, and laughed quietly at some amusing reminiscence. As Ingrid later told me, Lars Schmidt was good company, unaffected, easy to listen to. When he saw Ingrid to her hotel, he politely thanked her for a lovely evening, and asked if he might call her again.

"Yes, I would like it," said Ingrid, "but my daughter, Pia, will be coming from America to be with me for the summer. I shall have very little time. It has been so terribly long since I've seen her. But I'll be back with the play in September."

On July 8, 1957, Ingrid and Pia were tearfully reunited in an empty airliner at Orly Airport. Pia, now nineteen, had flown to Stockholm with her father, her stepmother, and her halfbrother, Peter Michael. They remained to vacation in Sweden while Pia, at her own insistence, flew on to Paris to spend the summer with her mother.

At Orly, Ingrid pleaded with an army of photographers and reporters to allow her complete privacy for this initial reconcilement, in return for which they could come to her hotel and take all the pictures they wished. They acceded and, when the plane taxied to a stop and all the passengers had debarked except Pia, Ingrid slipped aboard and deliriously clasped the daughter she had not seen since that dark memory of six years ago in London. As they clung to each other, Ingrid was not aware that a renegade photographer had hidden inside the plane and soundlessly snapped a picture—not until she saw it in the Paris *Match*, an illustrated weekly.

Pia, unable to suppress her feelings, buried her pretty head in her mother's bosom, and for a long time they clasped each other tightly, murmuring incoherent endearments, unwilling to let go. After a moment—emotions expended—Ingrid held her daughter at arm's length and hungrily feasted her eyes. Pia gazed at her mother. "You are so young," she said proudly. "You don't seem at all like my mother."

Minutes later, Pia, almost as tall as Ingrid, with the same Nordic coloring, appeared in the doorway to face a battery of spectators. Overwhelmed by the sight, she hesitated. Ingrid quickly stepped forward, took her arm and, turning on broad smiles, they walked down the plane's ramp.

On July 10th, after an eight-month run, *Tea and Sympathy*

closed for the summer and Ingrid took Pia to Santa Marinella. At long last, "Pia's room" was occupied by its tardy tenant.

All else became secondary to the reunion. Ingrid took her lovely daughter to Naples and Capri, and to Siena to see the annual *corsa del palio*, the spectacular horse races held in the cobblestoned square. She took her to Taormina, in Sicily, where in the ruins of the ancient Greek theater, with the Messina Straits as a backdrop, Pia sat in the front row and watched her mother receive the golden "David of Donatello" award for her performance in *Anastasia*.

"It was an unforgettable experience," Ingrid later told me. "It was a most thrilling sight, 'way on top of that mountain, watching the ceremonies with all those people who had come from all over Italy. The 'Donatello' is like the Academy Oscar, but what really made it exciting and wonderful was that Pia was with me."

Back in Rome they toured its treasure of antiquities, and went shopping on Via Condotti and the Piazza di Spagna. They swam and boated in the clear blue sea that lapped the Mediterranean villa. Pia played with the children and struck up a warm friendship with seven-and-a-half-year-old Robertino.

On August 18th, reluctant to part with her repossessed daughter, Ingrid accompanied her by plane to Copenhagen, Denmark, whence she would fly back to Stockholm to rejoin her waiting father. At the airport, when it was time for Pia to depart, they walked down the ramp, instinctively holding hands. When they neared the gate and saw the cluster of passengers, they stopped where they could be alone. Mother and daughter faced each other.

"I've had such a good time, Jenny." Pia wanted it that way, though she would always be Pia to Ingrid.

"I did too, Mother. I don't know how to thank you."

"You can thank me by coming again next summer. Will you?"

"If you want me to," said Pia, tremulously.

"Of course I want you to. I want you to come every summer. And when you have no more school, I want you to come and stay with me as long as you like."

"Then I'll come," said Pia, holding back her tears.

The passengers started filing through the gate. Mother and

daughter embraced and kissed. Then Ingrid watched until Pia turned before entering the plane door. They waved, and Pia vanished.

Then Ingrid walked happily and resolutely down the fenced-in ramp. She cried softly to herself.

Four days later, Ingrid wrote me, "It is unbelievable what a thrilling, happy time we had together. It seemed as if eight years were wiped out in just a couple of hours. We are so alike, and feel and think the same way, there was no need for explanations of any kind. I can hardly wait for next summer when Pia will come again. Isn't it all wonderful?"

On her return to Salt Lake City, Pia decided to quit the University of Colorado and switch to Mills College, Oakland, California, where she would be closer to home.

By the end of September, Ingrid was back in Paris, reappearing in *Tea and Sympathy*, and seeing Lars Schmidt with increasing frequency. Slowly, unconsciously, the two had found each other. The bells had begun to ring.

Of recent weeks the news from India had been sparse, but within days the unsavory reports erupted again. Rumors were rife that Sonali Das Gupta had secretly arrived in the city. Further, that she had issued an "ultimatum" to Ingrid to divorce her husband, which knowledge Ingrid denied.

As it turned out, Sonali had indeed flown to Paris on October 6th. Two weeks later, Rossellini himself arrived and Ingrid met him at Orly Airport. They hugged and kissed in the crowded waiting room, while photographers snapped pictures. He stroked her blond hair tenderly. It was a highly skilled joint performance. Press and public were convinced. For the present.

That evening Rossellini sat in her dressing room at the Théâtre de Paris. He had been absent in India for exactly eleven months. As Ingrid got herself ready for the show, he commented, "You are still doing this junk?"

On October 31st, Ingrid made her last appearance in *Tea and Sympathy*. The following day the Rossellinis flew to Rome to conclude a legal separation, the papers having already been filed by their Italian attorney, Ercole Graziadei. On November 7th they signed the necessary documents before Mario Elia, President of the Rome Civil Court.

Graziadei made the agreement public, announcing that Rossellini had agreed to provide $960.00 a month for his family's support. Since Rossellini was hopelessly in debt and his monetary obligations insolubly entangled, this last was palpably a face-saving measure. The separation gave Rossellini full free visitation rights with the children.

Echoing the ambiguities of the 1949 Messina statement issued by Ingrid and Lindstrom, Graziadei released a letter signed by Ingrid and Rossellini, addressed to himself, explaining the reason for the rift:

"For some time we have encountered difficulties in continuing our life together. The different directions which our artistic activities have taken during the past two years have also been affected by differences in viewpoints and interests which divided us and which already had been interpreted in this sense. All this has brought us, after long reflection, to the decision to separate for good.

"An unforgettable past, the love for our children and reciprocal profound affection guarantee the serenity of our future relations."

With no bitterness, Ingrid set her eyes towards London, where on November 17th she would begin the filming of *Indiscreet*. Presently, while reports persisted that Sonali was pregnant, Rossellini came to Ingrid with a personal problem.

"The Indian government will not let me take my film out of the country," he said. "I need it to cut and edit for European television. Without it, I am lost. Nehru is now in London. Please go to him and ask him to release it. You can do this for me."

Sooner than she had planned, Ingrid flew to London and sought out a friend, Ann Todd, the British film star, who was a friend of Nehru's sister, the Indian Ambassador to Britain. Ann Todd managed an appointment and Ingrid was presented to the Prime Minister at the Indian Embassy.

"I regret, Madame Bergman," said Mahatma Gandhi's successor, "that there is not much I can do about cinema intrigues." But Ingrid quickly assured him that this was not the object of her mission. With all the sincerity at her command, she pled her husband's cause, and the order went to India to release the film for shipment to Paris.

In the midst of shooting *Indiscreet*, Ingrid wrote me on November 28, 1957, from the Connaught Hotel in London. She said:

> The children are in Italy for the time being. I will go down for Christmas, when we have a five-day layoff, and bring them here. I will find a little house and we'll stay about a year, as after this one I'll be doing *Inn of the Sixth Happiness* for 20th Century-Fox. In the summer I might go to Santa Marinella, if it is still available. I am very happy I have these pictures lined up.
>
> Be assured that all is well with us. I honestly believe even Roberto will feel a relief at no longer being the husband of a star. He'll make great pictures once again. Let's face it, artistically we were not good for each other. I hope the bad press will soon be over and he can start a new life with more peace . . . Knowing how little time there will be next month, I had better say Merry Christmas right now. And you are the first to get my greetings.

Mike Connolly, a columnist for the *Hollywood Reporter*, stated in that paper that in the separation agreement Ingrid had "paid off" Rossellini with a sizable piece of her *Indiscreet* earnings. I sent her the item, saying, "I earnestly pray that you are now achieving some sort of financial security; that some wise business head—Kay Brown, perhaps—is investing your money where no one can touch it. Forgive Papa if he feels a bit concerned."

Ingrid replied, "The clipping you sent me is not true. I am finally planning to get rich. However, right now there is very much to take care of in Italy. Nevertheless, it won't be staggering for me. By the time I have finished these pictures, we will have 'champagne and caviar' every day!"

The "insecure, hand-to-mouth existence," to which she had referred in a recent interview, had come to an end.

The legal separation, *per se*, still was not the desired solution to their lives. Both Ingrid and Rossellini wanted complete, unqualified freedom, but they now faced a maze of complications:

(a) There is no divorce in Italy. An annulment is the sole recourse, obtainable only by corroborative evidence of a serious flaw in the original marriage, as in the Rossellini-de Marchis case.

(b) Robertino, Isabella and Ingrid, Jr., were Italian citizens.

(c) Though the separation agreement granted her custody, Ingrid had no wish to deprive the father of his children.

(d) If Ingrid bypassed an Italian annulment and obtained a divorce from Rossellini in some other country, then married again, she faced the possibility of being considered a bigamist in Italy. If, subsequently, she wanted to visit the children when they were with their father in Italy, she could be subjected to a number of legal hurdles and embarrassments.

(e) Ingrid was a Swedish citizen when she married Rossellini a few days after her Mexican divorce from Dr. Lindstrom.

(f) When the proxy marriage ceremony took place, the divorce had not yet been registered in Sweden. Because of this omission, insofar as Italian law was concerned, Ingrid was still the wife of Dr. Lindstrom when she married a second time.

The tangle of international technicalities appeared insurmountable until attorney Graziadei came up with the answer: If the divorce was not registered in Sweden at the time they were married in Juarez, then, *ipso facto*, the proxy marriage was illegal.

Based on this tenuous interpretation, Graziadei filed suit, late in December, 1957, in a Rome civil court for an annulment in behalf of Rossellini. As to the children's status under an annulment, in Italian law no child is illegitimate so long as the father acknowledges parenthood.

In London, Ingrid's optimistic plan to lease a house and have the children with her was thwarted by her husband's refusal to let them go. Philosophically, she resumed her work in *Indiscreet* and patiently prayed for an early ruling of the Italian court. Nineteen fifty-eight displaced the turbulent old year and she lived in the promise of better days to come.

In Paris, Rossellini labored on the Indian film, cutting it into short sequences for television. Periodically, he dashed to Rome to try to straighten out his multiplying business problems. He domiciled at the Raphael Hotel, a short distance from the Arc de Triomphe, where he and Ingrid had often stayed. It was rumored that Sonali Das Gupta occupied an adjoining room, but actually no one saw her. Her true whereabouts was unknown.

Early in March, while marking time for the nullification hearing, calendared for May 7th, Ingrid and Lars Schmidt took a trip together to Sweden, he on business, she to visit friends and relatives. Her countrymen were delighted to see her once again with a Swede. Newsmen asked if they planned to marry. "We neither deny nor confirm that," answered Schmidt, quietly and pleasantly. "I guess that says a lot, doesn't it?"

Ingrid went to work in London on *The Inn of the Sixth Happiness* on St. Patrick's Day, 1958, costarring with the English actor, Robert Donat, and the German actor, Curt Jurgens. The film's story concerned an Englishwoman, still living, who went to China as a missionary and ended, after suffering at the hands of bandits and Japanese invaders, by adopting more than one hundred children.

Three weeks later, Ingrid wrote from London:

> Roberto brought the children from Santa Marinella to Paris. I've been trying to get him to let them come and stay with me for a few days, but he has been difficult. Just as I was getting angry, little Ingrid came down with an appendix and had to go to the hospital. Now, thank goodness, she is well and should be able to make the trip in two weeks. I just hope Roberto will not make more trouble. He gets low and depressed, he says, and to have the children around is his only comfort. I guess it doesn't matter that I haven't seen them for five months!
>
> My plans are to finish this picture, then settle in a house in the Paris suburbs. Aside from that, my life is a bit confused

right now. The annulment comes up May 7th, but one never knows if it will be postponed again or even refused.

On June 24, 1958, Ingrid wrote on the stationery of The Hotel Portmeirion, Penrhyndeudraeth, Merionethshire, Wales, where her picture was shooting exteriors:

> Before we move back to London for three more weeks of work, I wanted you to see where I have been this last month. Try to pronounce *that* in a sober state! It's lovely country, but the weather is not for movies. Day after tomorrow we leave . . . but I am tired. It will be eighteen weeks' work when the picture is finished.
>
> The children have been with me and over this weekend I'll take them to Paris. Then Roberto will take them to Santa Marinella for two months of sunshine and swimming.
>
> The annulment hearing has been postponed three times by the Rome court. Now it is set for June 30th . . .

Formal hearings were held on that date in Rome's First District Court of Judge Mario Elia. The annulment was granted, but in accordance with Italian law, the public prosecutor, Martin Ferrauiolo, announced his intention to appeal the decision. The annulment would not be final until the appeal was heard, which, to everyone's discomfiture, might take months. Coincident with this action, Sonali Das Gupta filed suit in Bombay for divorce from her husband.

July came, and with it, Pia. They made the rounds of Paris, visited the Louvre, browsed among the bookstalls along the Left Bank. Looking more like sisters than mother and daughter, they shopped and dined, walked in the Bois, drove to Versailles, and climbed the Eiffel Tower.

"We were like old friends," wrote Ingrid. "We had so much fun together. Then we'd come home exhausted, and after dinner we'd sit up till all hours talking, talking, talking. She is such a lovely girl."

"Dear Ingrid," I wrote, a few weeks later. "I'm coming to Europe sometime in October and, needless to say, you are my

Number One objective. Number Two, Papa wants to meet this Lars Schmidt person! And, of course, the children. After that, I can go about my business."

She replied, "What a wonderful surprise your news was! You certainly shall meet Lars, and by then the children will be with me and you can see how beautifully they have grown since you last saw them . . ."

When September came, the Rome prosecutor's appeal to nullify the annulment had yet to be heard. Nevertheless, Ingrid's mind was made up as to her future course. With Lars Schmidt she set out to find a home against the day—soon they hoped—when they would marry. Through a Paris real-estate agent they found what they had envisioned—a manor house in the country, far from the world of tumult and temperament in which they both labored.

From Choisel (pronounced Shwa-zel), France, came a letter from Ingrid:

> Truly, it is a lovely house. We described to the agent exactly the kind of place we wanted, and he showed us this one. It was the first and only one we looked at, but we knew it was ours the minute we saw it. Not very large, but there are plenty of rooms for all of us. And there will be a room for Pia. There are many things that have to be done—painting, plumbing, redecorating, and a room to add on. But when it is all done, this will be home. We call it *La Grange aux Moineaux*, which means "a barn for sparrows."
>
> Soon you will be coming, and I am disappointed because I had hoped to have a room for you to stay. But workmen have been a big problem; they are so hard to get, due to all the building going on. So, I have to concentrate on the children's rooms and on the kitchen, which was very old-fashioned.
>
> The children will soon be here to start school in Paris. That is, if all goes well, because Roberto makes everything difficult, and I have to constantly see my lawyers. So you see, I cannot put you up in one of the children's rooms, even if your long legs could stand the short beds.
>
> Choisel is a very small village of about twenty houses. It

is about twenty-five miles from Paris. It has only one little inn-cafe, but I have no idea what it is like. I do all my grocery shopping at Chevreuse, which has two or three small hotels. However, that is four kilometers from here.

Now I must stop writing, because I am meeting Lars for lunch. He is a fine and kind person, Joe, and full of understanding. He is very honest and very uncomplicated. As Kay Brown says, "The first man in my life without a big ego."

Many people seemed shocked that so soon after the separation I fall in love. But no one will ever know how many years I lived without any love at all.

14.

Choisel

AT New York's Idlewild Airport the TWA ticket counter had run out of maps of Paris and environs. A young lady behind the counter, not in uniform, overheard my query. In a French accent—she said she was from the Paris office—she asked if she could be of assistance.

"Yes, thank you. I want to go to a little place outside Paris, called Choisel. If it's in the direction of Orly Airport, it would be foolish for me to take the bus to Paris and then backtrack to Choisel."

"Ah, yes," she said. "Choisel *is* near Orly. It is better you take a taxi from the airport."

Flying over the Atlantic, I mused over what information I had garnered about Lars Schmidt: he was the scion of an old shipping family in Göthenburg, born on the 11th of June, 1917, in an old family mansion in Lerum, a small town on the southwest coast of Sweden. His father was a retired army major. Schmidt was divorced and had a son who was killed in an accident in 1950 at the age of eight.

Always interested in the graphic and dramatic arts, during World War II Schmidt came to New York, purchased the Scandinavian rights to the Broadway hit, *Arsenic and Old Lace*, and produced it in Stockholm with great success. Subsequently, he imported scores of playscripts with considerable profit. He maintained headquarters in both Stockholm and Paris.

"He's quite a man, Joe," Kay Brown had said. "Forget that he's good-looking. They're a dime a dozen. Lars is highly civilized—solid."

My seat companion on the plane was a Mr. Renato Supino, an Italo-American from Demarest, New Jersey, engaged in international insurance, who also maintained a home near Paris. Still unsure of Choisel's whereabouts, I plied him with questions about my destination.

"The sound is familiar," he said, with an odd mixture of French and Italian accents. "Do you have any more address?"

"Yes. *Seine et Oise*."

"Ah, that is not in the direction of Orly. You should go first to Paris. I have a house at Le Vesines, in the same district. When we arrive at the terminal, we shall inquire."

At the Invalides Air Terminal in Paris Mr. Supino asked at the TWA desk how best to reach Choisel. Choisel? No one had ever heard of it. He tried the Air France desk and received the same blank looks. After an hour of this fruitless quest, he approached the telephone section.

"Tell them," I said, "it is where Ingrid Bergman lives." My benefactor did so. The effect was electrical. The hearty, full-breasted woman in charge not only pinpointed the elusive locale, but also cautioned that it was an expensive taxi ride. Ignoring the accumulating requests for service, this amazing lady called a railroad, and advised us that "*l'ami de Madame Bairgman*" should take an interurban train at the Gare de Luxembourg, which ran every few minutes. However, she counseled, the train only went as far as Chevreuse, where I would have to take a taxi for the remaining four kilometers to Choisel.

At the station, utilizing a gibberish of French, Italian, English, together with pantomime, I managed to have myself directed aboard the train. The autumn air was biting and damp. As dusk descended over the beautiful countryside the taxi from Chevreuse delivered me to the little inn at Choisel, but all its three rooms were taken. My driver suggested Cernay-la-Ville, a town of six hundred, three kilometers in another direction.

In twenty minutes I was snugly ensconced in a tiny room equipped with an enamel wash basin, a large pitcher of water, a bed piled high with coverlets, and an electric heater (?) consisting of a single six-inch coil. The sanitary facilities, *circa* Napoleon, were in a shed in the backyard. Madame Benoit, an attentive, motherly woman, was the landlady. The name of the inn was "*Le Week-end*," and its printed slogan "*Comme chez soi*" (like home itself).

Madame Benoit tried to put in a phone call to Ingrid for me, but the operator said her number had been changed and she was not permitted to give it out. Frazzled and hungry, I dined and retired. Morning brought with it a steady but gentle rain. Through Madame Benoit I located a young garage owner who agreed to drive me to Ingrid's house. Nothing stirred among the handful of mouse-gray houses called Choisel as we rolled along in a midget Peugeot. About half a mile from the village the driver pulled up before tall wooden gates flanked by a ten-foot-high stone wall.

I asked my chauffeur-friend to wait and entered through a small door within the gate. At this instant, as if on signal, the rain clouds parted and shafts of sunlight painted the landscape. A vista of extraordinary serenity and loveliness held my gaze. A hundred yards to the left, at the end of a broad gravel driveway, was the house. Built of quarried stone, its second floor of dormered windows sloped into a ridge of pastel gray, blue and red tiles. The garages and servants' quarters adjoined the house to form an L.

On the other side of the house spread a carpet of lush, verdant lawn—three acres, perhaps—overlorded by two majestic cypress trees plumb in the center. On all sides beyond the green rectangle was a forest primeval of pines and poplars, chestnuts and more cypress.

A big black shepherd barked once or twice, then came to greet me with wet paws. A white-jacketed young man emerged from the house, followed by a maid in white apron and lace cap.

Ostensibly the butler, the young man informed me in halting English that Madame Bergman was not at home; she was in Paris and he did not know when she would return. After elaborately identifying myself, I asked him to call her on the telephone. He shook his head and said, "I cannot do that, *M'sieur*. It is too early."

"Well, then, here is my name. I am stopping at Le Week-end in Cernay-la-Ville. I will go back and wait for her call. You telephone and give her the message."

Three hours later Madame Benoit fluttered with excitement: "*M'sieur! Madame Bergman téléphone!*"

"Hello–hello–Ingrid!"

"Halloo, Joe. My goodness, when did you arrive?–why didn't you let me know?–are you all right?–is your hotel all right?–what a funny name, Le Week-end!"

"Yes, yes, Ingrid. I'm okay. It's not exactly the Hampshire House, but the people are nice and the food is good–"

She laughed merrily. "My goodness, you are really here!"

"What are you doing in Paris?"

"I've been here the last two days, buying things for the house, getting winter clothes for the children. It's good that you're comfortable, Joe. I can't wait to see you. I'll come right back. Why don't you have lunch with me at the house–I'll send a car for you . . ."

It rained fitfully; between the downpours the sky turned a lambent blue. About one o'clock I stood in the entryway of the house and called out Ingrid's name. From upstairs responded her voice, vibrant and gay. She hurried down the hall and we met midway on the staircase.

"You are here!" Then, touching my ears, she exclaimed, "But where are your earmuffs?"

"Well, I'll be hanged! I completely forgot 'em." I drew them out of my overcoat pocket and put them on.

"That's more like it!" she chuckled.

The initial greetings over, she said, "The children were to have left Santa Marinella yesterday. Now they won't leave until next week. If they had come this morning I would have had to share your time with them. I haven't seen them for three months." Her face clouded. "Roberto promised they'd come two weeks ago. Now he says they'll be here next Monday."

"Is he with them?"

"No, he is in Paris. He lives at the Raphael. Come, I'll show you the house . . ."

In the kitchen: "All this is new—the pine walls—the cupboards. My, how hard it was to find a good carpenter. Everybody is so busy these days. And look, an electric range! And here is our jewel . . ." She pressed a button and the spits of an automatic *rôtisseur* began to revolve.

In the small dining room, which could seat no more than eight, and looked out across the lawn to the forest beyond, Ingrid gestured toward the scarlet wallpaper which teemed with white arabesques, and asked, "How do you like that?"

"Rather busy, I'd say."

"That's what Lars says. It came with the house. This is the only room I haven't done over. You get dizzy just looking at it. Well, when I get all the other things done, I'll find something quieter."

"When do I meet Lars?"

"Tonight. He'll be coming for dinner."

Down the carpeted hall: "This is my bedroom—still needs a few things." (Sparsely furnished, the room contained a mahogany double bed, a spread of rich chenille in broad red-and-white stripes. On a small dresser was a leather triptych, holding snapshots of her children, including Pia.)

"And here is the bath," said Ingrid. "Good and big. I like big bathrooms and big towels. And down here (at the end of the hallway) is the new addition to the house—a bedroom for Pia." (A plasterer was at work.)

In the large living room: "There is so much to do in here. Bookcases, cabinets, rugs, ugh, so much . . ."

A brick-and-stone fireplace occupied one corner. French doors led to a terrace paved with irregular slabs of cement. On a wall hung two oils painted by her father, a self-portrait and a wistful one of her mother. Opposite them hung a three-foot oil of herself as Joan of Arc, which RKO had made as a lobby display, and had sold to Ingrid for one hundred dollars when they had no further use for it. Beside a sofa was a magazine rack containing American, Swedish, French and Italian publications.

On a table stood the bronze figurine of Joan presented her in the *Joan of Lorraine* days by her leading man, Sam Wanamaker. On a desk, in leather and silver frames, reposed pictures of Arthur Honegger and Paul Claudel, composer and writer of *Joan at the Stake*, and of French comedian Maurice Chevalier, each affectionately autographed. Beside them was a white-bearded study of Ernest Hemingway, on which he had drawn on his right sleeve a heart pierced by an arrow.

"When I was doing *Joan at the Stake* in Paris," said Ingrid, "Claudel came to watch the rehearsals, but Honegger was very sick and could not leave his bed. I wrote him letters from the different cities where we played, and sent him a few pictures he had asked for. He wanted so much to come to Milan for the opening at La Scala. He sent me this picture when I was there."

With the photograph, the great modern composer had sent a letter saying that his life was running out, and that his only remaining consolation was spreading out her pictures and letters on the bed before him and just gazing at them.

"When I came to Paris I went to see him," said Ingrid. "He was seventy years old and seemed shrunken to nothing. I said, 'But you don't look a bit like your photograph.' He said, 'I didn't want you to see me as an ugly old man.' "

The butler announced luncheon and we went in to enjoy roast veal, assorted cheeses and white wine. She ate sparingly, and plied me with questions about my family, Ruth Roberts, and the state of Hollywood movies. Outside the window, the skies cleared and the sun sparkled on the moist terrain. Then we went out on the terrace where she became absorbed in some press clippings and magazine articles I had brought her.

She was dressed in powder-blue slacks, a cardigan sweater with white and blue vertical stripes, white socks and rope-soled shoes of blue canvas. Her shoulder-length hair was held back by a plain bandeau. On the third finger of her left hand she wore a ring of gold mesh designed like a strap and buckle.

Time had emphasized the lines around her mouth and her eyes. The warm color of her cheeks shone through a soft tan. Her skin clung closer to the bone and accentuated the chiseled conformation of her face. I was particularly struck by the alteration in the set of her jaws—tight and grim and full of determination.

With maturity had come a resurgent self-assurance absent in former years. Under the surface of tranquillity was a lurking belligerence.

During my two-week visit I was to witness frequent bursts of laughter and sudden flashes of anger.

Presently, Ingrid finished her reading. "Ugh, the things they write," she said. She mentioned an article by a well-known woman columnist. "She came on the set in London and talked with me for five minutes. Now she writes as if she spent the whole day with me. I never said half the things she writes."

She excused herself, went inside, and reappeared, wearing a heavy white coat sweater and short rubber boots. "Let's take a walk," she said, and promptly started off on a narrow, soggy path that bordered the great lawn. She took long vigorous strides and I followed as best I could.

"Isn't all this lovely, Joe?"

"Truly beautiful. Ever since I arrived I've been storing up the air to fortify me against the smog when I get back."

"It's wonderful for the children. They love it so." The black shepherd caught up with us. "Look at him, so friendly with you, yet he never saw you before. Lars got him for a watchdog, and all he does is make up to every stranger he sees. We'll have to get a watchdog to watch him."

The path took a sharp turn at the far end of the lawn and we headed for the jungled woods. Ingrid's throaty voice issued from deep down and flowed like water tumbling through pebbles. When she spoke of her children the words took on a lyric quality, as if accompanied by music.

"Where will the children go to school?"

"In Paris," she said. "The Leonardo da Vinci, Liceo Italiano."

"Italian?"

"Yes, but they'll study French also. They're very good with languages, but sometimes they answer French with Italian. They're quite bright, I'll have you know. Even now they know a little English. Choisel is only forty-five minutes from Paris, so it won't be too hard taking them back and forth. You remember Helena, the maid I had on Stromboli; I have her back again. She loves the children and they get along wonderfully. She's with them now in Santa Marinella. You'll be seeing her."

"What is the status of the annulment?"

Instantly, her tone changed. "Oh, it is awful—driving me crazy. The hearing of the prosecutor's appeal has been constantly postponed. Now Graziadei says it will be soon. I hope so. I'm tired of waiting so I can get married. Lars is such a fine man, Joe."

Then for a couple of minutes she was silent. There was nothing but the sound of crunching leaves and branches pushed aside. Her pace never abated.

"Roberto and I were simply not good for each other," she resumed, as if there were things that needed to be said. "He tried hard, very hard. And I tried, but we kept pulling apart. You were right on Stromboli, when you said that our happiness depended on our work.

"It hasn't been easy, but it is best for both of us this way. I think now it is the end of hunting for me. I mean I have found what I need—the children—my work—our house. And how very lucky I am to have found Lars."

She suddenly stopped and turned, her eyes beseeching understanding. I pressed her hand reassuringly. By the time we had made the circuit back to sit on the terrace, white clouds obscured the sun and the air grew chill. Ingrid fetched an automobile robe and wrapped it around her legs. Toward 5:30, as the sky darkened, we went inside. I put a match to the logs in the fireplace while Ingrid left the room. In a moment she returned holding a small glass pitcher.

"Here's some lemon juice—all we had," she grinned. "Maybe you can make enough for two Scotch sours, for old time's sake."

After going through the essential motions, I handed her a glass. "To your early marriage," I said.

"*That* is a very good toast," was her response.

Along about 6:30 Lars Schmidt arrived. "How do you do," he spoke in Oxfordian English. "I've heard much about you. Your flight was comfortable, I hope."

Tall and well-proportioned, his very blond hair, clear skin and well-organized features presented a youthful aspect. He was conservatively attired in a dark suit, white shirt and black tie. His blue eyes were framed by horn-rimmed glasses. His manner was debonair, yet reserved. He made you feel as if he had known you a lifetime.

On the third finger of his left hand there was a ring similar to the one worn by Ingrid. As we sat before the flaming logs I could almost touch the empathy between them; an unostentatious exchange of affection, respect and admiration. A feeling of peace and harmony and comfort hovered in the air.

Schmidt neither drank nor smoked while Ingrid and I finished our meager cocktails. When we went in for dinner, Schmidt indicated the wallpaper and said, "Has Joe seen this monstrosity?"

"Oh, yes. We've been through all that. He agrees with you."

"Then I must say he is a gentleman of taste. It takes a strong stomach to sit here and eat." And they beamed amiably at each other.

Dinner consisted of roast chicken, garden vegetables, a *tarte* of dwarf strawberries, white wine and camembert cheese, during which we talked about the weather, Le Week-end, and Ingrid's purchases of the last couple of days.

We returned to the living room and took the same positions as before, in front of the friendly fire; Ingrid and I on the sofa; Lars Schmidt opposite Ingrid, close enough to touch her.

In response to my question, Schmidt told of his current presentations both in Stockholm and Paris—*Cat on a Hot Tin Roof*, *The Diary of Anne Frank*, *Two for the Seesaw*, and *Brittanicus*. In an easy, relaxed manner, he spoke of the successful ones and those of doubtful prospects. His yellow hair fell carelessly over his well-shaped brow, and glistened under the reading lamp.

He seemed accessible and courteously communicative, urbane, and gallant and yet meditative at the same time. "How long are you going to be here?" he wanted to know. "Will you stop over in Paris? You know Paris, of course. Please take my telephone number and call me. Let us have lunch or dinner. If there is anything you need or anything we can do for you, please be sure that my office is at your service . . ."

Ingrid drew up her legs, eased comfortably against the end of the sofa, and contentedly let the two men get acquainted with each other. When she looked at Lars Schmidt, it was with the look of having come to the end of hunting. And when their glances met he reciprocated with gentle, unobtrusive warmth. An integrity of spirit and conscience flowed from one to the other, the kind of rapport that is born of genuine affinity. Absent was the possessiveness and domination I had known in her other domestic atmospheres.

Soon after midnight, Lars Schmidt dropped me off at Le Week-end and returned to his Boulevard Flandrin apartment in Paris.

One day, while walking less breathlessly through the woods, I asked Ingrid how the children were taking their parents' separation.

"Very well, thank goodness," she said. "Fortunately, they are used to one or both of us being away from them for long periods. Roberto was eleven months in India, you know. So when we told them about the separation, we explained that it was because our work kept us apart; for instance, when he was in India I was working in Paris or London and Wales. It was not difficult for them to understand. They accepted it and went on as before."

"How do they feel about Lars?"

"You see how easy it is to be with Lars. He doesn't force himself on you. He is so restful. They took a liking to him right away, but in the beginning Robertino was a little aloof. He loves his father very much—so do the twins—and Roberto is terribly wrapped up in them. I wouldn't want it any other way."

"Kay told me about the first time you met—but how did it all develop? Apparently, neither one of you was swept off your feet in the beginning."

"No, that is true," she said reminiscently. "I think it was good that way . . ."

Then, as she talked, I gathered that Lars Schmidt had not come upon the scene astride a white charger; that Ingrid was not a wide-eyed maiden, yearning for unattainable moons. Imperceptibly, without their awareness, the magic of like interests—the world of the theater, the art galleries, music, literature, the outdoors—had drawn them closer and closer. What had begun so casually, so innocently, had grown into a mature mutual appreciation, nourished by calm reflection and sober considerations. Lars Schmidt was staunch and comfortable and answered her need for leavening laughter.

"We laugh about the same things," said Ingrid. "That is important. We laugh all the time. I love to hear him laugh."

She told me how, on her visit with him to Sweden, he had taken her to the southwestern coast and showed her a two-acre island called Dannholmen. Of solid rock, barren of foliage, it was shaped like the back of a hippopotamus. On it he had built a small but modern bungalow.

"Lars is very fond of boating and fishing," she said. "Ten years ago, when he first saw the island, he fell in love with it and made up his mind that one day he would buy it. Two years ago, he did. Next summer we're going to spend our vacation there. We'll surely be married by that time."

Another day I asked Ingrid how she found Pia on her last visit. Her answer was tinged with pride and tenderness. "Oh, we had a wonderful time. I wish you could see her, Joe. She's grown into a fine young woman—and very pretty. We are awfully good friends."

"Is she studying anything special?"

"No. She just wants to finish college and then go to work at something. She has no particular boy friend and has no marriage plans—at least not now. She's got a lot of our stubbornness and has her own ideas about what she wants to do.

"Monday, when the children arrive, I want you to come and see them; then I want them all to myself the rest of the day. After that, we'll have more time together."

"Of course. I'll find something to do."

"You'll just have to spend your time at the bars and nightclubs of Cernay-la-Ville," she said, referring, no doubt, to Le Weekend. "But please don't get lost."

Monday came and Ingrid telephoned, her tone bristling with temper. "The children are not coming today. I don't know why. I can't get a sensible excuse. Now Roberto says they will leave Rome Wednesday. It's awful—I don't know what to do..."

Wednesday came and the episode was repeated. This time she hopped in the Simca station wagon and rushed off to Paris to see Rossellini. She returned with his assurance that the children would definitely arrive on Friday, the 17th. On the 16th she was frantic that their departure would again be postponed.

"Why don't you telephone Santa Marinella and find out if they have left?" I said.

She made the call and spoke to someone in Italian. After she hung up the receiver, she turned fretfully: "Ugh, the housekeeper says they have gone to Rome with Helena to take the train. I wish I could be sure."

"Anyone you can call in Rome?"

"Yes—Marcella—she would know."

She tried, but Marcella was out. "She's probably gone to the station to see them off," I said. The mounting strain dissolved from her countenance.

Confident that now I would be sure to see the youngsters before leaving for London, I announced my intention to go to Paris Friday evening, spend two days there, then fly out Sunday night. Lars Schmidt promptly took over; he would see to my hotel and plane reservations. "And let us have lunch on Saturday," he said.

About four o'clock on Friday, Ingrid's voice, in an extremely agitated state, came over the wall telephone in the kitchen of my inn.

"The children have arrived," she cried hoarsely, "but I have only the twins with me. Roberto took Robertino with him to the hotel. It was terrible at the station. We argued and argued. Are you all packed? Can you come right away? You can go with me to Paris—I'm going to see my lawyers..."

With the aid of the local garage owner I was at the house in ten minutes. Ingrid, the twins, Helena, the butler and the maid were all outside. Ingrid, in corduroy slacks and a camel's-hair overcoat, was pacing up and down impatient to be off. The twins were identically dressed in plaid pants, white sweaters, camel's-hair topcoats, and calf-length rubber boots. Red ribbons held back their long fair hair. Little Ingrid held the leash of a white curly-haired poodle.

Ingrid's eyes were crimson. Not since the febrile days of Stromboli and Rome in 1949 had I seen her look this way. Except that now her tears were bred of battle. She called her lovely, round-cheeked daughters.

"This is Ingrid," she said. Little Ingrid extended her hand, then turned a velvety cheek to be kissed.

"And this is Isabella," said Ingrid, gazing at them proudly. And Isabella held out her hand, then turned her own cheek to be kissed.

"Come on, Joe. Let's go," said Ingrid. "We'll talk on the way." She slid in behind the wheel of the station wagon and we slithered through narrow stony streets until we struck a broad divided highway.

Rigid with fury, she spoke in smoldering rage; she who hated loud words—words that wore "long boots, hard boots."

"We had a horrible scene at the station," she said. "As soon as they got off the train Roberto said they were coming with *him* to stay at the hotel—the Raphael—he insisted. Only for a few days, he said. They should have been here weeks ago. I've been waiting and waiting for them, but it didn't matter to him.

"We argued and argued—awful for the children to see. How lucky there were no photographers around. That would have been something. How they would have loved that!

"So finally he put Robertino in his car and started off. But I took the twins and Helena and drove like hell for Choisel.

"Now I've had all I can take. It's enough. I'm tired of giving in all the time. I want Robertino. You know how I hate trouble with lawyers and courts—now, if I have to, I'll go to court. I'll speak out—make all the trouble he wants . . ."

She drove rapidly, but skillfully, always watching the thickening traffic on the rain-wet highway. Her words gushed out in an angry torrent. Each declaration was punctuated by the clamp of her jaws. Her conscience had finally taken command, and the long years of yielding to inimical forces had come to an end.

Ingrid Bergman had grown as tall as the problems that hounded her. Here, at long last, at the wheel of the speeding car, was resolution and integration—and direction.

Now we were in Paris, and her mood began to simmer down to normal.

"Lars has a room for you at the Windsor," she said. "We'll meet him and he'll take you there. When I'm through at the lawyer's I'll call you at the hotel. I would have dinner with you and Lars, but I'm anxious to get back to my little girls."

When Lars Schmidt arrived at the Hotel Windsor, one block off the Champs Élysées, he was instantly hailed by the doorman, whose hand he shook. In the lobby, clerks and porters hastened from behind their desks to greet him.

"What is this?" I said. "Do you own the hotel?"

"Ah, no," he said embarrassedly. "I lived here three years ago."

"For how long?"

"About six months. They are very nice here. I think you will like it."

I suggested we wait in the bar for Ingrid's call. He ordered a vodka and water, took one sip and never touched the glass again. "Anything wrong with your drink?" I said. He shook his head: "The truth is I can't drink hard liquor. It makes me ill. I ordered it just to sit with you."

In about an hour Ingrid phoned to say that a meeting between herself, her lawyers, Rossellini and his attorneys had been set for eleven o'clock the next day. Following the meeting she would join Lars and me for lunch.

At noon of the next day, Saturday, Lars Schmidt and I sat in the Windsor lounge and waited for Ingrid. Shortly after twelve I was called to a telephone booth. "Must be Ingrid," said Schmidt, with deep concern.

My "Hello," was smothered by a shrill note of triumph. "I've won, Joe! I've won! I have Robertino with me—he is holding my hand—I'm taking him with me to Choisel! I can't have lunch with you—I want to take him right away."

"I understand, Ingrid. I'm very glad for you."

"When are you leaving tomorrow?"

"I'll check out of the hotel at nine o'clock."

"You just have to see Robertino," she said. "Tell Lars the good news and ask him to bring you in for lunch . . ."

Schmidt and I walked the one block to Fouquet's Restaurant on the Champs Élysées, where we ordered *sole meunière*, green salad, and white wine.

"Was there something special you wanted to do here?" Schmidt asked.

"Nothing in particular—just wander around and renew an old friendship with Paris. Go to the Louvre and look again at the Winged Victory."

"If you are interested in art you should not miss the Impressionist show. It is in a gallery at the Concorde end of the Tuileries."

"I will, indeed. I'll go this afternoon."

"Then why don't we go together after lunch?" he said. "We can share the pleasure. To enjoy art fully one should be with a companion."

After gorging for two hours on the great French painters, he dropped me off on the Rue Royale, where I wanted to make some purchases.

Sunday at noon, Lars Schmidt and I arrived at Choisel. The twins were chasing the poodle around the great lawn, their laughter tinkling like silver bells. Ingrid and Robertino were on the terrace.

"Hello, Robertino," I said.

"*M'sieur,*" he responded softly, at the same time extending his hand.

"You remember me from Santa Marinella?" He looked questioningly at his mother. Ingrid translated into Italian.

"*Si signor,*" he said vaguely, but politely.

He was attired in tan moccasins, tan corduroy trousers, and a white sweater that buttoned down the left side. His blond hair had grown slightly darker, and a lock drooped boyishly over his forehead. His luminous blue eyes were serious, inquiring, introspective. Nearly nine years of age, the strikingly handsome lad stood erect, attentive and respectful.

As Ingrid, Lars and I engaged in conversation, Robertino said, "*Scusi*." Then he glanced up at his mother for approval and, receiving it, he ran off to join his sisters.

"I hesitate to tear him away," said Schmidt, "but there is a religious rite that Joe must perform . . ." Ingrid looked quizzically from him to me. "Joe says he never leaves Paris without taking another look at the Winged Victory."

"Oh, that!" she laughed heartily. "Joe always liked everything that flies."

"Besides," said Schmidt, "there are a few things I must attend to."

"Good-bye, Joe," said Ingrid, as she hugged me. "It was good to see you again . . ."

The children were out of sight. "Say good-bye to the children for me," I said.

"Let me call them."

"No, no. Please don't disturb them . . ."

She stood in the doorway and watched after us until the car entered the gate. Here Schmidt stopped and we both turned and waved. Ingrid held up her arm and slowly waved her hand—slowly, right to left, left to right . . .

On Sunday, October 19, 1958, at nine P.M. as I was entering the taxicab a porter rushed out and said, "*M'sieur! M'sieur! Madame Bergman est au téléphone!*"

In the booth, Ingrid's voice rang clear and joyous: "Oh, Joe. I'm glad I caught you! I wanted to say good-bye again. It is so happy here now . . ."

The hearing of the Italian prosecutor's appeal to nullify the annulment was postponed for the third time, with the exasperating prospect of continuing postponements.

As the weeks passed, Ingrid's mounting resurgence determined her course. On December 5th she applied for and regained the

Swedish citizenship she had forfeited eight years before with her marriage to Rossellini. In Stockholm, a Cabinet meeting presided over by King Gustav Adolf VI granted, without discussion, her appeal.

On December 21st she was married in perfectly executed secrecy to Lars Schmidt in London's famed Caxton Hall, a favorite wedding place for notables who have been divorced. She was driven to the Hall, near Westminster Abbey, by her London attorney, Ambrose Appelbe. A minute later, Schmidt arrived with his closest friend, Baron Göran von Essen, and the Baroness. The only others present were Ingrid's dear friends, Sidney Bernstein and his wife.

The wedding party slipped out of Caxton Hall as unobserved as they had arrived, then rode to the Swedish Church in London, where the vicar pronounced a benediction and blessing.

The Associated Press quoted Attorney Appelbe: "There wasn't a person in the length and breadth of the whole street. It was lovely—a very simple show on a Sunday morning with the sun shining."

The newlyweds immediately flew back to Paris and Choisel, where the children had been left in the care of a friend.

Rossellini promptly filed an appeal with the Rome civil court to give him custody of the three children because of Ingrid's "relationship with Lars Schmidt." Ingrid countered by petitioning a French court for custody, through her Paris attorney, René Florpot.

On January 21, 1959, Ingrid and her former husband, Rossellini, met in a bitter, joyless reunion in the private chambers of Judge René Drouillat, in the Palace of Justice. Three days later, the judge rendered his decision; a provisional ruling which gave Ingrid custody of the children, but gave Rossellini what amounted to visiting rights on weekends. He also decreed that the children attend an Italian school in Paris and not be taken out of France until a final ruling was made, which was expected to take at least one year. Ingrid immediately took legal steps to start the process.

The new Bergman's direction was sharp and positive and unafraid.

On the 15th of February Ingrid telephoned from Choisel to tell me of her projected plan to attend the forthcoming Academy Awards (April 6th) in Hollywood. The sound of glory and gratitude and peace sparkled through the little black box on my desk.

"I have just put the children to bed, and Lars is waiting to say hello to you. I am so busy these days, there is little time to write. I get up at 6:30 every morning, work around the house, buy the groceries, and when the children come home from school I help them with their homework. Even Helena says she never saw me work so hard. But I have a good time, and I thank God every day for bringing Lars my way, and that he wanted me. I could never be a happier wife than I am with him.

"It is so quiet here now—like being wrapped up in a warm blanket . . ."

As she talked, I saw the house and I saw Ingrid—her gentle, glowing face; the children, serene in slumber; Lars Schmidt, standing by, gazing at Ingrid with quiet affection. The trials of her former years were rapidly receding into the dimming past.

I saw the stone house and the stretch of tender grass and the twin cypresses that sheltered each other. Now Ingrid was surrounded by beauty and the reality of beauty—and she had grown, at last, to understand it, and to be part of it. She no longer walked through life uncertainly.

Postscript

AT noon of April 3, ten turbulent years plus fifteen days since she had left Hollywood, Ingrid and Lars Schmidt landed at Los Angeles International Airport after a polar flight via Scandinavian Airlines.

Wearing a matching blue tweed Dior ensemble of coat, dress, and hat, she was radiant, vivacious, and sparkling with happiness as for forty minutes she was photographed and interviewed by some one hundred members of press, radio, and television, the sight of whom inhibited the exposure of my red earmuffs.

Asked when she had last been in Hollywood, she replied, "March 19, 1949—a day that changed my life. I shall always remember it—like a birthday or an anniversary."

When the session finally ended, producer Jerry Wald of 20th Century-Fox and Edd Henry of the MCA Agency accompanied Ingrid and her husband to the Beverly Hills Hotel, while I hurried to Hahn's Florist. There I had a nosegay of violets fixed in a vase encircled by the earmuffs. Enclosing no card, I had it promptly delivered to Bungalow 12 of the hotel.

At 5:30, as prearranged, I arrived at the bungalow and was admitted by Lars Schmidt. Ingrid stood in the middle of the room, wearing an enormous grin and—the earmuffs!

When the laughter subsided, I said, "You're really here, Ingrid. The circle has come complete."

"Yes," she said, her face a kaleidoscope of emotions, "it's really true. And what do you think? Pia's coming tomorrow, isn't it wonderful?" Ingrid's whole being was charged with joy. "She'll go to all the parties, and to the Awards—her first time. Then we'll take her to New York and see shows, shows, shows!"

Lars Schmidt, who kept watching her admiringly, now reached over and held her hand.

"It is a beautiful experience for Ingrid," he said. "I'm so glad she was given the opportunity to come here."

"I want to take Lars to the Beachcomber's." Ingrid changed the subject. "This is our only free evening. Do you think we can?"

I called the restaurant and by eight o'clock we were seated in a palm-leafed corner, ordering remaki and spareribs.

"And I want a navy grog," said Ingrid, referring to a rum concoction sipped through an ice-encased straw.

"What's that?" Schmidt asked. Then, after Ingrid's flowery description, "Well, I must try that," he said.

"Where is the rain?" Ingrid asked the waiter.

"I'm sorry, Miss Bergman, it broke down this afternoon."

"Oh, what a shame," she said. "I brought my husband all the way from Paris just to see the rain."

When the navy grogs were finished, I said, "Lars, I thought you couldn't drink hard liquor."

"Ah, but this is not hard." He laughed. "It's mostly ice."

"Lars is like me," said Ingrid. "He is full of curiosity."

They were constantly looking at each other, as though they had just met and had discovered wondrous things about each other.

"My goodness, Joe," said Ingrid, "it seems as if you and I were here only last week; suddenly, it seems as if I've never been away."

"You've never really been away, Ingrid. An important part of your life was here, and will always be here."

"So many people I want to see, and such little time. Gary Cooper, Hitch (Alfred Hitchcock), Leo McCarey. . . ."

"They'll all probably be at Buddy Adler's party tomorrow night."

"But so many people will be there," she said. "It's impossible to visit with anyone at a big party. I tried to call Ruth (Roberts) but they told me she left for Europe two days ago. I was so disappointed."

"She was, too. She left with Loretta Young to shoot some TV

shows. She said she would see you in Paris. Lars, when are you going to have an Ingrid Bergman Theater in Paris?"

He gazed at her in that quiet, gentle way of his, then, his eyes still on her, he said, "I can't say exactly when, but there will be one."

"Ingrid, I was disappointed that you weren't nominated for *The Inn*."

"Ugh, you are too prejudiced, Joe. You didn't used to be. I haven't seen all the pictures, but they're all wonderful actresses. Rosalind Russell, Elizabeth Taylor, Susan Hayward—my goodness!"

"Well, anyhow, you have two Oscars."

"Yes." She chuckled. "They make very good bookends. You should see the house now. We have it all fixed up."

"Except the dining-room wallpaper." Lars Schmidt smiled.

"That will be changed when we get back," Ingrid said. Then, wearied by the long journey and the drastic revision of hours, they called it an evening.

At eight o'clock the following night, the plush Crystal Room of the Beverly Hills Hotel was jammed with press photographers and the nearly three hundred guests of Mr. and Mrs. Buddy Adler who had come to honor the self-exiled star. Without question, they were the cream of Moviedom's elite.

Many had flown in from Europe, New York, and filming locations to participate in this unprecedented tribute. Present, too, were those who had spurned her a decade ago. Now they were on the Bergman bandwagon.

Ingrid was glamour personified in a ballet-length steel-gray dress. Around her neck was a glittering diamond necklace, a gift from Lars Schmidt. Pia's alabaster beauty was heightened by a deep-blue dress embroidered in white.

As mother and daughter posed with husband-stepfather, Lars Schmidt beamed at Pia and, turning to the horde of photographers, said, "Haven't I a beautiful daughter?"

It was ten o'clock when the dinner gong finally put an end to the picture-taking. At a ringside table, Cary Grant sat between Ingrid and Pia, along with the Adlers and Louella Parsons. Across the dance floor, Lars Schmidt enchanted those at his table, including Hedda Hopper, with his ease of manner and cosmopolitan charm.

When I danced with Pia, she said with some distress, "Please don't call me Pia."

"I'm sorry, Jenny. It's unconscious. Having fun here?"

"Oh, yes," she said. "It's very exciting for me, but I think it is so wonderful for Mother."

On Monday evening, April 6, Ingrid arrived at the Pantages Theater on Hollywood Boulevard, in company with Jenny Ann (Pia) and Lars Schmidt. A mob of three thousand well-dressed fans, who packed the street and the temporary bleachers outside the theater, rose with one accord and gave their prodigal daughter the greatest ovation of the evening.

Inside, as the classic ceremonies progressed, Cary Grant introduced her on the stage. Ingrid, gowned in a pink and beaded short evening dress, made her entrance to present the Oscar to producer Arthur Freed for *Gigi*, as the best production of 1958. Her appearance was the signal for another tremendous ovation. Once again, Ingrid Bergman was Hollywood's beloved and very special pride.

"It is so heart-warming to receive such a welcome," she said. "I feel that I am home. I am so deeply grateful. . . ."